R. Gupta's®

Popular Master Guide

HIGH COURT OF DELHI

Jr. Judicial Assistant/ Restorer

GROUP C

Recruitment Exam

According to Latest Pattern of Exam

2018 EDITION

RAMESH PUBLISHING HOUSE, New Delhi

Published by
O.P. Gupta *for* Ramesh Publishing House

Admin. Office
12-H, New Daryaganj Road, Opp. Officers' Mess,
New Delhi-110002 ✆ 23261567, 23275224, 23275124

E-mail: info@rameshpublishinghouse.com
Website: www.rameshpublishinghouse.com

Showroom
- Balaji Market, Nai Sarak, Delhi-6 ✆ 23253720, 23282525
- 4457, Nai Sarak, Delhi-6, ✆ 23918938

Book Code: R-1509

ISBN: 978-93-5012-277-8

Mode of Selection

Eligible candidates will be required to appear in a written test of two hours based on Multiple Choice Question pattern in English consisting of

I. Language Comprehension

II. General Awareness

III. General Mathematics &

IV. Reasoning Ability

Carrying a weightage of 180 marks. Those candidates who qualify in the written test shall be required to appear in comprehension/essay writing test (of 50 marks) and those who qualify the same shall be called for typing test in English on Computer of a duration of 10 minutes at the speed of 40 w.p.m. The candidates who qualify the typing test will be called for interview. Candidates with knowledge of operating Computer would be given weightage. Final merit of successful candidates will be prepared on the basis of aggregate of their performance in all examinations viz. objective type, comprehension/essay writing test & interview.

CONTENTS

Model Test Paper (Solved)

HIGH COURT OF DELHI

Junior Judicial Assistant /Restorer Exam

Reasoning Ability

1. How many meaningful English words, can be formed with the letters PCYO using all the letters but each letter only once in each word?

A. None B. One
C. Two D. Three

2. The positions of first and the fifth letters of the word SUITABLE are interchanged, similarly, the positions of second and sixth letters, third and seventh letters and fourth and eighth letters are interchanged. In the new arrangement how many letters are there in the English alphabetical series between the alphabet which is third from the left end and the alphabet which is second from the right end?

A. None B. One
C. Two D. Four

Directions (Qs. 3 and 4): *Read the following information carefully and answer the questions which follow:*

Among A, B, C, D and E each scored different marks in an examination. Only one person scored more than C. E scored more than A but less than D. D did not score the highest marks. The one who scored the second lowest, scored 71% marks. C scored 92% marks.

3. Who amongst the following is most likely to have scored 87% marks?

A. A B. B
C. D D. E

4. Which of the following percentages is most likely to be B's percentage in the exam?

A. 68% B. 71%
C. 84% D. 97%

Directions (Qs. 5-7): *The following questions are based upon the alphabetical series given below:*

M J L I T Q S R K U F H C B D E A V P O G N

5. What will come in place of question (?) mark in the following series based on the above alphabetical series?

N PO BDE ?

A. UKR B. SRKU
C. RKUF D. QSRK

6. If in a certain code 'BIND' is coded as "CLGB' and 'HELD' is coded as "FDJB' based on the series given above, how will 'FORK' be coded in the same code language?

A. HGKU B. UPKR
C. KPSR D. UPSR

7. 'HC' is related to 'KQ' in a certain way. Similarly 'OG' is related to 'AB' in the same way. To which of the following is 'RK" related to following the same pattern?

A. TJ B. SI
C. TI D. HD

8. Each vowel of the word SAVOURY is changed to the next letter in the English alphabetical order and each consonant is changed to the previous letter in the English alphabetical order. If the new alphabets thus formed are arranged in alphabetic order (from left to right), which of the following will be fifth from the right?

A. U B. R
C. Q D. P

9. How many such pairs of letters are there in the word PACKETS, each of which has as many letters between them in the word (in both forward and backward directions) as they have between them in the English alphabetical order?

A. One B. Two
C. Three D. Four

10. Point P is 10 m to the West of Point A. Point B is 2 m to the South of Point P. Point Q is 6 m to the East of Point B. Point C is 2 m to the North of Point Q. Which of the following three points fall in a straight line?

A. A, C, P B. B, C, P
C. Q, C, A D. A, B, Q

Directions (Qs. 11-15): *In these questions relationship between different elements is shown in the statements. The statements are followed by two conclusions.*

Give Answer (A) : If only Conclusion I is true.

Give Answer (B) : If only Conclusion II is true.

Give Answer (C) : If both Conclusions I and II are true.

Give Answer (D) : If neither Conclusion I nor II is true.

11. Statement : $H \geq I = J > K \leq L$
Conclusions : I. $K < H$
II. $L \geq I$

12. Statement : $S > C \geq O; P < C$
Conclusions : I. $O < P$
II. $S < P$

13. Statement : $A = B \leq C; A > R$
Conclusions : I. $B > R$
II. $R < C$

14. Statement : $D > E \leq F; J < F$
Conclusions : I. $D > J$
II. $E < J$

15. Statement : $P < Q > T; R \geq Q$
Conclusions : I. $R > P$
II. $T < R$

Directions (Qs. 16-20): *Study the following information to answer the given questions :*

Eight people are sitting in two parallel rows containing four people each, in such a way that there is an equal distance between adjacent persons. In row-1 A, B, C and D are seated (but not necessarily in the same order) and all of them are facing North. In row-2 P, Q, R and S are seated (but not necessarily in the same order) and all of them are facing South. Therefore, in the given seating arrangement each member seated in a row faces another member of the other row.

S sits second to left of Q. A faces the immediate neighbour of S. Only one person sits between A and C. P does not face A. B is not an immediate neighbour of A.

16. Which of the following is true regarding D?

A. D sits at one of the extreme ends of the line
B. A sits to immeditate left of D
C. Q faces D
D. C is an immediate neighbour of D

17. Who amongst the following faces C?

A. P B. Q
C. R D. S

18. Who amongst the following sits to the immediate right of the person who faces C?

A. P B. Q
C. R D. S

19. Four of the following five are alike in a certain way based on the given seating arrangement and thus form a group. Which is the one that does not belong to that group?

A. A B. Q
C. R D. S

20. Who amongst the following faces R?

A. A B. B
C. C D. D

Directions (Qs. 21-26): *Study the following information to answer the given questions :*

'time and money' is written as 'ma jo ki'

'manage time well' is written as 'pa ru jo'

'earn more money' is written as 'zi ha ma' and

'earn well enough' is written as 'si ru ha'.

21. What is the code for 'earn'?

A. si B. ru
C. ha D. ma

22. Which of the following represents 'more time'?

A. pa jo B. zi ki
C. ma ki D. jo zi

23. What is the code for 'manage'?

A. ru B. pa
C. jo D. ha

24. Which of the following may represent 'money matters'?

A. ki to B. ma pa
C. fi ma D. ha ma

25. What does 'ru' stand for?

A. well B. manage
C. time D. enough

26. Which of the following may represent 'good enough'?

A. ru si B. da ha
C. si pa D. si da

Directions (Qs. 27-33): *Study the following information carefully and answer the given questions.*

Eight friends A, B, C, D, E, F, G and H are sitting around a circle facing the centre, but not necessarily in the same order.

- D sits third to left of A. A is an immediate neighbour of both F and H.
- Only one person sits between C and F.
- B is not an immediate neighbour of D.
- Only one person sits between B and G.

27. A is related to G in a certain way. Similarly C is related to H in the same way following the given seating arrangement. To whom amongst the following is F related following the same pattern?

A. A　　B. B
C. C　　D. D

28. Who amongst the following sits second to the right of C?

A. F　　B. A
C. D　　D. G

29. What is the position of C with respect to the position of E?

A. Third to the left
B. Second to the left
C. Immediate right
D. Third to the right

30. Which of the following is true with respect to the given seating arrangement?

A. A sits to the immediate left of H
B. B sits exactly between C and G
C. F sits second to right of C
D. None of these

31. Which of the following pairs represents the immediate neighbours of G?

A. A, C　　B. C, D
C. D, H　　D. D, E

32. Who amongst the following sits exactly between C and F?

A. A　　B. D
C. G　　D. B

33. Starting from A, if all the friends are made to sit in the alphabetical order in clockwise direction, the positions of how many (excluding A) will remain unchanged?

A. None　　B. One
C. Two　　D. Three

Directions (Qs. 34-37): *In each question below are two statements followed by two conclusions numbered I and II. You have to take the two given statements to be true even if they seem to be at variance from commonly known facts and then decide which of the given conclusions logically follows from the given statements disregarding commonly known facts.*

Give Answer (A) : If only Conclusion I follows.

Give Answer (B) : If only Conclusion II follows.

Give Answer (C) : If both Conclusions I and II follow.

Give Answer (D) : If neither Conclusion I nor II follows.

34. Statements :

All exams are tests.

No test is a question.

Conclusions :

I. Atleast some exams are questions.

II. No exam is a question.

35. Statements :

No bangle is an earring.

Some earrings are rings.

Conclusions :

I. No ring is a bangle.

II. Some rings are definitely not earrings.

36. Statements :

Some banks are colleges.

All colleges are schools.

Conclusions :

I. Atleast some banks are schools.

II. All schools are colleges.

37. Statements :

All rivers are lakes.

All lakes are oceans.

Conclusions :

I. All rivers are oceans.

II. Atleast some oceans are lakes.

Directions (Qs. 38-40): *Each of the questions below consists of a question and two statements numbered I and II given below it. You have to decide whether the data provided in the statements are sufficient to answer the question. Read both the statements and–*

Give Answer (A) : If the data in Statement I alone are sufficient to answer the question, while the data in Statement II alone are not sufficient to answer the question.

Give Answer (B) : If the data in Statement II alone are sufficient to answer the question, while the data in Statement I alone are not suffi-cient to answer the question.

Give Answer (C) : If the data in both the Statements I and II together are necessary to answer the question.

Give Answer (D) : If the data neither in the Statement I nor II are sufficient to answer the question.

38. On which date of the month was Parul born?

I. Her mother correctly remembers that she was born after 15th but before 21st of April.

II. Her father correctly remembers that she was born after 18th but before 24th of April.

39. How many brothers does Meghna have? (Meghna is a girl)

I. Kishore, the father of Meghna is the only child of Kamal. Kamal has only two grand children.

II. Jyoti, the daughter-in-law of Kamal has a son and a daughter.

40. Among P, Q, R, S and T sitting in a straight line, facing North, who sits exactly in the middle of the line?

I. S sits third to left of Q. S is an immediate neighbour of both P and T.

II. Two people sit between T and R. R does not sit at any of the extreme ends. P sits second to right of T.

Directions (Qs. 41-45): *Select the one which is different from the other three responses.*

41. A. DGJMP B. HKNQT C. LORUW D. PSVYB

42. A. 6 B. 21 C. 24 D. 40

43. A. Amazon B. Nile C. Thames D. Kabul

44. A. Milk B. Curd C. Petrol D. Butter

45. A. ZXV B. XVT C. MKI D. NPR

Language Comprehension

Directions (Qs. 46-50): *Pick out the most effective word from the given words to fill in the blank to make the sentence meaningfully complete.*

46. The government is planning to set ....family welfare centres for slums in cities.

A. another B. with
C. for D. up

47. Economic independence and education have ....women more assertive.

A. prepared B. made
C. marked D. resulted

48. In the modern world the .... of change and scientific innovation is unusually rapid.

A. supplies B. context
C. pace D. fantasy

49. The unprecendented economic growth of China has .... worldwide attention.

A. perceived B. proposed
C. neither D. attracted

50. Each business activity........ employment to people who would otherwise be unemployed.

A. taking B. finds
C. creates D. provides

Directions (Qs. 51-60): *Read the following passage carefully and answer the questions given below it. Certain words have been printed in **bold** to help you locate them while answering some of the questions.*

The importance of communication skills cannot be underestimated especially so in the teaching-learning process. Teaching is generally considered as only fifty per cent knowledge and fifty per cent interpersonal or communication skills. For a teacher, it is not just important to give a lecture rich in content that provides **abundant** information about the subject or topic in question, but a successful teacher develops an **affinity** with, an understanding of and a harmonious interrelationship with her pupils. Building rapport becomes her primary task in the classroom. But what exactly is rapport? Rapport is a sympathetic relationship or understanding that allows you to look at the world from someone else's perspective. Making other people feel that you understand them creates a strong bond. Building rapport is the first step to better communication—the primary goal of all true educators. Communication skills for teachers are thus as important as their in-depth knowledge of the particular subject which they teach. To a surprising **degree,** how one communicates determines one's effectiveness as a teacher. A study on communication styles suggests that 7% of communication takes place through words, 38% through voice intonation and 55% through body language.

Much of teaching is about sending and receiving messages. The process of communication is composed of three elements; the source (sender, speaker, transmitter or instructor), the symbols used in the composing and transmitting of the message (words or signs), and the receiver (listener, reader or student). The three elements are dynamically interrelated since each element is dependent on the others for effective communication to take place. Effective communication is all about conveying your message to the other people clearly and unambiguously. It's also about receiving information the others are sending to you, with as little distortion as possible. Doing this involves effort from both the sender and the receiver. And it's a process that can be fraught with error, with messages **muddled** by the sender, or misinterpreted by the recipient. When this isn't detected it can cause tremendous confusion, wasted effort and missed opportunity.

Good communication skills are a prerequisite for those in the teaching profession. Carefully planned and skillfully delivered messages can issue invitations to students that school is a place to share ideas, investigate, and collaborate with others. Effective communication is essential for a well-run classroom. A teacher, who is able to communicate well with students, can inspire them to learn and participate in class and encourage them to come forth with their views thus creating a proper rapport. Although this **sounds** simple and obvious, it requires much more than a teacher saying something out loud to a student. They must also realise that all students have different levels of strengths and weaknesses.

Directions (Qs. 51 and 52): *Choose the word which is* ***most opposite*** *in* ***meaning*** *to the word/s printed in* **bold** *as used in the passage.*

51. ABUNDANT

A. Small B. Little
C. False D. Sufficient

52. MUDDLED
A. Skillfully organised
B. Strongly controlled
C. Clearly conveyed
D. Isolated

Directions (Qs. 53-55): *Choose the word which is* ***most similar*** *in* ***meaning*** *to the word/s printed in* **bold** *as used in the passage.*

53. SOUNDS
A. Seems B. Corrects
C. Noises D. Takes

54. AFFINITY
A. Partnership
B. Partiality
C. Weakness
D. Compatibility

55. DEGREE
A. Extent B. Goal
C. Affect D. Situation

56. Which of the following are essential for effective communication?
1. Conveying the message clearly.
2. Not to waste effort and opportunity.
3. Receiving the information with as little distortion as possible.

A. Only 1 and 3
B. Only 2
C. Only 1
D. Only 3

57. Which of the following is true about Rapport as per the passage?
1. It is a sympathetic relationship.
2. It is based on understanding of other people's frame of reference.
3. It helps in creating a strong bond.
4. It is important for teachers to build rapport with students.

A. Only 1 and 2
B. Only 2 and 4
C. Only 1, 2, 3 and 4
D. None of these

58. Which of the following must the teachers keep in mind to facilitate learning in students as per the passage?
A. To control the students such that they do not share ideas with others within the lecture hours.
B. To maintain rapport with students and compromise on the course content.
C. To realise that all students have different levels of strengths and weaknesses.
D. Only to keep the lecture rich in course content.

59. Which of the following are the three elements of communication as per the passage?
A. Source, Signs and Students
B. Source, Sender and Speaker
C. Signs, Words and Students
D. Instructor, Listener and Reader

60. Which of the following is the finding of a study on communication styles?
A. The body language and gestures account for 38% of

communication and outweighs the voice intonation.

B. Only 9% communication about content whereas the rest is about our tone and body language.

C. The tone of our voice accounts for 55% of what we communicate and outweighs the body languages.

D. More than 90% of our communication is not about content but about our tone and body language.

Directions (Qs. 61-70): *Read each sentence to find out whether there is any error in it. The error, if any, will be in one part of the sentence. The letter of that part is the answer. If there is no error, the answer is 'D'. (Ignore the errors of punctuation, if any).*

61. (A) The brakes and steering failed/(B) and the bus ran down the hill/(C) without anyone being able to control it./(D) No error.

62. (A) The polling was marred/(B) at many a place/(C) by attempts at rigging./(D) No error.

63. (A) He wanted to work all right/ (B) but we saw that he was completely worn/(C) and so we persuaded him to stop./(D) No error.

64. (A) When a whale is washed ashore by the tide,/(B) the people flock together to see it/ (C) wondering how so huge an animal can swim about in the water./(D) No error.

65. (A) Few scientists changed/(B) people's ideas as much as/(C) Darwin with his Theory of Evolution./(D) No error.

66. (A) Were he/(B) to see you,/(C) he would have been surprised./ (D) No error.

67. (A) The number of marks carried by each question/(B) are indicated/(C) at the end of the question./(D) No error.

68. (A) An animal/(B) can be just as unhappy in a vast area/(C) or in a small one./(D) No error.

69. (A) It is time/(B) we did something/(C) to stop road accidents./(D) No error.

70. (A) A free press is not a privilege/ (B) but the organic necessity/ (C) in a free society./(D) No error.

Directions (Qs. 71-80): *In the following passage there are blanks, each of which has been numbered. These numbers are printed below the passage and against each, five words are suggested, one of which fits the blanks appropriately. Find out the appropriate word in each case.*

The latest technology **(71)** put to use or about to arrive in market must be **(72)** to all entrepreneurs. The reason is that it may have an **(73)** effect on business. Value radios gave way to transistor radios and with micro chips, technology is giving way to digital equipment. Business has **(74)** the same but the technology has kept changing. A notable feature is that the size of the receivers decreased **(75)** so did the use of its material and consequently its price. The traditional flour mills are losing business **(76)** customers now buy flour **(77)** from the market. As a result of this, the business is **(78).** Following the same lines as technology, the social trends also go on changing and influence the market. The Indian sarees are being taken **(79)** by readymade stitched clothes. Every entrepreneur must note such changes in the environment and also the technology and plan in **(80)** with these to ensure the success of his endeavour.

71. A. to B. needed
C. decided D. being

72. A. hoped B. welcome
C. released D. known

73. A. approximate
B. huge
C. uniform
D. enormous

74. A. maintained B. remained
C. often D. mentioned

75. A. mainly B. and
C. how D. also

76. A. reason B. due
C. young D. as

77. A. knowingly B. ease
C. cheap D. directly

78. A. shrinking B. blooming
C. returned D. same

79. A. against B. to
C. over D. up

80. A. lines B. relativity
C. accordance D. proper

Directions (Qs. 81-85): *Rearrange the following five sentences 1, 2, 3, 4 and 5 in a proper sequence so as to form a meaningful paragraph, and then answer the questions given below :*

1. Understandably, the newly married woman herself wants to spend more time with the family.
2. They also worry that she might not be able to defend herself in case of trouble.
3. Once married, the in-laws exert a lot of pressure for similar cause of security.
4. Initially the family does not want the 'decent' girl going all around.
5. Retaining female workers at door-to-door sales jobs is just as hard as ever.

81. Which of the following should be the **SECOND** sentence?
A. 5 B. 2
C. 4 D. 3

82. Which of the following should be the **FOURTH** sentence?
A. 1 B. 3
C. 4 D. 2

83. Which of the following should be the **FIRST** sentence?
A. 4 B. 2
C. 3 D. 5

84. Which of the following should be the **THIRD** sentence?
A. 3 B. 1
C. 5 D. 2

85. Which of the following should be the **LAST (FIFTH)** sentence?

A. 2 B. 4
C. 3 D. 1

Directions (Qs. 86-88) : *Find the right word in the following questions which can substitute for the given statement :*

86. One who has a good taste for food and enjoys it :
A. Parasite B. Stoic
C. Gourmet D. Curator

87. A person who is fond of fighting :
A. Centipede B. Brunette
C. Bellicose D. Belligerent

88. A person who goes on horseback :
A. Epicurean B. Connisseur
C. Equestrian D. Pedestrian

Directions (Qs. 89 and 90) : *In the following questions find the antonyms of the given words.*

89. **CALCULATED**
A. Irritate B. Connected
C. Rash D. Pinnacle

90. **IMPLICIT**
A. Trust B. Uncertain
C. Vague D. Definite

General Mathematics

Directions (Qs. 91-105): *What should come in place of the question mark (?) in the following questions?*

91. ? ÷ 0.5 × 24 = 5652
A. 171.75 B. 117.25
C. 171.25 D. 117.75

92. 5 × ? = 4808 ÷ 8
A. 122.2 B. 112.2
C. 120.2 D. 102.2

93. 65% of 654 – ? % of 860 = 210.1
A. 25 B. 15
C. 20 D. 30

94. 35154 – 20465 – 5201 = ?
A. 9488 B. 9844
C. 9484 D. 9848

95. $\frac{8}{13} \div \frac{192}{559} = ?$
A. $1\frac{19}{24}$ B. $4\frac{19}{28}$
C. $2\frac{17}{28}$ D. $3\frac{17}{28}$

96. 243 × 124 – 25340 = ?
A. 4729 B. 4792
C. 4972 D. 4927

97. 92 ÷ 8 ÷ 2 ?
A. 4.75 B. 5.75
C. 4.25 D. 5.25

98. $(121)^3 \times 11 \div (1331)^2 = (11)^?$
A. 3 B. 2
C. 1 D. 0

99. 283.56 + 142.04 + 661.78 = ?
A. 1084.28
B. 1087.28
C. 1080.38
D. None of these

100. 7028 ÷ 25 = ?
A. 218.12
B. 281.21
C. 218.21
D. None of these

101. $390.5 \times \sqrt{?} = 284 \times 22$
A. $(256)^2$ B. 16
C. $\sqrt{16}$ D. 256

102. $12.5 \times 8.4 \times 7.6 = ?$
A. 787
B. 788
C. 799
D. None of these

103. $4477 \div (44 \times 5.5) = ?$
A. 24.5 B. 21.5
C. 16.5 D. 18.5

104. 33.5% of 250 = ?
A. 76.25 B. 82.25
C. 78.75 D. 83.75

105. $\frac{1}{2}$ of $\frac{3}{5}$ of $\frac{4}{9}$ of 5820 = ?
A. 766 B. 777
C. 776 D. 767

106. 12 men alone can complete a piece of work in 6 days. whereas 10 men and 21 women together take 3 days to complete the same piece of work. In how many days can 12 women alone complete the piece of work?
A. 10 B. 9
C. 11 D. 8

107. The owner of an electronic store charges his customer 11% more than the cost price. If a cutomer paid ₹ 1,33,200 for an LED T.V., then what ws the original price of the T.V.?
A. ₹ 1,20,000 B. ₹ 1,14,500
C. ₹ 1,22,500 D. ₹ 1,18,000

108. The average age of a woman and her daughter is 19 years. The ratio of their ages is 16 : 3 respectively. What is the daughter's age?
A. 9 years B. 3 years
C. 12 years D. 6 years

109. If the fractions $\frac{3}{5}, \frac{1}{4}, \frac{5}{6}, \frac{7}{9}$ and $\frac{8}{11}$ are arranged in ascending order of their values, which one will be the third?
A. $\frac{5}{6}$ B. $\frac{3}{5}$
C. $\frac{7}{9}$ D. $\frac{8}{11}$

110. A car covers a certain distance in 3 hours at the speed of 124 kms./hr. What is the average speed of a truck which travels a distance of 120 kms less than the car in the same time?
A. 88 kms./hr. B. 84 kms./hr.
C. 78 kms./hr. D. 73 kms./hr.

111. The cost of 4 Calculators and 2 Stencils is ₹ 6,200. What is the cost of 10 Calculators and 5 Stencils?
A. ₹ 15,500
B. ₹ 14,875
C. ₹ 16,200
D. Cannot be determined

112. Find the average of the following set of scores:
214, 351, 109, 333, 752, 614, 456, 547
A. 482
B. 428
C. 444
D. None of these

113. The average of four consecutive odd numbers A, B, C and D respectively is 54. What is the product of A and C?

A. 2907 B. 2805
C. 2703 D. 2915

114. The sum of 55% of a number and 40% of the same number is 180.5. What is 80% of that number?
A. 134 B. 152
C. 148 D. 166

115. There are 950 employees in an organization, out of which 28% got promoted. How many empolyees got promoted?
A. 226 B. 256
C. 266 D. 216

116. What is the **least** number to be added to 3000 to make it a perfect square?
A. 191 B. 136
C. 25 D. 84

117. What would be the compound interest obtained on an amount of ₹ 7,640 at the rate of 15 p.c.p.a after two years?
A. ₹ 2,634.9 B. ₹ 2,643.9
C. ₹ 2,364.9 D. ₹ 2,463.9

118. In an examination it is required to get 65% of the aggregate marks to pass. A student gets 847 marks and is declared failed by 10% marks. What are the **maximum** aggregate marks a student can get?
A. 1450
B. 1640
C. 1500
D. None of these

119. A juice centre requires 35 dozen guavas for 28 days. How many dozen guavas will it require for 36 days?
A. 50 B. 52
C. 40 D. 45

120. Mohan sold an item for ₹ 4,510 and incurred a loss of 45%. At what price should he have sold the item to have gained a profit of 45%?
A. ₹ 10,900
B. ₹ 12,620
C. ₹ 11,890
D. Cannot be determined

121. What will come in place of both the question marks (?) in the following question?

$$\frac{(?)^{1.5}}{288} = \frac{6}{(?)^{1.5}}$$

A. 6 B. 12
C. 7 D. 14

122. What would be the circumference of a circle whose area is 745.36 sq.cm?
A. 94.4 cm B. 88.8 cm
C. 96.8 cm D. 87.4 cm

Directions (Qs. 123-125): *What will come in place of the question mark (?) in the following number series?*

123. 5 15 35 75 155 (?)
A. 295 B. 315
C. 275 D. 305

124. 3 6 18 72 360 (?)
A. 2160 B. 1800
C. 2520 D. 1440

125. 688 472 347 283 256 (?)
A. 236 B. 229
C. 255 D. 248

Directions (Qs. 126-130): *In each of these questions an equation is given with a question mark (?) in place of the correct figure on the right hand side which satisfies the eqality. Based on the values on the left hand side and the symbol of equality given, you have to decide which of the following figures will satisfy the equality and thus come in place of the question mark.*

Symbols stand for
> (greater than)
= (equal to)
< (lesser than)
≥ (either greater than or equal to)
≤ (either lesser than or equal to)

126. $-[\{92 \div 184\} \times 1.5] < (?)$
A. –0.7 B. –0.753
C. –0.8 D. –0.75

127. $[\{84 - (3)^2\} \times 10] > (?)$
A. $\left(\sqrt{784}\right)^2$ B. $(28)^2$
C. 750 D. 749.9

128. $[85 - \{58 - 76\}] \geq (?)$
A. –103 B. $\sqrt{103}$
C. ± 51.5 D. ± 103

129. $\left[\left\{\sqrt{324} - \sqrt{256}\right\} \times -4.5\right] = (?)$
A. –7 B. 8
C. –8 D. 9

130. $\pm[(81 \div 6) + (45 \div 2)] \leq (?)$
A. $\sqrt{36}$ B. $-\sqrt{1296}$
C. $\sqrt{1296}$ D. –36

131. The cost of five chairs and three tables is ₹ 3,110. Cost of one chair is ₹ 210 less than cost of one table. What is the cost of two tables and two chairs?
A. ₹ 1,660
B. ₹ 1,860
C. ₹ 2,600
D. Cannot be determined

132. The respective ratio between the present ages of Ram, Rohan and Raj is 3 : 4 : 5. If the average of their present ages is 28 years then what would be the sum of the ages of Ram and Rohan together after 5 years?
A. 45 years B. 55 years
C. 52 years D. 59 years

133. The total area of a circle and a rectangle is equal to 1166 sq cm. The diameter of the circle is 28 cm. What is the sum of the circumference of the circle and the perimeter of the rectangle if the length of the rectangle is 25 cm ?
A. 186 cm
B. 182 cm
C. 184 cm
D. Cannot be determined

134. Raman scored 456 marks in an exam and Seeta got 54 per cent marks in the same exam which is 24 marks less than Raman. If the minimum passing marks in the exam is 34 per cent, then how much more marks did Raman score than the minimum passing marks?
A. 184 B. 196
C. 190 D. 180

135. Smallest angles of a triangle is equal to two-third the smallest angle of a quadrilateral. The ratio between the angles of the quadrilateral is 3 : 4 : 5 : 6. Largest angle of the triangle is twice its smallest angle. What is the sum of second largest angle of the triangle and largest angle of the quadrilateral?

A. 160° B. 180°
C. 190° D. 170°

General Awareness

136. Kuchipudi is the dance form of which state?

A. Uttar Pradesh
B. Andhra Pradesh
C. Karnataka
D. Rajasthan

137. 'Shakti-Sthal' is situated in

A. Allahabad B. Lucknow
C. Delhi D. Madak

138. As per census 2011, the population of Delhi is

A. 18,368,156 B. 16,787,941
C. 20,305,618 D. 14,690,507

139. On which day World Health Day is observed?

A. April 7 B. March 15
C. April 9 D. April 10

140. Where is Waterloo?

A. England B. France
C. Spain D. Belgium

141. Both Mahavira and Buddha preached during the reign of:

A. Ajatashatru
B. Bimbisara
C. Nandivardhan
D. Uday

142. Jahangiri Mahal is located in:

A. Delhi
B. Fatehpur Sikri
C. Agra Fort
D. Sikandara

143. How many litres blood remain present in the human body?

A. one litre B. four litres
C. six litres D. ten litres

144. Neuron is the unit of

A. Connective tissue
B. Muscular tissue
C. Epithelial tissue
D. Nerve tissue

145. The black hole theory was discovered by:

A. S. Chandrashekhar
B. Har Govind Khurana
C. C.V. Raman
D. S. Ramanujam

146. 'Bulls and Bears' is a term used in:

A. Stock Exchange
B. Bull Fight
C. Politics
D. None of these

147. "The Vedas contain all the truth" was interpreted by:

A. Swami Vivekanand
B. Swami Dayanand
C. Swami Shraddhanand
D. S. Radhakrishnan

148. The 29th State of India is:

A. Jharkhand
B. Chhattisgarh
C. Telengana
D. Uttarakhand

149. Economic Survey is published by—
A. Ministry of Finance
B. Reserve Bank of India
C. Central Statistical Organisation
D. Ministry of Commerce

150. Where is National Defence Academy located?
A. Bengluru
B. Coimbatore
C. Khadagvasla
D. Dehradun

151. Where is the Netaji Subhash Chandra Bose Institute of Sports?
A. Mumbai B. Kolkata
C. Delhi D. Pune

152. On which river is Sardar Sarovar Project located?
A. Krishna B. Godavari
C. Narmada D. Cauvery

153. The President can dissolve the Lok Sabha—
A. on the advice of Prime Minister
B. on the advice of Vice-President
C. on the advice of Speaker of the Lok Sabha
D. on the advice of Chief Justice of the Supreme Court

154. Who is the author of 'Post Office'?
A. Rabindra Nath Tagore
B. Mulkraj Anand
C. Bankim Chandra Chatterjee
D. Vishnu Sharma

155. The area of Delhi is
A. 1,780 sq km
B. 1,190 sq km
C. 1,890 sq km
D. 1,483 sq km

156. Which of the following is not correctly matched?
A. Sales Tax – State Government
B. Income Tax – State Government
C. Excise Duty – Central Government
D. Octroi – Municipal Corporation

157. Which of the following writs may be issued to enforce a Fundamental Right?
A. Habeas Corpus
B. Mandamus
C. Prohibition
D. Certiorari

158. A common High Court for two or more States and/or Union Territory may be established by:
A. President
B. Parliament by making law
C. Governor of State
D. Chief Justice of India

159. Who among the following does appoint Finance Commission?
A. Prime Minister
B. President
C. Ministry of Finance
D. Planning Commission

160. As per census 2011, which of the following has the lowest density of population?
A. Manipur B. Meghalaya
C. Nagaland D. Mizoram

161. The relics of Indus Valley Civilisation indicates that the main occupation of the people, was:

A. agriculture
B. cattle rearing
C. commerce
D. hunting

162. Which of the following is correctly matched?
A. Gulbarga – Karnataka
B. Midnapur – Gujarat
C. Wardha – Madhya Pradesh
D. Cochin – Tamil Nadu

163. U Thant Award is given for:
A. Contribution to east-west understanding
B. Community leadership
C. Social service
D. Journalism

164. The first electric railway was opened in:
A. 1853 B. 1885
C. 1905 D. 1925

165. Saina Nehwal is associated with which of the following games?
A. Chess
B. Badminton
C. Golf
D. None of these

166. The Girnar Hills are situated in which of the following states?
A. Gujarat
B. Karnataka
C. Madhya Pradesh
D. Maharashtra

167. Who is called the father of White Revolution?
A. Dr. Verghese Kurien
B. Nanjunda Swang
C. M.S. Swaminathan
D. U.R. Rao

168. Which of the following Union Territories has the highest literacy rate?
A. Puducherry
B. Lakshadweep
C. Delhi
D. Chandigarh

169. Which of the following sanctuaries is famous for one-horned rhinoceros?
A. Manas Sanctuary
B. Palamau Sanctuary
C. Periyar Sanctuary
D. Kaziranga National Park

170. The Barabar Hills, the cave dwellings of Ashokan era, are situated near
A. Patna B. Gaya
C. Sarnath D. Allahabad

171. Where is the National Metallurgical Laboratory located?
A. Jamshedpur
B. Nagpur
C. Thiruvananthapuram
D. Visakhapatnam

172. When did India carry out first underground nuclear explosion at Pokhran?
A. 1972 B. 1974
C. 1976 D. 1978

173. 'Grand Slam' is a term associated with
A. Tennis
B. Chess
C. Horse Racing
D. Shooting

174. Which country hosted the first Asian Games?
A. India B. Indonesia
C. Iran D. Malaysia

175. Normally the common wealth Games are held at intervals of
A. Three years
B. Four years

C. Five years
D. There is no fixed interval

176. The Chairperson of the Lok Sabha is designated as:
A. Sepaker
B. Chairman
C. Vice-President
D. President

177. "Oscar Awards" are given for the excellence in the field of:
A. Literature B. Sports
C. Politics D. Films

178. Many times we hear about GM food. What is full form of the term GM?
A. Globally Marketed
B. Greenwich Method
C. Genetically Modified
D. Grossly Mineralled

179. Who is the highest Law officer of a State?
A. Advocate General
B. Secretary General Law Department
C. Attorney General
D. Solicitor General

180. In which of the following states 'Koyana Hydro Electric Power Project' is located?
A. Madhya Pradesh
B. Kerala
C. Maharashtra
D. Odisha

Comprehension/Essay Writing Test

1. Read the following comprehension passage carefully and answer the questions given below:

Touching on the state of the economy, Mr. Thakre strongly defended the government's decision to cut subsidies in the recent Union Budget saying "carrying the burden of subsidies beyond a point is virtually impossible for any government."

He said people need to be explained that subsidy bills get carried over and it would be their children who would have to bear their burden. This was hardly conducive to a healthy economy, he added.

There were also other extraneous factors over which the government had no control. For instance, if world oil prices rise, the oil bill automatically shoots up and it would be unfair to expect the government to pick up this bill.

He said people need to be told that harsh decisions were needed to correct distortions in the economy just like a patient needing strong medicines to recover.

(*a*) What was the government's decision?
(*b*) Who defended this decision?
(*c*) What is impossible for any government?
(*d*) In what respect have the coming generations to suffer, according to Mr. Thakre?
(*e*) Name one extraneous factor over which the government has no control.

(*f*) What kind of decisions are essential to correct distortions in the economy?

(*g*) Assign a suitable heading to the passage.

2. Write an essay on any one of the follwing topics:

A. Clean India Drive

B. Corruption in India

C. The value of sports

ANSWERS

1	**2**	**3**	**4**	**5**	**6**	**7**	**8**	**9**	**10**
B	C	C	D	B	D	A	C	B	A
11	**12**	**13**	**14**	**15**	**16**	**17**	**18**	**19**	**20**
A	B	C	D	C	D	A	B	D	A
21	**22**	**23**	**24**	**25**	**26**	**27**	**28**	**29**	**30**
C	D	B	C	A	D	D	C	A	D
31	**32**	**33**	**34**	**35**	**36**	**37**	**38**	**39**	**40**
B	D	B	B	D	A	C	D	C	B
41	**42**	**43**	**44**	**45**	**46**	**47**	**48**	**49**	**50**
C	B	D	C	D	D	B	C	D	D
51	**52**	**53**	**54**	**55**	**56**	**57**	**58**	**59**	**60**
B	C	A	D	A	A	C	C	A	D
61	**62**	**63**	**64**	**65**	**66**	**67**	**68**	**69**	**70**
C	D	B	D	A	A	B	C	D	B
71	**72**	**73**	**74**	**75**	**76**	**77**	**78**	**79**	**80**
D	D	D	B	B	D	D	A	C	C
81	**82**	**83**	**84**	**85**	**86**	**87**	**88**	**89**	**90**
C	B	D	D	D	C	C	C	C	D
91	**92**	**93**	**94**	**95**	**96**	**97**	**98**	**99**	**100**
D	C	A	A	A	B	B	C	D	D
101	**102**	**103**	**104**	**105**	**106**	**107**	**108**	**109**	**110**
D	D	D	D	C	B	A	D	D	B
111	**112**	**113**	**114**	**115**	**116**	**117**	**118**	**119**	**120**
A	D	B	B	C	C	D	D	D	C
121	**122**	**123**	**124**	**125**	**126**	**127**	**128**	**129**	**130**
B	C	B	A	D	A	D	D	D	C
131	**132**	**133**	**134**	**135**	**136**	**137**	**138**	**139**	**140**
A	D	B	A	B	B	C	B	A	D
141	**142**	**143**	**144**	**145**	**146**	**147**	**148**	**149**	**150**
B	C	C	D	A	A	B	C	C	C
151	**152**	**153**	**154**	**155**	**156**	**157**	**158**	**159**	**160**
B	C	A	A	D	B	A	B	B	D

161	**162**	**163**	**164**	**165**	**166**	**167**	**168**	**169**	**170**
C	A	A	D	B	A	A	B	D	B
171	**172**	**173**	**174**	**175**	**176**	**177**	**178**	**179**	**180***
A	B	A	A	B	A	D	C	A	C

EXPLANATORY ANSWERS

1. Only one meaningful word ⇒ Copy

2. Given word : S U I T A B L E
According to the question
word after changing the position

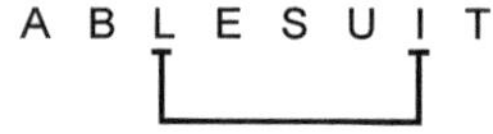

Alphabets between I and L

I [J K] L

3. Arrangement of students in ascending order according to their marks.

A < E < D < C < B

According to the question,

Second lowest marks is 71%, which is scored by E and C has gained 92% marks. So, it is higher probability that D has scored 87% marks.

4. As B is top scorer. Hence B has scored 97% marks.

16-20 : Line-1 Q P S R

Line-2 B C D A

Seating arrangements of eight friends is as it shown above.

16. C has been seating beside of D.

17. P is facing towards C.

18. Q has been seating in the right side of P. Here P is facing towards C.

19. Position of A, Q, R and B are at end points of line 1 and line 2, whereas 'S' is not at any point position.

20. A is facing towards R.

27–33 :

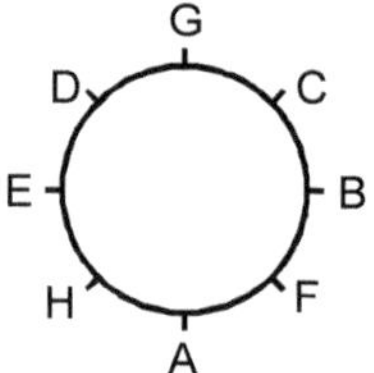

Circular seating arrangement of eight friends is as like shown above.

33.

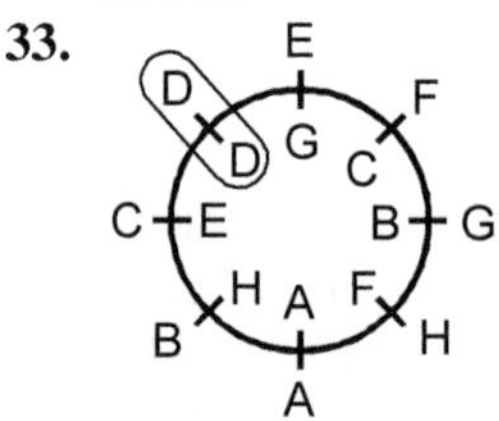

Arrangement of English alphabet in clockwise sense. Thus, only 'D' position is unchanged.

38. According to the statement-1, Parul's date of birth, lies between 16th April to 20th April.

Whereas according to statement-2, her birth day lies between 19th April to 23rd April.

*No. of Qs. may vary.

From these two statements, we cannot conclude her exact date of birth.

39. Kamal has only two grand childrens. And it is given that Meghna is a girl. Hence after going through statement-2, we can conclude that second grand children is a boy.

40. Statement-1

P/T S P/T R Q

either P or T is at mid point position.

Statement-2

T P R

P is at exact mid point position.

91. $x \div \frac{5}{10} \times 24 = 5652$

$\Rightarrow \quad x \times \frac{10}{5} \times 24 = 5652$

$\Rightarrow \quad x = \frac{5652}{24 \times 2} = \frac{5652}{48}$

$= \frac{1413}{12} = 117.75.$

92. $5 \times x = \frac{4808}{8} = 601$

$x = \frac{601}{5} = \frac{1202}{10}$

$= 120.2$

94. $x = 35154 - 20465 - 5201$

$\Rightarrow \quad x = 35154 - 25666$

$\Rightarrow \quad x = 9488$

95. $\frac{8}{13} \times \frac{559}{192} = x$

$\Rightarrow \quad x = \frac{43}{24} = 1\frac{19}{24}$

97. $x = \frac{92}{8 \times 2} = \frac{23}{4} = 5.75$

98. $\left[(11)^2\right]^3 \times 11 \div \left[(11)^3\right]^2 = (11)^x$

$\Rightarrow \quad 11^6 \times 11 \div 11^6 = 11^x$

$\Rightarrow \quad 11^{6+1-6} = 11^x$

$\Rightarrow \quad 11^1 = 11^x$

$\Rightarrow \quad x = 1$

100. $x = \frac{7028}{25} = \frac{7028 \times 4}{25 \times 4} = \frac{28112}{100}$

$= 281.12$

101. $390.5 \times \sqrt{x} = 284 \times 22$

$\Rightarrow \sqrt{x} = \frac{284 \times 22 \times 10}{3905} = 16$

$\therefore x = 16 \times 16 = 256$

107. $100 + 11 = 111$

When SP ₹ 111 then CP = ₹ 100

When SP ₹ 133200 then

$CP = \frac{100}{111} \times 133200$

= ₹ 120000

Hence, original price of the TV = ₹ 120000.

108. Let women's age = $16x$ years and daughter's age = $3x$ years

According to the question,

$16x + 3x = 19 \times 2$

$\Rightarrow \quad 19x = 38$

$\Rightarrow \quad x = 2$

Hence, daughter's age = 3×2 = 6 years.

113. Let x, $x + 2$, $x + 4$ and $x + 6$ are four consecutive odd numbers which are denoted by A, B, C, D

According to the question,

$$\frac{x+x+2+x+4+x+6}{4} = 54$$

$\Rightarrow$ $4x + 12 = 54 \times 4 = 216$

$\Rightarrow 4x = 216 - 12 = 204$

$\Rightarrow x = 51$ and $x + 4$

$= 51 + 4 = 55$

Now A × C = 51 × 55 = 2805.

114. $55\% + 40\% = 95\%$

$95\% = 180.5$

$$80\% = \frac{180.5}{95} \times 80$$

$$= \frac{180.5}{19} \times 16 = 9.5 \times 16 = 152$$

115. 28% of $950 = \frac{28}{100} \times 950$

$= 14 \times 19 = 266$

Hence, number of promoted employees = 266

116.

5	3000 25	54
104	500 416	
	86	

$55 \times 55 = 3025$

if we add 25 in 3000 then it becomes a perfect square. 3000 + 25 = 3025

Hence required number = 25.

117.

$$A = P\left(1 + \frac{r}{100}\right)^t$$

$$= 7640\left(1 + \frac{15}{100}\right)^2$$

$$= 7640 \times \frac{23}{20} \times \frac{23}{20}$$

$$= \frac{764 \times 529}{40}$$

$$= \frac{191 \times 529}{10}$$

$$= \frac{101039}{10} = 10103.9$$

Compound Interest = A – P

= 10103.9 – 7640 = ₹ 2463.9

118. Let maximum marks = x

According to the question,

65% of $x = 10\%$ of $x + 847$

$\Rightarrow$ 55% of $x = 847$

$$\Rightarrow \frac{55}{100} \times x = 847$$

$$\Rightarrow x = \frac{847 \times 100}{55} = 1540$$

Hence maximum number = 1540.

120. 100 – 45 = 55

When SP ₹ 55 then CP = ₹ 100

When SP ₹ 4510 then CP

$$= ₹\ \frac{100}{55} \times 4510$$

CP = ₹ 8200

100 + 45 = 145

When CP ₹ 100 then

SP = ₹ 145

When CP ₹ 8200 then

$$SP = ₹\ \frac{145}{100} \times 8200$$

SP = ₹ 145 × 82

= ₹ 11890

Hence for 45% profit, SP should be ₹ 11890.

121.

$$\frac{x^{1.5}}{288} = \frac{6}{(x)^{1.5}}$$

$\Rightarrow x^{1.5} \times x^{1.5} = 288 \times 6$

$\Rightarrow x^3 = 36 \times 8 \times 6$

$= 6 \times 6 \times 6 \times 2 \times 2 \times 2$

$$\Rightarrow \qquad x^3 = (6 \times 2)^3$$

$$\Rightarrow \qquad x = 12$$

Hence 12 will come at the place of question mark.

122. Area of circle = πr^2

$$745.36 = \frac{22}{7} \times r^2$$

$$\Rightarrow \qquad r^2 = \frac{745.36 \times 7}{22}$$

$$= 237.16$$

$$\Rightarrow \qquad r = \sqrt{237.16}$$

$$= 15.4 \text{ cm}$$

$$C = 2\pi r$$

$$= 2 \times \frac{22}{7} \times 15.4$$

$$= 2 \times 22 \times 2.2$$

$$= 44 \times 2.2$$

$$= 96.8 \text{ cm}$$

Hence circumference of circle = 96.8 cm.

Comprehension/Essay Writing Test

1. (*a*) The government's decision was to cut subsidies.

(*b*) Mr. Thakre.

(*c*) It is (virtually) impossible for any government to carry the burden of subsidies beyond a point.

(*d*) According to Mr. Thakre the coming generations will have to suffer to pay the subsidy bills which get carried over if they are not stopped.

(*e*) Of the extraneous factors over which the government has no control is the rise in oil prices the world over.

(*f*) Hare decisions are essential to correct distortions in the economy.

(*g*) The Burden of Subsidies.

or

A Case for Cessation of Subsidies.

2. (B) Corruption in India

Corruption is one of the burning topics of today. It is also one of the most serious problems of society these days.

Corruption is there in all the government departments. It is there from the lowest to the highest level. If you want to get any work done in any department, you have to grease the palms of many officials there. The peons, the clerks and the officers, all are corrupt. It has, however, to be admitted that some exceptions are also there. Those who do not take bribes can be counted on fingers.

Corruption is there in many countries. But it is not so common in developed countries. India is one of the most corrupt countries in the world. In this respect, her place is with Pakistan, Bangladesh, Nigeria, etc. The European countries are the least corrupt in the world.

In India, it is said, nobody can get a government job without paying bribe. This became clear when the biggest recruitment scam was unearthed a few years ago in Punjab.

Only the UPSC and the like may be an exception. As far as the state public service commissions are concerned, nothing can be said with certainty unless their working is thoroughly scrutinised by some investigative agency.

India has become a land of scams. During the last few decades, we have seen a number of scams unearthed. Some of them are 2G Spectrum scam, Coalgate, Railways scam, Securities scam, Hawala scam, Fodder scam, Bofors scam, Housing scam, Sugar scam, Wheat scam, Urea scam, Recruitment scam, Petrol pump scam, Coffingate, etc. Indeed, the list is endless. So many frauds are committed in banks. The money meant for the pension to the aged, widows, orphans and the handicapped is swindled. Unfortunately, this virus of corruption has spread even in the judiciary, at least at the lower level. It is heartening to note that the Supreme Court and the High Court are trying to root it out from judiciary. Let us hope for the best.

The biggest den of corruption is the political field. There is criminalisation of politics at the highest level. A fairly large number of our central and state legislators have a criminal background. The cases of corruption against many of them are going on in courts. The courts and the Election Commission are doing their best to end this criminalisation of politics.

We have the CBI, the central and state vigilance commissions and other investigative agencies. The Lok Pal, the Consumer Courts and other Courts and Tribunals are there to end corruption and injustice. But the corrupt people are very cunning. They can easily find loopholes in laws. They have the money and muscle power. They can get the laws twisted to their advantage.

Besides the loopholes in laws, the most serious thing is that the punishments are not harsh. Even when a person is convicted, he either goes scot free or gets very little punishment. The people are losing faith in the investigative agencies and even in the judiciary. It is common knowledge that only those who commit petty thefts and frauds, are punished. Those who indulge in most serious scams or crimes, hardly ever get any punishment. It is because they can engage famous, crafty lawyers who can prolong the case till it loses its teeth.

Laws are made and passed by the legislators. In many of them they themselves are criminals, how can we hope that they will make and pass good laws? They will always pass laws which are in their own favour and which can save them if they are caught.

If the democratic process has to be continued in the country and if the people are to be saved from losing all faith in the government, investigative agencies and the judiciary, something serious will have to be done. Otherwise, this country will go to the dogs, sooner or later.

GENERAL KNOWLEDGE

INDIAN HISTORY AND CULTURE

1. Which of following throws light on Harappan Culture?
A. Rock edicts
B. The writings in terracotta seals
C. Archaeological excavations
D. All of the above

2. The idol worship in India can be traced to:
A. the Pre-Aryan period
B. the later Vedic period
C. the Mauryan period
D. the Kushan period

3. Who was the court part of Samudra Gupta?
A. Asvaghosha
B. Nagarjuna
C. Harishena
D. Aryabhatta

4. The ruins of the glory of Vijayanagar and a place of historical importance for its architectural style is now found at:
A. Belur
B. Hampi
C. Srirangapatnam
D. Tanjore

5. The world famous rock cut Kailasa Temple at Ellora was built by the:
A. Mauryas
B. Pallavas
C. Chalukyas
D. Rashtrakutas

6. Which one of the following Silsilas of Sufism was against music:
A. Chishtiya
B. Suhrawardiya
C. Qadiriya
D. Naqshbandiya

7. From the excavations of which ancient site informations are gathered regarding brisk trade relations between India and Rome during early centuries of Christian era:
A. Madurai B. Tamralipti
C. Tondi D. Arikamedu

8. Greko-Roman Art has found a place in:
A. Ellora
B. Gandhara
C. Kalinga
D. Buddhist Art

9. How many 'Mandals' (Books) does the *Rig Veda* contain?
A. 7 B. 10
C. 11 D. 21

10. Which one of the following trees is shown in seals of the Indus Valley Civilisation in association with a deity?
A. Neem tree
B. Pipal tree
C. Banyan tree
D. Mango tree

11. Chinese pilgrim who visited India during Harshavardhan's period was:
A. Fa-hien B. Itsing
C. Nishka D. Hiuen Tsang

12. Chalukya King Pulakesin-II was defeated by:
A. Mahendra Varman-I
B. Narasimha Varman-I
C. Parameswara Varman-I
D. Jatila Parantaka

13. Lumbini, the birth place of Gautam Buddha, is in:
A. Bihar
B. Sikkim
C. Nepal
D. None of these

14. Which one of the following Sufis regarded Krishna among the awliyas:
A. Shah Mohammad Ghaus
B. Shah Waliullah
C. Shah Abdul Azeez
D. Khwaja Mir Dard

15. The Mughals borrowed the celebration of 'Nauroz' from:
A. Parsis B. Jews
C. Mangols D. Turks

16. The temple built in 1100 AD and dominating all other temples in Bhubaneshwar is:
A. Raja Rani Temple
B. Kandariya Mahadev
C. Tribhuvaneswara Lingaraja
D. Mukhteswara

17. The paintings in the Ajanta and Ellora caves are indicative of development of art under the:
A. Rashtrakutas B. Pallavas
C. Pandyas D. Chalukyas

18. Match List-I with List-II and select the correct answer with the help of the codes given below:

List-I	*List-II*
(*a*) Rigveda	1. Musical hymns
(*b*) Yajurveda	2. Hymns and rituals
(*c*) Samaveda	3. Charms and spells
(*d*) Atharvaveda	4. Hymns and prayers

Codes:

	(*a*)	(*b*)	(*c*)	(*d*)
A.	4	2	1	3
B.	3	2	4	1
C.	4	1	2	3
D.	2	3	1	4

19. Mughal painting reached its zenith under:
A. Shahjahan B. Akbar
C. Jahangir D. Aurangzeb

20. Who among the following Sikh Gurus compiled the 'Adi Granth'?
A. First Guru
B. Fifth Guru
C. Ninth Guru
D. Tenth and the last Guru

21. 'Mongols' intruded into India for the first time during the reign of:
A. Iltutmish
B. Firoz Shah Tughlaq
C. Balban
D. Alauddin Khilji

22. Which dynasty was well-known for excellent village administration?
A. Pallavas B. Cholas
C. Pandyas D. Chalukyas

23. Who of the following was the biographer of Akbar?
A. Abul Fazl
B. Faizi
C. Abdun Nabi Khan
D. Birbal

24. Match the following:

	List-I		*List-II*
(*a*)	Sanchi	1.	Chandela Art
(*b*)	Khajuraho	2.	Great Stupa
(*c*)	Thanjavur	3.	Pallava temples
(*d*)	Kanchipuram	4.	Chola temples

Codes:

	(*a*)	(*b*)	(*c*)	(*d*)
A.	1	2	3	4
B.	2	1	4	3
C.	3	4	2	1
D.	4	1	2	3

25. Who was called the "Second Founder of the Maratha Kingdom"?
A. Raja Ram
B. Balaji Viswanath
C. Baji Rao I
D. Balaji Baji Rao

26. The Mughal emperor who discouraged *Sati* was:
A. Babur B. Humayun
C. Akbar D. Jahangir

27. Which one of the following Saints' name is associated with Shivaji?
A. Rama Nand B. Ram Das
C. Chaitanya D. Tukaram

28. Tansen, the greatest musician of Akbar's court, belonged to:
A. Gwalior B. Kannauj
C. Delhi D. Agra

29. The tomb of Sufi saint Sheikh Salim Chishti is at:
A. Jaunpur
B. Sikandara
C. Fatehpur Sikri
D. Ajmer

30. Islam was abolished as the State religion during the rule of:
A. Akbar
B. Balban
C. Ibrahim Lodi
D. Ghias-ud-din Tughlaq

31. Who among the following founded the 'Sunga' dynasty?
A. Bimbisara B. Agnimitra
C. Ajatashatru D. Pushyamitra

32. Who among the following founded the 'Brahmo Samaj'?
A. Keshab Chandra Sen
B. Ramakrishna
C. Dayananda Saraswati
D. Raja Ram Mohan Roy

33. Akbar built Ibadatkhana at Fatehpur Sikri to:
A. Conduct mass prayer
B. Hold darbar
C. Hold religious discussions
D. Hear public grievances

34. Which one of the given Mughal buildings bears the inscription "If on Earth be on Eden of Bliss it is this, it is this none but this"?
A. Diwan-i-Aam

B. Diwan-i-Khas
C. Taj Mahal
D. Buland Darwaza

35. 'Mansabdars' during the Mughal period were:
A. Landlords and zamindars
B. Militia men
C. Officials of the state
D. Revenue Collectors

36. During Aurangzeb's reign which of the following were not employed by his government?
A. Rajputs
B. Pathans
C. Marathas
D. All of the above

37. The first Europeans who started trade with India were:
A. British B. Danish
C. Portuguese D. Dutch

38. The fulsome development of Mughal painting was the achievement of:
A. Humayun B. Akbar
C. Babur D. Jahangir

39. Moti Masjid in the Red Fort at Delhi was built by:
A. Akbar B. Jahangir
C. Shahjahan D. Aurangzeb

40. Who among the following Sultans of Delhi has been described by the historians as the 'mixture of opposites'?
A. Balban
B. Alauddin Khilji
C. Muhammad Bin Tughlaq
D. Ibrahim Lodi

41. Who was the last ruler of Lodi Dynasty?
A. Bahlol Lodi
B. Ibrahim Lodi
C. Daulat Khan Lodi
D. Sikander Lodhi

42. Which of the following Mughal emperors has vividly described Indian flora & fauna, seasons, fruits, etc. in his diary?
A. Akbar B. Jahangir
C. Babur D. Aurangzeb

43. The greatness of Shershah lies in his:
A. victories against Humayun
B. superior generalship
C. adminstrative reforms
D. religious tolerance

44. Who among the following Mughal emperors wrote his autobiography in Persian:
A. Babur B. Akbar
C. Jahangir D. Aurangzeb

45. Taxila was a famous site of:
A. Early Vedic Art
B. Mauryan Art
C. Gandhara Art
D. Gupta Art

46. The gold coins were introduced first time in India by:
A. The Kushanas
B. The Greeks
C. The Sakas
D. The Parthians

47. Which of the following dynasties conquered Sri Lanka and South-East Asian countries?
A. The Pandyas
B. The Chalukyas
C. The Cholas
D. The Rashtrakutas

48. Match the capitals of the ruling dynasties of early Medieval India:

	List-I		*List-II*
(*a*)	Pratiharas	1.	Kannauj
(*b*)	Chandelas	2.	Khajuraho
(*c*)	Paramaras	3.	Dhar
(*d*)	Chalukyas	4.	Anhilwad

Codes:

	(*a*)	(*b*)	(*c*)	(*d*)
A.	1	2	3	4
B.	1	3	4	2
C.	2	4	1	3
D.	2	1	3	4

49. 'Al Hilal' was a newspaper started for propagating nationalism by:

A. Abul Kalam Azad
B. Mohammed Ali
C. Zafar Ali Khan
D. Dr. Syed Mahmud

50. The famous monastery of Vikramsila was founded by the:

A. Guptas
B. Senas
C. Palas
D. Rashtrakutas

51. Fahein, the first Chinese pilgrim, visited India during the reign of:

A. Chandragupta Maurya
B. Chandragupta Vikramaditya
C. Harshavardhana
D. Ashoka the Great

52. Who amongst the following rulers belonged to the Holkar dynasty?

A. Balaji B. Shivaji
C. Tukoji D. Prithviraj

53. Who levied the tax known by the name "Chauth"?

A. Marathas B. Mughals
C. Cholas D. Chandelas

54. The most important feature in the economic measures pursued by Allauddin Khilji was:

A. Foreign trade
B. Minting of new coins
C. Development of agriculture
D. Market control

55. The era which is counted from 78 AD is the:

A. Kollam Era
B. Vikrama Era
C. Saka Era
D. Salivahana Era

56. Provincial Autonomy was a significant feature of:

A. The Indian Independence Act, 1947
B. The Government of India Act, 1919
C. The Government of India Act, 1909
D. The Government of India Act, 1935

57. The Simon Commission was appointed in:

A. 1928 B. 1929
C. 1930 D. 1926

58. Swarajya was declared as the goal of the Congress at its session in 1906 at:

A. Bombay B. Calcutta
C. Lucknow D. Madras

59. Gandhiji started the Dandi march from:

A. Ahmedabad B. Allahabad
C. Dandi D. Calcutta

60. The Congress adopted the Quit India Resolution in the year:
A. 1940 B. 1938
C. 1946 D. 1942

61. The art style which combines Indian and Greek features is called:
A. Sikhara B. Verna
C. Nagana D. Gandhara

62. Match the following:

	List-I		***List-II***
(*a*)	Fascism	1.	Adolf Hitler
(*b*)	Democracy	2.	Lenin
(*c*)	Nazism	3.	Mussolini
(*d*)	Socialism	4.	Woodrow Wilson

Codes:

	(*a*)	(*b*)	(*c*)	(*d*)
A.	1	4	2	3
B.	4	3	2	1
C.	3	4	1	2
D.	3	1	4	2

63. Which battle laid the foundation of Mughal rule in India?
A. Battle of Plassey
B. Battle of Talikota
C. First battle of Panipat
D. Battle of Haldighati

64. The site of Amritsar was bestowed by Mughal emperor Akbar upon:
A. Guru Tegh Bahadur
B. Guru Ram Das
C. Guru Amar Das
D. Guru Hari Kishan

65. Alexander advanced in India up to the river:
A. Ravi B. Satluj
C. Beas D. Yamuna

66. The water divide between Indus and Ganga river systems is formed by:
A. Vindhyan Range
B. Dhaula Dhar Range
C. Aravalli Range
D. Satpura Range

67. The Partition of Bengal was effected in 1905 by:
A. Lord Minto
B. Lord Lyton
C. Lord Curzon
D. Lord Lawrence

68. Revival of Vedas is associated with:
A. Swami Dayanand Saraswati
B. Swami Vivekananda
C. Acharya Rajneesh
D. Raja Ram Mohan Roy

69. At the time of independence of India in 1947, the Prime Minister of England was:
A. Lord Mountbatten
B. Clement Attlee
C. Winston Churchill
D. Neville Chamberlain

70. Who is known as the 'Iron man' of India?
A. Lala Lajpat Rai
B. Gopal Krishna Gokhale
C. Sardar Vallabhbhai Patel
D. Dr. B.R. Ambedkar

71. Iqtas were organised in India by:
A. Qutubuddin Aibak
B. Balban
C. Alauddin Khilji
D. Iltutmish

72. Literature in the Gupta period was written mostly in:
A. Sanskrit B. Telugu
C. Tamil D. Kannada

73. Who among the following was impeached on return to Britain for accepting bribes and committing atrocities on Indian rulers?
A. Warren Hastings
B. Sir John Share
C. Lord Clive
D. Lord Cornwallis

74. Gandhiji started **Satyagraha** in 1919 in protest against the:
A. Salt Law
B. Rowlatt Act
C. Act of 1909
D. Jallianwala Bagh Massacre

75. The immediate cause for the outbreak of the First World War was:
A. the assassination of Archduke Francis Ferdinand
B. the imprisonment of Lenin
C. the ambition of America to dominate the world
D. the sudden death of Lloyd George

76. The Opium Wars were fought between:
A. Britain and China
B. Britain and India
C. India and China
D. Britain and Japan

77. Of the following who was not a signatory to the historic Poona Pact of 1932?
A. B.R. Ambedkar
B. Madan Mohan Malviya
C. C. Rajagopalachari
D. M.K. Gandhi

78. On the first occasion, the Prime Minister of India was appointed by:
A. The Governor General
B. The British Emperor
C. Mahatma Gandhi
D. The Viceroy

79. The American publicist who was with Mahatma Gandhi during his 'Quit India' movement was:
A. Louis Fischer
B. William L. Shiver
C. Web Miller
D. Negley Farson

80. The most decisive battle that led to the establishment of supremacy of the British in India was:
A. The battle of Plassey
B. The battle of Buxar
C. The battle of Wandiwash
D. The third battle of Panipat

81. The person who returned his Token of Honour to Government of India on May 30, 1919 was:
A. Jamnalal Bajaj
B. Tej Bahadur Sapru
C. Mahatma Gandhi
D. Rabindranath Tagore

82. Match the following Lists I and II and select the correct answer from the codes given below:

	List-I (Authors)		***List-II (Books)***
(*a*)	Mahatma Gandhi	1.	India Divided
(*b*)	Ram Manohar Lohia	2.	India Wins Freedom

(*c*)	Dr Rajendra Prasad	3.	Hind Swaraj
(*d*)	Abul Kalam Azad	4.	The Wheel of History

Codes:

	(*a*)	(*b*)	(*c*)	(*d*)
A.	1	3	4	2
B.	4	3	2	1
C.	3	4	1	2
D.	2	3	4	1

83. Karamchand Gandhi was a Dewan of:
A. Porbandar
B. Rajkot
C. Wakaner
D. All of the above states

84. The Asiatic Society of Bengal (founded in 1784) owes its origin to:
A. Warren Hastings
B. Sir William Jones
C. Sir James Mackintosh
D. James Princep

85. A prominent leader of the Ghadar Party was:
A. P. Mitra
B. Hardayal
C. B.G. Tilak
D. Bipin Chandra Pal

86. Who propounded the theory of 'Drain of Wealth' from India to Great Britain?
A. Gopal Krishna Gokhale
B. Dadabhai Naoroji
C. Surendranath Banerjee
D. Lala Lajpat Rai

87. Which one of the following was the first to impose censorship of the Press:
A. Wellesley B. Hastings
C. John Adams D. Dalhousie

88. MacDonald's Communal Award did not provide separate electorates and reserved seats in provincial legislatures to:
A. Muslims
B. Sikhs
C. Scheduled Castes
D. Buddhists

89. On November 1, 1858 Queen Victoria Proclamation was read out at Allahabad by:
A. Lord William Bentinck
B. Lord Canning
C. Lord Burnham
D. Sir Harcourt Butler

90. The first census in India during the British period was held during the tenure of:
A. Lord Dufferin
B. Lord Lyton
C. Lord Mayo
D. Lord Ripon

91. Which one of the following names cannot be associated with the Revolt of 1857?
A. Begum Hazarat Mahal
B. Maulavi Ahmadullah
C. Peshwa Baji Rao II
D. Bahadur Shah II

92. The call 'Dilli Challo' was given by:
A. Lala Lajpat Rai
B. Dr Rajendra Prasad
C. Subhash Chandra Bose
D. Mahatma Gandhi

93. Who among the following attended all the three Round Table Conferences?

A. Jawaharlal Nehru
B. Dr B.R. Ambedkar
C. Vallabhbhai Patel
D. Dr Rajendra Prasad

94. The British Viceroy who took a number of measures for preserving ancient buildings and monuments of India was:
A. Lord Ripon
B. Lord Curzon
C. Lord Minto
D. Lord Irwin

95. Find the correct match:

	List-I		***List-II***
(*a*)	Abdul Gaffar Khan	1.	Mahatma
(*b*)	Dadabhai Naoroji	2.	Frontier Gandhi
(*c*)	Mohandas Karamchand Gandhi	3.	Grand Old Man of India
(*d*)	Rabindranath Tagore	4.	Gurudev

Codes:

	(*a*)	(*b*)	(*c*)	(*d*)
A.	3	1	4	2
B.	2	3	1	4
C.	4	1	2	3
D.	2	1	3	4

96. The first Governor-General of the East India Company in India was:
A. Robert Clive
B. Sir John Shore
C. Warren Hastings
D. Marquis of Hastings

97. The Stupa of Sanchi was built by:
A. Ashoka
B. Kanishka
C. Harshvardhan
D. Dharmpala

98. The prefix 'Mahatma' was added with the name of Gandhi:
A. During Champaran **Satyagraha**
B. During the **Satyagraha** against Rowlatt Act
C. In the Amritsar Session of the Indian National Congress 1919
D. At the beginning of **Khilafat** movement

99. The Harappans were the earliest people to produce:
A. Seals
B. Bronze implements
C. Cotton
D. Barley

100. The Megalithic culture (500 BC-AD 100) brings us to the historical period in South India. The Megaliths used:
A. weapons made of stone
B. tools and implements made of stone
C. graves encircled by big pieces of stones
D. articles of daily use made of stone

101. Which one of the following persons called Irwin and Gandhi as 'the two Mahatmas':
A. Mira Behn
B. Sarojini Naidu
C. Madan Mohan Malviya
D. Jawaharlal Nehru

102. Gandhi suspended his first non-cooperation movement because:
- A. it turned violent suddenly
- B. most of the leaders had been arrested and were in prison
- C. his experiment on all-India strike had succeeded
- D. he saw no chances of success for the movement

103. Indian National Army was headed by:
- A. Netaji Subhash Chandra Bose
- B. General Cariappa
- C. Field Marshal Manekshaw
- D. Chandra Shekhar Azad

104. 'Purna Swaraj' day was first celebrated in India on:
- A. 26 January, 1930
- B. 15 August, 1930
- C. 15 August, 1947
- D. 26 January, 1950

105. Who was the Viceroy of British India when Attlee's government decided to grant Independence to India?
- A. Lord Mountbatten
- B. Lord Linlithgow
- C. Lord Wavell
- D. Lord Wellington

106. When did the 'Quit India' movement begin?
- A. March 1930
- B. August 1942
- C. August 1945
- D. August 1947

107. The Mausoleum of Sher Shah Suri is at:
- A. Allahabad B. Agra
- C. Jaunpur D. Sasaram

108. The slogan 'Inquilab Zindabad' was given by:
- A. Chandra Shekhar Azad
- B. Mohammed Iqbal
- C. Bhagat Singh
- D. Mahatma Gandhi

109. 'Red Shirts' movement aimed at:
- A. creation of an independent Pakhtoonistan
- B. ensuring the creating of Pakistan
- C. making India a communist country at the dawn of independence
- D. throwing out the British from India

110. Bhagwad Gita was originally written in the language:
- A. Pali B. Prakrit
- C. Sanskrit D. Hindi

111. Megasthenes was sent by Seleukos Nikator to the court of
- A. Chandragupta Maurya
- B. Ashoka
- C. Chandragupta I
- D. Bimbisar

112. The aim of the Cripps Mission to India was to:
- A. appease the Indian public opinion
- B. decide the future of India immediately
- C. grant independence to India in stages
- D. decentralise power to provinces

113. Which party was in power in the UK when India became independent?

A. Labour
B. Conservative
C. Liberal
D. No party, since a National Government was there

114. Who evolved the national consciousness as a formal concept?
A. Bal Gangadhar Tilak
B. Mahatma Gandhi
C. Jawaharlal Nehru
D. Surendranath Banerjee

115. The Swaraj Party was founded by:
A. Motilal Nehru
B. Bal Gangadhar Tilak
C. C. Rajagopalachari
D. Vallabhbhai Patel

116. The aim of the Swaraj Party was to:
A. boycott the foreign goods
B. declare independence and establish a provisional Indian government
C. enter the Legislative Councils through elections in order to wreck the legislature from within
D. All of the above

117. The cause of the immediate precipitation of the Sepoy mutiny was:
A. the spread of Christianity
B. the Doctrine of Lapse
C. the disparity between the European soldiers and the native Sepoys in service conditions
D. The compulsion on the Sepoys to use cartridges greased with fat

118. When did Vikram era start?
A. 19 BC B. 58 BC
C. 78 AD D. 73 AD

119. Which of the following was a consequence of the invasion of Amir Timur?
A. Decline of the Mughal Empire
B. Fall of Lodi Dynasty
C. Decline of Tughlaq Dynasty
D. End of Khilji Dynasty

120. What is the correct chronological sequence of the following?
I. Gandhi-Irwin Pact
II. Nehru Report
III. Non-cooperation Movement
IV. Quit India Movement
A. III, IV, I, II B. III, II, I, IV
C. II, III, IV, I D. I, III, II, IV

121. What is the correct chronological order in which the following four appeared on the political scenario in India?
I. Lord Minto
II. Lord Reading
III. Lord Curzon
IV. Lord Irwin
A. II, III, I, IV B. IV, I, III, II
C. I, III, II, IV D. III, I, II, IV

122. Who was the first Governor-General of free India?
A. Lord Mountbatten
B. C. Rajagopalachari
C. Pandit Jawaharlal Nehru
D. Babu Rajendra Prasad

123. 'Jatakas' are the sacred books of the:
A. Vaishnavas B. Jains
C. Buddhists D. Shaivas

124. The Ajanta paintings belong to the:
A. Harappan period
B. Mauryan period
C. Buddhist period
D. Gupta period

125. The famous King of legendary Bhoja, belonged to the dynasty of:
A. the Pratiharas
B. the Chauhans
C. the Paramaras
D. the Chandelas

126. The Gandhara School of Art was influenced most by the:
A. Greeks B. Kushans
C. Persians D. Sakas

127. Rock cut temples have been discovered in:
A. Elephanta Caves
B. Ajanta Caves
C. Ellora Caves
D. None of the above

128. 'Sufi Sect' developed in the religion:
A. Hinduism B. Islam
C. Christianity D. Sikhism

129. The great Indian philosopher Sankara advocated:
A. Dvaita
B. Advaita
C. Vishishtadvaita
D. None of the above

130. The influence of Chaitanya was mainly confined to:
A. The Eastern India
B. The Southern India
C. Gujarat
D. North India

131. Which of the following classes participated the least in the Indian National Movement?
A. Capitalists
B. Princes of States
C. Government officials
D. The peasants

132. Who said first 'Swaraj is my birth right, and I shall have it'?
A. Bal Gangadhar Tilak
B. Gopal Krishna Gokhale
C. M.K. Gandhi
D. Lala Lajpat Rai

133. Who led the extremists before the arrival of Gandhi on the political scene for India's freedom struggle?
A. Dadabhai Naoroji
B. Surendranath Banerjee
C. Gopal Krishna Gokhale
D. Bal Gangadhar Tilak

134. The Home Rule movement was launched by:
A. Annie Besant and Bal Gangadhar Tilak together
B. Annie Besant and Bal Gangadhar Tilak separately
C. Annie Besant and Mahatma Gandhi together
D. The Congress when Mrs Besant was its President

135. Which of the following caves has the 'Trimurti' statue with the faces of Brahma, Vishnu and Mahesh?
A. Kanheri B. Ajanta
C. Elephanta D. Ellora

13

ANSWERS

1	2	3	4	5	6	7	8	9	10
C	A	C	B	D	D	D	B	B	B
11	**12**	**13**	**14**	**15**	**16**	**17**	**18**	**19**	**20**
D	B	C	A	A	C	A	A	C	B
21	**22**	**23**	**24**	**25**	**26**	**27**	**28**	**29**	**30**
A	B	A	B	B	C	B	A	C	A
31	**32**	**33**	**34**	**35**	**36**	**37**	**38**	**39**	**40**
D	D	C	B	C	C	C	D	D	C
41	**42**	**43**	**44**	**45**	**46**	**47**	**48**	**49**	**50**
B	B	C	C	C	A	C	A	A	C
51	**52**	**53**	**54**	**55**	**56**	**57**	**58**	**59**	**60**
B	C	A	D	C	D	A	B	A	D
61	**62**	**63**	**64**	**65**	**66**	**67**	**68**	**69**	**70**
D	C	C	B	C	C	C	A	B	C
71	**72**	**73**	**74**	**75**	**76**	**77**	**78**	**79**	**80**
D	A	A	B	A	A	B	A	A	B
81	**82**	**83**	**84**	**85**	**86**	**87**	**88**	**89**	**90**
D	C	B	B	B	B	A	D	B	C
91	**92**	**93**	**94**	**95**	**96**	**97**	**98**	**99**	**100**
C	C	B	B	B	C	A	B	C	B
101	**102**	**103**	**104**	**105**	**106**	**107**	**108**	**109**	**110**
C	A	A	A	C	B	D	C	D	C
111	**112**	**113**	**114**	**115**	**116**	**117**	**118**	**119**	**120**
A	A	A	D	A	C	D	B	C	B
121	**122**	**123**	**124**	**125**	**126**	**127**	**128**	**129**	**130**
D	A	C	D	A	A	A	B	B	A
131	**132**	**133**	**134**	**135**					
B	A	D	B	C					

INDIAN POLITY AND CONSTITUTION

1. The Constituent Assembly was presided over by:
A. Dr Rajendra Prasad
B. Dr B.R. Ambedkar
C. Pandit Jawaharlal Nehru
D. Dr K.M. Munshi

2. Under which article of the Constitution of India, a citizen can go to the Supreme Court for the enforcement of his Fundamental Rights?
A. Article 31
B. Article 29
C. Article 32
D. Article 10

3. Which of the following two words were added to the Preamble of the Indian Constitution by the 42nd Amendment?
A. Sovereign and Democratic
B. Secular and Socialist
C. Secular and Democratic
D. Democratic and Republic

4. By which Constitutional Amendment Bill was the voting age reduced from 21 years to 18 years?
A. 48th B. 57th
C. 61st D. 63rd

5. Which among the following is not a Fundamental Right now?
A. Right to Equality
B. Right to Property
C. Right to Constitutional Remedies
D. None of these

6. Secularism in the Constitution of India stands for:
A. equal respect to all religions
B. non-interference of the State in religious affairs
C. according the status of state religion to all religions in India
D. None of the above

7. Which of the following is not a condition for Indian citizenship?
A. Property B. Birth
C. Heredity D. Nationality

8. The President calls the joint sitting of both Houses of Parliament when:
A. any constitutional amendment bill is to be passed
B. a money bill is rejected by the Rajya Sabha
C. an ordinary bill is not passed by both Houses of Parliament
D. the President wished to do so

9. The Indian Constitution was adopted and enacted by the Constituent Assembly of India on:
A. 9 December, 1949
B. 26 January, 1946
C. 26 November, 1949
D. 26 January, 1950

10. The Preamble of our Constitution reads—India is a:
A. Sovereign Socialist Secular Democratic Republic

B. Sovereign Democratic Socialist Secular Republic
C. Socialist Democratic Secular Republic
D. Democratic Sovereign Secular Socialist Republic

11. The main feature of the Panchayati Raj in India is:
A. Rolling plan
B. Decentralisation of power
C. Money plan
D. Sharing of power between the Centre and the States

12. The President of India is elected by:
A. the people of India
B. all the members of Parliament
C. all the elected Members of Parliament
D. all the elected Members of the Parliament and of State Legislative Assemblies

13. The maximum strength of the Rajya Sabha is:
A. 250 B. 270
C. 300 D. 545

14. Who conducts elections to the Lok Sabha and Legislative Assemblies of the States?
A. President and Governor respectively
B. Prime Minister and Chief Minister respectively
C. Speakers of the Lok Sabha and the Legislative Assemblies
D. Chief Election Commissioner

15. The Comptroller and Auditor General of India may be removed:
A. by the President in his discretion
B. by the President on the advice of the Union Council of Ministers
C. by the President on the advice of the UPSC
D. by the President on an address by both Houses of Parliament

16. Salaries and allowances of the High Court judges are charged upon the:
A. Consolidated Fund of India
B. Consolidated Fund of the State
C. Contingency Fund of India
D. Contingency Fund of the State

17. Who was appointed as the Prime Minister without being a member of a House of the Parliament?
A. Gulzarilal Nanda
B. Rajiv Gandhi
C. Chandrashekhar
D. P.V. Narasimha Rao

18. What can be the maximum period of gap between any two sessions of the Indian Parliament?
A. Six months
B. Three months
C. One year
D. Ten weeks

19. The number of members nominated to Lok Sabha by the President is:

A. 2 B. 4
C. 5 D. 12

20. Which democratic country is said to be federal in form but unitary in character?

A. USA B. India
C. Ireland D. UK

21. Which of the following is not a charged expenditure on the Consolidated Fund of India?

A. Expenditure of Five-Year Plans
B. Expenditure on the Chairman and Members of the UPSC
C. Expenditure on the Judges of the Supreme Court
D. Debt charges of the Government of India

22. Which one of the following subjects is not contained in the Union list?

A. Currency
B. Agriculture
C. Foreign Affairs
D. Union Duties

23. The Speaker of the Lok Sabha is:

A. nominated by the President
B. nominated by the Prime Minister
C. nominated by the Vice-President
D. elected by the members of the Lok Sabha

24. Which writ is issued by a superior court to an individual or institution directing him to perform a public duty?

A. Habeas Corpus
B. Quo Warranto
C. Mandamus
D. Certiorari

25. The Council of Ministers of an Indian State is collectively responsible to the:

A. Legislative Council
B. Legislative Assembly
C. Governor of the State
D. Both houses of the State legislature

26. Who can legislate on those residual matters which are not mentioned in Central/State/ Concurrent lists?

A. State legislatures exclusively
B. Parliament alone
C. Parliament after State legislatures concur
D. Parliament or State legislatures as adjudicated by the Supreme Court

27. The salary of the Members of Parliament is decided by:

A. the Parliament
B. the Central Cabinet
C. the President
D. the Speaker

28. Which one of the following Fundamental Rights was described by Dr B.R. Ambedkar as the heart and soul of the Constitution?

A. Right to Religion

B. Right to Constitutional Remedies
C. Right to Property
D. Right to Education

29. The President of India addresses both Houses of Parliament assembled together at the commencement of the first session:
A. of each year
B. after each general election to the House of the People
C. Both A and B
D. Neither A nor B

30. Of the following, who held the offices of judge of the Supreme Court and the Speaker of Lok Sabha?
A. M. Hidayatullah
B. K.S. Hegde
C. Subba Rao
D. P.N. Bhagwati

31. No person shall be a citizen of India if he has:
A. lived in a foreign country for more than five years
B. been convicted by a foreign court of law
C. voluntarily acquired citizenship of another country
D. accepted employment in another country

32. The Balwant Rai Mehta Committee made important recommendations concerning:
A. Industrial policy towards the small scale industries
B. Policy towards foreign capital
C. Panchayati raj
D. Foodgrain policy

33. The Constituent Assembly of India was set up under the:
A. Simon Commission Proposals
B. Cripps' Mission Proposals
C. Mountbatten Plan
D. Cabinet Mission Plan

34. A Judge of the Supreme Court retires at the age of:
A. 65 years B. 55 years
C. 60 years D. 58 years

35. Match List-I with List-II and select your answer from the code given below:

List-I (Articles of the Constitution)	***List-II (Subject Matter)***
(*a*) Art. 40	1. Organisation of village panchayat
(*b*) Art. 41	2. Right to work
(*c*) Art. 44	3. Uniform Civil Code
(*d*) Art. 48	4. Organisation of agriculture and animal husbandry

Codes:

	(*a*)	(*b*)	(*c*)	(*d*)
A.	1	2	3	4
B.	2	3	1	4
C.	1	3	4	2
D.	3	2	4	1

36. The Council of Ministers is collectively responsible to
A. the President of India
B. the Prime Minister
C. the Parliament
D. the People

37. When the office of the President of India falls vacant, it must be filled by an election within:
A. eight months
B. six months
C. two months
D. nine months

38. The provisions as to disqualification on grounds of defection by a member of Parliament are contained in:
A. Article 191
B. Article 102
C. The Seventh Schedule
D. The Tenth Schedule

39. According to our Constitution, the Rajya Sabha:
A. is dissolved once in 2 years
B. is dissolved every 5 years
C. is dissolved every 6 years
D. is not subject to dissolution

40. Fundamental Duties were introduced in the Constitution by:
A. 40th Amendment
B. 42nd Amendment
C. 43rd Amendment
D. 44th Amendment

41. The jurisdiction of a High Court may be extended by the:
A. President
B. Governor of the State
C. Parliament
D. State Legislature

42. Linguistic reorganisation of state took place in:
A. 1947 B. 1950
C. 1956 D. 1971

43. The Union Council of Ministers is collectively responsible to the:
A. President
B. Lok Sabha
C. Rajya Sabha and Lok Sabha
D. Prime Minister

44. Who administers the oath of the office to the President in India?
A. Prime Minister
B. Speaker of Lok Sabha
C. Chief Justice of India
D. Vice-President

45. Which of the following qualifications is not essential for a person to become the Vice-President of India?
A. He must be an Indian citizen
B. He should be a graduate
C. He must not be less than 35 years of age
D. He must be qualified to be a member of the Rajya Sabha

46. The term "Fourth Estate" is used for:
A. The Press and Newspaper
B. Parliament
C. Judiciary
D. The Executive

47. Implementing Laws is the function of:
A. Executive B. Legislature
C. Judiciary D. Cabinet

48. Which one of the following is a Fundamental Right guaranteed by the Constitution of India?
A. Right to Govern
B. Right to Property
C. Right to Information
D. Right to Equality

49. Education is included in which of the following lists?
A. Central list
B. State list
C. Concurrent list
D. Local list

50. The Chief Jusitce of a High Court is appointed by:
A. The President
B. Chief Justice of the Supreme Court
C. Governor of the State
D. Chief Minister of the State

51. Can a person who is not a member of Parliament by appointed as a minister?
A. No
B. Yes
C. Yes, provided the Parliament approves of such an appointment
D. Yes, but he has to become a member of Parliament within six months of his appointment

52. Through which Constitutional Amendment was the Nagarpalika Bill passed?
A. 70th B. 72nd
C. 73rd D. 74th

53. The fourth schedule of the Constitution of India contains:
A. Directive Principles of State Policy
B. the Anti Defection Act
C. Fundamental Duties
D. Allocation of seats in the Council of State

54. Which of the following Article/ Articles read with the word 'Socialist' used in the Preamble of the Indian Constitution enabled the Supreme Court to deduce a fundamental right to equal pay for equal work?
A. Article 14
B. Article 14 and 15
C. Article 14, 15 and 16
D. Article 14 and 16

55. Under the Cabinet Mission Plan, the total number of seats allotted to each province in the Constituent Assembly was roughly in the ratio of one representative to the population of:
A. 8 lakh persons
B. 10 lakh persons
C. 12 lakh persons
D. 15 lakh persons

56. Which Article of the Constitution of India deals with the appellate jurisdiction of the Supreme Court in connection with constitutional cases:
A. Article 131
B. Article 132
C. Article 132 read with Article 134 A
D. Article 133 read with Article 134 A

57. Article 356 of the Constitution of India deals with:

A. autonomy of States

B. the proclamation of President's Rule in a State

C. the removal of a Chief Minister

D. the appointment of a Governor

58. Which one of the following constitutional amendments gives a constitutional status of the Panchayati Raj institutions?

A. 72nd B. 73rd

C. 74th D. 75th

59. Panchayati Raj system involves a three-tier arrangement. Which one of the following correctly represents this system?

A. Village level, corporation level, block level

B. Village level, block level, district level

C. Village level, town level, district level

D. Village level, district level, State level

60. The Election Commission is:

A. A legislative body

B. A constitutional body

C. An executive body

D. A non-formal body

61. Who is normally the Chancellor of the State Universities?

A. Chief Minister of the State

B. Governor of the State

C. Education Minister of the State

D. Advocate-General of the State

62. The *ex officio* Chairman of the Planning Commission of India is the:

A. Planning Minister

B. Finance Minister

C. Prime Minister

D. President

63. In which part of the Constitution the concept of Welfare State finds elaboration?

A. Preamble

B. Fundamental Rights

C. Fundamental Duties

D. Directive Principles of State Policy

64. Judges of the High Courts cannot practise, after retirement, in:

A. The Supreme Court

B. Any of the High Courts

C. The High Courts served by them

D. Any court in the country

65. The election of the President can be challenged:

A. before the Chief Election Commissioner

B. in the Supreme Court

C. before Union Parliament

D. before the Ministry of Law

ANSWERS

1	2	3	4	5	6	7	8	9	10
A	C	B	C	B	A	A	C	C	A
11	**12**	**13**	**14**	**15**	**16**	**17**	**18**	**19**	**20**
B	D	A	D	D	A	B	A	A	B
21	**22**	**23**	**24**	**25**	**26**	**27**	**28**	**29**	**30**
A	B	D	C	B	D	A	B	C	B
31	**32**	**33**	**34**	**35**	**36**	**37**	**38**	**39**	**40**
C	C	D	A	A	C	B	D	D	B
41	**42**	**43**	**44**	**45**	**46**	**47**	**48**	**49**	**50**
C	C	B	C	B	A	C	D	C	A
51	**52**	**53**	**54**	**55**	**56**	**57**	**58**	**59**	**60**
D	D	D	C	B	B	B	B	B	B
61	**62**	**63**	**64**	**65**					
B	C	D	C	B					

GEOGRAPHY OF INDIA AND WORLD

1. Which of the following soils in India is most fertile?
A. Regur B. Alluvial soil
C. Laterite soil D. Red soil

2. In which of the following States is the site of Nhava Sheva Port located?
A. Kerala
B. Karnataka
C. Andhra Pradesh
D. Maharashtra

3. Density of Earth's atmosphere is highest in the:
A. Troposphere B. Stratosphere
C. Mesosphere D. Ionosphere

4. Which one of the following is the driest region in India?
A. Telengana
B. Marwar
C. Vidarbha
D. Marathwada

5. The Equatorial Forests of the Amazon Basin in South America are known as:
A. Selva B. Taiga
C. Tundra D. Pampas

6. Which is a tropical food crop requiring a temperature of 27°C and a rainfall more than 100 cm?
A. Wheat B. Maize
C. Rice D. Barley

7. After which one of the following tribes of India; has a large continent of ancient geological history of the world been named?
A. Santhals B. Bhils
C. Marias D. Gonds

8. Which one of the following characteristics is associated with the 'Bread Basket' area of the USA?
A. Moderate rainfall in winter
B. Heavy rainfall throughout the year
C. Low rainfall in summer
D. Long winter with snow

9. Which of the following is largely used in textile industries in India?
A. Cotton
B. Wool
C. Synthetic fibres
D. Jute

10. Sun belt of USA is important for which one of the following industries?
A. Cotton textile
B. Petrochemical
C. Hi-tech electronics
D. Food processing

11. Coffee is a:
A. Sub-tropical shrub
B. Warm temperate shrub
C. Tropical shrub
D. Cool temperate shrub

12. The best variety of world's cotton is known as:
A. Sea Island
B. Upland American
C. Egyptian
D. Short staple Indian

13. How much land area in India is under forests?
A. About 17%
B. About 28%
C. About 18%
D. About 21.34%

14. Which one of the following statements is not true for laterite soils?
A. they are the soils of the humid tropical regions
B. they are highly leached soils
C. their fertility is low
D. they are rich in line

15. Which of the following States is the largest producer of mica in India:
A. Jharkhand
B. Karnataka
C. Rajasthan
D. Madhya Pradesh

16. The Industry for which Nepa Nagar is known is:
A. cement
B. fertilizer
C. handloom
D. newsprint paper

17. Which of the following is known as the morning star?
A. Saturn B. Jupiter
C. Venus D. Mars

18. The Nagarjuna Sagar project is constructed on the river:
A. Kaveri B. Krishna
C. Godavari D. Indus

19. The innermost layer of the earth is known as:
A. Lithosphere
B. Mesosphere
C. Asthenosphere
D. Barysphere

20. Which one of the following is not a cold ocean current?
A. California B. Oyashio
C. Kuroshio D. Canaries

21. The highest trophic level in an ecosystem is obtained by:
A. herbivores B. carnivores
C. decomposers D. omnivores

22. Which of the following absorbs part of the insolation and preserves earth's radiated hear?
A. Oxygen
B. Nitrogen
C. Water vapour
D. Carbon dioxide

23. Arakan Yoma is the extension of the Himalayas located in:
A. Baluchistan
B. Myanmar
C. Nepal
D. Kashmir (India)

24. The largest estuary in India is at the mouth of river:
A. Hooghly B. Bhagirathi
C. Godavari D. Krishna

25. Match Lists I and II and mark the correct answer using the codes given below:

	List-I (Places)	***List-II (Minerals)***
(*a*)	Ankaleshwar	1. Iron ore
(*b*)	Dalli-Rajhara	2. Petroleum
(*c*)	Kodarma	3. Copper
(*d*)	Khetri	4. Mica

Codes:

	(*a*)	(*b*)	(*c*)	(*d*)
A.	1	2	3	4
B.	2	1	4	3
C.	4	3	2	1
D.	3	2	1	4

26. When it is noon at IST meredian, what would be the local time at 120º East longitude:

A. 09.30 B. 14.30
C. 17.30 D. 20.00

27. Which one of the following is correctly matched?

A. Eskimo–Canada
B. Oran–Japan
C. Lapps–India
D. Gonds–Africa

28. The coniferous forests are not found in:

A. Amazonian
B. Scandinavia
C. Canada
D. Finland

29. Mexico is the largest producer of:

A. cotton B. rice
C. silver D. tea

30. Which food crop in India is sown in October-November and reaped in April?

A. Coconut B. Coffee
C. Rice D. Wheat

31. Which one of the following is the longest river in the world?

A. Amazon
B. Yangtze-Kiang
C. Nile
D. Mississipi-Missouri

32. The Alamatti Dam is constructed on the river:

A. Kaveri
B. Seeleru
C. Krishna
D. Tungabhadra

33. Which of the following States is most famous for its beautiful sea beaches?

A. Gujarat B. Goa
C. Tamil Nadu D. Odisha

34. Grassland is called 'Pampas' in:

A. Africa
B. South America
C. United Kingdom
D. the USA

35. The coastal part of water bodies of the oceans which is structurally part of the mainland of the continents is called the:

A. Isthmus
B. Oceanic Ridge
C. Continental Shelf
D. Continental Slope

36. Which one of the following is not the result of underground water action?

A. Stalactites B. Stalagmites
C. Sink holes D. Fiords

37. Which one of the following practices is adopted for restoring the fertility of soil?

A. Weeding B. Levelling
C. Fallowing D. Harrowing

38. The Eastern Coast of India is known as:

A. Eastern Plateau
B. Bengal Coast
C. Coromandel Coast
D. Cyclonic Coast

39. Which of the following dams is the largest?

A. Mython Dam
B. Bhakra-Nangal Dam
C. Hirakud Dam
D. Nagarjuna Sagar Dam

40. Which of the following States is the largest producer of lignite?
A. Odisha
B. Bihar
C. West Bengal
D. Tamil Nadu

41. The International date line passes through:
A. Gibraltar strait
B. Bering strait
C. Florida strait
D. Malacca strait

42. The direction of ocean currents is reversed with seasons:
A. in the Pacific ocean
B. in the Indian ocean
C. in the Atlantic ocean
D. in the Mediterranean sea

43. The importance of ozone layer is that it shields:
A. plants from radiation
B. life on earth from cosmic bombardment
C. earth from meteorites
D. life on earth from the ultraviolet rays of the sun

44. The ideal monsoon system is developed in:
A. Mexico B. India
C. Thailand D. China

45. The State which occupies the first place in India in the production of Tobacco is:
A. Tamil Nadu
B. West Bengal
C. Andhra Pradesh
D. Maharashtra

46. Why is rent earned by land even in the long-run?
A. Land has original and indestructible powers
B. Land is a man-made factor
C. Its supply is inelastic in the short run
D. Its supply is inelastic in the long-run

47. The largest brackish water lake of India is in the State of:
A. Jammu & Kashmir
B. Maharashtra
C. Odisha
D. West Bengal

48. Which of the following represents the zone between Tropic of Cancer and Tropic of Capricorn?
A. Frigid Zone
B. Torrid Zone
C. Temperate Zone
D. Sub-tropical Zone

49. Maharashtrian Plateau is made up of:
A. alluvial soil B. coral reef
C. sandstone D. lava

50. Which gets first monsoon in summer?
A. Western Ghats
B. Himalayas
C. Eastern Ghats
D. Gangetic Plains

51. Which country is called the Sugar Bowl of the world?
A. Cuba B. India
C. Argentina D. Brazil

52. What is the maximum known depth of an ocean?
A. 8 km B. 10 km
C. 11 km D. 22 km

53. A line drawn on a weather map connecting places that receive equal amounts of sunshine is called:
A. Isohyet B. Isotherm
C. Isobar D. Isohel

54. Palk Strait connects:
A. India and Sri Lanka
B. North Korea and South Korea
C. Saudi Arabia and Burma (Myanmar)
D. Britain and France

55. Black Pagoda is found at:
A. Konark B. Khajuraho
C. Madurai D. Egypt

56. Earthquakes occur owing to:
A. changes in earth crust
B. movements in the interior layers of the earth
C. volcanic eruptions
D. None of the above

57. What is the International Date Line?
A. A line connecting places of the same longitude as Greenwich
B. The line near 180° longitude, while crossing which date changes
C. The line of the Globe which will have daytime throughout the year
D. None of the above

58. In which region do we find the belt of doldrum?
A. Polar region
B. Sub-tropical region
C. Temperate region
D. Equatorial region

59. The grasslands of Argentina are called:
A. Steppes B. Pampas
C. Campos D. Prairies

60. On which one of the following longitudes is the Indian Standard Time determined?
A. 68½ E B. 68½ W
C. 82½ E D. 82½ W

61. The origin of earth dates back to approximately:
A. 3.6 billion years
B. 4.6 billion years
C. 5.6 billion years
D. 6.6 billion years

62. The period by which the entire country in India comes under southwest monsoon is:
A. Ist - 10th June
B. 10th - 20th June
C. 20th - 30th June
D. Ist - 15th July

63. The most extensive soil cover of India comprises:
A. laterite soils
B. black soils
C. alluvial soils
D. marshy soils

64. Evergreen rain forest is mainly found in regions having well distributed annual rainfall:
A. below 50 cm
B. 50 - 100 cm
C. 100 - 200 cm
D. more than 200 cm

65. Which one of the following organisations is responsible for publishing topographical sheets?

A. Geological Survey of India (GSI)
B. National Atlas & Thematic Mapping Organisation (NATMO)
C. Indian Meteorological Department (IMD)
D. Survey of India (SOI)

66. Humidity is measured by:
A. Lactometer
B. Polarimeter
C. Thermometer
D. Hygrometer

67. Which of the following is not a terrestrial planet?
A. Mercury
B. Earth
C. Jupiter
D. Mars

68. Access to raw material is the main basis for the location of:
A. sugarcane industry
B. aluminium industry
C. electronic industry
D. hi-tech industry

69. Which of the following Himalayan peaks is situated in Assam?
A. Nanda Devi
B. Namche Barwa
C. Dhaulagiri
D. Kedarnath

70. Among the world oceans, the widest continental shelves are observed around the:
A. Atlantic ocean
B. Arctic ocean
C. Indian ocean
D. Pacific ocean

71. Mozambique current forms part of currents of:
A. North Pacific
B. South Pacific
C. Indian Ocean
D. South Atlantic

72. The average time interval between successive high and low tides is:
A. 3 hours and 13 minutes
B. 6 hours and 26 minutes
C. 12 hours and 36 minutes
D. 24 hours and 52 minutes

73. Which of the following shipping canals joins the North sea and the Baltic sea?
A. Suez B. Keil
C. Soo D. Manchester

74. High temperature and low pressure over the Indian subcontinent during the summer season, draws air from the Indian ocean leading to the in blowing of the:
A. South-east monsoon
B. South-west monsoon
C. Trade winds
D. Westerlies

75. Through which of the following countries does the river Tigris flow?
A. Egypt B. Iran
C. Italy D. Iraq

76. Imaginary lines drawn on a global map from pole-to-pole and from the perpendicular to the equator are called:
A. Contours B. Isobars
C. Meridians D. Steppes

77. The 23½° South latitude is known as:
A. the Tropic of Cancer
B. the Tropic of Capricorn
C. the Equator
D. the Prime Meridian

78. 'Equinox' means:
A. days are longer than nights
B. days and nights are equal
C. days are shorter than nights
D. None of these

79. The hills that have the Dodda Bettah Peak are:
A. Annamalai B. Nilgiri
C. Palani D. Kutralam

80. Which one of the following processes is responsible for changing the colour of a rock into yellow or red?
A. Hydration B. Exfoliation
C. Carbonation D. Oxidation

81. The food crop sown in the largest area in India is:
A. maize B. paddy
C. wheat D. jawar

82. Find the mismatched pair:
A. Mathura—Oil refinery
B. Visakhapatnam—Aircraft
C. Sindri—Fertiliser
D. Kapurthala—Railway coaches

83. Which one of the following is the largest lake in the world?
A. Lake Superior
B. Caspian Sea
C. Lake Baikal
D. Lake Victoria

84. Chilka Lake is located in:
A. Bihar
B. West Bengal
C. Assam
D. Odisha

85. Seasonal movement of people from mountains to plains and vice versa is called:
A. migration
B. transhumance
C. commutation
D. transportation

86. What do you call a narrow neck of land that connects two large landmarks?
A. Peninsula B. Isthmus
C. Cape D. Strait

87. What is the colour of laterite soil?
A. Yellow B. Brown
C. Red D. Pink

88. What are Doldrums?
A. The trade winds
B. Area of great humidity
C. A low pressure belt round the Equator where there are very light winds and calm seas
D. Area where seas are calm

89. The Thermal Equator coincides with the Tropic of Cancer on:
A. 21st March
B. 21st June
C. 23rd September
D. 22nd December

90. The total length of India's coastline is approximately:
A. 5500 km B. 7516 km
C. 6500 km D. 8500 km

ANSWERS

1	2	3	4	5	6	7	8	9	10
B	D	A	B	A	C	D	A	A	B
11	**12**	**13**	**14**	**15**	**16**	**17**	**18**	**19**	**20**
A	D	D	D	A	D	C	B	D	B
21	**22**	**23**	**24**	**25**	**26**	**27**	**28**	**29**	**30**
D	C	B	A	B	B	A	A	C	D
31	**32**	**33**	**34**	**35**	**36**	**37**	**38**	**39**	**40**
C	C	B	B	C	D	C	C	B	D
41	**42**	**43**	**44**	**45**	**46**	**47**	**48**	**49**	**50**
B	B	D	B	C	A	C	C	D	A
51	**52**	**53**	**54**	**55**	**56**	**57**	**58**	**59**	**60**
A	A	D	A	A	B	B	D	B	C
61	**62**	**63**	**64**	**65**	**66**	**67**	**68**	**69**	**70**
B	D	C	C	B	D	C	A	B	D
71	**72**	**73**	**74**	**75**	**76**	**77**	**78**	**79**	**80**
C	C	B	B	D	C	B	B	B	D
81	**82**	**83**	**84**	**85**	**86**	**87**	**88**	**89**	**90**
B	B	B	D	A	B	B	C	B	B

INDIAN ECONOMY

1. According to the 2011 Census the population of India is:
   A. 1 billion 21 crore
   B. 1 billion 2 crore
   C. 1 billion 2 crore 7 lakh
   D. 1 billion
2. What is the density of population in India?
   A. 273 B. 382
   C. 416 D. 216
3. The sex ratio (females per thousand males) in India is:
   A. 927 B. 963
   C. 943 D. 993
4. The decadal growth rate of population during the decade 2001-2011:
   A. 17.7 per cent
   B. 18.5 per cent
   C. 12.8 per cent
   D. 13.7 per cent
5. The principal means of transport of goods in India is:
   A. Railways
   B. Roadways
   C. Inland waterways
   D. Airways
6. Which one of the following is the most densely populated state of India?
   A. UP B. Bihar
   C. West Bengal D. Kerala
7. Which of the following states has the highest literacy rate?
   A. Kerala
   B. Arunachal Pradesh
   C. Nagaland
   D. Maharashtra
8. Which one of the following Union Territories has the highest literacy rate:
   A. Puducherry
   B. Daman and Diu
   C. Lakshadweep
   D. Chandigarh
9. Unemployment in India is due to:
   A. poor manpower planning
   B. population explosion
   C. inappropriate educational system
   D. All of the above
10. The policy of family planning was adopted by the government in:
    A. 1947 B. 1952
    C. 1956 D. 1962
11. The Second Five Year Plan focussed on:
    A. agriculture
    B. education
    C. heavy industries
    D. health
12. Which one of the following measures has been taken to modernise Indian agriculture?
    A. Area under irrigation increase
    B. High yielding variety seeds
    C. Credit and facilities to villages
    D. All of the above

13. Seasonal unemployment refers mainly to:
A. Private sector industry
B. Public sector industry
C. Agriculture
D. Banks

14. Open unemployment refers to people:
A. who are not willing to work
B. who are willing but do not get work
C. who leave their jobs in search of better ones
D. who have been dismissed because of incorrect practices

15. Which one of the following is not a source of revenue of the Union Government?
A. Income tax
B. Corporation tax
C. Land revenue
D. Customs duties

16. Bank rate means:
A. the official rate of interest charged by the Central Bank of the country
B. rate of profit of the banking institutions
C. interest rate charged by the scheduled banks
D. interest rate charged by the moneylenders

17. Marginal revenue will be zero if the elasticity of demand is:
A. negative
B. unity
C. greater than one
D. equal to zero

18. The term "market" in Economics means:
A. a central place
B. presence of competition
C. place where goods are stored
D. shops and superbazars

19. Commercial banking system in India is:
A. mixed banking
B. unit banking
C. branch banking
D. None of the above

20. The gilt edged market in the capital market of India refers to:
A. long term private securities
B. market dealing in existing securities
C. market for corporate securities
D. market for Government securities

21. Which of the following yields the largest revenue to the Government of India?
A. Sales tax
B. Corporate tax
C. Income tax
D. Entertainment tax

22. Sustainable agriculture means:
A. Self-sufficiency
B. To be able to export and import under WTO norms
C. To utilise land so that its quality remains intact
D. To utilise waste land for agricultural purposes

23. Which one of the following crops is the greatest beneficiary of the Green Revolution in both production and productivity?
A. Jowar B. Maize
C. Rice D. Wheat

24. Per capita income means:
   A. average income of the wage-earners
   B. income necessary for an individual to meet his daily expenses
   C. total income of the group divided by the number of the people in the group
   D. average income of family

25. The agency estimating the national income of India is:
   A. NITI Aayog
   B. Ministry of Finance
   C. RBI
   D. CSO

26. The most serious economic problems of India are:
   A. underdevelopment, not poverty
   B. poverty and unemployment
   C. unemployment, not poverty
   D. stagnation, not poverty

27. National product includes goods:
   A. only those consumed by the producers
   B. all whether exchanged or not
   C. both exchanged in markets and retained by producers for addition to their stock
   D. only exchanged in markets but not those consumed by producers

28. Marginal utility is:
   A. total minus average utility
   B. addition to total utility because of one unit increase in commodity
   C. total utility divided by the number of units
   D. total plus average utility

29. Demand of a commodity mainly depends on:
   A. desire to purchase
   B. power to purchase
   C. tax policy
   D. advertisement

30. Which one of the following is in the State list?
   A. Railway Police
   B. Corporation Tax
   C. Census
   D. Economic and Social Planning

31. In a highly developed country the relative contribution of agriculture to Gross Domestic Product (GDP) is:
   A. relatively high
   B. relatively low
   C. the same as that of other sectors
   D. zero

32. Match List-I with List-II and select the correct answer using the codes given below:

	List-I (Industry)	***List-II (Production Centre)***
(*a*)	Jute Textile	1. Bhadohi
(*b*)	Silk Textile	2. Ludhiana
(*c*)	Woollen Hosiery	3. Bangalore
(*d*)	Woollen Carpet	4. Titagarh

Codes:

	(*a*)	(*b*)	(*c*)	(*d*)
A.	3	4	2	1
B.	4	3	2	1
C.	1	3	4	2
D.	4	1	3	2

33. The credit control operation in India is performed by:
A. Rural banks
B. Commercial banks
C. Reserve Bank of India
D. State Bank of India

34. Division of labour is limited by:
A. the number of workers
B. hours of work
C. extent of the market
D. working space

35. The four factors of production are:
A. land, labour, capital, organisation
B. land, electricity, water, labour
C. labour, capital, land, rainfall
D. labour, climate, land, tools

36. What is the main purpose of currency?
A. Currency Chest
B. Standard of Postponed Payments
C. Standard of Money
D. Medium of Exchange

37. National Income accounting is the study of the income and expenditure of the entire:
A. family
B. state
C. economy
D. organisation

38. The problem of Economics arises from:
A. plenty of goods
B. scarcity of goods
C. more wants and less goods
D. All of these

39. Agricultural income-tax is a source of revenue to:
A. Central Government
B. State Government
C. Local Administration
D. Central and State Governments

40. Beyond a certain point, deficit financing will certainly lead to:
A. inflation
B. deflation
C. recession
D. economic stagnation

41. In public budgets, zero-based budgeting was first introduced in:
A. USA B. UK
C. France D. Sweden

42. To achieve economic self-reliance was the main objective of which of the following Five-Year Plans?
A. First Plan
B. Second Plan
C. Third Plan
D. Fourth Plan

43. The preparation of National Income Estimates is the responsibility of the:
A. Planning Commission
B. National Development Council
C. National Sample Survey
D. Central Statistical Organisation

44. Which one of the following is the most sensitive indicator of the health of a community?
A. Birth rate

B. Infant mortality rate
C. Death rate
D. Maternal mortality rate

45. Banks in India were nationalised for the first time in the year:
A. 1950 B. 1960
C. 1969 D. 1979

46. The objectives of Indian Planning are:
A. increasing national income
B. reducing inequalities in income wealth
C. elimination of poverty
D. All of the above

47. The Gandhian economy was based on the principle of:
A. State control
B. Competition
C. Trusteeship
D. Rural cooperation

48. Fiscal policy is concerned with:
A. public revenue
B. public expenditure and debt
C. bank rate policy
D. Both A and B

49. Devaluation of a currency refers to:
A. decrease in the internal value of money
B. decrease in the external value of money
C. decrease both in the external and internal values of money
D. Government withdrawal of a currency not of a denomination

50. The maternal mortality rates in Asia are the highest in:
A. Bangladesh B. India
C. Indonesia D. Nepal

51. To get the Net National Product we deduct what from the Gross National Product?
A. Direct Taxes
B. Imports
C. Interim Payments
D. Loss

52. 'Protection' means:
A. restrictions imposed on import trade
B. protection to home industries
C. no free exchange of goods and services between two countries
D. All of these

53. The Reserve Bank of India:
A. provides direct finance to agriculture
B. provides finance to primary cooperative societies
C. provides finance to State cooperative banks
D. does not provide finance to agriculture

54. In which sector of the Indian economy is productivity the highest?
A. Manufacturing
B. Transport, Communication and Commerce
C. Agriculture
D. Other sectors

55. Which of the following is not a method of estimating national income?
A. Income method

B. Value-added method
C. Expenditure method
D. Export-import method

56. As per the 2011 Census, the literacy rate in India has gone up to:
A. 70.0% B. 78.0%
C. 80.5% D. 73.0%

57. Population explosion in a country means:
A. high birth rate and high death rate
B. high birth rate and low death rate
C. low birth rate and high death rate
D. low birth rate and low death rate

58. The measurement of poverty line is based on the criteria of:
A. their dwelling houses
B. the nature of employment
C. caloric consumption
D. level of education

59. Elasticity of demand is a tendency of demand to:
A. increase or decrease on the change of price
B. increase on the rising of price
C. decrease on the falling of price
D. consistency of demand on rising and falling prices

60. Capital is that wealth:
A. which is used for the production of wealth
B. which is kept in boxes and lockers
C. which is buried in the land
D. which is stored for consumption

61. Function of an entrepreneur is:
A. organisation of labour
B. collection of capital
C. showing efficiency in collection of loans from the banks and the market
D. risk-taking

62. How many banks were nationalised on 19th July, 1969?
A. 14 B. 20
C. 19 D. 23

63. The poverty line has been defined in the:
A. Seventh Five-Year Plan
B. Sixth Five-Year Plan
C. Eighth Five-Year Plan
D. Fifth Five-Year Plan

64. In Centre-State financial relations in India, the Gadgil Formula is used in:
A. division of tax revenue
B. formulating the policy for fresh borrowings
C. writing off states indebtedness to the Centre
D. allocating Central Plan assistance between States

65. Which of the following is a cash crop?
A. Wheat B. Rice
C. Maize D. Sugarcane

66. According to the Reserve Bank of India, the term 'Open Market Operation' means sale and purchase of:
A. gold

B. government securities
C. iron and steel
D. foreign exchange

67. Reserve Bank of India was established on:
A. January 1, 1934
B. April 1, 1934
C. January 1, 1935
D. April 1, 1935

68. What is India's trade policy?
A. Increase in both exports and imports
B. Decrease in both exports and imports
C. Neither increase nor decrease in both imports and exports
D. Export promotion and import substitution

69. The Centre gives grants-in-aid to States:
A. to augment the financial resources of the States
B. to maintain good relations with the States
C. to ensure balanced and quick economic growth throughout the country
D. to ensure social justice in India

70. Temporary tax levied to obtain additional revenue is called:
A. Cess B. Rate
C. Fee D. Surcharge

71. Finance Commission is constituted every:
A. three years B. six years
C. four years D. five years

72. 'Mixed economy' means co-existence of:
A. heavy industries and light industries
B. agrarian economy and industrialised economy
C. the poor and the rich
D. public sector and private sector

73. The largest share of India's National income originates in the:
A. Primary sector
B. Secondary sector
C. Tertiary sector
D. None of the above

74. Which one of the following taxes is levied by the State Government only?
A. Entertainment tax
B. Wealth tax
C. Income tax
D. Corporation tax

75. Which one of the following States has the lowest per capita income in India?
A. Odisha B. Bihar
C. Jharkhand D. Rajasthan

Answers

1	**2**	**3**	**4**	**5**	**6**	**7**	**8**	**9**	**10**
A	B	C	A	A	B	A	C	D	B
11	**12**	**13**	**14**	**15**	**16**	**17**	**18**	**19**	**20**
C	D	C	D	C	A	B	B	C	C

21	**22**	**23**	**24**	**25**	**26**	**27**	**28**	**29**	**30**
B	C	D	A	D	B	B	B	B	A
31	**32**	**33**	**34**	**35**	**36**	**37**	**38**	**39**	**40**
B	B	C	B	A	D	C	B	B	A
41	**42**	**43**	**44**	**45**	**46**	**47**	**48**	**49**	**50**
A	D	D	B	C	D	C	D	B	A
51	**52**	**53**	**54**	**55**	**56**	**57**	**58**	**59**	**60**
D	D	D	C	D	D	B	C	A	A
61	**62**	**63**	**64**	**65**	**66**	**67**	**68**	**69**	**70**
D	A	D	A	D	B	D	D	A	D
71	**72**	**73**	**74**	**75**					
D	D	C	A	B					

SCIENCE

1. Which of the following is the hardest metal?
A. Gold B. Iron
C. Platinum D. Tungsten

2. Bakeries use yeast in bread-making because it:
A. makes the bread hard
B. makes the bread soft and spongy
C. enhances the food values
D. keeps the bread fresh

3. The chemical name of 'laughing gas' is:
A. nitric oxide
B. nitrogen dioxide
C. nitrogen pentoxide
D. nitrous oxide

4. Brass is an alloy of:
A. lead and tin
B. zinc and copper
C. antimony, tin and lead
D. zinc, tin and copper

5. The length of its day and tilt of its axis are almost identical to those of the earth. This is true of:
A. Uranus B. Neptune
C. Saturn D. Mars

6. The milky way is classified as:
A. spiral Galaxy
B. electrical Galaxy
C. irregular Galaxy
D. round Galaxy

7. The energy of the sun is produced by:
A. ionisation
B. nuclear fusion
C. nuclear fission
D. oxidation

8. Which one of the following is not correctly matched?
A. Decibel—unit of loudness of sound
B. Horse power—unit of power
C. Nautical mile—unit of distance in navigation
D. Celsius—unit of heat

9. The common name of Sodium Bicarbonate is:
A. baking soda
B. washing soda
C. caustic soda
D. soda lime

10. Which variety of glass is heat resistant?
A. Flint glass B. Hard glass
C. Bottle glass D. Pyrex glass

11. Which of the following is a source of ready energy that one athlete can use after strenuous exercises?
A. Milk
B. Glucose
C. Sucrose
D. Tomato soup

12. The renewable source of energy:
A. petroleum B. kerosene
C. coal D. tree

13. The filament of an electric bulb is made of:
A. copper B. soft iron
C. cast iron D. tungsten

14. The natural wax and lac are obtained as:

A. petroleum products
B. resins of forest plants
C. by-products of sugar indsutry
D. insect secretions

15. Which hormone is known as 'fight or flight' hormone:

A. insulin B. adrenaline
C. estrogen D. oxytocin

16. "Pacemaker" is associated with:

A. kidney B. brain
C. heart D. lungs

17. The velocity of sound is more in:

A. water B. air
C. steel D. wood

18. Which planet orbits closest to the earth?

A. Mars B. Jupiter
C. Venus D. Mercury

19. It causes clotting of blood:

A. thrombin
B. haemoglobin
C. pectin
D. All of the above

20. Hardness of water is caused by soluble salts of:

A. sodium and potassium
B. potassium and ammonium
C. sodium and calcium
D. calcium and magnesium

21. The purification of a substance which evaporates without melting can be carried out by:

A. Crystallisation
B. Distillation
C. Steam distillation
D. Sublimation

22. Which of the following is the largest part of the human brain?

A. Cerebellum
B. Midbrain
C. Cerebrum
D. Medulla Oblongata

23. The total number of ear bones are:

A. 2 B. 4
C. 6 D. 8

24. An element in the form of gaseous atoms is converted into negative ions is called:

A. bond energy
B. electron affinity
C. electronegativity
D. ionization energy

25. Match the following:

	List-I* *(Name of Instruments)		***List-II* *(The Quantites they Measure)***
(*a*)	Anemometer	1.	Speed Rotation
(*b*)	Ammeter	2.	High temperature
(*c*)	Tachometer	3.	Wind speed
(*d*)	Pyrometer	4.	Electric current
		5.	Pressure difference

Codes:

	(*a*)	(*b*)	(*c*)	(*d*)
A.	4	3	1	5
B.	3	4	1	2
C.	3	5	2	1
D.	1	4	5	2

26. Diamond is a form of:
A. carbon B. nitrogen
C. oxygen D. hydrogen

27. The method used to obtain alcohol from molasses is called:
A. Distillation B. Hydrolysis
C. Fermentation D. Oxidation

28. Which of the following is the least inflammable fabric?
A. Cotton B. Nylon
C. Rayon D. Silk

29. Which of the following is required to build new tissues in the human body?
A. Carbohydrates
B. Fat
C. Protein
D. Water

30. The Vitamin which is required for proper clotting of blood in human body is:
A. vitamin E B. vitamin A
C. vitamin B_{12} D. vitamin K

31. Electron was discovered by:
A. Ernest Rutherford
B. Max Planck
C. Joseph Thomson
D. Albert Einstein

32. The number of amino acids which are found in nature is:
A. 20 B. 10
C. 15 D. 105

33. Bacteria were first seen, described and sketched by:
A. Jenner
B. Linnaeus
C. Pasteur
D. Leeuwenhock

34. The outstanding discovery of J.C. Bose, the Indian Scientist, is:
A. crescograph B. boson
C. cosmic rays D. ionograph

35. Density of a metal—when it is heated:
A. remains the same
B. increases
C. decreases
D. melts

36. Which of the following elements has been known to man from prehistoric times?
A. Sulphur B. Uranium
C. Platinum D. Arsenic

37. Our Solar system is a small unit of:
A. milky way galaxy
B. crab nebula galaxy
C. an independent galaxy
D. None of the above

38. Nights are cooler in the deserts because:
A. the sky is generally clear
B. the sky is generally cloudy
C. sand radiates heat less quickly as compared to earth
D. sand radiates heat more quickly as compared to the earth

39. Storage batteries commonly contain:
A. copper B. mercury
C. lead D. iron

40. Which of the following is a polymer?
A. Vinyl chloride
B. Urea
C. Starch
D. Styrene

41. What is common between a whale and a monkey?
A. Both have on external ear
B. Both have a long balancing tail
C. Both have body-hair throughout life
D. Both give birth to young ones

42. The hormone which regulates the basal metabolism in our body is secreted from:
A. pituitary
B. thyroid
C. adrenal cortex
D. pancreas

43. The acid used in car battery is:
A. hydrochloric acid
B. boric acid
C. sulphuric acid
D. carbonic acid

44. The boiling point of water is unaffected by:
A. the external pressure
B. the temperature of heat source
C. the kind of dissolved substances
D. the amount of dissolved substances

45. What is the velocity of sound in the air?
A. 330 cms per sec.
B. 330 metres per sec.
C. 760 metres per sec.
D. 1120 cms per sec.

46. The gas used in discharge tubes for optical decoration and advertising is:
A. carbon dioxide
B. ammonia
C. sulphur dioxide
D. neon

47. The substances present at the centre of the sun are in:
A. solid, liquid and gaseous states
B. liquid state only
C. gaseous state only
D. Both B and C

48. Blank capsules used in dispensing are made of:
A. egg-white B. gum
C. starch D. gelatine

49. Which one of the following is not an explosive?
A. trinitrotoluene
B. trinitroglycerine
C. cyclotrimethylene trinitramine
D. nitrochloroform

50. An ordinary clock loses time in summer; this is because:
A. the length of the pendulum increases and time period decreases
B. the length of the pendulum increases and time period increases
C. the length of the pendulum decreases and time period increases
D. the length of the pendulum decreases and time period decreases

51. When ice cubes floating in a beaker of water melt, the level of water in the beaker:

A. goes up
B. goes down
C. remains same
D. fall or rise depending on the number of ice cubes present in the beaker

52. Which of the following is an element?
A. Silica B. Magnesia
C. Glass D. Graphite

53. A characteristic gas smells near the unclear public urinals. Which is this gas?
A. Ammonia
B. Chlorine
C. Sulphur dioxide
D. Carbon monoxide

54. Kilowatt is a unit to measure:
A. power B. work
C. energy D. current

55. The apparent weight of a man in a lift will be less than his real weight:
A. when the lift is stationary
B. at no time
C. when the lift is going up with uniform acceleration
D. when the lift is going down with uniform acceleration

56. A natural sweetening agent obtained from a plant (but not sugar) is:
A. saccharin
B. santonine
C. cyclomates
D. None of these

57. Alkaloids are by-products of the metabolism of:
A. animals B. bacteria
C. plants D. viruses

58. Atom bomb is based on:
A. artificial radioactivity
B. nuclear fission
C. nuclear fusion
D. chemical reaction

59. Which gas in the atmosphere absorbs ultraviolet rays?
A. Methane B. Nitrogen
C. Ozone D. Helium

60. Which of the following is essential for the plants to help them in the formation of chlorophyll?
A. Potassium
B. Magnesium
C. Calcium
D. Phosphorus

61. The material used for bleaching paper pulp is:
A. lime
B. alum
C. caustic soda
D. sodium hypochlorite

62. Which of the following is used as a preservative of food articles?
A. sodium bicarbonate
B. sodium benzoate
C. sodium carbonate
D. sodium chloride

63. Milk in natural form has a certain amount of sugar. This sugar is called:
A. fructose B. glucose
C. sucrose D. lactose

64. Blood is classified biochemically as a:
A. cell B. liquid
C. tissue D. cartilage

65. Foxglove plant yields a drug which is a stimulant to:

A. kidney B. brain
C. lungs D. heart

66. The function of a catalyst in a reaction is to:

A. decrease the rate of the reaction
B. increase the rate of the reaction
C. increase the pressure of the reactants
D. decrease the pressure of the reactants

67. Which of the following gases is used for refrigeration?

A. Sulphur dioxide
B. Chlorine
C. Freon
D. Phosphine

68. Which plant stores food in the stem?

A. Ginger B. Carrot
C. Raddish D. Groundnut

69. When a ship enters a sea from a river, its level:

A. remains same
B. falls
C. rises
D. rises or falls depending on the condition and material of the ship

70. The sky is blue in colour because of:

A. combination of various lights producing blue colour
B. the moisture present in the air
C. the accumulation of smoke in the sky
D. the scattering of light by dust particles or air molecules

71. If a body is taken from the earth to the moon:

A. its mass will not be affected
B. its mass will decrease
C. its weight will become more
D. Both its mass and weight will decrease

72. An iron nail floats on mercury but sinks in water because:

A. mercury is a metal and water is not
B. upper layer of mercury is strong
C. mercury is a liquid metal and iron is a solid metal
D. iron is less dense than mercury

73. An electric bulb produces a loud sound when broken, because:

A. the glass is brittle
B. the gas inside the bulb suddenly expands
C. the gas makes the explosion
D. the air rushes into the partial vacuum in the bulb

74. A person climbing a hill bends forward so as to:

A. reduce chances of slipping
B. increase his stability
C. increase his stamina
D. move faster

75. The freezer in a refrigerator is fitted near the top:

A. without any specific and particular purpose

B. because it is convenient
C. so that it can cool the whole interior by setting up convection current
D. to keep it away from the hot compressor

76. The cover of a solar cooker is made of glass:
A. because glass allows heat radiation from the sun into the container but not out of it
B. to enable us to see the food cooking
C. because heat is radiated without absorption by glass
D. as glass is a good conductor of heat and cheap

77. Chlorine is a/an:
A. halogen B. alloy
C. metal D. noble gas

78. Which of the following is not an alloy?
A. brass B. bronze
C. steel D. zinc

79. Which of the following is an insecticide?
A. TNT B. DDT
C. Urea D. Alcohol

80. 'IC chips' for computers are usually made of:
A. chromium B. lead
C. silicon D. gold

81. Which of the following is used as dry ice?
A. Carbon dioxide
B. Ammonia
C. Oxygen
D. Ice with raw dust

82. The normal unit of measurement of distance of a star is:
A. kilometre B. light year
C. nautical mile D. knot

83. Solution of washing soda in water will be:
A. alkaline
B. acidic
C. neutral
D. None of these

84. Vitamin C is also called:
A. ascorbic acid
B. nucleic acid
C. lactic acid
D. hydrochloric acid

85. Pearls are found in:
A. turtles B. snails
C. tortoises D. oysters

86. Coal burns in air because air contains:
A. hydrogen
B. oxygen
C. nitrogen
D. carbon dioxide

87. A substance which glows and is used in watch dials is:
A. sodium B. sulphur
C. phosphorus D. chlorine

88. Which of the following chemical is used by photographers?
A. Sodium sulphide
B. Silver bromide
C. Potassium cyanide
D. Ivory powder

89. The process of coating iron with zinc is known as:
A. vulcanisation
B. electroplating
C. polishing
D. galvanising

90. The best source of iron is:
A. milk
B. egg
C. cauliflower
D. green vegetables

91. Vitamins are useful to the body for:
A. replacing the energy lost
B. the body growth
C. regulating the functions of the body
D. maintaining the body temperature

92. The metals used for the manufacture of stainless steel are:
A. chromium and carbon
B. aluminium and carbon
C. copper and nickel
D. chromium and zinc

93. In refrigerator, the refrigerant liquid is:
A. carbon dioxide
B. nitrogen
C. liquid helium
D. ammonia

94. Which of the following is the least inflammable fabric?
A. Cotton B. Nylon
C. Rayon D. Silk

95. Which of the following contains carbon?
A. Chromite
B. Bauxite
C. Lignite
D. Phosphorite

96. Which of the following blood groups is the universal donor?
A. A B. B
C. AB D. O

97. Which of the following fight infections in the body?
A. WBCs
B. RBCs
C. Blood plasma
D. Haemoglobin

98. The term 'refraction of light' means:
A. bending of light rays when they enter from one medium to another medium
B. splitting of white light into seven colours when it passes through the prism
C. bending of light round the corners of obstacles and apertures
D. coming back of light from a bright smooth surface

99. In the visible spectrum, the colour having the shortest wavelength is:
A. green B. red
C. violet D. blue

100. What is used to disintegrate bladder stones?
A. Infrared
B. Ultraviolet rays
C. X-rays
D. Ultrasonics

101. Mica is used in an electric iron, because it is a:
A. bad conductor of heat
B. good conductor of heat
C. good conductor of electricity
D. bad conductor of electricity

102. A line on a map joining places having equal atmospheric pressure is called:

A. Isotherm B. Isobar

C. Isocryme D. Isoheline

103. On addition of salt to water, its:

A. boiling point increases

B. boiling point decreases

C. boiling point is not affected

D. freezing point increases

104. If the velocity of a particle is reduced to half of its initial value, then the kinetic energy of the particle will:

A. get doubled

B. become four times

C. reduce to half its original value

D. reduce to one-fourth of its original value

105. A lunar eclipse occurs when:

A. Sun, Moon and Earth are not in the same line

B. Earth comes between the Sun and the Moon

C. Moon comes between the Sun and the Earth

D. Sun comes between the Earth and the Moon

106. Red light is used in traffic signals because:

A. it has the longest wavelength

B. it is beautiful

C. it is visible to people even with bad eyesight

D. None of these

107. The oil in the wick of a lamp rises up due to:

A. pressure difference

B. low viscosity of oil

C. capillary action

D. gravitational force

108. A thick glass tumbler cracks more easily than a thin one when hot water is poured into it. Why?

A. Thick glass is more brittle than thin glass

B. Thick glass is of inferior quality

C. The inner surface of the tumbler expands more than its outer surface

D. The outer surface of the tumbler expands more than its inner surface

109. How many cells are there in the hen's egg?

A. 1 B. 10

C. 100 D. 1000

110. The mirror placed near the driver of a bus is:

A. plane mirror

B. convex mirror

C. concave mirror

D. cooling mirror

111. Beri-Beri is a disease, caused by the deficiency of:

A. vitamin B B. vitamin C

C. vitamin K D. protein

112. Following are the great discoveries in physics:

1. X-rays
2. Theory of Relativity
3. Super Conductivity
4. Raman Effect

The chronological order in which they were discovered is:
A. 1, 3, 2, 4 B. 1, 2, 3, 4
C. 2, 1, 4, 3 D. 4, 1, 2, 3

113. Heliotropism is:
A. harmful effects of helium
B. helicopter flight control
C. medicine used to cure heart diseases
D. movement of plant organs towards sunlight

114. The isotope of uranium which is very much radioactive is:
A. U 235
B. U 238
C. U 233
D. All of the above

115. The human skull consists of:
A. 8 bones
B. 14 bones
C. 21 bones
D. 42 bones

Answers

1	**2**	**3**	**4**	**5**	**6**	**7**	**8**	**9**	**10**
D	B	D	D	D	A	B	D	A	D
11	**12**	**13**	**14**	**15**	**16**	**17**	**18**	**19**	**20**
B	D	D	D	B	C	A	C	A	D
21	**22**	**23**	**24**	**25**	**26**	**27**	**28**	**29**	**30**
D	C	C	B	B	A	C	A	C	D
31	**32**	**33**	**34**	**35**	**36**	**37**	**38**	**39**	**40**
C	A	D	A	C	A	A	D	C	C
41	**42**	**43**	**44**	**45**	**46**	**47**	**48**	**49**	**50**
D	B	C	B	B	D	C	C	D	B
51	**52**	**53**	**54**	**55**	**56**	**57**	**58**	**59**	**60**
C	D	C	A	D	D	C	B	C	B
61	**62**	**63**	**64**	**65**	**66**	**67**	**68**	**69**	**70**
D	B	D	C	D	B	C	A	C	D
71	**72**	**73**	**74**	**75**	**76**	**77**	**78**	**79**	**80**
A	D	D	B	C	A	A	D	D	C
81	**82**	**83**	**84**	**85**	**86**	**87**	**88**	**89**	**90**
A	B	A	A	D	B	C	B	D	D
91	**92**	**93**	**94**	**95**	**96**	**97**	**98**	**99**	**100**
C	A	D	A	C	D	A	A	C	C
101	**102**	**103**	**104**	**105**	**106**	**107**	**108**	**109**	**110**
A	A	A	D	B	A	C	C	A	C
111	**112**	**113**	**114**	**115**					
A	B	D	A	C					

SCIENCE AND TECHNOLOGY

1. Which one of the following techniques can be used to establish the paternity of child?
   A. Protein analysis
   B. Chromosome counting
   C. Quantitative analysis of DNA
   D. DNA finger printing

2. The first Indian artificial satellite was named:
   A. Aryabhatta B. Explorer-I
   C. Sputnik-1 D. Luna-3

3. The first computer of India is known as:
   A. Dharam B. Siddharth
   C. Param D. Gati

4. The symptom of anaemia is:
   A. loose or wrinkled skin
   B. difficulty in breathing
   C. yellowish eyes
   D. Oedema of liver

5. In surgery, what is arthroplasty:
   A. open heart surgery
   B. kidney transplant
   C. hip-joint replacement
   D. blood transfussion

6. The intermediate range nuclear-capable missile developed indigenously is named:
   A. Agni B. Prithvi
   C. Nag D. Trishul

7. The computer was invented by:
   A. Faraday B. Maxwell
   C. Babbage D. Bill Gates

8. Which of the following is the name of the first indigenously developed Indian Super Computer?
   A. Param B. Shakti
   C. Dharam D. Gati

9. The instrument which measures the movement of clouds by casting their images through a peephole on to a black mirrored surface is called:
   A. Periscope
   B. Nephoscope
   C. Stethoscope
   D. Gyroscope

10. Genetic engineering is possible only due to the role of certain specific enzymes that cut DNA at particular points of the sequence. These enzymes are called:
    A. nucleuses
    B. restriction enzymes
    C. DNA polymerases
    D. nitrogenases

11. The intensity of the waves generated by an earthquake and its time of occurrence is recorded by a:
    A. Barometer
    B. Thermometer
    C. Seismograph
    D. Galvanometer

12. A genetic disorder characterised by poor blood circulation and

abnormal haemoglobin molecules is better known as:
A. Sickel-cell anaemia
B. Haemophilia
C. Phenyl ketonuria
D. Huntington's chorea

13. The process of preparation of soap is known as:
A. Saponification
B. Calcification
C. Hydroxylation
D. Methylation

14. Who amongst the following initiated the age of genetic engineering in 1973 by inserting an amphibian ribosomal RNA gene into a bacterial plasmid?
A. Cohen and Boyer
B. J.C. Sanford
C. Watson and Crick
D. Roger Beachy

15. Superconductivity results when matter is:
A. heated to very high temperature
B. compressed to very high pressure
C. subjected to very low pressure
D. cooled to very low temperature

16. All of the following diseases are caused by viruses except:
A. jaundice
B. influenza
C. mumps
D. typhoid

17. Penicillin is given a patient in order to:
A. cure hereditary disease
B. cure all diseases
C. prevent any rise in body temperature
D. prevent the growth of several types of diseases caused by bacteria

18. BCG is:
A. curative medicine for tuberculosis
B. a preventive medicine for tuberculosis
C. a disinfectant
D. an antiseptic

19. What is "Lakshya"?
A. Pilotless target aircraft
B. Missile
C. Radar
D. Satellite Launch Vehicle

20. What is a 'Robot':
A. a type of rocket
B. a bomb
C. a machine that resembles a person and does mechanical routine tasks on command
D. an animal found in the jungles of Africa

21. MAB stands for:
A. Man and Biosphere Programme
B. Man and Biology Programme
C. Mammals and Biosphere Programme
D. None of the above

22. Element used for atomic power is:
A. calcium B. sodium
C. beryllium D. uranium

23. A pure semiconductor:
A. has low resistance
B. is called an intrinsic semi-conductor
C. Both of the above
D. None of the above

24. AIDS disease is caused by:
A. virus
B. sexual contact
C. bacteria
D. protozoa

25. The first indigenously built missile boat is named as:
A. INS Vibhuti
B. INS Vikrant
C. INS Shilpi
D. INS Mana

26. Which of the following is an example of Bio-technology?
A. Using electron microscope
B. Using technology to stabilise the life processes
C. Using modern techniques to understand the evolution of life
D. Using micro-organisms to synthesise insulin

27. Autopsy means:
A. curing a disease through self-medication
B. postmortem examination of a human body
C. curing a disease through auto-suggestion
D. becoming diseased through abuse of drugs

28. Introduction of a steel plough in the place of a wooden plough is an instance of:
A. advanced technology
B. appropriate technology
C. redundant technology
D. absolute technology

29. For appropriate technology what factors are of immediate concern?
I. skilled manpower
II. capital
III. infrastructure
IV. latest innovation
A. I and II   B. III and IV
C. I and IV   D. II and IV

30. Eco mark is given to Indian products that are:
A. pure and unadulterated
B. rich in protein
C. environment friendly
D. economically viable

31. 'Dolly' is the first clone mammal in the world of:
A. buffalo   B. goat
C. sheep   D. monkey

32. India's biggest nuclear research reactor is known as:
A. Apsara   B. Dhruva
C. Cirus   D. Purnima

33. We use the term 'mach number' in connection with:
A. sound
B. submarines
C. aircraft
D. spacecraft

34. Which of the following units measures the memory of the computer?
A. Volts   B. Amperes
C. Ohms   D. Bits

35. Maximum 'gobar gas' is produced during:
A. summer
B. winter
C. rainy season
D. All seasons

36. The first Indian satellite, Aryabhatta, was launched into space from a cosmodrome of:
A. France
B. USA
C. USSR
D. West Germany

37. The Vikram Sarabhai Space Centre is at:
A. Ahmedabad
B. Bangalore
C. Sriharikota
D. Trivandrum

38. The science dealing with the study of inheritance and variation is called:
A. Genetics
B. Evolution
C. Morphology
D. Cytology

39. Games are made up of:
A. histones
B. non-histones
C. proteins
D. polynucleotides

40. Which is the first artificial satellite to be put into orbit on October 4, 1957?
A. Sputnik-1
B. Apollo-7
C. Explorer-1
D. Solar Max

41. CNG (Compressed Natural Gas) is used for:
A. protecting pollution
B. saving diesel
C. avoiding the use of petrol
D. All of the above

42. Bronchitis is a disease of:
A. blood
B. liver
C. intestine
D. respiratory tract

43. The molecules responsible for storing the genetic code are:
A. DNA
B. RNA
C. protein
D. chromosome

44. Test tube baby means:
A. ovum fertilised and developed in test tube
B. ovum fertilised in test tube and developed in test tubes
C. ovum fertilised in test tubes and developed in uterus
D. ovum developed without fertilisation in test tubes

45. What is the basic characteristic of antigens:
A. They are capable of stimulating the formation of haemoglobin in the blood
B. They destroy haemoglobin
C. They are capable of defending themselves against attack by antibodies
D. They are capable of stimulating the formation of antibodies

46. What was the disease that led to the discovery of first anti viral vaccine?
A. Cancer
B. Tetanus
C. Polio
D. Small pox

47. Which is the most fast spreading disease?
A. Malaria
B. Plague
C. Poliomyelitis
D. Leprosy

48. The Central Food Technological Research Institute is located at:
A. Kolkata
B. Kanpur
C. Mysore
D. Ranchi

49. The International Rice Research Institute is located in:
A. Philippines
B. Thailand
C. Indonesia
D. Malaysia

50. "AIDS" affects:
A. blood cells of human body
B. immune system of human body
C. growth of human body
D. All of the above

51. Which of the following fertilisers is used after sowing the seeds:
A. nitrate
B. potash
C. green manure
D. phosphorus

52. Swelling of a strained foot is reduced by soaking in hot water containing a large amount of common salt. This is because of phenomenon called:
A. Osmosis
B. Plasmolysis
C. Electrolysis
D. None of these

53. Match List-I with List-II and select the correct answer using the codes given below the lists:

List-I	*List-II*
(*a*) Trishul	1. Anti-tank missile
(*b*) Prithvi	2. Intermediate range ballistic system
(*c*) Agni	3. Short range surface to air missile
(*d*) Nag	4. Surface to surface missile

Codes:

	(*a*)	(*b*)	(*c*)	(*d*)
A.	1	2	3	4
B.	4	3	2	1
C.	3	4	2	1
D.	2	1	4	3

54. In paints, the pigment is responsible for:
A. durability
B. colour
C. smoothness
D. glossy face

55. The working principle of a washing machine is:
A. centrifugation
B. dialysis
C. reverse osmosis
D. diffusion

56. Who invented 'radar':
A. J.H. Van Tassell
B. Wilhelm K. Roentgen
C. P.T. Farnsworth
D. A.H. Taylor and Zeo C. Young

57. Which one of the following is a useful functional association between fungi and the roots of higher plants?

A. Biofertiliser
B. Coralloid root
C. Lichen
D. Mycorrhiza

58. Low temperatures (cryogenics) find application in:

A. space travel, surgery and magnetic levitation
B. surgery, magnetic levitation and telemetry
C. space travel, surgery and telemetry
D. space travel, magnetic levitation and telemetry

59. Pure silicon is used as a:

A. conductor
B. insulator
C. non-conductor
D. semiconductor

60. The most common type of fingerprint encountered are:

A. whorls
B. loops
C. arches
D. composites

61. Indian farmers are unhappy over the introduction of 'Terminator Seed Technology' because the seeds produced by this technology are expected to:

A. show poor germination
B. form low-yielding plants despite the high quality
C. give rise to sexually sterile plants
D. give rise to plants incapable of forming viable seeds

62. Which one of the following genetic diseases is sex linked?

A. Royal haemophilia
B. Tay Sachs disease
C. Cystic fibrosis
D. Hypertension

63. Guided missiles are:

A. missiles that guide the soldiers in the army
B. unmanned self-propelled space or air vehicles carrying explosive war head
C. missiles that are launched by the gliders
D. ordinary war planes with a very sharp striking power and deep thrust

64. Prithvi is:

A. indigenously developed intermediate range ballistic missile
B. indigenously developed nuclear bomb
C. indigenously developed nuclear reactor
D. indigenously developed surface to surface missile

65. National Institute of Immunology and National Institute of Science, Technology and Development Studies are located in:

A. Hyderabad
B. Bangalore
C. Mumbai
D. New Delhi

Answers

1	2	3	4	5	6	7	8	9	10
C	A	B	D	C	A	C	A	B	B
11	**12**	**13**	**14**	**15**	**16**	**17**	**18**	**19**	**20**
C	A	C	A	D	D	D	B	A	C
21	**22**	**23**	**24**	**25**	**26**	**27**	**28**	**29**	**30**
A	D	B	A	A	B	B	A	A	C
31	**32**	**33**	**34**	**35**	**36**	**37**	**38**	**39**	**40**
C	B	C	D	C	C	D	A	D	A
41	**42**	**43**	**44**	**45**	**46**	**47**	**48**	**49**	**50**
D	D	A	C	D	D	B	C	A	B
51	**52**	**53**	**54**	**55**	**56**	**57**	**58**	**59**	**60**
A	A	C	B	A	D	A	A	B	B
61	**62**	**63**	**64**	**65**					
D	A	B	D	D					

AWARDS AND HONOURS

1. Who among the following is the first person to receive the Bharat Ratna award?
   A. C. Rajagopalachari
   B. S. Radhakrishnan
   C. C.V. Raman
   D. M. Visweswaraiya
2. Who among the following is the first person who was given the Bharat Ratna award posthumaously?
   A. K. Kamraj
   B. Lal Bahadur Shastri
   C. B.R. Ambedkar
   D. Vallabhbhai Patel
3. Which of the following is the highest order of gallantry award in India?
   A. Mahavir Chakra
   B. Vir Chakra
   C. Paramveer Chakra
   D. Ashok Chakra
4. The Arjuna awards are given to outstanding persons in the field of:
   A. science
   B. sports
   C. social services
   D. literature
5. The Bhartiya Jnanpith award is given to:
   A. sportspersons
   B. scientists
   C. coaches
   D. creative writers
6. Dada Saheb Phalke award is given in the field of:
   A. social services
   B. cinema
   C. creative writing
   D. politics
7. Who among the following is the first to receive 'Dada Saheb Phalke award'?
   A. Sivaji Ganesan
   B. Dr. Raj Kumar
   C. Devika Rani
   D. Majrooh Sultanpuri
8. Which of the following awards is given to the eminent coaches who successfully trained international sportspersons and teams:
   A. Dronacharya award
   B. K.K. Birla Foundation sports award
   C. Jamnalal Bajaj award
   D. Arjuna award
9. Lata Mangeshkar award is given by Madhya Pradesh Government in the field of:
   A. music B. cinema
   C. drama D. dance
10. The Kalinga Prize is given for the popularisation of Science and Research, by which of the following:
    A. UNICEF B. UNESCO
    C. Odisha Govt. D. Indian Govt.
11. Indira Gandhi International award is given in the field of:
    A. peace
    B. disarmament

C. development
D. All of the above

12. Which of the following prizes is considered to be the most prestigious in the world?
A. Magsaysay award
B. Nobel prize
C. Japan prize
D. Pulitzer award

13. Dhanvantari prize is given in which of the following fields:
A. medicine
B. agriculture
C. journalism
D. international understanding

14. The Nobel prize is not given in which of the following fields:
A. peace B. physics
C. economics D. agriculture

15. Match the following:

List-I (Nobel Prize Recipients)	***List-II (Fields in which given)***
(*a*) C.V. Raman	1. Economics
(*b*) Hargobind Khorana	2. Peace
(*c*) Mother Teresa	3. Medicine
(*d*) Amartya Sen	4. Literature
(*e*) Rabindra Nath Tagore	5. Physics

Codes:

	(*a*)	(*b*)	(*c*)	(*d*)	(*e*)
A.	5	3	2	1	4
B.	5	2	3	1	4
C.	3	4	2	1	5
D.	3	4	2	5	1

16. How many Oscar awards did the film Slumdog Millionaire win?
A. 7 B. 8
C. 9 D. 11

17. Which of the following is not a Civilian award?
A. Padma Vibhushan
B. Bharat Ratna
C. Padma Bhushan
D. Param Vishist Seva Medal

18. Which of the following is not a Gallantry award?
A. Paramveer Chakra
B. Mahavir Chakra
C. Padma Shri
D. Ashoka Chakra

19. Vikram Sarabhai Puraskar is given for:
A. outstanding contribution in science and technology
B. the popularisation of science and research
C. outstanding contribution in space and research
D. significant contribution in medicine

20. Which of the following is the highest order of Scientific award in India?
A. Shanti Swaroop Bhatnagar Puraskar
B. Homi Jahangir Bhabha Puraskar
C. Vikram Sarabhai Puraskar
D. G.D. Birla Science Puraskar

21. Which of the following awards is not conferred by Indian Government?
A. Ambedkar International award

B. Mahatma Gandhi Peace award
C. Padma Bhushan
D. Mahatma Gandhi award

22. C.K. Naidu award is given to a person for:
A. excellence in athletics
B. outstanding performance in games
C. outstanding contribution in cricket
D. best performance in hockey

23. Who among the following cinestars is awarded Pakistan's highest civil award in recognition of his services in improving Indo-Pak relations:
A. Manoj Kumar
B. Dilip Kumar
C. Raj Kumar
D. Ashok Kumar

24. The Saraswati Samman the highest and most prestigious literacy award of the country is given by:
A. Bharati Jnanpith
B. Sahitya Akademi
C. K.K. Birla Foundation
D. Human Resources Ministry, Indian Government

25. The Nobel prize for economics was awarded for the first time in 1969 by:
A. Swedish Central Bank
B. World Bank
C. International Monetary Fund
D. Nobel Foundation Committee

26. The UNESCO peace award is regarded as little Nobel prize conferred by:
A. UNESCO
B. Nobel Foundation Committee, Sweden
C. US Government
D. None of these

27. Govind Ballabh Pant award is given to:
A. the honestman of the year
B. the best parliamentarian
C. the best sportsman of the year
D. None of these

28. Which of the following samman is not conferred by Madhya Pradesh Government?
A. Tansen Samman
B. Kalidas Samman
C. Tulsi Samman
D. Vyas Samman

29. What name is given to the highest award for self-sacrifice or brave, daring and proeminent act of valour?
A. Param Vishist Seva Medal
B. Mahavir Chakra
C. Paramveer Chakra
D. Vir Chakra

30. 'Global 500' awards are given for achievements in:
A. population control
B. campaign against terrorism
C. protection of environment
D. campaign against drugs

31. The first Indian to win Nobel prize was:
A. C.V. Raman
B. Rabindra Nath Tagore
C. Hargobind Khorana
D. Amartya Sen

32. In which one of the following scientific fields Borlaug award is given:

A. medicine
B. space research
C. agriculture
D. atomic physics

33. 'Stri Shakti Puraskar' is given to women for:

1. excellence in athletics
2. outstanding performance in games
3. courage and enterprise for betterment of women
4. contribution to the nation and the people

Select your answer from the codes given below:

Codes:

A. 1 and 2 B. 2 and 3
C. 3 and 4 D. 1 and 4

34. The highest civilian award of India, Bharat Ratna has been awarded to only two foreigners so far. One of them is Khan Abdul Ghaffar Khan, the other is:

A. Mikhail Gorbachev
B. George Bush
C. Nelson Mandela
D. Helmut Kohl

35. Match the following:

I.	Arjuna award	(*a*)	Persons of cine world
II.	Oscar award	(*b*)	Journalists
III.	Dronacharya award	(*c*)	Sports persons
IV.	Pulitzer prize	(*d*)	Coaches

Codes:

A. I-(*a*), II-(*b*), III-(*d*), IV-(*c*)
B. I-(*c*), II-(*a*), III-(*d*), IV-(*b*)
C. I-(*b*), II-(*a*), III-(*c*), IV-(*d*)
D. I-(*c*), II-(*d*), III-(*a*), IV-(*b*)

36. Match List-I with List-II and select the correct answer by using the codes given below the lists:

List-I (Field in which given)	***List-II (Name of Award)***
(*a*) Science	1. Ghalib award
(*b*) Films	2. Arjuna award
(*c*) Poetry and prose	3. Phalke award
(*d*) Sports	4. Shanti Swarup Bhatnagar Memorial award

Codes:

	(*a*)	(*b*)	(*c*)	(*d*)
A.	4	3	2	1
B.	3	4	1	2
C.	3	4	2	1
D.	4	3	1	2

37. Which India-born scientist was awarded the Nobel prize in Astrophysics?

A. Prof. Chandrasekhar
B. Sir C.V. Raman
C. Satyendra Nath Bose
D. Vikram Sarabhai

38. Which of the following awards is not conferred by K.K. Birla Foundation?

A. Bihari award
B. Shankar award
C. Bharat Bharti Samman
D. Vyas Samman

39. The Vachaspati award is given for the outstanding contribution in the field of:

A. Hindi literature
B. Sanskrit literature
C. Bengali literature
D. Malayalam literature

40. The Ramon Magsaysay award, considered to be the Asia's Nobel prize is not given in which of the following fields:

A. government services
B. public services
C. community leadership
D. peace and disarmament

ANSWERS

1	**2**	**3**	**4**	**5**	**6**	**7**	**8**	**9**	**10**
A	B	C	B	D	B	C	A	A	B
11	**12**	**13**	**14**	**15**	**16**	**17**	**18**	**19**	**20**
D	B	A	D	A	B	D	C	C	A
21	**22**	**23**	**24**	**25**	**26**	**27**	**28**	**29**	**30**
D	C	B	C	A	A	B	D	C	C
31	**32**	**33**	**34**	**35**	**36**	**37**	**38**	**39**	**40**
B	C	C	C	B	D	A	C	B	D

GAMES AND SPORTS

1. Which is the national game of India?
A. Football B. Cricket
C. Hockey D. Kabaddi

2. Who among the following sportsmen is called the 'magician of Hockey'?
A. Dhyanchand
B. Dhanraj Pillai
C. Pargat Singh
D. Baljit Singh Dhillon

3. Which one of the following teams won the First One-Day Cricket World Cup held in 1975?
A. England B. Australia
C. Pakistan D. West Indies

4. In India the game of polo was introduced by the:
A. Greeks
B. Englishmen
C. Turks
D. Mughals

5. The term 'Tricks' is associated with which of the following games?
A. Polo B. Billiards
C. Bridge D. Croquet

6. P.V. Sindhu is associated with which of the following sport?
A. Weightlifting
B. Swimming
C. Tennis
D. Badminton

7. The name of Abhinav Bindra is associated with this sport?
A. Shooting B. Cricket
C. Football D. Basketball

8. 'Deodhar Trophy' is associated with which of the following games?
A. Hockey B. Cricket
C. Football D. Basketball

9. 'Free-throw' is given in which of the following sports?
A. Volleyball
B. Basketball
C. Badminton
D. Cricket

10. Match the following:

List-I (Countries)	***List-II (Sports)***
1. Australia	(*a*) Bull fighting
2. USA	(*b*) Ice hockey
3. Spain	(*c*) Cricket
4. Japan	(*d*) Basketball
	(*e*) Ju Jitsu

Codes:
A. 1-(*c*), 2-(*d*), 3-(*b*), 4-(*a*)
B. 1-(*d*), 2-(*b*), 3-(*c*), 4-(*e*)
C. 1-(*c*), 2-(*d*), 3-(*a*), 4-(*e*)
D. 1-(*c*), 2-(*b*), 3-(*a*), 4-(*e*)

11. How many players participate in a polo team?
A. 4 B. 8
C. 11 D. 7

12. In a cricket game when the umpire raises his right hand's index finger high:

A. batsman is not out
B. batsman is out
C. batsman is retired
D. batsman scores a six

13. What is the maximum duration of playing a football match?
A. 60 minutes B. 90 minutes
C. 80 minutes D. 70 minutes

14. The longest swimming course in the world is:
A. Dardenelles strait
B. Palk strait
C. English channel
D. Magellan strait

15. 'Subroto Cup' is associated with which of the following games?
A. Hockey B. Football
C. Basketball D. Cricket

16. Which of the following is the distance of running in a Marathon race?
A. 26 miles
B. 26 miles, 385 yards
C. 26 miles, 225 yards
D. 26 miles, 365 yards

17. Which is the correct weight of the cricket ball?
A. 4¼ oz B. 5¾ ioz
C. 4 oz D. 6 oz

18. The term 'butterfly stroke' is associated with which of the following games?
A. Swimming B. Cricket
C. Gliding D. Football

19. The term 'put' is associated with the sport:
A. Billiards B. Golf
C. Cricket D. Baseball

20. The Olympic Symbol (Summer Games) comprises of five rings or circles linked together to represent:
A. the sporting friendship of all
B. the five continents
C. Both A and B
D. None of these

21. Select a pair which is not properly matched:
A. Diego Maradona—Hockey
B. Gary Kasparov—Chess
C. Pete Sampras—Tennis
D. Ronaldo—Football

22. Santosh Trophy is associated with this sport:
A. Hockey B. Cricket
C. Badminton D. Football

23. Who was the first Indian woman to swim across the English channel?
A. Rita Faria
B. Shanta Rangaswami
C. Arati Saha
D. P.T. Usha

24. The 'Hall of Fame' tournament is associated with which of the following games:
A. Cricket B. Football
C. Hockey D. Tennis

25. The term 'Silly Point' is associated with the sport:
A. Billiards B. Bridge
C. Chess D. Cricket

26. The term 'Bunker' is associated with:
A. Polo
B. Golf

C. Basketball
D. Table Tennis

27. 'Arthur Walker Trophy' is associated with the sport:
A. Basketball
B. Billiards
C. Boat rowing
D. Bridge

28. Geet Sethi is associated with the sports:
A. Athletics
B. Billiards
C. Shooting
D. Weightlifting

29. Saina Nehwal is associated with the sport:
A. Shooting
B. Badminton
C. Boxing
D. Weightlifting

30. How many players participate in a volleyball team?
A. 6 B. 7
C. 8 D. 9

31. The Sports Day is observed on:
A. August 27 B. August 29
C. October 25 D. October 27

32. The first Asian Games were held in 1951 at:
A. Tokyo, Japan
B. Jakarta, Indonesia
C. Bangkok, Thailand
D. New Delhi, India

33. Australia won the world cup cricket in 2015 by defeating which of the teams?
A. England
B. Australia
C. New Zealand
D. None of these

34. 'Checkmate' is associated with which of the following sports:
A. Boxing B. Bridge
C. Chess D. Golf

35. Eden Gardens is a famous place associated with which of the following games?
A. Football
B. Hockey
C. Lawn Tennis
D. Cricket

36. The first Modern Olympic Games were held in 1896 in which of the following places?
A. Athens
B. Paris
C. Los Angeles
D. Sarajevo

37. The Winter Olympic Games came into being in 1924 was held at:
A. Chamonix (France)
B. St. Moritz (Switzerland)
C. Lake Placid (New York)
D. Oslo (Norway)

38. In the game of Baseball, distance between each base in a Diamond shaped ground is:
A. 56 ft B. 72 ft
C. 80 ft D. 90 ft

39. The Davis Cup is associated with which of the following games?
A. Lawn Tennis
B. Tennis
C. Cricket
D. Soccer

40. The Olympic Games are held every:
A. two years
B. four years
C. five years
D. six years

41. In which of the following years, the Olympic Games were not held:
A. 1916 B. 1940
C. 1944 D. All of these

42. Baron Pierre de Coubertin, father of the modern Olympic Games, belongs to:
A. Greece B. USA
C. France D. Italy

43. What is the national sport of Japan?
A. Karate B. Sumo
C. Ju-Jitsu D. Mikado

44. Which of the following cups is not associated with Hockey?
A. Agha Khan Cup
B. Azlan Shah Cup
C. Singer Cup
D. Indira Gandhi Gold Cup

45. Match the following:

List-I (Game)	***List-II (Term)***
1. Badminton	(*a*) Dribbling
2. Basketball	(*b*) Smash
3. Baseball	(*c*) Cue
4. Billiards	(*d*) Strike

Codes:
A. 1-(*b*), 2-(*a*), 3-(*d*), 4-(*c*)
B. 1-(*a*), 2-(*b*), 3-(*c*), 4-(*d*)
C. 1-(*d*), 2-(*b*), 3-(*a*), 4-(*c*)
D. 1-(*b*), 2-(*a*), 3-(*c*), 4-(*d*)

46. Who among the following has become the first women in the world to swim across seven seas?
A. Shikha Tandon
B. Bula Chowdhury
C. Amanda Beard
D. Arati Saha

47. In which of the following years were women athetes admitted to Olympic Games?
A. 1900 B. 1904
C. 1908 D. 1912

48. The term 'Gambit' is associated with the game of:
A. Golf B. Boating
C. Bridge D. Chess

49. 'Thomas Cup Trophy' is associated with which of the following sports?
A. World Chess
B. World Badminton
C. World Cricket
D. World Hockey

50. Match the following:

List-I (Sportsmen)	***List-II (Sports)***
I. Pele	(*a*) Ocean swimming
II. Sachin Tendulkar	(*b*) Athletics
III. Anju B. George	(*c*) Cricket
IV. Bula Chowdhury	(*d*) Football

Codes:
A. I-(*a*), II-(*b*), III-(*c*), IV-(*d*)
B. I-(*d*), II-(*c*), III-(*b*), IV-(*a*)
C. I-(*d*), II-(*c*), III-(*a*), IV-(*b*)
D. I-(*c*), II-(*d*), III-(*b*), IV-(*a*)

Answers

1	2	3	4	5	6	7	8	9	10
C	A	D	C	C	D	A	B	B	C
11	**12**	**13**	**14**	**15**	**16**	**17**	**18**	**19**	**20**
D	B	B	C	B	B	B	A	B	C
21	**22**	**23**	**24**	**25**	**26**	**27**	**28**	**29**	**30**
A	D	C	D	D	A	B	B	B	A
31	**32**	**33**	**34**	**35**	**36**	**37**	**38**	**39**	**40**
B	D	C	C	D	A	A	D	A	B
41	**42**	**43**	**44**	**45**	**46**	**47**	**48**	**49**	**50**
D	C	C	C	A	B	A	D	B	B

MISCELLANEOUS

1. Who is popularly known as the 'Nightingale of India'?
   A. Saronjini Naidu
   B. M.S. Subbulakshmi
   C. Mahadevi Verma
   D. Lata Mangeshkar
2. The first Speaker of the Lok Sabha was:
   A. Rabi Ray
   B. M. Ananthasayanam Ayangar
   C. Hukam Singh
   D. G.V. Mavalankar
3. The book *Prison Diary* was written by:
   A. Mahatma Gandhi
   B. V.D. Savarkar
   C. Jaya Prakash Narain
   D. Morarji Desai
4. The new name given to Calcutta city is:
   A. Kalighat B. Kalicutta
   C. Kolkatta D. Kolkata
5. ISI mark is not given to which of the following products?
   A. Electrical goods
   B. Hosiery goods
   C. Biscuits
   D. Cloth
6. Which day every year is observed as the World Health Day?
   A. May 13
   B. June 30
   C. April 7
   D. September 30
7. The origin of the phrase "United Nations" is associated with which one of the following personalities?
   A. Jawaharlal Nehru
   B. Franklin Roosevelt
   C. Charles de Gaulle
   D. Woodraw Wilson
8. The Economic and Social Commission for Asia and Pacific (ESCAP) is located at:
   A. Kuala Lumpur
   B. Bangkok
   C. Manila
   D. Singapore
9. Which of the following is the headquarters of the World Bank?
   A. The Hague
   B. Washington
   C. Paris
   D. London
10. Which one of the following countries is not a member of the Shanghai-5?
    A. China
    B. Kazakhistan
    C. Russia
    D. Vietnam
11. What is the currency of South Africa?
    A. Guilder B. Pound
    C. Shekel D. Rand
12. Who was the first woman the following to become the Prime

Minister of a country in the world?

A. Benazir Bhutto
B. Indira Gandhi
C. Margaret Thatcher
D. Sirimavo Bandarnaika

13. Which animal is the symbol of the World Wildlife Fund?

A. Tiger
B. Giant Panda
C. Hornbill
D. White Bear

14. Who was the first President of All India Trade Union Congress?

A. Dewan Chaman Lal
B. Lala Lajpat Rai
C. N.G. Ranga
D. Swami Sahajanand

15. Which one of the following is an important tribe of the Dhauladha Range?

A. Abor B. Gaddi
C. Lepcha D. Tharu

16. Which one of the following cities is not connected by National Highway No. 3?

A. Agra B. Bhopal
C. Dhule D. Gwalior

17. Which one of the following cities does not have the special economic zone?

A. Chennai B. Kandla
C. Kochi D. Surat

18. Which one of the following programmes is not included in the Swarna Jayanti Gram Swarojgar Yojna?

A. IRDP B. TRYSEM
C. DWCRA D. JRY

19. Who took the charge of Prime Ministership immediately after the death of Jawaharlal Nehru?

A. Indira Gandhi
B. Morarji Desai
C. Gulzarilal Nanda
D. Lal Bahadur Shastri

20. Which one among the following is least like the others?

A. Kathakali
B. Bhangra
C. Kuchipudi
D. Bharat Natyam

21. Which one of the following is not correctly matched?

A. Fiji—Suva
B. Finland—Oslo
C. Guyana—George Town
D. Lebanon—Beirut

22. The author of the book "Animal Farm" is:

A. Leo Tolstoy
B. George Orwell
C. John Dryden
D. S.M. Ali

23. Which one of the following is referred to as the 'Golden Hand Shake'?

A. Honouring VIP's
B. Voluntary Retirement Scheme
C. Wishing bon voyage
D. Receiving distinguished guests

24. "India House" is located in:

A. New Delhi B. Kolkata
C. London D. NewYork

25. The largest flightless bird which can run at a great speed:
A. Penguin B. Kiwi
C. Ostrich D. Emu

26. International Finance Corporation is the ancillary institution of the:
A. UNO B. IDO
C. IMF D. IBRD

27. The Pradhan Mantri Gram Sadak Yojna is:
A. to augment road connectivity and provide foodgrains to the poorest of the poor at cheaper rates.
B. to facilitate patrolling of the area to prevent misuse of electricity by unauthorised persons
C. to help the police to reach the place of crime more swiftly to control crime-spurt
D. to develop community life in villages which are not well connected

28. Losoong is a festival which is celebrated in:
A. Tibet
B. Arunachal Pradesh
C. Sikkim
D. Kerala

29. Which of the following countries is now known as Myammar?
A. Kampuchea
B. Northern Rhodesia
C. Burma
D. Laos

30. Who said 'Man is a political animal'?
A. Socrates B. Plato
C. Aristotle D. Dante

31. "Persons may change but rules should not change" is the principle of:
A. Absolute Monarchy
B. Constitutional Government
C. Unwritten Constitution
D. Republic

32. 'Kuchipudi' is a dance style which originated from:
A. Kerala
B. Andhra Pradesh
C. Manipur
D. Tamil Nadu

33. Currency of Japan is called:
A. Yen B. Dollar
C. Pound D. Lira

34. The first Secretary-General of the United Nations was:
A. Dag Hammarskjoeld
B. U. Thant
C. Kurt Waldheim
D. Trygve Lie

35. Padma Subramaniam is an exponent of classical dance:
A. Kuchipudi
B. Odissi
C. Bharatnatyam
D. Manipuri

36. Shiv-Hari, the popular musical duo, plays which of the following instruments?
A. Tabla and Guitar
B. Santoor and Flute
C. Piano and Drums
D. None of these

37. Which of the following is called the 'Mother of Parliaments'?
A. The German Parliament
B. The American Parliament
C. The French Parliament
D. The British Parliament

38. Which of the following places is not in Pak-occupied Kashmir?
A. Gilgit
B. Skardu
C. Muzaffarabad
D. Kargil

39. Who amongst the following was not a Vice-President before becoming President of India?
A. V.V. Giri
B. R. Venkataraman
C. S. Radhakrishnan
D. Giani Zail Singh

40. Which one of the following projections is used chiefly in navigation?
A. Mercator's B. Mollweid's
C. Bonne's D. Lambert'

41. Which of the following years is known as the "Year of great divide" with regard to population growth in India?
A. 1911 B. 1921
C. 1947 D. 1951

42. Which one of the following is the World Environment Day?
A. 22nd April B. 1st May
C. 31st May D. 5th June

43. The cost of next-best alternative is known as:
A. Real Cost
B. Social Cost
C. Opportunity Cost
D. Over-head Cost

44. "Kamasutra" is written by:
A. Kalamandalam Nair
B. Ananda Coomaraswamy
C. Birju Maharaj
D. S.H. Vatsyayan

45. December 10, is regarded as a red-letter-day for the whole world because it is the:
A. International Labour Day
B. Human Rights Day
C. United Nations Day
D. Science Day

46. Given below is a list of traditional dresses of women along with States. Which one of them is not correctly matched?
A. Boku–Sikkim
B. Mekhala–Assam
C. Mundu–Chhattisgarh
D. Pheran–Kashmir

47. The book "The Proudest Day" deals with the story of:
A. Integration of Indian States
B. India's independence
C. Pokhran nuclear explosion
D. Formation of the NDA Government at the Centre

48. March 8th, is observed as:
A. World Environment Day
B. Heritage Day
C. International Women's Day
D. Youth Day

49. The 'Kumbha Mela' comes round once in:
A. 7 years B. 5 years
C. 10 years D. 12 years

50. Who among the following has written the book entitled 'Autobiography of an Unknown Indian'?
A. Kuldip Nayyar
B. V.S. Naipaul
C. Nirad C. Choudhuri
D. N.A. Palkhivala

51. The abbrivation IGNOU stands for:
A. Indian Government's Nuclear Option Ultimatum
B. Indira Gandhi National Open University
C. Inter-Governmental and Non-Official Understandings
D. Informal Group on National Occupational Utilities

52. The author of the book 'The Gin Drinkers' is:
A. Arundhati Roy
B. Anita Desai
C. Sagarika Ghose
D. Shobha De

53. 1st December, of every year is observed to mark:
A. World Habitat Day
B. Universal Children's Day
C. World AIDS Day
D. Anniversary of United Nations

54. The famous Salar Jung Museum is situated in:
A. Assam
B. Andhra Pradesh
C. Jammu and Kashmir
D. Uttar Pradesh

55. The International Nautical Mile is equal to:
A. 1852 metres
B. 1825 metres
C. 2000 metres
D. 1582 metres

56. Consumer Day is celebrated every year on:
A. April 1
B. October 23
C. March 15
D. December 5

57. Subhas Mukhopadhyay is associated with which one of the following fields?
A. Politics
B. Sports
C. Literature
D. Social service

58. The Asian Development Bank has its headquarters in:
A. Kathmandu B. Manila
C. Colombo D. Tokyo

59. Who among the following Indians has presided over the UNESCO?
A. Dr. Zakir Hussain
B. Dr. Ramaswami Mudaliar
C. Dr. S. Radhakrishnan
D. Maulana Abul Kalam Azad

60. World Health Day is observed on:
A. April 7 B. April 9
C. April 18 D. April 20

61. Which of the following countries is now known as Cambodia?
A. Northern Rhodesia
B. Laos
C. Kampuchea
D. Comoros

62. Who was the first Indian to become the member of British Parliament?
A. W.C. Bannerjee
B. M. Malabari
C. D.N. Wacha
D. Dadabhai Naoroji

63. Who is the writer of the book 'Interpreter of Maladies'?
A. Jhumpa Lahiri
B. Arundhati Roy
C. Vikram Seth
D. Geeta Mehta

64. Which of the following is a morning 'Raag'?
A. Sohini B. Bhairavi
C. Kalabati D. Sarang

65. Who is the writer of the poetry 'Deep Shikha'?
A. Ramdhari Singh Dinkar
B. Shankar Dayal Sharma
C. Subhadara Kumari Chauhan
D. None of these

66. The compilation of 'Meri Ekawan Kavitayen' (My 51 Poems) is written by:
A. Atal Behari Vajpayee
B. Harivanshrai Bachchan
C. Dharam Vir Bharati
D. Shivmangal Singh 'Suman'

67. Who among the following is the writer of 'Anand Math'?
A. Harindra Nath Chattopadhyay
B. Rabindranath Tagore
C. Mulk Raj Anand
D. Bankim Chandra Chatterjee

68. In which Shakespearian drama is *Desdemona* a character?
A. Hamlet
B. Othello
C. Merchant of Venice
D. As You Like It

69. The famous work of Leo Tolstoy is:
A. Merchant of Venice
B. Illiad
C. War and Peace
D. Great Expectations

70. Who said, "Fools rush in where angels fear to tread"?
A. The Bible
B. John Milton
C. Alexander Pope
D. Dr. Samuel Johnson

71. Who is the writer of the novel "God of Small Things"?
A. Arundhati Roy
B. Jhumpa Lahiri
C. Kamal Subramaniyam
D. Mahashweta Devi

72. The capital of Mizoram is:
A. Imphal B. Shillong
C. Kohima D. Aizawl

73. Who is the author of the book 'The Namesake'?
A. Shashi Desh
B. Jhumpa Lahiri
C. Kapil Dev
D. Benazir Bhutto

74. Which of the following is the 29th State of India?
A. Telangana
B. Uttarakhand
C. Chhattisgarh
D. Goa

75. Guernica was painted by:
A. Leonardo da Vinci
B. Michelangelo
C. Picasso
D. Raphael

76. The 'Last Supper' is a world famous painting by:
A. Paul Gaugin
B. Leonardo da Vinci
C. Raphael
D. Rembrandt

77. 'Bhogali Bihu' is a festival of:
A. Assam B. Odisha
C. Gujarat D. Rajasthan

78. Classical dance having its roots in Tamil Nadu is:
A. Kathakali
B. Kathak
C. Kuchipudi
D. Bharat Natyam

79. Jamini Roy distinguished himself in:
A. dancing
B. colour photography
C. instrumental music
D. painting

80. Which of the following countries is not a member of the UNO?
A. Sweden B. Taiwan
C. Australia D. Norway

81. Which Indian jurist held the office of the President of International Court of Justice?
A. H.R. Khanna
B. K.S. Hegde
C. Nagendra Singh
D. R.S. Pathak

82. Who was the first Indian to be the President of UN General Assembly?
A. Natwar Singh
B. V.K. Krishna Menon
C. Mrs. Vijayalakshmi Pandit
D. Romesh Bhandari

83. What is the correct sequence of the formation of the following States of India?
1. Andhra Pradesh
2. Haryana
3. Kerala
4. Meghalaya
A. 1, 3, 2, 4
B. 1, 3, 4, 2
C. 3, 1, 2, 4
D. 3, 1, 4, 2

84. The 'first lady' of the Indian silver screen is:
A. Madhubala
B. Devika Rani
C. Durga Khote
D. Nargis Dutt

85. Arunachal Pradesh has borders with:
A. Bhutan, China and Myanmar
B. Bhutan, Bangladesh and Myanmar
C. Bangladesh, China and Myanmar
D. Bhutan, China and Bangladesh

86. The talkie film Alam Ara was produced in:
A. 1912 B. 1913
C. 1931 D. 1934

87. The headquarters of UNESCO is:
A. Paris
B. Washington DC
C. Geneva
D. Switzerland

88. The headquarters of WHO is:
A. Paris
B. Geneva
C. Washington DC
D. Rome

89. The author of the book 'India Wins Freedom' is:
A. Abul Kalam Azad
B. Rajendra Prasad
C. Annie Besant
D. Lala Lajpat Rai

90. Television was introduced in India in:
A. 15 September, 1959
B. 5 September, 1959
C. 25 September, 1959
D. 30 September, 1959

Answers

1	**2**	**3**	**4**	**5**	**6**	**7**	**8**	**9**	**10**
A	D	C	D	D	C	B	B	B	D
11	**12**	**13**	**14**	**15**	**16**	**17**	**18**	**19**	**20**
D	D	B	B	B	B	A	D	C	B
21	**22**	**23**	**24**	**25**	**26**	**27**	**28**	**29**	**30**
B	B	B	C	C	D	D	C	C	C
31	**32**	**33**	**34**	**35**	**36**	**37**	**38**	**39**	**40**
B	B	A	D	C	B	D	D	D	A
41	**42**	**43**	**44**	**45**	**46**	**47**	**48**	**49**	**50**
B	D	C	D	B	C	C	C	D	C
51	**52**	**53**	**54**	**55**	**56**	**57**	**58**	**59**	**60**
B	C	C	B	B	C	C	B	C	A
61	**62**	**63**	**64**	**65**	**66**	**67**	**68**	**69**	**70**
C	D	A	B	D	A	D	B	C	C
71	**72**	**73**	**74**	**75**	**76**	**77**	**78**	**79**	**80**
A	D	B	A	C	B	A	D	D	B
81	**82**	**83**	**84**	**85**	**86**	**87**	**88**	**89**	**90**
C	C	A	B	A	C	A	B	A	A

Quantitative Aptitude

1

NUMBERS

A number tells us how many times a unit is contained in a given quantity. It therefore signifies one or more units, or denotes one or more distinct objects of the same kind. For example, *one* rupee, *six* pencils, *nine* cats, *thirty* paise, etc. The words in italics denote numbers.

Whole Numbers: The numbers 0, 1, 2, 3, 4, 5, 6, 7, 8, 9, 10, 11, ... are called whole numbers or integers. So 84 is an integer while 6¼ is not an integer.

Even Numbers: The numbers, which are divisible by two are called even numbers. *For example,* 2, 4, 6, 8, 10, 12, 28, 36, etc.

Odd Numbers: The numbers, which cannot be divided by two are called odd numbers. *For example,* 1, 3, 5, 7, 9, 11, 13, 15, 17, 19, etc.

Prime Numbers: The numbers, which are divisible only by themselves and one are called prime numbers. *For example,* 2, 3, 5, 7, 11, 13, etc.

Composite Numbers: The numbers, which are not prime called composite numbers. Thus, the prime numbers and composite numbers make up the set of natural numbers.

Consecutive Numbers: A collection of numbers is consecutive if each number is the successor of the number which precedes it. *For example,* 4, 5, 6, 7, 8 and 9 are consecutive, but 4, 5, 6, 8, 10 are not. 6, 8, 10, 12 are consecutive even numbers. 11, 13, 17, 19 are consecutive prime numbers.

Any whole number can be written as a product of factors which are prime numbers.

How to write a number as a product of prime factors?

(*i*) Divide the number by 2 if possible; continue to divide by 2 until the factor you get, is not divisible by 2.

(*ii*) Divide the result from (i) by 3 if possible; continue to divide by 3 until the factor you get, is not divisible by 3.

(*iii*) Divide the result from (ii) by 5 if possible; continue to divide by 5 until the factor you get, is not divisible by 5.

(*iv*) Continue this procedure by dividing by 7, 11, 13, and so on; until all the factors are prime.

EXAMPLES :

Example 1. *Express 2310 as a product of prime factors.*

Solution.

2	2310
2	1155
5	385
7	77
	11

$\therefore$ $2310 = 2 \times 3 \times 5 \times 7 \times 11.$

Example 2. *Resolve 1026 into prime factors.*

Solution.

2	1026
3	513
3	171
3	57
	19

$\therefore$ $1026 = 2 \times 3 \times 3 \times 3 \times 19$

A number n is a common multiple of two other numbers a and b if it is a multiple of each of them. For example, 24 is a common multiple of 2 and 3, since $2 \times 12 = 24$ and $3 \times 8 = 24$. But 21 is not a common multiple of 3 and 6, because 21 is not a multiple of 6.

A number x is a common factor of two other numbers a and b if x is a factor of a and x is a factor of b.

L.C.M.: The least common multiple of two numbers is the smallest number which is a common multiple of both numbers.

How to find the least common multiple of two numbers a and b?

(i) Write a and b as products of *primes* separately.

(ii) If there are any common factors delete them in one of the products.

(iii) Multiply the remaining factors to get L.C.M.

PROPERTIES OF NUMBERS

1. The product of any two consecutive numbers is divisible by 2

For example,

$2 \times 3 = 6$	is divisible by 2
$3 \times 4 = 12$	is divisible by 2
$4 \times 5 = 20$	is divisible by 2
$15 \times 16 = 240$	is divisible by 2

2. The product of any three consecutive numbers is divisible by 6.
For example,

$2 \times 3 \times 4 = 24$ is divisible by 6
$3 \times 4 \times 5 = 60$ is divisible by 6
$4 \times 5 \times 6 = 120$ is divisible by 6
$10 \times 11 \times 12 = 1320$ is divisible by 6
$40 \times 41 \times 42 = 68880$ is divisible by 6

3. The product of any four consecutive numbers is divisible by 24.
For example,

$2 \times 3 \times 4 \times 5 = 120$ is divisible by 24.
$$4 \times 5 \times 6 \times 7 = 24 \times 5 \times 7$$
$$6 \times 7 \times 8 \times 9 = 3 \times 2 \times 7 \times 8 \times 9$$
$$= 24 \times 2 \times 7 \times 9$$
$$10 \times 11 \times 12 \times 13 = 2 \times 5 \times 11 \times 12 \times 13$$
$$= 24 \times 5 \times 11 \times 13$$

4. The product of any five consecutive numbers is divisible by 120.
For example,

$$2 \times 3 \times 4 \times 5 \times 6 = 120 \times 6$$
$$3 \times 4 \times 5 \times 6 \times 7 = 120 \times 21$$
$$4 \times 5 \times 6 \times 7 \times 8 = 120 \times 56$$

5. Every square number is a multiple of 3 or exceeds of multiple of 3 by unity.
For example,

$$3^2 = 9 = 3 \times 3$$
$$4^2 = 16 = 3 \times 5 + 1$$
$$5^2 = 25 = 3 \times 8 + 1$$
$$6^2 = 36 = 3 \times 12$$
$$7^2 = 49 = 3 \times 16 + 1$$

6. Difference of the squares of any two odd numbers is always divisible by 8.
For example,

$$5^2 - 3^2 = 25 - 9 = 16 = 8 \times 2$$
$$7^2 - 5^2 = 49 - 25 = 24 = 8 \times 3$$
$$9^2 - 5^2 = 81 - 25 = 56 = 8 \times 7$$
$$11^2 - 3^2 = 121 - 9 = 112 = 8 \times 14$$

7. A number is exactly divisible by 11 when the difference between the sums of the digits in the odd and even places respectively is zero or a multiple of 11.
For example, Consider the number 1569942

Sum of the odd digits $= 1 + 6 + 9 + 2 = 18$
Sum of the even digits $= 5 + 9 + 4 = 18$

Difference between the sums of the odd and even digits

$$= 18 - 18 = 0$$

Hence, 1569942 is divisible by 11.

8. The product of two consecutive odd or even numbers increased by unity is a perfect square.

For example,

$$3 \times 5 + 1 = 16 = 4^2$$
$$4 \times 6 + 1 = 25 = 5^2$$
$$5 \times 7 + 1 = 36 = 6^2$$
$$6 \times 8 + 1 = 49 = 7^2$$

9. The sum of any two consecutive numbers is equal to the difference of their squares.

For example,

$$3 + 4 = 7 = 4^2 - 3^2 = 7$$
$$5 + 4 = 9 = 5^2 - 4^2 = 9$$
$$7 + 6 = 13 = 7^2 - 6^2 = 13$$

10. The sum of the cubes of any three consecutive numbers is divisible by the sum of the numbers themselves.

For example, $2^3 + 3^3 + 4^3 = 8 + 27 + 64 = 99 = (2 + 3 + 4)\ 11$

$$4^3 + 5^3 + 6^3 = 64 + 125 + 216 = 405$$
$$= (4 + 5 + 6)\ 27$$

EXERCISE

1. 2, 4, 6, 8, 10, ... are:

A. prime numbers
B. odd numbers
C. even numbers
D. natural numbers

2. 1, 2, 3, 4, ... are :

A. Natural numbers
B. Odd numbers
C. Prime numbers
D. Composite numbers

3. 1, 2, 3, 4, 5, 7, 11 and 13 are:

A. even numbers
B. odd numbers
C. prime numbers
D. natural numbers

4. The prime numbers between 1 to 100 are:

A. 20 B. 22
C. 25 D. 30

5. The only even prime number is:

A. 2 B. 67
C. 79 D. 98

6. Which of the following is not a prime number?

79, 83, 87, 97

A. 79 B. 83
C. 87 D. 97

7. Which of the following is a prime number?

117, 147, 149, 159

A. 117 B. 147
C. 149 D. 159

8. The next number in the sequence 1, 7, 3, 9, 5, 11, ... is :
A. 7 B. 13
C. 15 D. 17

9. In the sequence 4, 9, ...25, 36, the missing number is :
A. 14 B. 16
C. 20 D. 21

10. In the sequence 17, ..., 18, 15, 19, 14, 20, 13, the missing number is:
A. 5 B. 10
C. 12 D. 16

Directions. *For questions 11 to 14, let * means add the first number to twice the second number.*

11. The value of 5*4 is:
A. 20 B. 9
C. 11 D. 13

12. The value of 7*0 is:
A. 7 B. 9
C. 14 D. 0

13. The value of [1*2] * 3 is:
A. 5 B. 7
C. 9 D. 11

14. The value of 3* [0*6] is:
A. 18 B. 23
C. 27 D. 29

Directions. *For questions 15 to 17, let Δ means square the first number and add the second.*

15. The value of 2 Δ 10 is:
A. 12 B. 14
C. 27 D. 102

16. The value of 6 Δ 7 is:
A. 42 B. 43
C. 54 D. 59

17. The value of [3 × 2] Δ 9 is :
A. 42 B. 45
C. 87 D. 91

Directions. *For questions 18 to 20, let ** means increase the first number by 2 and then multiply by the second number.*

18. The value of 5** 3 is :
A. 15 B. 25
C. 21 D. 17

19. The value of [3**3]**4 is:
A. 68 B. 60
C. 54 D. 36

20. The value of [5**0]**3 is :
A. 0 B. 6
C. 15 D. 21

21. The smallest whole number which is divisible by 3 and also by the next two greater prime number is:
A. 15 B. 21
C. 60 D. 105

22. A number is called perfect, when it is equal to the sum of all its divisions excluding the number itself, e.g., 6 = 1 + 2 + 3. The other perfect number less than 32 is:
A. 8 B. 12
C. 16 D. 28

23. The smallest number of four digits is:
A. 1001 B. 0001
C. 0010 D. 1000

24. The largest number of four digits is:

A. 1000 B. 9000
C. 9009 D. 9999

25. If 'a' is an odd number, 'b' is an even number and 'c' is odd then, $a + b + c$ is:

A. odd number
B. even number
C. prime number
D. any number

26. The product of two prime numbers is a :

A. prime number
B. even number
C. odd number
D. composite number

27. Prime factors of a number are 2, 2, 3, 7. The number is :

A. 14 B. 41
C 48 D. 84

28. The largest number which is a factor of 56 as well as 84 is :

A. 2 B. 7
C. 14 D. 28

29. H.C.F. of 72, 108, 56 is :

A. 3 B. 4
C. 6 D. 8

30. L.C.M. of 6, 9, 12, 18 is :

A. 28 B. 36
C. 38 D. 42

31. If 'x' and 'y' are both odd numbers, which of the following numbers must be an even number?

A. $x + y$
B. $x \times y$
C. $xy + 2$
D. $2x + y$

32. 'a' is less than 'b', which of the following numbers is greater than 'a' and less than 'b' :

A. $\frac{a+b}{2}$ B. $\frac{ab}{2}$
C. $b^2 - a^7$ D. ab

33. $a + b + c + d$ is a positive number, a minimum of 'x' of the numbers a, b, c and d must be positive, where 'x' is equal to :

A. 1 B. 2
C. 3 D. 4

34. Which of the following is largest?
$[2 + 2 + 2]^2$, $[(2 + 2)^2]^2$,
$[2 \times 2 \times 2]^2$, $[4]^2$

A. $[2 + 2 + 2]^2$
B. $[(2 + 2)^2]^2$
C. $[2 \times 2 \times 2]^2$
D. $[4]^2$

35. The sum of two numbers is 84. If one of them exceeds the other by 12, the numbers are :

A. 62, 22 B. 36, 24
C. 48, 36 D. 35, 47

36. Take a number. Double it and add 15 to it. If the result is 81, the number is :

A. 30 B. 32
C. 33 D. 66

37. Take a number, find its square root and add 20 to it. If the result is 30, the number is :

A. 5 B. 1
C. 20 D. 100

38. There are four numbrs A, B, C and D. Average of the first three, i.e., A, B and C is 15 and that of

B, C and D is 16. If the last number, i.e. D is 19, then the first number is:

A. 15 B. 16
C. 17 D. 18

39. Think of a number, divide it by 9 and add 9 to it, if the result is 27, the number is :

A. 18 B. 21
C. 100 D. 162

40. Of the three numbers, the first is twice the second and thrice the third. If the average of three is 22, the three numbers are:

A. 12, 18, 36 B. 18, 12, 36
C. 36, 12, 18 D. 36, 18, 12

41. The number which when added to itself 10 times gives 264. The number is:

A. 20 B. 22
C. 24 D. 26

42. If a person is standing on the sixth number in the queue from both the ends, the total persons in the queue are:

A. 9 B. 11
C. 12 D. 13

43. A number increased by itself and 5 gives 17. The number is :

A. 2 B. 3
C. 5 D. 6

44. Consider a number 'x'. Divide it by 4 and add 9. If the result is 15, the value of 'x' is :

A. 20 B. 24
C. 23 D. 28

45. A number 'x' when multiplied by 5 and added to three times its own gives 64, the number is:

A. 8 B. 12
C. 14 D. 18

46. If the sum of two numbers 'x' and 'y' is equal to twice the first number, the second number 'y' is:

A. $> x$
B. $< x$
C. $= x$
D. negative number

47. The excess of thrice a certain number over 11 is 19. The number is:

A. 8 B. 9
C. 10 D. 11

48. The difference between the squares of two consecutive numbers is 25. The numbers are:

A. 13, 12 B. 12, 13
C. 15, 14 D. 14, 13

49. The sum of two digits of a number is 15. If 9 is added to the number, the digits are reversed. The number is :

A. 78 B. 87
C. 69 D. 96

50. A number which when multiplied by 11 is as much above 180 as it was originally below it. The number is:

A. 25 B. 30
C. 40 D. 45

51. Divide ₹ 53 among X, Y, Z so that X may receive ₹ 7 more than Y, and Y may receive ₹ 8 more than Z.

A. 10, 15, 18 B. 18, 10, 25
C. 20, 12, 27 D. 25, 18, 10

EXPLANATORY ANSWERS

1. C : The numbers divisible by 2 are called even numbers since, 4, 6, 8, 10, are divisible by 2, hence these are even numbers.

2. A : The numbers written in natural sequence are natural numbers.

3. C : The numbers which are not divisible by 2, 3, 5, 7, 11 and 13 (*i.e.*, by any numbers except themselves and one) are called prime numbers.

4. C : To find out prime numbers between 1 and 100, write all numbers between 1 to 100.

✗	(2)	(3)	4	(5)	6	(7)	8	9	10
(11)	12	(13)	14	15	16	(17)	18	(19)	20
21	22	(23)	24	25	26	27	28	(29)	30
(31)	32	33	34	35	36	(37)	38	39	40
(41)	42	(43)	44	45	46	(47)	48	49	50
51	52	(53)	54	55	56	57	58	(59)	60
(61)	62	63	64	65	66	(67)	68	69	70
(71)	72	(73)	74	75	76	77	78	(79)	80
81	82	(83)	84	85	86	87	88	(89)	90
91	92	93	94	95	96	(97)	98	99	100

(*i*) Cross out 1 which is not a prime number.

(ii) Cross out all numbers divisible by 2, except 2 which is a prime number.

(*iii*) Cross out all numbers divisible by 3, except 3 itself.

(*iv*) Cross out all numbers divisible by 5, except 5 itself.

(*v*) Cross out all numbers divisible by 7, except 7 itself.

The numbers remaining are the prime numbers between 1 and 100 which are circled and are 25 in all.

5. A : 2 is the only even prime number.

6. C : 87 is divisilble by 3, therefore it is not a prime number.

7. C : 149 is not divisible by any number, therefore it is a prime number.

8. A : In the sequence 1, 7, 3, 9, 5, 11..... the alternate numbers differ by 2, i.e., first and third number differ by 2, similarly the difference of second and fourth number is 2. Thus, next number in the series should be 5 + 2 = 7.

9. B : The sequence 4, 9, ..., 25, 36 contains the square of natural numbers, *i.e.*, 2^2, 3^2, 4^2, 5^2, 6^2. Thus the missing number is 4^2, *i.e.*, 16.

10. D : In the sequence 17, ..., 18, 15, 19, 14, 20, 13, the next alternate number is one more than the previous alternate number, i.e., 17 + 1 = 18, 18 + 1 = 19, 19 + 1 = 20. Also the second number and fourth number differ by 1, i.e., 13 + 1 = 14, 14 + 1 = 15, 15 + 1 = 16 is the required missing number).

[**means add the first number to the twice of the second number*].

11. D : 5 + [2 × 4] = 5 + 8 = 13

12. A : 7 + [2 × 0] = 7 + 0 = 7.

13. D : [1 * 2]* 3 = [1 + 2 × 2]* 3 = 5* 3 = 5 + 3 × 2 = 11.

14. C : 3 * [0 * 6] = 3 *[0 + 2 × 6] = 3* 12 = 3 + 2 × 12 = 27

[Δ *means square the first number and add the second number.*]

15. B : 2 Δ 10 = 2 × 2 + 10 = 14

16. B : 6 Δ 7 = 6 × 6 + 7 = 43

17. B : [3 × 2] Δ 9 = 6 Δ 9 = 6 × 6 + 9 = 45

[** *means increase the first number by 2 and then multiply by the second number*].

18. C : 5**3 = [5 + 2] × 3 = 21

19. A : [3**3]**4 = [(3 + 2) × 3]**4 = 15**4 = [15 + 2] × 4 = 68

20. B : [5**0]**3 = [(5 + 2) × 0] = **3 = 0**3 = [0 + 2] × 3 = 6

21. D : The number should be divisible by 3, 5, and 7. Thus L.C.M. of 3, 5, 7 is equal to 105 which is the required number.

22. D : 28 is multiple of 1, 2, 4, 7, 14.
Also 1 + 2 + 4 + 7 + 14 = 28

23. D. 24. D.

25. A : Out of *a, b, c* ; a is odd and *c* is odd while b is even. The sum of two odd numbers is even, *i.e.*, $a + c$ = even = d. Also the sum of two even numbers is even, i.e., d + b = even.
∴ $a + b + c$ = Even number.

26. D : Product of two prime numbers is not a prime number but it is always composite number.

27. D : The number is equal to the product or prime factors.
∴ 2 × 2 × 3 × 7 = 84 is the required number.

28. D : Find H.C.F. of 56, 84 which is equal to 28.

29. B.

30. B.

31. A : Since the sum of two odd numbers is always even number, therefore, $x + y$ is even number.

32. A : Average of two different numbers is always between the two numbers.

33. A : If all the numbers were not positive, then the sum could not be positive. If a, b, c were all –1 and d were 5, then $a + b + c + d$ would be positive, so B, C, D are incorrect.

34. B :

$$(2 + 2 + 2)^2 = 6^2 = 36$$

$$[(2 + 2)^2]^2 = [4^2]^2 = [4 \times 4]^2 = 16 \times 16 = 256$$

$$[2 \times 2 \times 2]^2 = (8)^2 = 64$$

$$(4)^2 = 4 \times 4 = 16.$$

35. C : Let the numbers be x and y

$$x + y = 84$$

$$x + (x + 12) = 84, \text{ or } 2x = 84 - 12 = 72,$$

or $$x = \frac{72}{2} = 36$$

$$y = x + 12 = 36 + 12 = 48.$$

36. C : Let the number be x

$\therefore$ $$2x + 15 = 81, \text{ or } 2x = 81 - 15 = 66$$

$\therefore$ $$x = \frac{66}{2} = 33.$$

37. D : Let the number be x

$\therefore$ $$\sqrt{x} + 20 = 30, \text{ or } \sqrt{x} = 30 - 20 = 10$$

$\therefore$ $$\left(\sqrt{x}\right)^2 = (10)^2, \text{ or } x = 100.$$

38. B :

$$\frac{A+B+C}{3} = 15, \text{ or, } A + B + C = 15 \times 3 = 45 \quad ...(i)$$

$$\frac{B+C+D}{3} = 16, \text{ or } B + C + D = 48 \quad ...(ii)$$

$$D = 19$$

$\therefore$ $B + C + 19 = 48$ or, $B + C = 48 - 19 = 29$

But, $A + B + C = 45$

Putting the value of $B + C = 29$ in the above equationi (i), we get

$$A + 29 = 45$$

$\therefore$ $$A = 45 - 29 = 16$$

39. D : Let the number be x.

$\therefore \quad \frac{x}{9}+9 = 27$ or, $\frac{x}{9} = 27 - 9 = 18$

$\therefore \quad x = 18 \times 9 = 162$

40. D : Let the third number $= x$

$\therefore$ First number $= 3x$, Second number $= \frac{3x}{2}$

$\therefore \quad \frac{1}{3}\left[x+3x+\frac{3x}{2}\right] = 22$ or, $\frac{11}{2}x = 66$

or, $\quad x = \frac{66 \times 2}{11} = 12 =$ Third number,

$12 \times 3 = 36 =$ First number,

$\frac{12 \times 3}{2} = 18 =$ Second number.

41. C : Let the number be x.

Then, $\quad x + 10x = 264$

or, $\quad 11x = 264, \quad \therefore \; x = \frac{264}{11} = 24$

42. B : If the person is standing at sixth number in the queue from both sides, that means there are five persons ahead and five persons behind him. Hence, total number of person in the queue is $5 + 1 + 5 = 11$.

43. D : Let the number is x.

$\therefore \quad x + x + 5 = 17$, or $2x = 17 - 5 = 12$

$\therefore \quad x = \frac{12}{2} = 6$

44. B : $\quad \frac{x}{4}+9 = 15$

$\frac{x}{4} = 15 - 9 = 6$

$\therefore \quad x = 6 \times 4 = 24.$

45. A : $5 \times x + 3x = 64$ or, $8x = 64, \quad \therefore \; x = \frac{64}{8} = 8$

46. C : $\quad x + y = 2x$

$\therefore \quad y = 2x - x = x$

47. C : Let the number be x.

$\therefore \quad 3x - 11 = 19, \quad$ or $3x = 19 + 11 = 30$

$\therefore \quad x = \frac{30}{3} = 10.$

48. A : Let the numbers are x and $(x + 1)$

$\therefore \quad (x + 1)^2 - x^2 = 25$

or, $\quad x^2 + 1 + 2x - x^2 = 25$

or, $\quad 2x + 1 = 25$

or, $\quad 2x = 25 - 1 = 24, \quad \therefore x = \frac{24}{2} = 12$

$\therefore \quad x + 1 = 12 + 1 = 13$

Hence, the numbers are 12, 13.

49. A : Let x be the digit in units place. Digit in ten's place is then $15 - x$.

$\therefore$ The number $= 10(15 - x) + x$

The new number with reserve digits $= 10 \times x + (15 - x)$

$\therefore \quad 10(15 - x) + x + 9 = 10x + 15 - x$

$150 - 10x + x + 9 = 9x + 15$

or, $\quad 18x = 144, \quad \therefore x = \frac{144}{18} = 8$

The digit of ten's place $= 15 - 8 = 7$

$\therefore$ The required number = 78

50. B : Let the number is x

$\therefore \quad 180 - x = 11x - 180$

or, $\quad 180 + 180 = 11x + x, \; 360 = 12x,$

or, $\quad x = \frac{360}{12} = 30$

51. D : Let Y receives ₹ a.

Then X receives ₹ $a + 7$ and Z receives ₹ $a - 8$.

But, $a + 7 + a + a - 8 =$ ₹ 53

or, $\quad 3a - 1 = 53, \; 3a = 53 + 1$

$\therefore \; 3a = 54, \;$ or, $\; a = \frac{54}{3}$

= ₹ 18. = Y's share

X's share= $a + 7 = 18 + 7 =$ ₹ 25,

Z's share= $a - 8 = 18 - 8 =$ ₹ 10.

2

FRACTIONS AND DECIMALS

A fraction is a number that represents a ratio or division of two whole numbers. A fraction is written in the form x/y, the number on the top, 'x' is called numerator; the number on the bottom, 'y' is called denominator. The denominator tells how many equal parts there are; and the numerator tells how many of these equal parts are taken.

> **Sets of equal fractions can be obtained by multiplying, or dividing, the numerator and denominator by the same number.**

For example,

$$\frac{3}{4}=\frac{3\times 2}{4\times 2}=\frac{3\times 2\times 2}{4\times 2\times 2}=\frac{3\times 3}{4\times 3}=\frac{3\times 4}{4\times 4}$$

Mixed Numbers: A mixed number consists of a whole number and a fraction.$3\frac{1}{4}$ is a mixed number, it means $3 + \frac{1}{4}$.

How to change mixed number into fraction?

(*i*) Multiply the whole number by the denominator of the fraction.

(*ii*) Add the numerator of the fraction to the result of step (*i*)

(*iii*) Use the result of step (*ii*) as the numerator and use the denominator of the fractional part of the mixed number as the denominator. This fraction is equal to the mixed number.

> **In calculations involving mixed numbers, always change the mixed numbers into fractions.**

Multiplication of Fractions: While multiplying, two fractions multiply their numerators and divide this by the product of their denominators.

Note: *In word problems,* **of** *always indicates multiplication.*

Division of Fractions: This can be done either by multiplying by the L.C.M. of the denominators of the fractions, or by multiplying by such a number which can make the denominator 1.

It may be noted that one fraction is a reciprocal of another if their product is 1. So $\frac{1}{3}$ and 3 are reciprocals. To find the reciprocal of a fraction, simply interchange the numerator and deno-minator. This is known as inverting fractions. To divide one fraction by another fraction, invert the divisor and multiply. *For example :*

$$\frac{3}{8} \div \frac{1}{2} = \frac{3}{8} \times 2 = \frac{6}{8} = \frac{3}{4}$$

Addition of Fractions: If the fractions have same denominator, then the denominator is called a common denominator. In such cases, add the numerators and use this sum as the new numerator with the common denominator as the denominator of the sum. *For example,*

$$\frac{3}{15} + \frac{7}{15} = \frac{3+7}{15} = \frac{10}{15} = \frac{2}{3}$$

If the fractions have different denominators, then L.C.M. is called the least common denominator and as has been said for the case when the fractions had the same denominator, *For example,*

$$\frac{1}{3} + \frac{9}{4} + \frac{3}{5} = ?$$

In this case, common denominator is L.C.M. of 3, 4, 5, which is equal to 60,

$$\frac{1}{3} = \frac{20}{60}, \frac{9}{4} = \frac{135}{60}, \frac{3}{5} = \frac{36}{60}$$

$$= \frac{20}{60} + \frac{135}{60} + \frac{36}{60} = \frac{191}{60}$$

Subtracting Fractions: When the fractions have the same denominator, subtract the numerators and place the result over the denominator.

For example,

$$\frac{5}{8} - \frac{3}{8} = \frac{5-3}{8} = \frac{2}{8}$$

When the fractions have different denominators,

(*i*) First of all, find the common denominator:

(*ii*) Express the fractions as equivalent fractions with the same denominator.

(*iii*) Subtract as has been said above, *for example,*

$$\frac{5}{8} - \frac{1}{5} = ?$$

Common denominator in this case is 40,

$$\frac{5}{8} = \frac{25}{40}, \frac{1}{5} = \frac{8}{40}$$

$$\frac{25}{40} - \frac{8}{40} = \frac{25-8}{40} = \frac{17}{40}$$

Equivalent Fractions: Two fractions may be equivalent or equal if they represent the same ratio of number. *For example,*

$$\frac{2}{5}=\frac{4}{10}=\frac{6}{15}=\frac{20}{50}$$

Combined Operations: Sometimes in simplifying fractions, we may come across the following signs :

(i) Brackets – ( ), { }, [ ]
(ii) Of – means multiplication

while dealing with such problems,

(i) first of all brackets should be removed,
(ii) then *of* followed by,
(iii) division and multiplicaiton, then
(iv) addition and subtraction.

Note: *Terms enclosed within brackets are to be treated as one quantity.*

When an expression within a bracket is preceded by the sign (+), the bracket may be removed without making any change in the sign of the quantities or terms within the bracket.

When an expression within a bracket is preceded by the sign (–), the bracket may be removed only after changing the sign of every term within it.

Complex Fractions: A fraction whose numerator and denominator are themselves fractions is called a complex fraction.

For example, $\frac{3/8}{4/5}$

It can be simplified by dividing the fractions. Thus,

$$\frac{3/8}{4/5}=\frac{3}{8}\div\frac{4}{5}=\frac{3}{8}\times\frac{5}{4}=\frac{15}{32}$$

DECIMALS

A collection of digits after a period (decimal point) is called decimal fraction. *For example,* .513, .317, .219, .6, etc. Every decimal represents a fraction.

How to find a fraction represented by decimal?

(i) Take a fraction whose denominator is 10, and whose numerator is the first digit to the right of decimal point.

(ii) Take the fraction whose denominator is 100, and whose numerator is the second digit to the right of decimal point.

(iii) Continue the procedure untill all the digits to the right of the decimal point have been used up. The denominator in each case is 10 times the denominator in the previous step.

(*iv*) The sum of the fractions obtained in (i), (ii) and (iii) is the fraction represented by the decimal point. For example, the fraction represened by 0.317 may be found out as follows:

$$\frac{3}{10}+\frac{1}{100}+\frac{7}{1000}=\frac{300}{1000}+\frac{10}{1000}+\frac{7}{1000}=\frac{317}{1000}$$

Any number of zeros may be added to the right of a decimal fraction without changing its value.

Addition and Subtraction of Decimals: While adding decimals we put decimal under decimal, units under units, tens under tens and hundreds under hundreds.

For example, 23.4621 + 102.019 + 0.961 =?

$$\begin{array}{r} 23.4621 \\ 102.0190 \\ 0.9610 \\ \hline 126.4421 \\ \hline \end{array}$$

Multiplicaiton of Decimals: When we multiply the decimal fractions by 10, the hundredths become tenths (10 × 1/100 = 1/10), the tenths become units (10 × 1/10 = 1) and the units become tens (1 × 10 = 10) and so on.

For example, 2.45 × 10 = 24.5.

Decimals are multiplied like whole numbers. The decimal point of the product is placed in such a way that the number of decimal places in the product is equal to the total of the number of decimal places in all the numbers multiplied.

Division of Decimals: While dividing one decimal by another decimal :

(*i*) Move the decimal point in the divisor to the right until there is no decimal fraction in the divisor.

(*ii*) Move the decimal point in the dividend the same number of places to the right as you moved the decimal point in step *(i)*.

(*iii*) Divide the result of *(ii)* by the result of *(i)*.

(*iv*) The number of decimal places in the result should be equal to the number of decimal places in the result of step *(ii)*.

For example, 66.957 ÷ 0.11

$$=\frac{66.957}{0.11}=\frac{66.957\times100}{0.11\times100}=\frac{6695.7}{11}=608.7$$

Relation between Decimal Fraction and Normal Fraction: A fraction can be converted into a decimal fraction by dividing the numerator by denominator. *For example*, 1/2 = 1.0/2 = 0.5.

$$\frac{1}{5}=\frac{1.0}{5}=0.2, \qquad \frac{1}{10}=\frac{1\cdot0}{10}=0\cdot1$$

$\frac{1}{4} = \frac{1 \cdot 00}{4} = 0 \cdot 25,$

$\frac{3}{4} = \frac{3 \cdot 00}{4} = 0 \cdot 75,$

$\frac{1}{20} = \frac{1 \cdot 00}{20} = 0.05,$

$\frac{1}{16} = \frac{1 \cdot 0000}{16} = 0 \cdot 0625,$

$\frac{1}{100} = \frac{1 \cdot 00}{100} = 0 \cdot 01$

$\frac{1}{1000} = \frac{1 \cdot 000}{1000} = 0.001$

$\frac{3}{8} = \frac{3.000}{8} = 0 \cdot 375$

$\frac{7}{8} = \frac{7 \cdot 000}{8} = 0 \cdot 875$

EXERCISE

1. Which of the following is equivalent to $\frac{15}{25}$?

A. $\frac{150}{25}$ B. $\frac{15}{250}$

C. $\frac{3}{5}$ D. $\frac{60}{75}$

2. Which of the following is not equivalent to $\frac{13}{20}$?

A. $\frac{26}{40}$ B. $\frac{130}{200}$

C. $\frac{39}{60}$ D. $\frac{52}{60}$

3. If $\frac{9*3}{3*7}$ is equivalent to $\frac{9}{7}$, the sign * is replaced by :

A. ÷ B. ×

C. + D. –

4. $\frac{5}{6}$ of an hour is equal to :

A. half an hour B. 40 minutes

C. 50 minutes D. 55 minutes

5. An aircraft uses 2/5 of its fuel in flying 1,250 kilometres. The distance travelled on remaining fuel is :

A. 1875 km B. 2125 km

C. 250 km D. 475 km

6. If $\frac{4}{3} * \frac{3}{4} = \frac{16}{9}$, then * means :

A. + B. –

C. × D. ÷

7. If $\frac{3}{15} * \frac{17}{5} = \frac{51}{75}$, then * means :

A. + B. –

C. × D. ÷

8. If $5x = 1$, then x is equal to :

A. .20 B. .02

C. $\frac{1}{2}$ D. 5

9. Which of the following is the largest fraction?

A. $\frac{3}{15}$ B. $\frac{5}{20}$

C. $\frac{8}{64}$ D. $\frac{25}{1000}$

10. Which of the following is the smallest fraction?

A. $\frac{1}{10}$ B. $\frac{1}{100}$

C. $\frac{9}{1000}$ D. $\frac{500}{10000}$

11. Six times x increased by 12 is equal to :

A. $\frac{x}{2}$ B. $2x$

C. $6x + 12$ D. $12x + 6$

12. Five times y diminished by 20 is equal to :

A. $5y - 20$ B. $5y + 20$

C. $y/4$ D. $4y$

13. The number less than 15 by 7 is:

A. $15x - 7$ B. 15/7

C. 15 D. 8

14. The excess of thrice a certain number over 16 is 32. The number is :

A. 17 B. 16

C. 12 D. 10

15. If 21 is added to four times a number, the result is 57. The number is :

A. 7 B. 8

C. 9 D. 10

16. A number, the sum of whose fourth and fifth parts exceeds their third part by 28, is :

A. 120 B. 240

C. 220 D. 160

17. Which fraction should be added to the sum of $5\frac{3}{4}$, $4\frac{4}{5}$ and $7\frac{3}{8}$ to make the result a whole number?

A. $\frac{1}{40}$ B. $\frac{2}{40}$

C. $\frac{3}{40}$ D. $\frac{4}{40}$

18. $\frac{1}{15}+\frac{3}{15}+\frac{5}{15}+\frac{6}{15}=?$

A. $\frac{10}{15}$ B. $\frac{3}{5}$

C. $\frac{4}{5}$ D. 1

19. A number one-sixth of which exceeds its one-ninth by 100 is :

A. 600 B. 900

C. 1500 D. 1800

20. The sum of $\frac{1}{2}, \frac{1}{4}$ and $\frac{1}{8}$ of a number is 28. The number is :

A. 28 B. 32

C. 36 D. 42

21. The sum of $\frac{1}{9}, \frac{1}{3}, \frac{1}{6}$ and $\frac{7}{18}$ of a number is 150. The number is :

A. 120 B. 130

C. 140 D. 150

22. Which is the greatest? .999, .1011, .1995, .9985

A. .999 B. .1011

C. .1995 D. .9985

23. In decimal system, $9\frac{1}{8}$ may be represented as:

A. 9.18 B. 9.125

C. 9.025 D. 9.225

24. $2.205 \div 0.15 = ?$

A. 1.47 B. 14.7

C. 147 D. 0.147

25. G.C.M. of .24, 3.2 and 16.0 is :
A. 80 B. 8
C. .8 D. .08

26. L.C.M. of .24, 3.2 and 16.0 is :
A. .48 B. 4.8
C. 48 D. 480

27. A pole has 0.5 of its length in mud, 0.25 of its length in water and 2 metres above water. The total length of the pole is :
A. 8 metres B. 5 metres
C. 4 metres D. 2 metres

28. $\sqrt{1/3}$ is equal to :
A. 0.57 B. 0.35
C. 0.30 D. 3.00

29. How many times does 2/3 of 1/2 go into half of one third?
A. 2 B. 1/2
C. 1/3 D. 2/3

30. The eleventh part of $990\frac{990}{990}$ is:
A. 99.0 B. 99.99
C. 90 D. 90.9

31. A train started from Delhi at 6.00 A.M. On the next (second) station 1/3 passengers got down and 96 got in. On the next (third) station, 1/2 of the total passengers present in the train got down and 12 came in. Now there were 248 passengers in the train. When the tain started from Delhi, total number of passengers were :
A. 435 B. 564
C. 654 D. 736

32. 1 ÷ [1 + 1 ÷ {1 + 1 ÷ 1(1 + 1 ÷ 2)}] is equal to:
A. 1 B. 2
C. $\frac{5}{8}$ D. zero

33. L.C.M. of 6, 7, 8 and 10 is equal to :
A. 840 B. 830
C. 820 D. 800

34. By how much does $\frac{6}{7/8}$ exceed $\frac{6/7}{8}$:
A. $6\frac{2}{3}$ B. $6\frac{3}{4}$
C. $7\frac{1}{2}$ D. $8\frac{3}{4}$

35. $\frac{.03}{1000}$ is equal to :
A. 3×10^{5} B. 3×10^{-3}
C. 3×10^{-6} D. 3×10^{-5}

36. $10\frac{1}{25}$ is equal to :
A. 10.25 B. 10.125
C. 10.04 D. 10.025

37. 1.25 × 1.25 + 2.75 × 2.75 + 2 × 1.25 × 2.75 is equal to :
A. 4.000 B. 16.000
C. 26.1250 D. 28.3250

38. What fraction of an hour is a second ?
A. $\frac{1}{24}$ B. $\frac{1}{60}$
C. $\frac{1}{120}$ D. $\frac{1}{3600}$

39. G.C.M. of 1.6 and 0.72 is equal to :
A. 8 B. .8
C. .08 D. .008

40. $\frac{4}{5}$ of 0.025 is equal to :
A. 0.0002 B. 0.002
C. 0.02 D. 0.2

EXPLANATORY ANSWERS

1. C : $\frac{15}{25} = \frac{3 \times 5}{5 \times 5} = \frac{3}{5}$.

2. D : $\frac{26}{40} = \frac{2 \times 13}{2 \times 20} = \frac{13}{20}, \frac{39}{60} = \frac{13 \times 3}{20 \times 3} = \frac{13}{20}$

$\frac{130}{200} = \frac{13 \times 10}{20 \times 10} = \frac{13}{20}, \frac{52}{60} = \frac{13 \times 4}{20 \times 3} = \frac{13}{20} \times \frac{4}{3}$

Hence, $\frac{52}{60}$ is not equal to $\frac{13}{20}$.

3. B : $\frac{9 * 3}{3 * 7} = \frac{9}{7}$, or, $\frac{9 \times 3}{7 \times 3} = \frac{9}{7}$, $\therefore$ The sign * is ×.

4. C : $\frac{5}{6}$ of 1 hr = $\frac{5}{6} \times 60$ minutes = 50 minutes.

5. A : Remaining fuel = $1 - \frac{2}{5} = \frac{5-2}{5} = \frac{3}{5}$

Distance flown by $\frac{2}{5}$ of fuel = 1250 km.

Distance flown by full fuel = $\frac{1250}{2/5} = \frac{1250 \times 5}{2}$ km.

Distance flown by $\frac{3}{5}$ of fuel = $\frac{1250 \times 5 \times 3}{2 \times 5} = 1875$ km.

6. D. **7. C.**

8. A : $5x = 1$, $\therefore x = \frac{1}{5} = .20$.

9. B : $\frac{3}{15} = \frac{1}{5}, \frac{8}{64} = \frac{1}{8}, \frac{5}{20} = \frac{1}{4}, \frac{25}{1000} = \frac{1}{40}$,

$\frac{1}{5}, \frac{1}{4}, \frac{1}{8}, \frac{1}{40}$, $\frac{16, 20, 10, 2}{80}$

$\therefore$ The largest fractin is $\frac{1}{4} = \frac{5}{20}$.

10. C : $\frac{1}{10} = .1,\ \frac{9}{1000} = .009$

$\frac{1}{100} = .01.\ \frac{500}{10000} = \frac{5}{100} = .05$

The smallest of these quantities is $.009 = \frac{9}{1000}$.

11. C : $x \times 6 + 12 = 6x + 12$.

12. A : $5 \times y - 20 = 5y - 20$.

13. D : $15 - 7 = 8$.

14. B : Let the number be x

$$3x - 16 = 32$$

$\therefore \quad 3x = 32 + 16 = 48$, or $x = \frac{48}{3} = 16$.

15. C : Let the number is x

$\therefore\ 4x + 21 = 57$ or, $4x = 57 - 21 = 36$, or, $x = \frac{36}{4} = 9$.

16. B : Let the number is x.

$\therefore \frac{x}{4} + \frac{x}{5} = \frac{x}{3} + 28,\ \frac{9x}{20} = \frac{x}{3} + 28$, or, $\frac{9x}{20} - \frac{x}{3} = 28$

or, $\frac{27x - 20x}{60} = 28$ or, $7x = 28 \times 60\ \therefore\ x = \frac{28 \times 60}{7} = 240$.

17. C : $5\frac{3}{4} + 4\frac{4}{5} + 7\frac{3}{8} = \frac{23}{4} + \frac{24}{5} + \frac{59}{8} = \frac{717}{40}$

717/40 becomes whole number when 3/40 is added to it, i.e.,

$\frac{717}{40} + \frac{3}{40} = \frac{720}{40} = 18$ which is a whole number.

18. D : $\frac{1}{15} + \frac{3}{15} + \frac{5}{15} + \frac{6}{15} = \frac{1+3+5+6}{15} = \frac{15}{15} = 1$.

19. D : Let the number is x.

$\frac{x}{6} = \frac{x}{9} + 100$ or, $\frac{x}{6} - \frac{x}{9} = 100$, or, $\frac{x}{18} = 100$

or, $x = 100 \times 18 = 1800$.

20. B : Let the number is x.

$$\therefore \frac{x}{2}+\frac{x}{4}+\frac{x}{8}=28, \text{ or, } \frac{7x}{8}=28 \therefore 7x = 28 \times 8 \text{ or, } x=\frac{28\times 8}{7}=32.$$

21. D : Let the number is x.

$$\therefore \frac{x}{9}+\frac{x}{3}+\frac{x}{6}+\frac{7x}{18}=150 \quad \text{or, } \frac{2x+6x+3x+7x}{18} = 150 \Rightarrow \frac{18x}{18}=150$$

$$\text{or, } x=\frac{150\times 18}{18}=150.$$

22. A : .999 is the greatest.

23. B : $9\frac{1}{8}=9+\frac{1}{8}=9+.125=9.125.$

24. B : $2.205 \div 0.15 = \frac{2.205}{0.15}=\frac{2205}{1000}\times\frac{100}{15}=\frac{2205}{150}=14.7.$

25. D : G.C.M. of .24, 3.2 and 16.0

$$= \text{G.C.M. of } \frac{24, 320 \text{ and } 1600}{100}=\frac{8}{100}=0.08.$$

26. C : L.C.M. of .24, 3.2 and 16.0 = L.C.M. of

$$\frac{24, 320 \text{ and } 1600}{100}=\frac{4800}{100}=48.$$

27. A : Let total length of the pole = x
Pole above water = $x - [0.5x + 0.25x] = 0.25x$;
$0.25x = 2$ metres

$$\therefore x=\frac{2\times 100}{25}=8 \text{ metres}.$$

28. A : $\sqrt{\frac{1}{3}}=\frac{\sqrt{1}}{\sqrt{3}}=\frac{1}{\sqrt{3}}=\frac{1}{1.732}=\frac{1000}{1732}=0.57.$

29. B : $\frac{2}{3}$ of $\frac{1}{2}=\frac{2}{3}\times\frac{1}{2}=\frac{1}{3}$, $\frac{1}{2}$ of $\frac{1}{3}=\frac{1}{6}$ $\therefore \frac{1}{6}\div\frac{1}{3}=\frac{1}{6}\times\frac{3}{1}=\frac{1}{2}.$

30. C : Eleventh part of $990\frac{990}{990}=990\frac{990}{990}\div 11 = \frac{991}{11} = 90.09.$

31. B : When train started from Delhi let number of passengers was x. On next station, 1/3 got down and 96 got in.

Now passengers in train = $x - \frac{x}{3} + 96 = \frac{2x}{3} + 96$

On next station 1/2 of it got down and 12 got in, i.e.,

$\frac{1}{2}\left[\frac{2x}{3} + 96\right]$ got down and 12 got in

Now passengers in train = $\frac{2x}{3} + 96 - \left[\frac{x}{3} + 48\right] + 12$

$= \frac{2x}{3} - \frac{x}{3} + 96 - 48 + 12 = 248 \quad \therefore x = [248 - 60] \times 3 = 188 \times 3 = 564.$

32. C.

33. A : The L.C.M. of 6, 7, 8 and 10 is calculated as follows :

2	6, 7, 8, 10
3	3, 7, 4, 5
4	1, 7, 4, 5
5	1, 7 1, 5
7	1, 7, 1, 1
	1, 1, 1, 1

L.C.M. = 2 × 3 × 4 × 5 × 7 = 840.

34. B : $6 \div \frac{7}{8} = \frac{6}{1} \times \frac{8}{7} = \frac{48}{7}$ or $\frac{6}{7} \div 8 = \frac{6}{7} \times \frac{1}{8} = \frac{3}{28}$

$\frac{48}{7} - \frac{3}{28} = \frac{192 - 3}{28} = \frac{189}{28} = 6\frac{21}{28} = 6\frac{3}{4}$.

35. D. **36. C.**

37. B : Put 1.25 = a and 2.75 = b, then,
1.25 × 1.25 + 2.75 × 2.75 + 2 × 1.25 × 2.75
$= a^2 + b^2 + 2ab = (a + b)^2 = (1.25 + 2.75)^2 = (4)^2 = 16.000$.

38. D. **39. C.**

40. C : $\frac{4}{5} \times 0.025 = \frac{4}{5} \times \frac{25}{1000} = \frac{1}{50} = 0.02$.

3

Powers, Exponents and Roots

If 'x' is any number and 'n' is a whole numbr greater than 0, x^n means that the product of n factors each of which is equal to x. Thus,

$$x^n = x \, . \, x \, . \, x \, . \, x \, ...x \; n \text{ times}$$

$$2^4 = 2 \times 2 \times 2 \times 2 = 16$$

$$3^5 = 3 \times 3 \times 3 \times 3 \times 3 = 243$$

$$\left(\frac{x}{y}\right)^n = \frac{x^n}{x^n}$$

$$\left(\frac{3}{7}\right)^2 = \frac{3 \times 3}{7 \times 7} = \frac{9}{49}.$$

In the expression x^n, x is called the base and n is called the exponent. The laws of exponents are :

$$x^n \times x^m = x^{n+m}$$

$$\frac{x^n}{x^m} = x^{n-m}$$

$$(x^m)^n = x^{mn}$$

$$(xy)^m = x^m y^m$$

Negative Exponents: $x^0 = 1$, for any non-zero number x. By one of the law of exponents,

$$x^n \times x^0 = x^{n+0} = x^n$$

i.e., $x^0 = 1$

Also, $x^{-n} = \dfrac{1}{x^n}$

Roots : If a number 'x' is raised to nth power and the result is 'a', then 'x' is called the *nth* root of 'a', which is usually written as $\sqrt[n]{a} = x$, *For example,*

$$2^4 = 16, \text{ or } \sqrt[4]{16} = 2$$

The second root is called the square root, the third root is called the cube root.

$$x^{1/n} \times y^{1/n} = (x.y)^{1/n}$$

or,

$$\sqrt[n]{x \times y} = \sqrt[n]{x} \times \sqrt[n]{y}$$

A number which is a prfect square must end in one or another of the digits 0, 1, 4, 5, 6, 9.

It may be noted that the square of,

1 & 9 both end in 1.
2 & 8 both end in 4.
3 & 7 both end in 9.
4 & 6 both end in 6.
5 end in 5.

(1, 9); (2, 8); (3, 7); (4, 6); (5, 5) are pairs of complementary digits, i.e., the sum of the digits in each pair is 10.

If two numbers end in complementary digits, their squares will have the same final digit.

If a number end in zero, its square should contain 2 zero and if a number ends in 2 zeros, its square should end in 4 zeros, and so on.

A number ending in an odd number of zeros cannot be a perfect square.

EXERCISE

1. $\sqrt{\frac{1}{3}} = ?$

A. 0.30
B. 0.57
C 0.89
D. 3.00

2. $\frac{6^4}{3^3} = ?$

A. 24
B. 42
C 48
D. 2

3. $\left(\frac{1}{2}\right)^{-1} = ?$

A. $-\frac{1}{2}$

B. $+\frac{1}{2}$

C. -2

D. $+2$

4. $125^\circ = ?$

A. 125   B. 1
C. 1250   D. 12.5

5. $8^{1/3} = ?$

A. $\frac{8}{3}$ B. $\frac{3}{8}$

C. 4 D. 2

6. $4^4 \times 4^{17} = ?$

A. 8^{17} B. 4^{21}

C. 8^{21} D. 4^{13}

7. $\frac{10x^8}{5x^4} = ?$

A. $2x^4$ B. $2x^2$

C. $2x^8$ D. $2x^{12}$

8. $2^{3^2} = ?$

A. 2^6 B. 2^9

C. 2^5 D. 8^4

9. $(2^3)^2 = ?$

A. 8 B. 64

C. 312 D. 512

10. $(36)^{1/2} = ?$

A. 18 B. 9

C. 6 D. 3

11. $x^{3/4} . x^{3/4} = ?$

A. $2x^{3/1}$ B. $x^{9/16}$

C. $x^{6/8}$ D. $x^{3/2}$

12. $(x^{3/4})^{1/2} = ?$

A. $x^{3/8}$ B. $x^{4/6}$

C. $x^{2/5}$ D. $x^{3/2}$

13. $\sqrt{32} = ?$

A. 4 B. $2\sqrt{4}$

C. $4\sqrt{2}$ D. $2^3\sqrt{2}$

14. $5\sqrt{3} = ?$

A. $\sqrt{75}$ B. $\sqrt{50}$

C. $\sqrt{25}$ D. $\sqrt[3]{5}$

15. $x^{b-c} \times X^{c-a} \times X^{a-b} = ?$

A. x^{a+b+c} B. x^{a-b-c}

C. $x^{2a-2b-2c}$ D. 1

16. When 16000 is expressed as a product of powers of 4 and 10, then it equals :

A. $4^2 \times 10^2$ B. $4^2 \times 10^3$

C. $4^3 \times 10^3$ D. $4^2 \times 10^4$

17. When 1800 is expressed as a product of powers of prime numbers, then it equals :

A. $2 \times 9 \times 10^2$ B. $2 \times 3^2 \times 10^2$

C. $2 \times 3^2 \times 5^2$ D. $2^3 \times 3^2 \times 5^2$

18. 27×243 is equal to :

A. 3^8 B. 3^9

C. 3^{10} D. 3^{11}

19. The sum of the squares of two numbers is 26 and difference is 8. The numbers are :

A. 9, 17 B. 3, 17

C. $9, \sqrt{17}$ D. $3, \sqrt{17}$

20. $\left[\left(\frac{x}{y}\right)^3\right]^{-2} = ?$

A. $\left(\frac{x}{y}\right)^{-6}$ B. $\left(\frac{x}{y}\right)^{1}$

C. $\left(\frac{x}{y}\right)^{6}$ D. $\left(\frac{x}{y}\right)^{5}$

21. $(x^4)^3$ is equal to :

A. x^{6+2} B. x^{12}

C. $x^{4/13}$ D. X^{4-3}

22. $(27)^{-4/3}$ is equal to :

A. 81 B. 54

C. $\frac{1}{21}$ D. $\frac{1}{81}$

23. $x^{1/8} \div x^{3/4}$ is equal to :

A. $x^{5/8}$ B. $x^{2/4}$

C. $x^{2/3}$ D. $\frac{1}{x^{5/8}}$

24. $\left[27^{-2/3}\right]^{1/2}$ is equal to :

A. $\frac{27}{54}$ B. $\frac{2}{3}$

C. $\frac{1}{3}$ D. $\frac{1}{9}$

25. $\sqrt{72}$ is equal to :

A. $6\sqrt{2}$

B. $4\sqrt{6}$

C. $9\sqrt{6}$

D. $2\sqrt{6}$

EXPLANATORY ANSWERS

1. B : $\sqrt{\frac{1}{3}} = \sqrt{0.3333} = 0.57$.

2. C : $\frac{6^4}{3^3} = \frac{6\times6\times6\times6}{3\times3\times5} = 2\times2\times2\times6 = 48$.

3. D : $\left(\frac{1}{2}\right)^{-1} = (2)^{+1} = 2$.

4. B : Any number raise to power zero = 1.

5. D : (8)1/3 = $(\sqrt[3]{8})^1 = \sqrt[3]{8} = 2$.

6. B : Since, $a^x \times a^x = a^{x+y}$

$\therefore$ $4^4 \times 4^{17} = 4^{4+17} = 4^{21}$.

7. A : $\frac{10x^8}{5x^4} = \frac{2x^8}{x^4} = 2x^8 \times x^{-4} = 2x^{8-4} = 2x^4$.

8. B : $2^{3^2} = 2^{3\times3} = 2^9$.

9. B : $(2^3)^2 = (2\times2\times2)^2 = 2\times2\times2\times2\times2\times2 = 64$.

10. C : $(36)^{1/2} = \sqrt{36} = 6$.

11. D : $x^{3/4}.x^{3/4} = x^{3/4+3/4} = x^{6/4} = x^{3/2}$.

12. A : $(x^{3/4})^{1/2} = x^{3/4.1/2} = x^{3/8}$.

13. C : $\sqrt{32} = \sqrt{4\times4\times2} = \sqrt{(4)^2.2} = 4\sqrt{2}$.

14. A : $5\sqrt{3} = \left(\sqrt{5}\right)^2.\sqrt{3} = \sqrt{5}.\sqrt{5}.\sqrt{3} = \sqrt{5.5.3} = \sqrt{75}$.

15. D : $x^{b-c} \cdot x^{c-a} \cdot x^{a-b} = x[b - c + c - a + a - b] = x^0 = 1.$

16. B : $16000 = 16 \times 1000 = (4)^2 \times (10)^3 = 4^2 \times 10^3.$

17. D : The prime factors of 1800 are, $2 \times 2 \times 2 \times 3 \times 3 \times 5 \times 5$
$= 2^3 \times 3^2 \times 5^2.$

18. A : $27 \times 243 = [3 \times 3 \times 3] \times [3 \times 3 \times 3 \times 3 \times 3] = 3^3 \cdot 3^5 = 3^8.$

19. D : Let the numbers are x and y

$$\therefore \quad x^2 + y^2 = 26 \quad \ldots(i)$$

$$x^2 - y^2 = 8 \quad \ldots(ii)$$

Adding (*i*) and (*ii*), we get

$$2x^2 + y^2 - y^2 = 26 + 8 = 34$$

$$\text{or,} \quad 2x^2 = 34, \quad \text{or} \quad x^2 = \frac{34}{2} = 17$$

$$\therefore \quad x = \sqrt{17}$$

$$\text{Since,} \quad x^2 + y^2 = 26$$

$$\text{or,} \quad 17 + y^2 = 26$$

$$\therefore \quad y^2 = 26 - 17 = 9$$

$$\therefore \quad y = \sqrt{9} = 3$$

Hence, the numbers are 3 and $\sqrt{17}$.

20. A : $\left[\left(\frac{x}{y}\right)^3\right]^{-2} = \left(\frac{x}{y}\right)^{3\times-2} = \left(\frac{x}{y}\right)^{-6}$

21. B : $(x^4)^3 = x^4 \cdot x^4 \cdot x^4 = x^{4+4+4} = x^{12}.$

22. D : $(27)–4/3 = \frac{1}{(27)^{4/3}} = \frac{1}{\sqrt[3]{(27)^4}} = \frac{1}{3^4} = \frac{1}{3\times3\times3\times3} = \frac{1}{81}.$

23. D :

$$x^{1/8} \div x^{3/4}$$

$$\text{or} \quad x^{1/8 - 3/4}$$

$$\text{or} \quad x^{-5/8} = \frac{1}{x^{5/8}}.$$

24. C : $[27^{-2/3}]^{1/2} = 27^{-2/3 \times 1/2} = 27^{-1/3} = \frac{1}{27^{1/3}} = \frac{1}{3}.$

25. A : $\sqrt{72} = \sqrt{36\times2} = \sqrt{6\times6\times2} = 6\sqrt{2}.$

4

PERCENTAGE

Percent, or per centum means 'for every hundred'. A percentage is a fraction expressed with 100 as its denominator and the rate per cent as its numerator. Thus, 5 per cent means 5 out of 100, or it can be expressed as 5/100 = 1/20. The symbol % is used to denote the term 'per cent'.

A decimal is converted to percentage by multiplying the decimal by 100, or by moving the decimal point two places to the right.

A percentage can be converted into decimal by dividing it by 100, or by moving the decimal point two places to the left.

For example, 12.5% = 0.125

and, 25% = .25

A fraction can be converted into a percentage by changing the fraction to a decimal and then changing the decimal to a percentage. A percentage can be changed into a fraction by first converting the percentage into a decimal and then changing the decimal to a fraction. *For example,*

1% = .01 = 1/100, 100% = 1.0 = 1

2% = .02 = 2/100, 120% = 1.2 = 12/10

5% = .05 = 1/20, 12.5% = 0.125 = 1/8

Remember :

1. To change a fraction or mixed number to a per cent; multiply the fraction or mixed number by 100. Reduce, if possible and add % sign.
2. To remove a % sign attached to a decimal and to keep it as decimal, divide the decimal by 100.
3. To remove a % sign attached to a decimal and to change the number to a fraction; divide the decimal by 100, change the result to a fraction, and reduce if necessary.
4. To remove a % sign attached to a fraction or mixed number and to keep it as fraction, divide the fraction or mixed number by 100.
5. To remove a % sign attached to a fraction or mixed number and to change the number to a decimal; divide the fraction by 100 and change the result to decimal.
6. In percentage problems, the whole is 100%. *For example,* if a problem involves 20% of a quantity, the rest of the quantity is 100 – 20 = 80%.

EXERCISE

1. 20% is equal to :

A. $\frac{1}{3}$ B. $\frac{1}{4}$

C. $\frac{1}{5}$ D. $\frac{2}{5}$

2. 5/8 may be expressed as:

A. 50/80%

B. 62.5%

C. 55.5%

D. 70.5%

3. 15% of ₹ 50 is equal to:

A. ₹ 25 B. 12.50

C. ₹ 9.50 D. 7.50

4. What rate per cent is one minute 12 seconds to an hour?

A. 2% B. 3%

C. 4% D. 5%

5. A student has to secure 40 per cent marks to pass. If he gets 20 marks and fails by 20 marks, the maximum marks are:

A. 20 B. 40

C. 80 D. 100

6. A person spends 75% of his salary and saves ₹ 150 per month. His monthly salary is:

A. ₹ 750 B. ₹ 600

C. ₹ 400 D. ₹ 300

7. Standard gold contains 22 parts of pure gold to 2 parts of alloy. The percentage of alloy in a sovereign which is made of standard gold is:

A. 11% B. 12%

C. $8\frac{1}{3}\%$ D. $11\frac{1}{3}\%$

8. The catalogue price of an article is ₹ 250. A reduction of 12% is made for cash purchase. The case price is:

A. ₹ 250

B. ₹ 220

C. ₹ 200

D. ₹ 180

9. 20% of ₹ 5 is :

A. Re. 1 B. ₹ 2

C. ₹ 3 D. ₹ 4

10. 15% of 3 metres is :

A. 30 cm

B. 45 cm

C. 60 cm

D. 25 cm

11. 5% of a number is 15. The number is :

A. 150 B. 200

C. 250 D. 300

12. 75% of what area is 15 square metres?

A. 10 square metres

B. 15 square metres

C. 20 square metres

D. 25 square metres

13. What per cent of ₹ 30 is ₹ 10?

A. 30% B. 33.3%

C. 35% D. 40%

14. What per cent of 6.25 is 1.25?

A. 10% B. 15%

C. 20% D. 25%

15. What per cent of 3 metres is 75 cm?

A. 10% B. 15%

C. 20% D. 25%

16. 62.5% may be written as :

A. $\frac{3}{8}$ B. $\frac{4}{8}$

C. $\frac{5}{8}$ D. $\frac{6}{8}$

17. 125% may be expressed in fractions as :

A. $\frac{4}{5}$ B. $\frac{5}{4}$

C. $\frac{3}{5}$ D. $\frac{6}{5}$

18. 97% of students were present in a school and 18 students were absent. The total number of students in the school is:

A. 400 B. 450
C. 500 D. 600

19. The population of a town increased from 50,000 to 52,000. The increase per cent is:

A. 4%
B. 3%
C. 2%
D. 1%

20. At a clearance sale, goods were sold at a reduction of 20 per cent. A student purchased a pen for ₹ 12 at the clearance sale. The usual price of the pen was:

A. ₹ 12
B. ₹ 13
C. Rs 14
D. ₹ 15

21. In a college election, a candidate who got 40% of total votes was defeated by his rival by 160 votes. the total number of votes polled was:

A. 900 B. 800
C. 700 D. 600

22. In an election, 4000 votes were polled. One of the candidates got 40% votes. He was defeated by:

A. 2400 votes
B. 1600 votes
C. 800 votes
D. 600 votes

23. The selling price of a certain commodity was reduced by 25%. As a result of it, the sales increased by 30%. What was the effect of it on cash collected by daily sales?

A. 5% increase
B. 5% decrease
C. 2.5% increase
D. 2.5 decrease

24. If the price of kerosine be raised by 10%, find by how much per cent a house holder must reduce his consumption of kerosine so that not to increase his expenditure?

A. 10%
B. 9.09%
C. 9.0%
D. 8.25%

25. A towel was 50 cm broad and 100 cm long. When bleached, it was found to have lost 20% of its length and 10% of breadth. The percentage of decrease in area is:

A. 28%
B. 20%
C. 10.08%
D. 10%

EXPLANATORY ANSWERS

1. **C :** $20\% = \frac{20}{100} = \frac{1}{5}$.

2. **B :** $\frac{5}{8} \Rightarrow \frac{5}{8} \times 100 = \frac{500}{8} = 62.5\%$.

3. **D :** 15% of ₹ 50 = $\frac{15}{100}$ × ₹ 50 = ₹ 7.50.

4. **A :** 1 minute 12 seconds = 60 + 12 = 72 second

   1 hour = 60 × 60 = 3600 seconds

   $\therefore \quad \frac{72 \times 100}{3600} = 2\%$.

5. **D :** Marks required to pass = 40% = 20 + 20

   $\therefore \quad$ Maximum marks $= \frac{100 \times 40}{40} = 100$.

6. **B :** Saving = 100% – 75% = 25% = ₹ 150

   $\therefore \quad$ Total salary = $\frac{100}{25}$ × 150 = ₹ 600.

7. **C :** Total parts = 22 parts + 2 parts = 24 parts; 24 parts contain 2 parts alloy

   $\therefore$ 100 parts contain $\frac{2}{24} \times 100 = \frac{25}{3} = 8\frac{1}{3}\%$.

8. **B :** Reduction at 12% on ₹ 250 = $\frac{12}{100}$ × 250 = ₹ 30

   $\therefore \quad$ Cash price = Catalogue price – Reduction

   = ₹ 250 – ₹ 30 = Rs. 220.

9. **A :** 20% of ₹ 5 = $\frac{20}{100} \times 5$ = Re. 1.

10. **B :** 15% of 3 metres = 15% of 300 cm = $\frac{15}{100} \times 300$ = 45 cm.

11. D : Let the number = x

$\therefore$ 5% of $x = 15$

or, $\frac{5}{100} \times x = 15$

$\therefore$ $x = \frac{15 \times 100}{5} = 300.$

12. C : Let the area = x m^2

$\therefore$ 75% of $x = 15$ sq. m

or $\frac{75}{100} \times x = 15$

$\therefore$ $x = \frac{15 \times 100}{75} = 20$ sq. m.

13. B : $\frac{10}{30} \times 100 = 33.3\%.$

14. C : $\frac{1.25}{6.25} \times 100 = 20\%.$

15. D : $\frac{75}{300} \times 100 = 25\%.$

16. C : $62.5\% = \frac{62.5}{100} = \frac{625}{1000} = \frac{5}{8}.$

17. C : $125\% = \frac{125}{100} = \frac{5}{4}.$

18. D : Number of students absent = 100% – 97% = 3% = 18

$\therefore$ $100\% = \frac{18 \times 100}{3} = 600.$

19. A : Increase in population = 52,000 – 50,000 = 2000

$\therefore$ % increase $= \frac{2000}{50{,}000} \times 100 = 4\%.$

20. D : S.P. = ₹ 12 = 80% of usual price

$\therefore$ Usual price $= \frac{100}{80} \times 12 =$ ₹ 15.

21. B : Candidate who won the election got 100 – 40 = 60% votes;

Difference of votes = 60% – 40% = 20% = 160

$$\therefore \quad \text{Total votes polled} = \frac{160}{20} \times 100 = 800.$$

22. C : Candidates who lost election got 40% of 4000

$$= \frac{40}{100} \times 4000 = 1600 \text{ votes}$$

Candidates who won the election got 60% of 4000

$$= \frac{60}{100} \times 4000 = 2400 \text{ votes}$$

Difference of votes = 2400 – 1600 = 800 votes.

23. D : Selling price = 100 – 25 = 75%, Daily sales = 100 + 30 = 130%;

0.75 × 1.30 = 0.975 = Cash collected = 97.5%;

100% – 97.5% = 2.5% decrease.

24. B : Raised price of kerosine is 110/100 of the original price. Hence, the consumption should become 100/110 of the original consumption so as to keep the expenditure same.

$$\therefore \quad \text{Reduction} = \left(1 - \frac{100}{110}\right) \text{ of original consumtion}$$

$$= \frac{10}{110} \text{ of original consumption}$$

$$\text{Reduction } \% = \frac{10}{110} \times 100 = 9.09\%.$$

25. A : Original area = 100 × 50 = 5000 sq. cm.

Reduced length = 80% of 100 cm = 80 cm.

Reduced breadth = 90% of 50 cm. = 45 cm.

Reduced area = 80 × 45 = 3600 sq. cm.

Reduction in area = 5000 – 3600 = 1400 sq. cm.

$$\therefore \quad \% \text{ Reduction} = \frac{1400}{5000} \times 100 = 28\%.$$

5

RATIO AND PROPORTION

Ratio: The relation which one quantity bears to another quantity of the same kind, showing the number of times one quantity is contained in another, is called ratio between the two quantities. Thus, the relation between ₹ 48 and ₹ 6 is the same as the relation between ₹ 8 and Re. 1. This relation or the ratio is written as 8 : 1.

Since, a ratio is a fraction, it is not altered if both of its terms are divided or multiplied by the same number.

For example,

$$\frac{2}{3}=\frac{4}{6}=\frac{8}{12}=\frac{20}{30}$$

Both the quantities are called the terms of the ratio. The quantity in the numerator is called *antecedent* and the quantity in the denominator is called *consequent.*

Inverse Ratio: When antecedent and consequent of one ratio become respectively the consequent and antecedent of the other, the second ratio is called the inverse or reciprocal ratio of the first.

For example, 3/5 or 3 : 5 is the inverse ratio of 5/3 or 5 : 3.

Compound Ratio: When the antecedents and consequents of two or more ratios are multiplied to get a new antecedent and a new consequent, the new ratio formed is called their compound ratio.

For example,

the compound ratio of 2 : 3, 3 : 4, 5 : 6 is

$$\frac{2}{3}\times\frac{3}{4}\times\frac{5}{6}=\frac{5}{12} \text{ or } 5 : 12$$

Proportion: Four quantities may be in proportion when the ratio of first to the second is the same as the ratio of third to the fourth. Thus the ratio 2 : 5 and 12 : 30 are equal and the four numbers 2, 5, 12 and 30 are in proportion and are writen as 2 : 5 : :12 : 30

If four quantities are in proportion, the product of the extremes is equal to the product of the means.

EXERCISE

1. The ratio between two numbers is 3 : 4 and their sum is 490. The numbers are:
A. 200 and 290
B. 210 and 280
C. 220 and 270
D. 230 and 260

2. The ratio between two numbers is 3 : 4 and the sum of their squares is 625. The numbers are:
A. 6 and 8 B. 15 and 20
C. 18 and 24 D. 20 and 25

3. Which of the following is greatest?
3 : 4, 4 : 5, 5 : 6, 6 : 7
A. 3 : 4 B. 4 : 5
C. 5 : 6 D. 6 : 7

4. In an examination, 25 students out of 70 scored less than 50% marks. The ratio of number of students who scored 50% marks or more to the number of students who scored less than 50% marks is:
A. 1 : 2 B. 3 : 5
C. 9 : 5 D. 5 : 7

5. The fraction that bears the same ratio to 4/9 that 3/11 does to 5/33 is:
A. 4 : 5 B. 5 : 6
C. 6 : 5 D. 7 : 5

6. If the consequent be 15 and the value of the ratio 3/5, then the value of antecedent is:
A. 7 B. 8
C 9 D. 10

7. If A : B = 5 : 7 and B : C = 9 : 11, then A : C = ?
A. 9 : 11 B. 45 : 77
C. 45 : 66 D. 39 : 77

8. Three numbers are in the ratio of 2 : 3 : 4 and the sum of the squares of the numbers is 116. The numbers are:
A. 4 : 6 : 8
B. 5 : 6 : 7
C. 6 : 9 : 12
D. 8 : 12 : 16

9. Sides of two squares are in the ratio of 3 : 4. Their perimeters are in the ratio of:
A. 3 : 4 B. 7 : 8
C. 5 : 6 D. 6 : 7

10. Two cubical boxes made of card-board have their edges in the ratio of 3 : 4. The ratio of the amounts of card-board in each of them is:
A. 3 : 4 B. 5 : 6
C. 6 : 7 D. 9 : 16

11. The angles of a triangle are in the ratio of 1 : 2 : 3. The largest angle is of:
A. 30° B. 60°
C. 90° D. 120°

12. The salaries of two persons are in the ratio of 4 : 7. Both of them spend 80 per cent of salaries and save rest of the money. The ratio of their savings is:
A. 8 : 2
B. 4 : 7
C. 7 : 5
D. 5 : 3

13. The mean proportion between 9 and 25 is:

A. 10 B. 12
C. 15 D. 17

14. The third proportional to 12 and 30 is:

A. 40 B. 45
C. 50 D. 75

15. The fourth proportional to 3, 4 and 15 is:

A. 20 B. 18
C. 17 D. 15

16. 75 : 15 = x : 7, the value of x is:

A. 25 B. 35
C. 40 D. 45

17. x : 7.5 = 7 : 17.5, the value of x is:

A. 1.0 B. 2.5
C. 3.0 D. 3.5

18. The mean proportional to 5 and 125 is:

A. 10 B. 15
C. 20 D. 25

19. The inverse ratio of 12 to 18 is:

A. $\frac{3}{2}$ B. $\frac{2}{3}$
C. $\frac{1}{3}$ D. $\frac{3}{1}$

20. Two numbers are in the ratio of 2: 3 and if 8 is added to each of them, they become in the ratio of 3 : 4. The number are:

A. 2 and 3
B. 4 and 6
C. 8 and 12
D. 16 and 24

21. If $x : y = 3 : 2$, then $(x + y) : (x - y) = ?$

A. 1 : 5 B. 5 : 1
C. 3 : 5 D. 5 : 2

22. If $x : y = y : z$, then $x = ?$

A. z B. $\frac{z}{y^2}$
C. $\frac{y^2}{z}$ D. $\frac{y}{z}$

EXPLANATORY ANSWERS

1. B : Ratio is 3 : 4, sum = 490
If sum is 7, the numbers are 3 and 4.
If sum is 490, the numbers are $\frac{3}{7} \times 490$ and $\frac{4}{7} \times 490$ *i.e.*, 210 and 280.

2. B : Ratio is 3 : 4. Sum of the squares of 3 and 4 is 9 + 16 = 25. If sum of the squares is 25, the squares of numbers are 9 and 16.
If sum of the squares is 625, the squares of numbers are $\frac{9}{25} \times 625$ and $\frac{16}{25} \times 625$ *i.e.,* 225 and 400.
Hence, the numbers are $\sqrt{225}$ and $\sqrt{400}$, *i.e.,* 15 and 20.

3. D : $\frac{3}{4}, \frac{4}{5}, \frac{5}{6}, \frac{6}{7}$

$\frac{315,\ 336,\ 350,\ 360}{420}$. Hence, the ratio 6 : 7 is the greatest.

4. C : Total students = 70.

Number of students scoring less than 50% marks = 25; Number of students scoring 50% or more than 50% marks = 70 – 25 = 45.

∴ The ratio of number of students who scored 50% marks or more to the number of students who scored less than 50% marks

= 45 : 25 = 9 : 5.

5. A : Let the required fraction is x. Then

$$\frac{x}{4/9} = \frac{3/11}{5/33} = \frac{3}{11} \times \frac{33}{5} = \frac{9}{5}$$

$$\therefore \quad x = \frac{9}{5} \times \frac{4}{9} = \frac{4}{5}, \text{ or }, 4 : 5.$$

6. C :

$$\text{Ratio} = \frac{3}{5} = \frac{\text{Antecedent}}{\text{Consequent}} = \frac{x}{15}$$

$$\therefore \quad x = 9, \text{ only then } \frac{9}{15} = \frac{3}{5}$$

7. B : $A : B = 5 : 7$; $B : C = 9 : 11$; $A : C = ?$

$$\frac{A}{B} = \frac{5}{7}, \quad \frac{B}{C} = \frac{9}{11}, \quad \frac{A}{C} = x$$

$$\frac{A}{B} \times \frac{B}{C} = \frac{5}{7} \times \frac{9}{11}, \text{ or, } \frac{A}{C} = \frac{45}{77}$$

$$\therefore \quad A : C = 45 : 77$$

8. A : Ratio of numbers = 2 : 3 : 4.

Ratio of squares of numbers = 4 : 9 : 16

If sum of the squares is 29, the squares of the numbers are 4, 9, 16.

If sum of the squares is 116, the squares of the numbers are

$$\frac{4}{29} \times 116, \frac{9}{29} \times 116, \frac{16}{29} \times 116 = 16, 36, 64$$

∴ The numbers are $\sqrt{16}, \sqrt{36}, \sqrt{64} = 4, 6, 8$.

9. A : Let the sides of two squares are $3x$ and $4x$.
Their perimeters are $4(3x)$ and $4(4x) = 12x$ and $16x$.
Ratio of permieters $= 12x : 16x = 3 : 4$.

10. D : Let the sides of two cubes are $3x$ and $4x$. Surface areas of two cubes are $6(3x)^2$ and $6(4x)^2$.
Ratio of surface areas $= 6(3x)^2 : 6(4x)^2 = 54x^2 : 96x^2 = 9 : 16$.

11. C : Ratio of the angles of triangle $= 1 : 2 : 3$
Sum of the angles of triangle $= 180^o$

$$\text{Largest angle} = \frac{3}{6} \times 180 = 90^o$$

12. B : Let the salaries be $4x$ and $7x$.
Savings are $100 - 80 = 20\%$

$$\text{Ratio of savings} = 20\% \text{ of } 4x : 20\% \text{ of } 7x$$

$$= \frac{20}{100} \times 4x : \frac{20}{100} \times 7x = 4 : 7$$

13. C : The mean proportion between any two numbers is equal to the square root of their product.
Let x be the mean proportion between 9 and 25.

$\therefore$ $9 : x = x : 25$

or, $x^2 = 25 \times 9$, or, $x = \sqrt{25 \times 9} = \sqrt{225} = 15$.

14. D : Let x be the third proportional to 12 and 30.

Then, $12 : 30 = 30 : x$

or, $12x = 30 \times 30$

$\therefore$ $x = \dfrac{30 \times 30}{12} = 75$.

15. A : Let x be the fourth proportional to 3, 4, 15.

Then, $3 : 4 = 15 : x$

Since, product of the extremes = Product of the means

$\therefore$ $3x = 15 \times 4$, or, $x = \dfrac{15 \times 4}{3} = 20$.

16. B : $75 : 15 = x : 7$

$$75 \times 7 = 15 \times x \text{ or, } x = \frac{75 \times 7}{15} = 35.$$

17. C : $x : 7.5 = 7 : 17.5$

$$x \times 17.5 = 7.5 \times 7.0$$

$$\therefore \quad x = \frac{7.5 \times 7.0}{17.5} = 3.0.$$

18. D : Let x be the mean proportional to 5 and 125.

Then, $5 : x = x : 125$ or, $x^2 = 125 \times 5$

$$\therefore \quad x = \sqrt{125 \times 5} = \sqrt{625} = 25.$$

19. A : The inverse ratio of 12 : 18 *i.e.,*

$\frac{12}{18}$ is $\frac{18}{12} = \frac{3}{2}$.

20. D : Let the numbers be $2x$ and $3x$.

Then we have, $\frac{2x+8}{3x+8} = \frac{3}{4}$, or, $8x + 32 = 9x + 24$

or, $9x - 8x = 32 - 24$, or, $x = 8$

$\therefore$ The numbers are 2×8 and 3×8 *i.e.,* 16 and 24

21. B : $x : y = 3 : 2$, $x + y = 3 + 2$

and $x - y = 3 - 2$

$$\therefore \quad (x + y) : (x - y) = 5 : 1$$

22. C : $x : y = y : z$, or, $\frac{x}{y} = \frac{y}{z}$

$$\therefore \quad x = \frac{y}{z} . y = \frac{y^2}{z}$$

6

PROFIT AND LOSS

Profit and Loss: The terms profit and loss are largely used in business. When the selling price (S.P.) is greater than cost price (C.P.) there is always some profit. When the selling price is less than the cost price, there is always loss.

It should be noted that profit or loss is calculated on the cost price, generally in the form of per cent.

For example, a man buys an article for ₹ 50 and sells it for ₹ 65. The gain per cent is calculated as follows:

$$\text{Profit} = \text{Selling Price} - \text{Cost Price}$$
$$= ₹\ 65 - ₹\ 50 = ₹\ 15$$

$$\%\ \text{Profit} = \frac{15}{50} \times 100 = 30\%$$

When cost price and profit or loss % are given, then

$$\text{S.P.} = \frac{[100 + \text{gain}\%]}{100} \times \text{C.P.}$$

or

$$\text{S.P.} = \frac{[100 - \text{Loss}\%]}{100} \times \text{C.P.}$$

When selling price and profit or loss % are given,

$$\text{C.P.} = \frac{\text{S.P.} \times 100}{100 + \text{Gain}\ \%} \quad \text{or} \quad \text{C.P.} = \frac{\text{S.P.} \times 100}{100 - \text{Loss}\ \%}$$

(i) To find the cost price when the selling price and the % profit based on cost price is given:

Establish a relation between S.P. and C.P. and solve it to find C.P.

For example, an article is sold for Rs.10 which is a 10% profit of C.P.

In this case, S.P. = ₹ 10 = C.P. + 10% of C.P. (Profit)

$\therefore$ S.P. = 100% of C.P.

or, $$\text{C.P.} = ₹\ \frac{10 \times 100}{110} = ₹\ 9.09.$$

(ii) To find the S.P. when the profit based on S.P. is given:

Establish a relation between the S.P. and C.P. and solve it to find the S.P.

For example, a person buys a book for ₹ 27 and sells it at a profit of 10% of S.P. Find the S.P.

₹ 27 + Profit = S.P.

Since, profit is 10% of S.P., the C.P. must be 90% of S.P.

∴ ₹ 27 = 90% of S.P.

$$\therefore \quad \text{S.P.} = \frac{27 \times 100}{90} = ₹\ 30.$$

(iii) To find S.P. when the % loss on the S.P. is given:

Establish a relation between C.P. and S.P. and solve it to find S.P.

For example, an article was bought for ₹ 10. Due to some breakage, it was sold for 25% loss on the S.P. Find the S.P. of the article.

₹ 10 – Loss = S.P.

Since, the loss is 25% of the S.P., the C.P. must be 125% of S.P.

∴ ₹ 10 = 125% of S.P.

$$\therefore \quad \text{S.P.} = \frac{\text{Rs. } 10 \times 100}{125} = ₹\ 8.$$

(iv) To find S.P. when the list price and % discount are given:

Multiply the list price by % discount to find the discount in terms of money and subtract it from the list price.

For example, the list price of an article is ₹ 90. Find its selling price if it is sold at 10% discount.

List price = ₹ 90.00, Discount = 10% of ₹ 90.00

$$= \frac{10 \times 90}{100} = ₹\ 9.00$$

∴ Selling price = ₹ 90.00 – ₹ 9.00 = ₹ 81.00

(v) To find S.P. when list price and a series of discounts are given:

(a) Multiply the list price by first % discount.

(b) Subtract it from the list price.

(c) Multiply the remainder by second discount.

(d) Subtract the product from the remainder.

(e) Continue the same procedure if more discounts are given.

For example, find the selling price of an article listed at ₹ 200 on which there are discounts of 10% and 20%.

First discount = 10% of ₹ 200

$$= \frac{10 \times 200}{100} = ₹\ 20$$

First selling price = ₹ 200 – ₹ 20 = ₹ 180.

Second discount = 20% of ₹ 180

$$= \frac{20 \times 180}{100} = ₹\ 36$$

Second selling price = ₹ 180 – ₹ 36 = ₹ 144

(vi) To find the single equivalent discount of a series of discounts :

(a) Add first two discounts.

(b) Multiply first two discounts.

(c) Subtract this product from the sum to find the equivalent discount of the first two discounts.

(d) If there is third discount, add the equivalent of first two discounts to the third.

(e) Multiply the equivalent of first two discounts by third.

(f) Subtract this product from the sum to find the equivalent of the three discounts.

(g) Continue the same procedure, if there are more discounts.

For example, what is the single discount equivalent to discount series 10%, 20%, 30%.

10% + 20% = 0.1 + 0.2 = 0.3

10% × 20% = 0.1 × 0.2 = 0.02

0.30 – 0.02 = 0.28

0.28 + 30% = 0.28 + 0.3 = 0.580

0.28 × 30% = 0.28 × 0.3 = 0.084

0.580 – 0.084 = 0.496 = 49.6%

Hence, the single equivalent discount of 10%, 20% and 30%, is 49.6%.

EXERCISE

1. A man buys an article for ₹ 25 and sells it for ₹ 30. His profit is:

A. 16.67% B. 20%

C. 25.5% D. 25.67%

2. If an article is sold at 10% profit, then the selling price in terms of cost price is:

A. 10/11 B. 11/10

C. ₹ 110 D. ₹ 90

3. If an article is sold at gain of x%, the cost price in terms of selling price is:

A. $\frac{100}{100+x}$ B. $\frac{100+x}{100}$

C. $\frac{100}{100-x}$ D. $\frac{100-x}{100}$

4. If an article is sold at gain of y%, the selling price in terms of cost price is:

A. $\frac{100}{100-y}$ B. $\frac{100-y}{100}$

C. $\frac{100}{100+y}$ D. $\frac{100+y}{100}$

5. If an article is sold at a loss of 25%, the selling price in terms of cost price is:

A. $\frac{1}{2}$ B. $\frac{2}{3}$

C. $\frac{3}{4}$ D. $\frac{4}{5}$

6. If an article is sold at a loss of 50%, the cost price in terms of selling price is:

A. $\frac{1}{2}$

B. 2

C. 2.5

D. None of the above

7. If S.P. of an article is 4/3 of C.P., the profit is:

A. $\frac{1}{3}\%$ B. $33\frac{1}{3}\%$

C. $25\frac{1}{5}\%$ D. $20\frac{1}{2}\%$

8. If C.P. of an article is 3/2 of S.P., the profit or loss percentage is:

A. $33\frac{1}{3}\%$ loss B. $33\frac{1}{3}\%$ profit

C. $33\frac{1}{8}\%$ loss D. $33\frac{1}{8}\%$ profit

9. If S.P. of an article is 6 times the loss, the loss percentage is:

A. $14\frac{5}{9}\%$ B. $15\frac{2}{8}\%$

C. $16\frac{3}{5}\%$ D. $14\frac{2}{7}\%$

10. If gain is 1/4 of C.P., the profit percentage is:

A. 4% B. 25%

C. 50% D. 75%

11. If loss is 1/3 of S.P., the loss percentage is:

A. 33% B. 25%

C. 20% D. 17%

12. A man bought certain articles at 8 for ₹ 7 and sold them at 6 for ₹ 5. The gain or loss percentage is:

A. $4\frac{16}{21}\%$ gain

B. $4\frac{16}{21}\%$ loss

C. No profit no loss

D. None of the above

13. A man bought a number of oranges at 3 for a rupee and an equal number at 2 for a rupee. At what price per dozen should be sell them to make a profit of 20%?

A. ₹ 4 B. ₹ 5

C. ₹ 6 D. ₹ 7

14. A machine was bought for ₹ 9000. For how much should it be sold to gain 15%?

A. ₹ 10,150 B. ₹ 10,250

C. ₹ 10,300 D. ₹ 10,350

15. Find the selling price if a fountain pen costing ₹ 6.20 is sold at a loss of 10%?

A. ₹ 6.92 B. ₹ 5.58

C. ₹ 6.00 D. ₹ 5.92

16. A carpet is sold for ₹ 585 at a loss of 10%. The cost price is:

A. ₹ 650 B. ₹ 640

C. ₹ 630 D. ₹ 620

17. A machine is sold at a profit of 20%. If it had been sold at a profit of 25%, it would have fetched ₹ 35 more. The cost price of the machine is:

A. ₹ 650 B. ₹ 700
C. ₹ 750 D. ₹ 800

18. By selling a book for ₹ 31 a person loses 7% of his outlay. If he sells the same book for ₹ 35, the bargain is:

A. 4% loss B. 4% profit
C. 5% loss D. 5% profit

19. The cost price of 12 articles is equal to the selling price of 9 articles. The gain per cent is:

A. 25.0% B. 33.3%
C. 30.0% D. 67.7%

20. At a clearance sale, the prices had been reduced by 20%. If a transistor was being sold at ₹ 150 before reduction, the price at clearance sale was:

A. ₹ 130
B. ₹ 125
C. ₹ 120
D. ₹ 115

EXPLANATORY ANSWERS

1. B : Profit = ₹ 30 – ₹ 25 = ₹ 5, % Profit = $\frac{5}{25} \times 100 = 20\%$.

2. B : If the profit is 10%, then S.P. = 110% of C.P. = $\frac{110}{100}$ of C.P. = $\frac{11}{10}$ of C.P.

3. A : Gain = x%, S.P. = [100 + x] % of C.P. $\therefore$ C.P. = $\frac{100}{100+x}$ S.P.

4. D : Gain = y%, S.P. = [100 + y] % of C.P.

$$\text{S.P.} = \frac{100+y}{100} \times \text{C.P.}$$

5. C : Loss = 25%, C.P. = 100, S.P. = 100 – 25 = 75

or, S.P. = 75% of C.P. = $\frac{3}{4}$ of C.P.

6. B : Let C.P. = 100, Loss = 50%, S.P. = 100 – 50 = 50%;
or, S.P. = 50% of C.P. or, C.P. = 200% of S.P. or, C.P. = 2 × S.P.

7. B : C.P. = 1, S.P. = $\frac{4}{3}$, Profit = $\frac{4}{3} - 1 = \frac{1}{3}$

% Profit = $100 \times \frac{1}{3} = 33\frac{1}{3}\%$.

8. A : C.P. = 1, S.P. = $\frac{2}{3}$ of C.P., Loss = $1 - \frac{2}{3} = \frac{1}{3}$.

% Loss = $\frac{1}{3} \times 100 = 33\frac{1}{3}\%$.

9. D : S.P. = 6 times the Loss or, Loss = $\frac{1}{6}$ of S.P.

C.P. = S.P. + Loss = S.P. + $\frac{1}{6}$ of S.P. = $\frac{7}{6}$ of S.P.

or, S.P. = $\frac{6}{7}$ of C.P. $\therefore$ Loss = 1 – $\frac{6}{7}$ of C.P. = $\frac{1}{7}$ of C.P.

% Loss = $100 \times \frac{1}{7} = 14\frac{2}{7}\%$

10. B : C.P. = 1, Gain = $\frac{1}{4}$ of C.P. = $\frac{1}{4}\times 1 = \frac{1}{4}$

% Gain = $\frac{1}{4}\times 100 = 25\%$.

11. B : Loss = $\frac{1}{3}$ of S.P.

C.P. = S.P. + Loss = S.P. + $\frac{1}{3}$ of S.P. = $\frac{4}{3}$ of S.P.

or, S.P. = $\frac{3}{4}$ of C.P. $\therefore$ Loss = $\frac{1}{4}$ of C.P.

% Loss = $\frac{1}{4}$ × 100 of C.P. = 25% of C.P.

12. B : C.P. of one article = ₹ $\frac{7}{8}$, S.P. of one article = ₹ $\frac{5}{6}$

Loss = C.P. – S.P. = $\frac{7}{8}-\frac{5}{6}=\frac{1}{24}$

% Loss = $\frac{1}{24}\times\frac{8}{7} \times 100 = \frac{100}{21} = 4\frac{16}{21}\%$

13. C : Let 1 dozen oranges were bought at 3 for a rupee and one dozen oranges were bought at 2 for a rupee.

$\therefore$ C.P. of 1 dozen = ₹ 4

C.P. of 1 dozen = ₹ 6

C.P. of 2 dozens = ₹ 6 + ₹ 4 = ₹ 10

% Profit 20% = 20% of ₹ 10 = ₹ 2

$\therefore$ S.P. = C.P. + Profit = ₹ 10 + ₹ 2

= ₹ 12

S.P. of 2 dozen oranges = ₹ 12

$\therefore$ S.P. of 1 dozen oranges = ₹ $\frac{12}{2}$ = ₹ 6

14. D : C.P. = ₹ 9000, Gain = 15% of ₹ 9000 = $\frac{15}{100} \times 9000$ = ₹ 1350.

∴ S.P. = ₹ 9000 + ₹ 1350 = ₹ 10,350.

15. B : C.P. = ₹ 6.20, Loss = 10% of C.P. = 10% of ₹ 6.20

$= \frac{10}{100} \times 6.20 = 62$ paise

S.P. = C.P. – Loss = ₹ 6.20 – 62 paise

= ₹ 5.58

16. A : S.P. = ₹ 585, Loss = 10% of C.P.

$$\text{C.P.} = \frac{\text{S.P.} \times 100}{[100 - \text{Loss\%}]} = \frac{585 \times 100}{100 - 10} = \frac{585 \times 100}{90} = ₹\ 650.$$

17. B : Let, C.P. = ₹ 100

Ist S.P. = ₹ 120, IInd S.P. = ₹ 125

Difference = ₹ 125 – ₹ 120 = ₹ 5

If difference is ₹ 5, C.P. = ₹ 100

If difference is ₹ 35, C.P. = $\frac{100}{5} \times 35$ = ₹ 700

18. D : S.P. = ₹ 31, Loss = 7%

∴ C.P. = $\frac{31 \times 100}{93}$ = ₹ $\frac{100}{3}$

IInd S.P. = ₹ 35, Profit = ₹ 35 – ₹ $\frac{100}{3}$ = ₹ $\frac{5}{3}$

∴ % Profit = $\frac{5}{3} \times \frac{3}{100} \times 100 = 5\%$.

19. B : Let C.P. of one article = ₹ 1

∴C.P. of 12 articles = ₹ 12

C.P. of 12 articles = S.P. of 9 articles = ₹ 12

∴ S.P. of 12 articles = $\frac{12}{9} \times 12$ = ₹ 16

Profit = ₹ 16 – ₹ 12 = ₹ 4

% Profit = $\frac{4}{12} \times 100 = 33.3\%$

20. C : S.P. before reduction = ₹ 150

S.P. after reduction = 100 – 20 = 80% of ₹ 150

= $\frac{80}{100} \times 150$ = ₹ 120.

7

INTEREST

Interest is the sum which is paid for the use of other's money. If it is payable yearly, it is called rate per cent per annum. Thus, 6% per annum means ₹ 6 paid as interest on each ₹ 100 for one year. The money borrowed is called *Principal.* The sum of the principal and interest is called *Amount.*

In the Case of Simple Interest:

$$\text{Simple Interest} = \frac{\text{Principal} \times \text{Rate\%} \times \text{Time (in years)}}{100}$$

$$\text{Amount} = \text{Principal} + \text{Interest}$$

When time, rate% and interest are given,

$$\text{Principal} = \frac{\text{Interest} \times 100}{\text{Rate} \times \text{Time (in years)}}$$

When principal, interest and time are given,

$$\text{Rate} = \frac{\text{Interest} \times 100}{\text{Principal} \times \text{Time}}$$

When principal, interest and rate are given,

$$\text{Time} = \frac{\text{Interest} \times 100}{\text{Principal} \times \text{Rate}}$$

Example 1. A sum of money amounts to ₹ 6000 in 2 years. If the interest on the sum for that time is ₹ 1000. Find the rate of simple interest.

Solution. Amount = ₹ 6000, Interest = ₹ 1000

Principal = ₹ 6000 – ₹ 1000 = ₹ 5000

Time = 2 years

$$\text{Rate} = \frac{\text{Interest} \times 100}{\text{Principal} \times \text{Time}} = \frac{1000 \times 100}{5000 \times 2} = 10\%$$

Example 2. What principal with yield ₹ 600 as simple interest at 12% per annum in 1 year?

Solution. Interest = ₹ 600, Rate = 12%, Time = 1 year

$$\text{Principal} = \frac{\text{Interest} \times 100}{\text{Rate} \times \text{Time}} = \frac{\text{Rs. } 600 \times 100}{12 \times 1} = ₹\ 5000.$$

Example 3. At what time will the interest on a sum of money will equal to the principal at 10% per annum?

Solution. Let, Principal = x, ∴ Interest = x, Rate = 10%

$$\text{Time} = \frac{\text{Interest} \times 100}{\text{Principal} \times \text{Rate}} = \frac{x \times 100}{x \times 10} = 10 \text{ years.}$$

Example 4. Three years back, a sum of money was remitted in a bank at 12% per annum S.I. The accounts are now cleared, the bank paying a sum of ₹ 6,800. What was the sum originally invested?

Solution. Interest for 3 years = 3 × 12 = 36% of the principal. The amount in 3 years = 100 + 36 = 136% of the principal = ₹ 6800.

$$\therefore \quad \text{Original sum invested} = \frac{6800 \times 100}{136} = ₹\ 5000.$$

In the Case of Compound Interest:

$$\text{Amount} = \text{Principal} \left[1 + \frac{\text{Rate}}{100}\right]^{\text{Time(in year)}}$$

If rate of compound interest differs from year to year, then

$$\text{Amount} = \text{Principal} \left[1 + \frac{\text{Rate}_1}{100}\right]\left[1 + \frac{\text{Rate}_2}{100}\right]\left[1 + \frac{\text{Rate}_3}{100}\right]\ldots\ldots\ldots$$

Example 5. Find the compound interest on ₹ 2000 for 2 years at 10%.

Solution. $\text{Amount} = \text{Principal} \left[1 + \frac{\text{Rate}}{100}\right]^2$

$$= ₹\ 2000 \left[1 + \frac{10}{100}\right]^2 = ₹\ 2000 \times \frac{11}{10} \times \frac{11}{10}$$

$$= ₹\ 2420$$

$$\text{Compound Interest} = ₹\ 2420 - ₹\ 2000 = ₹\ 420$$

Example 6. Find the compound interest on ₹ 4000 for 1.5 years at 10% interest payable half- yearly.

Solution. (In such cases, double the time and half the rate)

$$\text{Amount} = 4000 \left(1 + \frac{5}{100}\right)^3$$

$$= ₹\ 4000 \times \frac{21}{20} \times \frac{21}{20} \times \frac{21}{20} = ₹\ 4630.50$$

$$\text{Compound Interest} = ₹\ 4630.50 - ₹\ 4000 = ₹\ 630.50$$

Example 7. In what time ₹ 12000 will amount to ₹ 13230 at 5% C.I.?

Solution. Principal $\left[1+\frac{\text{Rate}}{100}\right]^n$ = Amount

$$\therefore \quad ₹\ 13230 = ₹\ 12000 \left[1+\frac{5}{100}\right]^n$$

$$\therefore \quad \left[1+\frac{5}{100}\right]^n = \frac{\text{Rs. } 13230}{\text{Rs. } 12000}$$

$$\text{or,} \quad \left[\frac{21}{20}\right]^n = \frac{441}{400} = \frac{21}{20} \times \frac{21}{20} = \left[\frac{21}{20}\right]^2$$

$$\therefore \quad n = 2 \text{ years}$$

When interest is calculated half-yearly, halve the rate and double the time. When interest is calculated quarterly, divide the rate by 4 and multiply the time by 4.

EXERCISE

1. S.I. on ₹ 5000 for 5 years at 10% p.a. is equal to:
A. ₹ 250 B. ₹ 2000
C. ₹ 2500 D. ₹ 2800

2. What principal will yield ₹ 120 as S.I. at 6% p.a. in 10 years?
A. ₹ 100 B. ₹ 125
C. ₹ 150 D. ₹ 200

3. In how many years will the sum of money double itself at 10% per annum S.I.?
A. 4 years B. 5 years
C. 8 years D. 10 years

4. What sum of money will produce an interest of ₹ 80 in 5 years at the rate of 5% per annum?
A. ₹ 320 B. ₹ 380
C. ₹ 420 D. ₹ 500

5. If S.I. on ₹ 5000 in 2 years is ₹ 500, the amount is:
A. ₹ 4500 B. ₹ 5500
C. ₹ 5575 D. ₹ 6000

6. The simple interest on a certain sum of money is ₹ 49 and the rate per cent is equal to the number of years. The rate per cent is:
A. 10% B. 9%
C. 7% D. 6%

7. If the rate of interest is 2 paise per rupee per month, then the interest on ₹ 200 in one year will be:
A. ₹ 4 B. ₹ 24
C. ₹ 48 D. ₹ 50

8. What annual payment will discharge a debt of ₹ 440 due in 5 years? Simple interest reckoned at 5%.
A. ₹ 80 B. ₹ 90
C. ₹ 100 D. ₹ 105

9. Compound interest on ₹ 2000 for 3 years at 5% p.a. is:
A. ₹ 300 B. ₹ 315.25
C. ₹ 325.50 D. ₹ 333.75

10. Find the compound interest on ₹ 1000 is one year at 5% per annum when the interest is calculated half-yearly?
A. ₹ 50.20 B. ₹ 50.62
C. ₹ 50.82 D. ₹ 55.62

11. The difference between C.I. and S.I. on ₹ 2500 for 2 years at 4% p.a. is:
A. ₹ 2 B. ₹ 3
C. ₹ 4 D. ₹ 5

12. What sum lent at C.I. at 5% p.a. will amount to ₹ 441 in 2 years?
A. ₹ 200 B. ₹ 250
C. ₹ 450 D. ₹ 400

13. For a sum of ₹ 1000, during same time at the same rate, highest quantity will be:
A. S.I. B. C.I.
C T.D. D. B.G.

14. S.I. is equal to C.I. for a certain sum when:
A. rate is same
B. time is same
C. interest is computed annually and time is one year
D. None of the above

15. Simple interest on the sum due of a bill for the time from when the bill is discounted to the due date of bill is called:
A. Simple Interest
B. Compound Interest
C. True Discount
D. Banker's Discount

16. A sum becomes double in 15 years at simple interest. It will become triple in:
A. 20 years B. 30 years
C. 35 years D. 40 years

17. In 5 years the interest on certain sum amounts to one-fourth of the sum. The rate of interest per annum is:
A. 4% B. 5%
C. 6% D. 10%

EXPLANATORY ANSWERS

1. C : $\text{S.I.} = \dfrac{\text{Principal} \times \text{Time} \times \text{Rate}}{100} = \dfrac{5000 \times 5 \times 100}{100} = ₹\ 2500.$

2. D : $\text{Principal} = \dfrac{\text{S.I.} \times 100}{\text{Time} \times \text{Rate}} = \dfrac{120 \times 100}{6 \times 10} = ₹\ 200$

3. D : Let Principal = x

$\therefore$ Amount = $2x$, Hence, Interest = $2x - x = x$

$$\text{Rate} = 10\%, \text{Time} = \frac{\text{Interest} \times 100}{\text{Principal} \times \text{Rate}} = \frac{x \times 100}{x \times 10} = 10 \text{ years.}$$

4. A : Principal $= \dfrac{\text{Interest} \times 100}{\text{Rate} \times \text{Time}} = \dfrac{80 \times 100}{5 \times 5} =$ ₹ 320.

5. B : Amount = ₹ 5000 + ₹ 500 = ₹ 5500.

6. C : Let the Principal = ₹ 100, Time = x years, Rate = x%

$$\text{S.I.} = \frac{100 \times x \times x}{100} = x^2 = ₹\ 49$$

$$\therefore \quad x = \sqrt{49} = 7 = 7\%$$

7. C : Rate of interest = 2% per month
= 24% per year

$$\therefore \quad \text{Interest} = \frac{200 \times 24 \times 1}{100} = ₹\ 48$$

8. A.

9. B :

$$\text{Amount} = ₹\ 2000 \left(1 + \frac{5}{100}\right)^3$$

= ₹ 2315.25

C.I. = Amount – Principal = 2315.25 – 2000
= ₹ 315.25.

10. B : When interest is calculated half-yearly, convert 1 year into 2 half years and take half of the rate.

Thus, rate = 2.5%, n = 2

$$\text{Amount} = ₹\ 1000 \left(1 + \frac{2.5}{100}\right)^2$$

= ₹ 1050.62

Interest = 1050.62 – 1000 = ₹ 50.62.

11. C. **12. D.** **13. B.** **14. C.** **15. D.** **16. B.**

17. B : Let sum = x, ∴ Interest = $x/4$,

Time = 5 years,

$$\text{Rate} = \frac{\text{Interest} \times 100}{\text{Sum} \times \text{Time}} = \frac{x/4 \times 100}{x \times 5} = 5\%.$$

8

DISCOUNT

Discount in the general term is the reduction or an allowance made from the amount of a bill in lieu of its immediate cash payment. The reduction made in consideration of making immediate payment is called discount or true discount. The immediate cash payment or cash equivalent is called present worth or present value.

$$\text{Sum Due} = \text{Present Worth} + \text{True Discount}$$

$$\text{True Discount} = \text{Sum Due} - \text{Present Worth}$$

$$\text{True Discount on Sum Due} = \text{Interest on Present Worth}$$

$$\text{Present Worth} = \frac{100 \times \text{Sum Due}}{100 + [\text{Rate} \times \text{Time}]}$$

$$\text{True Discount} = \frac{\text{Sum Due} \times \text{Rate} \times \text{Time}}{100 + [\text{Rate} \times \text{Time}]}$$

Example. *Find the present worth and true discount on ₹ 6000 due 2 years at 10% per annum S.I.*

Solution.

$$\text{P.W.} = \frac{100 \times \text{Sum Due}}{100 + [\text{Rate} \times \text{Time}]}$$

$$= \frac{100 \times 6000}{100 + [10 \times 2]} = \frac{100 \times 6000}{120} = ₹\ 5000$$

$$\text{T.D.} = \frac{\text{Sum Due} \times \text{Rate} \times \text{Time}}{100 + [\text{Rate} \times \text{Time}]}$$

$$= \frac{6000 \times 10 \times 2}{100 + [10 \times 2]} = \frac{6000 \times 10 \times 2}{120} = ₹\ 1000.$$

Banker's Discount: In business when a trader buys goods from a wholesaler, the payment is generally made by a bill of exchange which is a kind of undertaking in writing to pay for the goods after a certain time. When the wholesaler wants money at earlier date, in such case, the bill is sold to the banker for ready money and it is said to be discounted and the amount which the banker deducts is called Banker's discount.

Banker's Discount (B.D.) is the same as the simple interest on the amount of bill for the number of days the bill has yet to run.

$$\text{Banker's Gain (B.G.)} = \text{Banker's Discount} - \text{True Discount}$$

$$\text{Banker's Discount} = \text{True Discount} + \text{Interest on True Discount}$$

$$\text{Sum Due} = \frac{\text{B.D.} \times \text{T.D.}}{\text{B.D.}-\text{T.D.}}$$

$$\text{T.D.} = \sqrt{\text{P.W.} \times \text{B.G.}}$$

Example 1. *True discount on a certain sum of money due 1 year hence is ₹ 48 and interest on the same sum for the same time is ₹ 50. Find the sum and the rate per cent.*

Solution.

$$\text{Sum} = \frac{\text{Interest} \times \text{Discount}}{\text{Interest} - \text{Discount}}$$

$$= \frac{\text{Rs. } 50 \times \text{Rs. } 48}{\text{Rs. } 50 - \text{Rs. } 48} = ₹\ \frac{50 \times 48}{2} = ₹\ 1200$$

Now, ₹ 50 is the interest on ₹ 1200 in one year,

$$\therefore \qquad \text{Rate} = \frac{50 \times 100}{1200 \times 1} = 4\frac{1}{6}\%$$

Example 2. The banker's discount and true discount on a certain sum of money at 5% S.I. are ₹ 30 and ₹ 25 respectively. Find the sum.

Solution.

$$\text{Sum} = \frac{\text{B.D.} \times \text{T.D.}}{\text{B.D.} - \text{T.D.}} = \frac{30 \times 25}{30 - 25} = ₹\ 150$$

Example 3. *Find the banker's discount and banker's gain on a bill of ₹ 4000 at 10% if it is cashed 3 months in advance.*

Solution.

$$\text{Banker's discount} = \frac{\text{Rs. } 4000 \times 10 \times 3}{12 \times 100} = ₹\ 100$$

Cash received by the bill holder = ₹ 4000 – ₹ 100 = ₹ 3900

Interest on ₹ 100 = ₹ 2.50

Amount = ₹ 100 + ₹ 2.50 = ₹ 102.50

If amount is ₹ 102.50, T.D. = ₹ 2.50

If amount is ₹ 4000, $\text{T.D.} = \frac{2.50}{102.50} \times 4000 = ₹\ 97.56$

B.G. = B.D. – T.D. = ₹ 100 – ₹ 97.56 = ₹ 2.44.

Example 4. *Banker's gain on a bill is ₹ 18 whose present worth is ₹ 450. Find true discount.*

Solution.

$$\text{T.D.} = \sqrt{\text{P.W.} \times \text{B.G.}}$$

$$= \sqrt{450 \times 18} = \sqrt{8100} = ₹\ 90.$$

Example 5. *True discount on a bill of ₹ 5400 is ₹ 900. Find the banker's discount and also banker's gain.*

Solution. Amount = ₹ 5400, T.D. = ₹ 900,

P.W. = Amount – T.D. = ₹ 5400 – ₹ 900

= ₹ 4500

S.I. on ₹ 4500 = ₹ 900

∴ S.I. on ₹ 5400 = ₹ $\frac{900 \times 5400}{4500}$ = ₹ 1080

∴ B.D. = ₹ 1080

∴ B.G. = B.D. – T.D. = ₹ 1080 – ₹ 900 = ₹ 180.

EXERCISE

1. Present worth of a money is equal to:

A. $\frac{100 \times \text{Sum Due}}{100 + \text{Rate} + \text{Time}}$

B. $\frac{100 \times \text{Sum Due}}{(100 + \text{Rate})\ \text{Time}}$

C. $\frac{100 + (\text{Rate} \times \text{Time})}{100 \times \text{Sum Due}}$

D. $\frac{100 \times \text{Sum Due}}{100 + (\text{Rate} \times \text{Time})}$

2. Find the present worth of ₹ 1248 due 2 years hence at 2% per annum simple interest

A. ₹ 1200 B. ₹ 1210
C. ₹ 1220 D. ₹ 1242

3. Find the present worth of ₹ 460 due 3 years hence at 5% per annum S.I.

A. ₹ 450 B. ₹ 420
C. ₹ 410 D. ₹ 400

4. Find the discount on ₹ 1010 due 3 months hence at 4% p.a. S.I.

A. ₹ 8 B. ₹ 9
C. ₹ 10 D. ₹ 12

5. Find the reduction made on a bill of ₹ 1150 paid 1.25 years before it is due when the rate of interest is 12%

A. ₹ 100 B. ₹ 150
C. ₹ 200 D. ₹ 225

6. Find the difference between S.I. and T.D. on ₹ 5100 for half-year at 4% p.a.

A. Re. 0.50 B. Re. 1.00
C. ₹ 1.50 D. ₹ 2.00

7. If the true discount on a bill due 2 years hence at 5% p.a. is ₹ 25, the amount of the bill is:

A. ₹ 125 B. ₹ 220
C. ₹ 250 D. ₹ 275

8. If the present worth of a bill of ₹ 660 due 2 years hence is ₹ 600, the rate per cent per annum is:

A. 4% B. 5%
C. 6% D. 10%

9. The true discount on a sum of money due 1 year is ₹ 100 and banker's discount on the same sum and for the same time is ₹ 104. The sum is:

A. ₹ 2500 B. ₹ 2550
C. ₹ 2600 D. ₹ 2700

10. The true discount on a sum of money due 12 months is ₹ 200 and banker's discount on the same sum and for the same time is ₹ 208. The rate of interest is:

A. 4% B. 5%

C. 6% D. 7%

11. The true discount on a certain sum of money for 2 years is 3/4 the banker's discount. The rate of interest is:

A. 15% B. 16.67%

C. 20% D. 20.33%

12. The T.D. on a bill is 5/6 of B.D. and the rate is 4%. The time is:

A. 5 years B. 4 years

C. 3 years D. 2 years

13. A trader's terms are 20% discount for cash payment and interest is charged after one year. What rate of interest per annum does the customer get on his money for cash payment?

A. 15% B. 20%

C. 25% D. 30%

14. The T.D. on a bill due 1 year hence at 5% p.a. is ₹ 40. The amount is:

A. ₹ 840 B. ₹ 900

C. ₹ 950 D. ₹ 1000

15. The interest on ₹ 5000 is equal to the true discount on ₹ 5050 at 4% p.a. The latter is due after:

A. 3 months B. 4 months

C. 5 months D. 6 months

EXPLANATORY ANSWERS

1. D : $\text{P.W.} = \dfrac{100 \times \text{S.D.}}{100 + (\text{Rate} \times \text{Time})}$.

2. A : $\text{P.W.} = \dfrac{100 \times \text{S.D.}}{100 + (\text{Rate} \times \text{Time})} = \dfrac{100 \times 1248}{100 + (2 \times 2)} = \dfrac{100 \times 1248}{104} = ₹\ 1200.$

3. D : $\text{P.W.} = \dfrac{100 \times \text{S.D.}}{100 + (\text{Rate} \times \text{Time})} = \dfrac{100 \times 460}{100 + (3 \times 5)} = \dfrac{100 \times 460}{115} = ₹\ 400.$

4. C : $\text{T.D.} = \dfrac{\text{Sum} \times \text{Rate} \times \text{Time}}{100 + (\text{Rate} \times \text{Time})} = \dfrac{1010 \times 1/4 \times 4}{100 + (1/4 \times 4)} = \dfrac{1010}{101} = ₹\ 10$

5. B : $\text{Reduction} = \text{T.D.} = \dfrac{1150 \times 12 \times 5/4}{100 + (12 \times 5/4)} = \dfrac{1150 \times 15}{115} = ₹\ 150.$

6. D :

$$\text{S.I.} = \frac{5100 \times 4 \times 1/2}{100} = ₹\ 102$$

$$\text{T.D.} = \frac{5100 \times 4 \times 1/2}{100 + (4 \times 1/2)} = \frac{5100 \times 2}{102} = ₹\ 100$$

$$\text{S.I.} - \text{T.D.} = ₹\ 102 - ₹\ 100 = ₹\ 2.$$

7. D : Let P.W. = ₹ 100

$$\text{S.I. on ₹ 100 at 5\% for 2 years} = \frac{100 \times 5 \times 2}{100} = ₹\ 10$$

Amount = 100 + 10 = ₹ 110,
₹ 10 is the T.D. on ₹ 110
If T.D. is ₹ 10, amount = ₹ 110

If T.D. is ₹ 25, amount = $\frac{110}{10} \times 25$ = ₹ 275.

8. B : P.W. = ₹ 600, Interest = ₹ 660 – ₹ 600 = ₹ 60,

Time = 2 years, Rate = $\frac{60 \times 100}{600 \times 2} = 5\%$.

9. C : Sum = $\frac{\text{B.D.} \times \text{T.D.}}{\text{B.D.} - \text{T.D.}} = \frac{104 \times 100}{104 - 100} = \frac{104 \times 100}{4}$ = ₹ 2600.

10. A : Sum = $\frac{\text{B.D.} \times \text{T.D.}}{\text{B.D.} - \text{T.D.}} = \frac{208 \times 200}{208 - 200} = \frac{208 \times 200}{8}$ = ₹ 5200.

Now, ₹ 208 is the interest on ₹ 5200 for 1 year.

∴ Rate = $\frac{208 \times 100}{5200 \times 1} = 4\%$.

11. B : If B.D. = x, T.D. = $3/4x$, Sum = $\frac{x \times 3/4x}{x - 3/4x} = 3x$,

Since, B.D. is the interest on sum due, ∴ Rate = $\frac{x \times 100}{3x \times 2} = \frac{100}{6} = 16.67\%$.

12. A : If, B.D. = x, T.D. = $6/5x$, Sum = $\frac{x \times 5/6x}{x - 5/6x} = 5x$

Since, B.D. is the interest on sum due, ∴ Time = $\frac{x \times 100}{5x \times 4}$ = 5 years.

13. C : Let amount of Bill = ₹ 100, Discount for cash payment = 20% = ₹ 20
∴ Cash price = ₹ 100 – ₹ 20 = ₹ 80
i.e., ₹ 20 is interest earned on ₹ 80 for one year.

∴ Rate = $\frac{20 \times 100}{80 \times 1}$ = ₹ 25%.

14. A : T.D. = Interest on P.W. = ₹ 40

Time = 1 year, Rate = 5% P.W. = $\frac{40 \times 100}{5 \times 1}$ = ₹ 800.

∴ Amount = 800 + 40 = ₹ 840

15. A : Interest on P.W. = T.D. on amount
Now, Interest on ₹ 5000 = T.D. on ₹ 5050
∴ ₹ 5000 is the P.W. of ₹ 5050 due at 4%
∴ Interest on ₹ 5000 = Sum due – P.W. = ₹ 5050 – ₹ 5000 = ₹ 50

∴ Time = $\frac{50 \times 100}{5000 \times 4} = \frac{1}{4}$ year = 3 months

9

TIME, WORK AND WAGES

While dealing with problems of time and work, it should be kept in mind that,

(*i*) If a man can do a piece of work in 5 days, It is evident that in one day he will finish 1/5 of his whole work; and vice versa.

(*ii*) If the number of persons engaged to do a certain job be increased in a certain ratio, the time required to do the same job will be decreased in the same ratio, and vice-versa. Thus, if the number of persons be changed in the ratio of 3 : 5, the time required to finish the job will be changed in the ratio of 5 : 3.

(*iii*) If A is twice as good workman as B, then A will take one-half of the time taken by B to do the same job.

(*iv*) While dealing with problems on wages, it may be kept in mind that the money obtained is always divided in the ratio of the work done by each person.

In the problems based on time and work, it is always assumed that a person works at uniform rate, unless and until specified in the problem.

Example. *A can do a piece of work in 4 days and B can do the same work in 6 days. How long will A and B take to do the work together?*

Solution. A's work in one day $= \frac{1}{4}$ of the total work

B's Work in one day $= \frac{1}{6}$ of the total work

$(A + B)$'s work in one day $= \frac{1}{4}+\frac{1}{6} = \frac{5}{12}$ of the total work

$\therefore$ Number of days taken by A + B to finish the work $= \frac{12}{5} = 2.4$ days.

EXERCISE

1. A can do a certain job in 6 days and B can finish the same job in 10 days. A and B together will finish the same job in:

A. less than 10 days but more then 6 days

B. more than 10 days

C. less than 6 days

D. 2 days

2. A can make a table in 3 days while his friend can make it in 6 days. A and his friend together will make the table in:

A. 3 days B. 2 days
C. 1 day D. 1/2 days

3. X and Y together can do a certain job in 10 days while X alone can do the same job in 15 days. Y alone will do the same job in:

A. 15 days B. 20 days
C. 25 days D. 30 days

4. Amit can do 1/2 of a piece of work in 8 days, while Aslam can do 1/3 of the same work in 8 days. In how many days can both do it together?

A. 9.6 days B. 10.5 days
C. 11.2 days D. 16.0 days

5. X, Y and Z together can do a piece of work in 8 days while X and Z together can do it in 12 days. Y alone will do the same work in:

A. 16 days B. 20 days
C. 24 days D. 28 days

6. 24 persons can assemble a machine in 12 days. In how many days 36 persons will assemble the same machine?

A. 8 days B. 12 days
C. 16 days D. 20 days

7. X, Y and Z can do a certain job in 8, 10 and 8 days respectively. How long would they take to complete the same job when all work together?

A. $2\frac{1}{7}$ days B. $2\frac{3}{7}$ days

C. $2\frac{5}{7}$ days D. $2\frac{6}{7}$ days

8. If m men can do $1/n$ of a piece of work in P days, find the expression for the number of persons required to do the whole work in q days?

A. mn/pq B. mnq/p
C. mnp/q D. mp/nq

9. In the above Q. No. 8 if $m = 15$, $n = 4$, $p = 12.5$ and $q = 20$, then the number of persons required to do the same work is:

A. 38 B. 34
C. 30 D. 26

10. A piece of work can be done by 6 men and 5 women in 6 days or 3 men and 4 women in 10 days. In how many days can it be done by 9 men and 15 women?

A. 1 day B. 2 days
C. 3 days D. 4 days

11. X and Y undertook a contract to do a certain job for ₹ 4200. X alone could do the job in 3 weeks and Y alone in 4 weeks. If both of them finished the job working together, in what ratio should money be divided (X : Y)?

A. 3 : 4 B. 4 : 3
C. 1 : 1 D. 2 : 3

12. X and Y did a piece of work together and received ₹ 300. If X alone can do that piece of work in 2 weeks and Y alone in 3 weeks, how should the money be divided between them?

A. X = ₹ 180, Y = ₹ 120
B. X = ₹ 120, Y = ₹ 180
C. X = ₹ 150, Y = ₹ 150
D. X = ₹ 200, Y = ₹ 100

13. A, B and C did a work together and earned ₹ 195. If the ratio of work of A : B : C be as 4 : 6 : 3, the money obtained by C is:

A. ₹ 90 B. ₹ 60
C. ₹ 45 D. ₹ 30

14. To finish a certain job X takes twice as long as Y and Z together and Z three times as long as X and Y together. If X, Y and Z working together complete the job in 6 days, how long would X take to complete the work alone?

A. 16 days B. 18 days
C. 24 days D. 28 days

15. In the above question, how long would Z take to complete the work alone?

A. 16 days B. 18 days
C. 20 days D. 24 days

SOME SELECTED EXPLANATORY ANSWERS

1. C : Work done by A in one day $= \frac{1}{6}$

Work done by B in one day $= \frac{1}{10}$

Work done by (A + B) in one day $= \frac{1}{6}+\frac{1}{10} = \frac{8}{30}$

$\therefore$ A + B together will finish the work in $\frac{30}{8}$ days $= 3\frac{6}{8}$ days which is less than 6 days.

2. B : Work done by A and his friend in one day $=\frac{1}{3}+\frac{1}{6}=\frac{3}{6}$

$\therefore$ Both will finish the work in $\frac{6}{3}$ = 2 days

3. D : Work done by X + Y in one day $= \frac{1}{10}$

Work done by X alone in one day $= \frac{1}{15}$

Work done by Y alone in one day $= \frac{1}{10}-\frac{1}{15}=\frac{1}{30}$

$\therefore$ Y alone will finish the work in 30 days.

4. A : Amit alone can do the whole work in $8 \times 2 = 16$ days

$\therefore$ Work done by Amit in one day $= \frac{1}{16}$

Aslam alone can do the whole work in $8 \times 3 = 24$ days

$\therefore$ Work done by Aslam in one day $= \frac{1}{24}$

Work done by Amit and Aslam in one day $= \frac{1}{16} + \frac{1}{24} = \frac{5}{48}$

$\therefore$ Amit and Aslam will finish the work in $\frac{48}{5} = 9.6$ days.

5. C : Work done by X + Y + Z in one day $= \frac{1}{8}$

Work done by X + Z in one day $= \frac{1}{12}$

Work done by Y in one day $= \frac{1}{8} - \frac{1}{12} = \frac{1}{24}$

$\therefore$ Y alone will finish the work in 24 days.

6. A : $\because$ 24 persons can assemble in 12 days.

$\therefore$ 1 person can assemble in 12×24 days

$\therefore$ 36 persons can assemble in $\frac{12 \times 24}{36} = 8$ days

7. D : Work done by X + Y + Z in one day $= \frac{1}{8} + \frac{1}{10} + \frac{1}{8} = \frac{7}{20}$

$\therefore$ X + Y + Z will complete the work in $\frac{20}{7} = 2\frac{6}{7}$ days.

8. C : m men can do $1/n$ of work in p days

$\therefore$ Number of men required to do the work in one day $= mnp$

Hence, number of men required to do the whole work in q days $= mnp/q$.

9. A : $mnp/q = \frac{15 \times 4 \times 12.5}{20} = 38.$

10. C :

$$6 \text{ days} \rightarrow 6\ m + 5\ w$$
$$1 \text{ day} \rightarrow 36\ m + 30\ w$$

Similarly,

$$10 \text{ days} \rightarrow 3\ m + 4\ w$$
$$1 \text{ day} \rightarrow 30\ m + 40\ w$$
$$36\ m + 30\ w = 30\ m + 40\ w$$

or, $$6\ m = 10\ w$$

or, $$1\ m = \frac{5}{3}\ w$$

Therefore, $$6\ m + 5\ w = 15\ w$$

and $$9\ m + 15\ w = 30\ w$$

The problem now reduce to

$$15\ w \rightarrow 6 \text{ days}$$

$\therefore$ $$30\ w \rightarrow 6 \times \frac{15}{30} = 3 \text{ days}$$

11. B : Ratio of working capacity of X and Y is 4 : 3

$\therefore$ Ratio of money to be divided = 4 : 3

12. A : Ratio of working capacity of X and Y is 3 : 2

$\therefore$ X's share $= \frac{3}{5} \times 300 =$ ₹ 180,

Y's share $= \frac{2}{5} \times 300 =$ ₹ 120.

13. C : Money obtained byC $= \frac{3}{13} \times 195 =$ ₹ 45.

14. B : 2 times X's daily work = (Y + Z)'s daily work

Adding X's daily work to both sides we get

3 times X's daily work = (X + Y + Z)'s daily work = 1/6

$\therefore$ X's daily work $= \frac{1}{6} \times \frac{1}{3} = \frac{1}{18}$

$\therefore$ X alone can finish the work in 18 days.

15. D : 3 times Z's daily work = (X + Y)'s daily work

Adding Z's daily work to both sides, we get

4 times Z's daily work = (X + Y + Z)'s daily work = 1/6

$\therefore$ Z's daily work $= \frac{1}{6} \times \frac{1}{4} = \frac{1}{24}$

$\therefore$ Z alone can finish the work in 24 days.

10

SPEED, TIME AND DISTANCE

Important Formulae :

$$\text{Distance} = \text{Speed} \times \text{Time}$$

$$\text{Speed} = \frac{\text{Distance}}{\text{Time}}$$

$$\text{Time} = \frac{\text{Distance}}{\text{Speed}}$$

EXERCISE

1. Speed of a moving car is 36 km/hr. Its speed in metres per second is:

A. 10 m/s B. 15 m/s
C. 20 m/s D. 25 m/s

2. Two trains start at the same time from two stations X and Y, 900 km apart; and proceed towards each other at an average speed of 38 and 22 km per hour respectively. They will meet after

A. 12 hours B. 13 hours
C. 14 hours D. 15 hours

3. A scooterist completes a journey in 10 hours, the first half at the rate of 21 km/hr and the second half at the rate of 24 km/hr. The total distance travelled is :

A. 256 km B. 224 km
C. 204 km D. 192 km

4. A train 100 m long is running at the speed of 60 km per hour. Time taken by the train to pass a telegraph post is:

A. 4 sec B. 5 sec
C. 6 sec D. 3 sec

5. A train 150 m long is running at the speed of 90 km/hr. Time taken by the train to pass through a tree is :

A. 3 sec B. 4 sec
C. 6 sec D. 8 sec

6. A train 100 m long is running at the speed of 65 km/hr. Time taken by the train to pass through a man walking at the rate of 5 km/hr in the direction of the train is :

A. 8 sec B. 6 sec
C. 4 sec D. 2 sec

7. A train 100 m long is running at the rate of 55 km/hr. Time taken by the train to pass through a man walking at the rate of 5 km/hr moving in opposite direction is :

A. 10 sec B. 8 sec
C. 6 sec D. 4 sec

8. Two persons start from the same place and walk in the opposite directions at 5 km and 4 km per hour respectively. At the end of 3 hours, distance between them is

A. 12 km B. 15 km
C. 27 km D. 30 km

9. A person starts from a place P at 6 A.M. and walks to Q at 3 km per hour. Another person starts from P at 8 A.M. and follows the first on bicycle at 6 km per hour. Both of them reach Q at the same time. The distance from P to Q is:

A. 12 km B. 10 km
C. 8 km D. 6 km

10. A person can row at the rates of x km/hr up a stream and at the rate of y km/hr down the stream. The rate in still water is:

A. $x + y$ B. $x - y$
C. $\frac{x-y}{2}$ D. $\frac{x+y}{2}$

11. In Q. 10, the rate of flow of stream is :

A. $x + y$ B. $x - y$
C. $y - x$ D. $\frac{y-x}{2}$

12. A person can row down a stream at 6 km/hr and up the same stream at 3 km/hr. His rate in still water is :

A. 9 km/hr B. 4.5 km/hr
C. 1.5 km/hr D. 1.0 km/hr

13. In Q. 12, the rate of flow of the stream is :

A. 1.5 km/hr B. 2.5 km/hr
C. 4.5 km/hr D. 18.0 km/hr

14. A man can row at the rate of 9 km per hr in still water. At what rate can he row against a stream flowing 7 km per hour?

A. 8 km/hr B. 7 km/hr
C. 2 km/hr D. –2 km/hr

15. To walk one kilometre A takes m minutes and B, n minutes. In one hour, the difference of distance travelled by A and B is:

A. $m - n$ B. $60m - 60n$
C. $\frac{60}{m} - \frac{60}{n}$ D. $\frac{60}{mn}$

EXPLANATORY ANSWERS

1. A : Speed $= \frac{36\text{ km}}{1\text{ hr}} = \frac{36000\text{ m}}{3600\text{ sec}} = 10$ m/s.

2. D : Distance covered by two trains in 1 hour = 38 + 22 = 60 km.

$$\text{Distance} = 900 \text{ km}$$

$$\text{Time taken} = \frac{900}{60} = 15 \text{ hours.}$$

3. B : Let distance = x km.

Time taken in travelling $\frac{x}{2}$ km at the rate of 21 km/hr

$$= \frac{1}{21} \times \frac{x}{2} = \frac{x}{42} \text{ hr.}$$

Time taken in travelling $\frac{x}{2}$ km at the rate of 24 km/hr

$$= \frac{1}{24} \times \frac{x}{2} = \frac{x}{48} \text{ hr}$$

But $\frac{x}{42} + \frac{x}{48} = 10$

$$\frac{8x + 7x}{336} = 10$$

$$15x = 3360$$

$\Rightarrow$ $x = 224$ km.

4. C : Distance = 100 m

$$\text{Speed} = \frac{60\text{ km}}{1\text{ hr}} = \frac{60000\text{ m}}{3600\text{ sec}} = \frac{50}{3} \text{ m/sec}$$

$$\text{Time} = \frac{\text{Distance}}{\text{Speed}} = \frac{100}{50/3} = \frac{100 \times 3}{50} = 6 \text{ sec.}$$

5. C : $\text{Speed} = \frac{90\text{ km}}{1\text{ hr}} = \frac{90000\text{ m}}{3600\text{ sec}} = 25$ m/sec.

Distance = 150 m.

$$\text{Time} = \frac{\text{Distance}}{\text{Speed}} = \frac{150}{25} = 6 \text{ sec.}$$

6. B : Net speed = Speed of train – speed of man = 65 – 5 = 60 km/hr

$$\text{Speed} = \frac{60\text{ km}}{1\text{ hr}} = \frac{60000\text{ m}}{3600\text{ sec}} = \frac{50}{3} \text{ m/s}$$

$$\text{Time} = \frac{\text{Distance}}{\text{Speed}} = \frac{100}{50/3} = \frac{100 \times 3}{50} = 6 \text{ sec.}$$

7. C : Net speed = speed of train + speed of man = 55 + 5 = 60 km/hr

For rest of the answer see Q. 6.

8. C : Since, both the persons are moving in opposite direction and start from the same place, distance them after one hour = 5 + 4 = 9 km.

$\therefore$ Distance after 3 hours = 9 × 3 = 27 km.

9. A : Let distance from P to $Q = x$ km

$$\text{Speed of first person} = 3 \text{ km/hr}$$

$$\text{Time taken} = \frac{x}{3} \text{ hr}$$

$$\text{Speed of second person} = 6 \text{ km/hr}$$

$$\text{Time taken} = \frac{x}{6} \text{ hr}$$

According to problem, $\frac{x}{3} - \frac{x}{6} = 2$

$$\frac{2x - x}{6} = 2$$

$$x = 12$$

$\therefore$ Distance from P to Q = 12 km.

10. D : Rate in still water $= \frac{x+y}{2}$.

11. D : Rate of flow of stream $= \frac{y-x}{2}$.

12. B : Rate of still water $= \frac{6+3}{2} = 4.5$ km/hr.

13. A : Rate of flow of stream $= \frac{6-3}{2} = 1.5$ km/hr.

14. C : Rate of rowing against flowing water

= Rate of rowing of man – Rate of flow of the stream

= 9 – 7 = 2 km/hr.

15. C : Distance travelled by A in 1 hour $= \frac{60}{m}$ km

Distance travelled by B in 1 hour $= \frac{60}{n}$ km

$\therefore$ Difference of distance travelled by A and B in 1 hour $= \frac{60}{m} - \frac{60}{n}$.

11

AVERAGE

EXERCISE

1. The heights of 5 students (in cm) are 140, 135, 142, 138, 140. Their average height is :
   A. 136
   B. 138
   C. 139
   D. 140

2. Marks obtained by 10 students are 22, 35, 37, 38, 29, 27, 34, 36, 28, 34. The average marks are :
   A. 30 B. 31
   C. 32 D. 34

3. Average of class I to class V is 29. Average of class I to class III is 31. Average of class IV to class V is:
   A. 25 B. 26
   C. 27 D. 28

4. The average age of a group of 13 boys is 13 years. When two more boys joined the group, the average rose by 2 years. The sum of the ages of the two new boys is :
   A. 50 years
   B. 30 years
   C. 56 years
   D. 26 years

5. A boy of height 165 cm is replaced by another, which decreases the average height of the group of 34 boys by 1 cm. The height of the new boy is :
   A. 132 cm B. 129 cm
   C. 130 cm D. 131 cm

6. The average of five consecutive even numbers, starting with 2, is:
   A. 4 B. 6
   C. 7 D. 5

7. The average of 4, 5, 3.5, 7.5, 9.5 and 6.5 is :
   A. 6.0 B. 5.2
   C. 5.5 D. 5.0

8. The average of 8 numbers is 12. If each number is increased by 2, the average of the new set of numbers is:
   A. 14 B. 12
   C. 15 D. 13

9. The weights of 5 balls in gms are as under 50, 54, 53, 56, 52. The average weight is :
   A. 53 B. 54
   C. 52 D. 51

10. The lengths of 5 pieces of a string in cms are : 5, 5.2, 6.3, 7.2, 6.3. The average length of a piece is:
    A. 5.8 B. 6.0
    C. 6.1 D. 6.2

EXPLANATORY ANSWERS

1. C : Average height $= \frac{140+135+142+138+140}{5} = \frac{695}{5} = 139.$

2. C : Average marks $= \frac{22+35+37+38+29+27+34+36+28+34}{10}$

$= \frac{320}{10} = 32.$

3. B : Total students in class I to V = 29 × 5 = 145

Total students in class I to III = 31 × 3 = 93

Total students in class IV and V = 145 – 93 = 52

Average of class IV and V $= \frac{52}{2} = 26.$

4. C : Total age of 13 boys = 13 × 13 = 169 years

Total age of 15 boys = 15(13 + 2) = 15 × 15 = 225 years

Total age of two new boys = 225 – 169 = 56 years.

5. D : Average decrease in height of 34 boys = 1 cm

Total decrease in height of 34 boys = 34 × 1 = 34 cm

∴ Height of the new boy = 165 – 34 = 131 cm.

6. B : Sum of five consecutive even numbers starting with 2

= 2 + 4 + 6 + 8 + 10 = 30

Average = 30 ÷ 5 = 6.

7. A.

8. A : New average = 12 + 2 = 14.

9. A : Average weight $= \frac{50+54+53+56+52}{5} = \frac{265}{5} = 53.$

10. B : Average length $= \frac{5+5.2+6.3+7.2+6.3}{5} = \frac{30.0}{5} = 6.0.$

12

PARTNERSHIP

EXERCISE

1. *X*, *Y* and *Z* invested in a common business. *X* invested ₹ 6000 for 2 months, *Y* invested ₹ 7000 for 4 months and *Z* invested ₹ 6400 for 5 months. Out of a profit of ₹ 900, *X*'s share is:

A. ₹ 400 B. ₹ 350
C. ₹ 150 D. ₹ 110

2. *X*, *Y* and *Z* invested ₹ 2400, ₹ 3600 and ₹ 4800 in a business. Out of a profit of ₹ 1260, *X*'s share is :

A. ₹ 280 B. ₹ 420
C. ₹ 560 D. ₹ 140

3. *A*, *B* and *C* invested in a common business. *A* invested ₹ 5000 for 2 months, *B* invested ₹ 6000 for 3 months and *C* invested ₹ 4000 for 5 months. Out of a profit of ₹ 960, *A*'s share is:

A. ₹ 360 B. ₹ 200
C. ₹ 400 D. ₹ 300

4. *A*, *B* and *C* invested in a common business. *A* invested ₹ 10000 for 3 months, *B* invested ₹ 15000 for 4 months and *C* invested ₹ 12000 for 5 months. Out of a profit of ₹ 1020, *A*'s share is :

A. ₹ 204 B. ₹ 408
C. ₹ 612 D. ₹ 816

5. *X*, *Y* and *Z* invested in a common business. *X* invested ₹ 4000 for 2 months, *Y* invested ₹ 2500 for 4 months and *Z* invested ₹ 3000 for 6 months. Out of a profit of ₹ 1800, *X*'s share is :

A. ₹ 400 B. ₹ 500
C. ₹ 800 D. ₹ 900

6. *X*, *Y* and *Z* invested ₹ 4800, ₹ 7200 and ₹ 9600 in a business. Out of a profit of ₹ 2520, *Z*'s share is:

A. ₹ 280 B. ₹ 560
C. ₹ 840 D. ₹ 1120

7. *A*, *B* and *C* invested ₹ 600, ₹ 900 and ₹ 1200 in a business. Out of a profit of ₹ 549, *A*'s share is:

A. ₹ 61 B. ₹ 122
C. ₹ 183 D. ₹ 244

8. *A*, *B* and *C* invested in a common business. *A* invested ₹ 2000 for 5 months, *B* invested ₹ 1200 for 6 months and *C* invested ₹ 2500 for 3 months. Out of a profit of ₹ 494, A's share is :

A. ₹ 144 B. ₹ 200
C. ₹ 150 D. ₹ 300

9. *X*, *Y* and *Z* invested ₹ 10000, ₹ 7200 and ₹ 7500 in a common business. Out of a profit of ₹ 988, *X*'s share is :

A. ₹ 400 B. ₹ 288
C. ₹ 300 D. ₹ 247

10. *A*, *B* and *C* invested ₹ 1200, ₹ 1800 and ₹ 2400 in a common business. Out of a profit of ₹ 1098, *A*'s share is :

A. ₹ 244 B. ₹ 586
C. ₹ 488 D. ₹ 366

11. *A* and *B* invested ₹ 30000 and ₹ 34000 in a common business. Out of a profit of ₹ 1600, *A*'s share is :

A. ₹ 800 B. ₹ 750
C. ₹ 850 D. ₹ 900

12. Mohan and Ramesh invested ₹ 8000 and ₹ 1000 respectively in a common business. Out of a profit of ₹ 9630, Mohan's share is:

A. ₹ 3210 B. ₹ 4280
C. ₹ 5350 D. ₹ 6420

13. *X*, *Y* and *Z* invested ₹ 2880, ₹ 3600 and ₹ 1800 in a common business. Out of a profit of ₹ 9600, *X*'s share is :

A. ₹ 3360 B. ₹ 4200
C. ₹ 2100 D. ₹ 6300

14. *A*, *B* and *C* invested ₹ 2400, ₹ 3600 and ₹ 4800 in a common business. Out of a profit of ₹ 981, *A*'s share is :

A. ₹ 109 B. ₹ 218
C. ₹ 327 D. ₹ 436

EXPLANATORY ANSWERS

1. C : *X*'s investment for 1 month = ₹ 6000 × 2 = ₹ 12000
Y's investment for 1 month = ₹ 7000 × 4 = ₹ 28000
Z's investment for 1 month = ₹ 6400 × 5 = ₹ 32000
12000 : 28000 : 32000
3 : 7 : 8
Sum of ratio = 3 + 7 + 8 = 18

$$X\text{'s share in the profit} = \frac{3}{18} \times 900 = ₹\ 150.$$

2. A :

X		*Y*		*Z*
₹ 2400	:	₹ 3600	:	₹ 4800
2	:	3	:	4

Sum of ratio = 2 + 3 + 4 = 9

$$X\text{'s share in the profit} = \frac{2}{9} \times 1260 = ₹\ 280.$$

3. B : *A*'s investment for 1 month = ₹ 5000 × 2 = ₹ 10000
B's investment for 1 month = ₹ 6000 × 3 = ₹ 18000
C's investment for 1 month = ₹ 4000 × 5 = ₹ 20000
Ratio = 10000 : 18000 : 20000
5 : 9 : 10
Sum of ratio = 5 + 9 + 10 = 24

$$A\text{'s share in the profit} = 960 \times \frac{5}{24} = ₹\ 200.$$

4. A : *A*'s investment = ₹ 10000 × 3 = ₹ 30000
B's investment = ₹ 15000 × 4 = ₹ 60000
C's investment = ₹ 12000 × 5 = ₹ 60000
Ratio = 30000 : 60000 : 60000
1 : 2 : 2
Sum of ratio = 1 + 2 + 2 = 5

A's share in the profit = ₹ $1020 \times \frac{1}{5}$ = ₹ 204.

5. A : *X*'s investment = ₹ 4000 × 2 = ₹ 8000
Y's investment = ₹ 2500 × 4 = ₹ 10000
Z's investment = ₹ 3000 × 6 = ₹ 18000
X : Y : Z = 8000 : 10000 : 18000
4 : 5 : 9
Sum of ratio = 4 + 5 + 9 = 18.

X's share in the profit = $\frac{4}{18} \times 1800$ = ₹ 400.

6. D :

X		*Y*		*Z*
4800	:	7200	:	9600
2	:	3	:	4

Sum of ratio = 2 + 3 + 4 = 9

Z's share in the profit = $\frac{4}{9} \times 2520$ = ₹ 1120.

7. B :

A		*B*		*C*
600	:	900	:	1200
2	:	3	:	4

Sum of ratio = 2 + 3 + 4 = 9

A's share in the profit = $\frac{2}{9} \times 549$ = ₹ 122.

8. b : *A*'s investment = ₹ 2000 × 5 = ₹ 10000
B's investment = ₹ 1200 × 6 = ₹ 7200
C's investment = ₹ 2500 × 3 = ₹ 7500
Ratio = 10000 : 7200 : 7500
100 : 72 : 75
Sum of ratio = 100 + 72 + 75 = 247

A's share in the profit = $\frac{100}{247} \times 494$ = ₹ 200.

9. A :

X		Y		Z
10000	:	7200	:	7500
100	:	72	:	75

Sum of ratio = 100 + 72 + 75 = 247

X's share in the profit = $\frac{100}{247} \times 988$ = ₹ 400.

10. A :

A		B		C
1200	:	1800	:	2400
2	:	3	:	4

Sum of ratio = 2 + 3 + 4 = 9

A's share in the profit = $\frac{2}{9} \times 1098$ = ₹ 244.

11. B :

A		B
30000	:	34000
15	:	17

Sum of ratio = 15 + 17 = 32

A's share in the profit = $\frac{15}{32} \times 1600$ = ₹ 750.

12. B : Mohan's investment = ₹ 8000
Ramesh's investment = ₹ 10000

Ratio = 8000 : 10000 = 4 : 5

Sum of ratio = 4 + 5 = 9

Mohan's share in the profit = $\frac{4}{9} \times \text{Rs.}9630$ = ₹ 4280.

13. A :

X		Y		Z
2880	:	3600	:	1800
8	:	10	:	5

Sum of ratio = 9 + 10 + 5 = 23

X's share in the profit = $\frac{8}{23} \times 9660$ = ₹ 3360.

14. B :

A		B		C
2400	:	3600	:	4800
2	:	3	:	4

Sum of ratio = 2 + 3 + 4 = 9

A's share in the profit = $\frac{2}{9} \times 981$ = ₹ 218.

13

MIXTURE AND ALLIGATION

1. Rule of Alligation:

$$\frac{\text{Amount of Cheaper ingredient}}{\text{Amount of Dearer ingredient}} = \frac{\text{Cost price of Dearer} - \text{Mean Price}}{\text{Mean Price} - \text{Cost Price of Cheaper}}$$

Here cost price of unit quantity of the mixture is called the *Mean Price.* The above rule may be represented schematically as under:

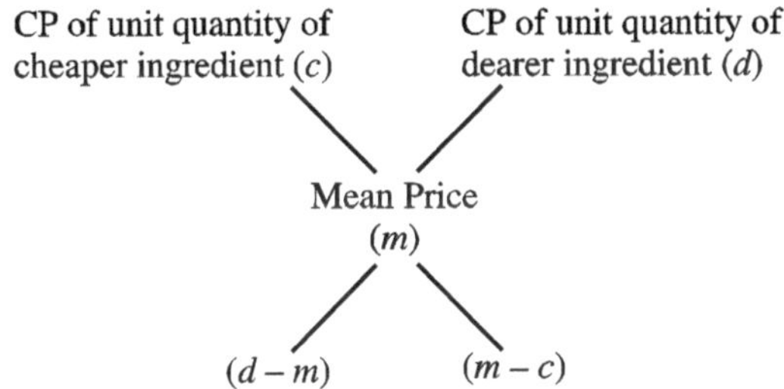

$$(\text{Cheaper quantity}) : (\text{Dearer quantity}) = (d - m) : (m - c)$$

This relationship is very helpful in solving problems on mixture involving percentage values, rates, prices, speeds etc.

2. m gm of sugar solution has x % sugar in it. To increase the sugar content in the solution to y %,

quantity of sugar need to be added $= \dfrac{m(y-x)}{100-y}$

3. A vessel contains x litres of liquid A. y litres are withdrawn and replaced by liquid B. Next y litres of the mixture is withdrawn and again replaced by liquid B.

This operation is repeated n times.

$$\frac{\text{Quantity of liquid A left after } n\text{th operation}}{\text{Whole quantity of liquid A initially present}} = \left(\frac{x-y}{x}\right)^n \text{ or } \left(1-\frac{y}{x}\right)^n$$

EXERCISE

1. Two vessels A and B contain mixture of milk and water in the ratio 4 : 1 and 9 : 11 respectively. They are mixed in the ratio of 3 : 2. Find the ratio of milk : water in the resulting mixture.

A. 34 : 16 B. 33 : 17
C. 16 : 34 D. 17 : 33

2. In what ratio must water be added to spirit to gain 25% by selling it at cost price?

A. 1 : 4 B. 4 : 1
C. 3 : 4 D. 4 : 3

3. A person has ₹ 5000. He invests a part of it at 3% per annum and the remainder at 8% per annum simple interest. His total income in 3 years is ₹ 750. Find the sum invested at different rates of interest.

A. ₹ 2000 and ₹ 3000
B. ₹ 2500 and ₹ 2500
C. ₹ 3000 and ₹ 2000
D. ₹ 2750 and ₹ 2250

4. A person covers a distance of 100 kms in 10 hours, partly by walking at 7 km/hr and rest by running at 12 km/hr. Find the distance covered in each part.

A. 48 kms B. 72 kms
C. 108 kms D. 124 kms

5. A vessel contains 80 litres of milk. 16 litres of milk was taken out of the vessel and replaced by water. Then 16 litres of mixture was withdrawn and again replaced by water. The operation was repeated for third time. How much milk is now left in the vessel?

A. 96.40 litres
B. 50.36 litres
C. 40.96 litres
D. 32.76 litres

6. If 4 kg of an alloy made of 1/4th iron and rest is mixed with 6 kg of another alloy made of 2/3rd iron and rest tin, find the ratio of iron to tin in the resultant mixture.

A. 1 : 1 B. 2 : 1
C. 1 : 2 D. 3 : 2

7. In a courtyard there are many chickens and goats. If heads are counted, it comes to 100 but when legs are counted, it comes to 320. Find the number of chickens and goats in the courtyard.

A. 20, 50 B. 30, 70
C. 40, 60 D. 50, 50

8. A container is full of milk. One-third of milk is taken out of it and replaced by same quantity of water. Then again one-third of the mixture is taken out of it and replaced by the same quantity of water. The process is repeated 4 times. If 16 litres of milk is left in the container at the end of 4th operation, find the capacity of the container.

A. 76 litres B. 81 litres
C. 82 litres D. 85 litres

9. The cost of type-I rice is ₹ 15 per kg and type-II is ₹ 20 per kg. If both type I and type II are mixed in the ratio of 2 : 3, then find the price per kg of the mixed variety.

A. ₹ 19.50

B. ₹ 19

C. ₹ 18.50

D. ₹ 18

10. A cask full of wine from which 8 litres are drawn and is then filled with water. This operation is performed three more times. The ratio of quantity of wine left in the cask to that of the water is 16 : 81. How much wine did the cask hold originally?

A. 42 litres B. 32 litres

C. 24 litres D. 18 litres

EXPLANATORY ANSWERS

1. B: Fraction is

	Milk	*Water*
A :	$\frac{4}{5}$	$\frac{1}{5}$
B :	$\frac{9}{20}$	$\frac{11}{20}$

$$(3A + 2B) = A \text{ and } B : \left(\frac{12}{5} + \frac{9}{10}\right) \quad \left(\frac{3}{5} + \frac{11}{10}\right)$$

$$\frac{33}{10} \qquad \frac{17}{10}$$

So, Ratio of milk : water in the resulting mixture = 33 : 17.

2. A: Let cost price of spirit be Re. 1 per litre.

Then SP of mixture = Re. 1 per litre

Gain = 25%

So, CP of mixture $= 1 \times \frac{100}{125} = \text{Re. } \frac{4}{5}$

We assume that CP of water is zero.

Using alligation rule on cost price,

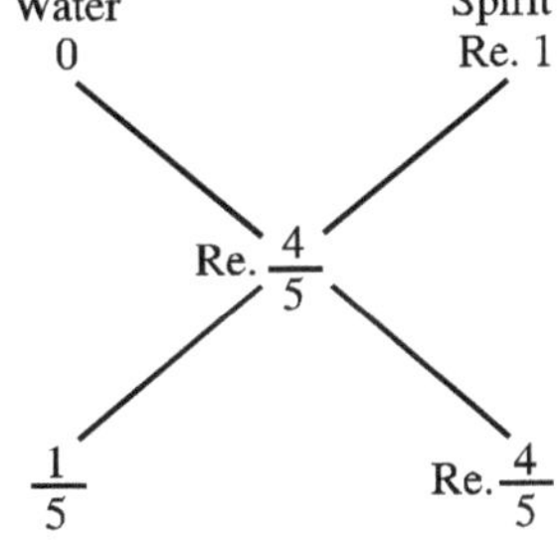

Water should be mixed to spirit in the ratio $\frac{1}{5} : \frac{4}{5}$ or 1 : 4.

3. C: Average rate of interest $= \dfrac{100 \times 750}{5000 \times 3} = 5\%$ per annum

Investment at 3% per annum

$= \dfrac{3}{3+2} \times 5000 =$ ₹ 3000

Investment at 8% per annum

$= \dfrac{2}{3+2} \times 5000 =$ ₹ 2000.

3   8
5
3   2

4. B: Average speed $= \dfrac{100}{10} = 10$ km/hr.

Ratio of time taken at 7 km/hr to 12 km/hr = 2 : 3

Time taken at 7 km/hr $= \dfrac{2}{2+3} \times 10 = 4$ hrs.

Distance covered at 7 km/hr = 7 × 4 = 28 km.
Distance covered at 12 km/hr = 100 – 28 = 72 km.

7   12
10
2   3

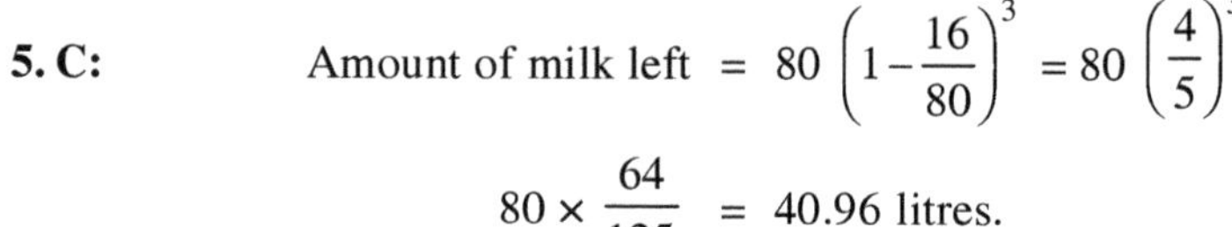

5. C: Amount of milk left $= 80\left(1-\dfrac{16}{80}\right)^3 = 80\left(\dfrac{4}{5}\right)^3$

$80 \times \dfrac{64}{125} = 40.96$ litres.

6. A: Total quantity of iron $= 4\left(\dfrac{1}{4}\right)+6\left(\dfrac{2}{3}\right) = 1 + 4 = 5$ kg.

Total quantity of tin $= (4 + 6) - 5$

$= 5$ kg.

In the resultant mixture, iron : tin = 5 : 5 or 1 : 1.

7. C: Average no. of legs per head

$= \dfrac{320}{100} = \dfrac{16}{5}$

or, 3 : 2

No. of goats $= \dfrac{3}{3+2} \times 100 = 60$

No. of chickens $= 100 - 60 = 40.$

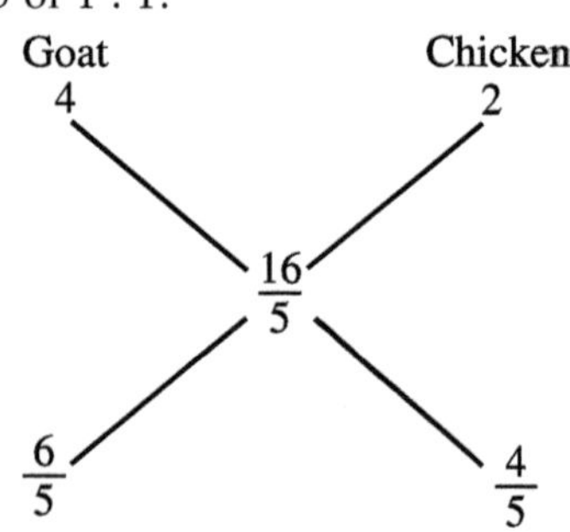

8. B: Let capacity of the container be x litre; then

$$x(1-1/3)^4 = 16 \Rightarrow x\left(\frac{2}{3}\right)^4 = 16 \quad \Rightarrow x \times \frac{16}{81} = 16 \quad \therefore x = 81 \text{ litres}$$

9. D: Let the price per kg of mixed variety be ₹ x; then

By the rule of alligation,

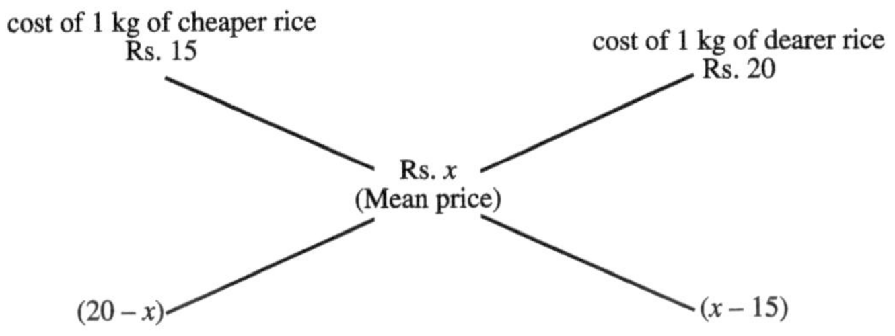

Now, $\frac{20-x}{x-15} = \frac{2}{3} \quad \Rightarrow 60 - 3x = 2x - 30 \quad \Rightarrow 5x = 90 \therefore x = ₹\ 18$

10. C: Let x litres wine cask hold originally, then

$$\frac{x\left(1-\frac{8}{x}\right)^4}{x} = \frac{16}{81} \Rightarrow \left(1-\frac{8}{x}\right)^4 = \left(\frac{2}{3}\right)^4 \Rightarrow \left(1-\frac{8}{x}\right) = \frac{2}{3}$$

$$\Rightarrow \frac{8}{x} = 1 - \frac{2}{3} \quad \Rightarrow \frac{8}{x} = \frac{1}{3} \quad \therefore x = 24 \text{ litres}$$

14

MENSURATION

Triangle

1. Perimeter = 3 × side (Equilateral triangle)
2. Area $= \frac{1}{2} \times \text{base} \times \text{height}$, or

   Area $= \sqrt{s(s-a)(s-b)(s-c)}$

   where *a, b, c,* are the lengths of the sides of triangle and $s = \frac{a+b+c}{2}$

Equilateral Triangle : All three sides are equal in length and all three angles are equal to 60°.

$$\text{Area} = \frac{\sqrt{3}}{4} \times (\text{Side})^2$$

Isosceles Triangle : Two sides are equal in lengths.

1. Area $= \frac{b}{4}\sqrt{4a^2 - b^2}$

   where a = lengths of equal sides $\qquad b$ = length of unequal side
2. In an isosceles right triangle,

   (a) Hypotenuse $= \sqrt{2} \times \text{congruent side (a)}$

   (b) Area $= \frac{1}{2} \times a^2$

   (c) Perimeter $= \sqrt{2} \times a\left(\sqrt{2} + 1\right)$

Rectangle :

1. Area = length(l) × breadth(b)
2. Perimeter = $2(l + b)$
3. Diagonal $= \sqrt{l^2 + b^2}$

Square :

1. Area = $(\text{Side})^2$
2. Perimeter = 4 × side
3. Diagonal = $\text{side} \times \sqrt{2}$

Parallelogram: Area = Base × Height.

Trapezium : Area = $\frac{1}{2} \times \text{Height} \times$ (Sum of parallel sides). Here, height is the distance between the two parallel sides.

Rhombus :

1. Area = $\frac{1}{2} \times \text{Product of diagonals}$
2. Side = $\sqrt{\left(\frac{d_1}{2}\right)^2 + \left(\frac{d_2}{2}\right)^2}$, where d_1 and d_2 are diagonals
3. Perimeter = 4 × side

Quadrilateral : Area = $\frac{1}{2} \times \text{One diagonal} \times$ (Sum of perpendicular to it from the opposite vertices) = $\frac{1}{2} \times d \times (a+b)$

Circle :

1. Diameter = 2 × Radius
2. Area = $\pi r^2 = \frac{\pi}{4} d^2$; where d = diameter = $\sqrt{\frac{4A}{\pi}}$
3. Circumference = $2\pi r = \pi d$
4. Radius = $\frac{\text{Circumference}}{2\pi} = \frac{\sqrt{\text{Area}}}{\pi}$
5. Length of an Arc = $\frac{\theta}{360°} \times 2\pi r$
6. Area of sector = $\frac{\theta}{360°} \times \pi r^2 = \frac{1}{2} \times \text{Arc} \times r$

Polygon :

1. Interior angle + Exterior angle = 180°
2. Each interior angle = $\left(\frac{2n-4}{n}\right) \times 90°$

where n = number of sides

3. Sum of Exterior angles = 360°
4. Perimeter = Number of sides × Length of side.
5. For an equilateral triangle of side 'a'

(*a*) radius of inscribed circle $=\dfrac{a}{2\sqrt{3}}$

and side of the triangle $= 2\sqrt{3}r$,

(*b*) radius of circumcircle $= \dfrac{a}{\sqrt{3}}$

6. Area of regular polygon $=\dfrac{1}{2}$(No. of sides) (Radius of the inscribed circle)

7. Area of regular hexagon $= \dfrac{3\sqrt{3}}{2}(\text{side})^2 = 2.598\ (\text{side})^2$

8. Area of a regular octagon $= 2\left(\sqrt{2}+1\right)(\text{side})^2 = 4.828\ (\text{side})^2$

9. Area of quadrilateral, A $= \sqrt{s(s-a)(s-b)(s-c)(s-d)}$

where, $s = \dfrac{a+b+c+d}{2}$

VOLUME AND SURFACE AREA OF SOLIDS

Cuboid : A cuboid has six faces, each one a ractangle. It has 12 edges. For example, a rectangular brick.

Let Length = l, Breadth = b and Height = h, then,

1. Volume = (Length × Breadth × Height)
2. Whole Surface Area = $2(lb + bh + lh)$
3. Diagonal $= \sqrt{l^2 + b^2 + h^2}$
4. Area of 4 walls of a room $= 2 \times h\ (l + b)$

Cube : In a cube, Length = Breadth = Height

1. Volume = $(l)^3$
2. Length $= \sqrt[3]{\text{Volume}}$
3. Whole Surface Area = $6\ l^2$
4. Diagonal $= l \times \sqrt{3}$
5. Lateral Surface Area = $4\ l^2$

Cylinder :

1. Volume = $\pi r^2 h$
2. Curved Surface Area = $2\pi rh$
3. Total Surface Area = $2\pi r(r + h)$
   where r = radius, h = height

Spherical Cell :

1. Volume = $\frac{4}{3}\pi\left(R^3 - r^3\right)$
2. Total Surface Area= $4\pi(R^2 - r^2)$
   where R = Outer radius
   r = Inner radius

Sphere :

1. Volume = $\frac{4}{3}\pi r^3$
2. Surface Area = $4\pi r^2$

Semi-sphere :

1. Volume = $\frac{2}{3}\pi r^3$
2. Curved surface area = $2\pi r^2$
3. Total surface area = $3\pi r^2$

Cone :

1. Slant height (l) = $\sqrt{r^2 + h^2}$
2. Volume = $\frac{1}{3}\pi r^2 h$
3. Curved surface area = πrl
4. Total surface area = $\pi r\,(l + r)$
5. If the depth of the frustum of a cone be k and the radii of its ends are r_1 and r_2, then
   (i) Slant height of the frustum of a cone

   $$= \sqrt{k^2 + (r_1 - r_2)^2}$$

   (ii) Curved surface of the frustum = $\pi(r_1 + r_2)\,l$.

   (iii) Volume = $\frac{\pi k}{3}\left(r_1^2 + r_1 r_2 + r_2^2\right)$

EXERCISE

1. What is the area of a circle whose radius is equal to the side of a square whose perimeter is 112 metres?
A. 176 sq m
B. 2504 sq m
C. 284 sq m
D. None of these

2. The sum of the circumference of a circle and the perimeter of a rectangle is 132 cm. The area of the rectangle is 112 sq cm and breadth of the rectangle is 8 cms. What is the area of the circle?
A. 616 sq cm
B. 540 sq cm
C. 396 sq cm
D. Cannot be determined

3. The total area of a circle and a rectangle is equal to 1166 sq cm. The diameter of the circle is 28 cm. What is the sum of the circumference of the circle and the perimeter of the rectangle if the length of the rectangle is 25 cm?
A. 186 cm
B. 182 cm
C. 184 cm
D. Cannot be determined

4. What would be the cost of laying a carpet on a floor which has its length and breadth in the respective ratio of 32 : 21 and where its perimeter is 212 feet, if the cost per square foot of laying the carpet is ₹ 2.5?
A. ₹ 6,720
B. ₹ 5,420
C. ₹ 7,390
D. None of these

5. A triangle's perimeter is 25 cms. Which of the following may be true or is a possibility?
(*a*) The sides are 7 cms., 7 cms. and 11 cms.
(*b*) It is an equilateral triangle.
(*c*) The value of sides can be in integer only.
A. Only (*a*)
B. Only (*a*) and (*b*)
C. Only (*c*)
D. Only (*b*) and (*c*)

6. What will be the cost of building a fence around a circular field with area equal to 18,634 sq. metres; if the cost of building the fence per metre is ₹ 365?
A. ₹ 1,76,660 B. ₹ 68,01,410
C. ₹ 2,43,250 D. ₹ 56,60,220

7. The area of a square is 196 sq cms whose side is half the radius of a circle. The circumference of the circle is equal to breadth of a rectangle. If perimeter of the rectangle is 712 cm. What is the length of the rectangle?
A. 196 cm B. 186 cm
C. 180 cm D. 190 cm

8. The circumference of a circular plot is 484 metres Find out the area of that circular plot—
A. 15246 metre^2
B. 18634 metre^2
C. 20328 metre^2
D. 13552 metre^2

9. A room measures 22 dm by 16 dm. I wish to buy a carpet for the floor leaving an uncarpeted margin 2 dm wide along each of the shorter sides of the room and a margin 0.5 dm wide along each of the longer sides of the room. If the price of the carpet is ₹ 500 per sq. metre, what is the cost of the whole carpet required?

A. ₹ 500 B. ₹ 2700
C. ₹ 2000 D. ₹ 1350

10. A paper is in the form of a rectangle ABCD where AB = 22 cm and BC = 14 cm. A semi-circular portion with segment BC as a diameter is cut off. Find the area of remaining paper.

A. 231 cm^2 B. 213 cm^2
C. 321 cm^2 D. 200 cm^2

11. How many plants can be put in a circular flower bed whose circumference is 880 dm allowing 35 dm^2 for each plant?

A. 880 B. 1760
C. 1000 D. 1500

12. An athletic track 14 m wide consists of two straight sections 120 m long joining semi-circular ends whose inner radius is 35 m. Calculate the area of the track :

A. 5670 m^2 B. 7065 m^2
C. 5670 m^2 D. 7056 m^2

13. A square park has each side of 100 m. At each corner of the park, there is a flower bed in the form of a quadrant of radius 14 m. Then the area of the remaining part of the park is :

A. 9384 m^2 B. 9834 m^2
C. 9000 m^2 D. 8900 m^2

14. The length of minute hand of a clock is 14 cm. Then the area swept by the minute hand in one minute.

A. 10 m^2 B. 12.26 m^2
C. 20.26 m^2 D. 10.26 m^2

15. Find the area of ring between two concentric circles whose circumference are 77 cm and 55 cm.

A. 770 cm^2 B. 321 cm^2
C. 231 cm^2 D. 230 cm^2

16. A rectangle water reservoir is 10.8 metres long and 3.75 metres wide at base. Water flows into it at the rate of 18 m per sec. through the pipe having the cross section 7.5 cm × 4.5 cm. Then the height to which the water will rise in the reservoir in 30 minutes is :

A. 7.2 m B. 2.7 m
C. 3.7 m D. 7.3 m

17. A rectangular sheet of 44 cm × 18 cm is rolled along its length and a cylinder is formed. Then the volume of cylinder is :

A. 7227 cm^2 B. 7272 cm^2
C. 2727 cm^2 D. 2772 cm^2

18. How many metres of cloth 5 metre wide will be required to make a conical tent, the radius of whose base is 7 metre and height is 24 metre?

A. 100 m B. 110 m
C. 550 m D. 55 m

19. The surface area of a sphere whose volume is 4851 cubic metres is :

A. 1386 m^2 B. 1380 m^2
C. 1286 m^2 D. 3186 m^2

20. A hollow sphere of external and internal diameter 4 cm and 2 cm respectively, is melted into a cone of base diameter 8 cm. Then the height of the cone is :

A. 12 cm B. 14 cm
C. 20 cm D. 24 cm

21. The diamensions of a metallic rod are 19 cm × 4 cm × 2 cm and each side of a metallic cube is 4 cm. Both are melted and recast into a new cube. Find the length of edge of cube so formed.

A. 4 cm B. 5 cm
C. 6 cm D. 7 cm

22. An agricultural field is in the form of a rectangle of length 35 metres and width 15.4 metres. A pit 5.5 metres long, 4 metres wide and 2.5 metres deep is dug in the corner of the field and the earth taken out of the pit is spread uniformly over the remaining area of the field. The extent to which the level of the field has been raised is :

A. 16.6 cm B. 10.6 cm
C. 16.1 cm D. 6.10 cm

23. The side of a square exceeds the side of the another square by 4 cm and the sum of areas of two squares is 400 sq. cm. Find the dimensions of the square.

A. 8 cm, 12 cm
B. 10 cm, 14 cm
C. 12 cm, 16 cm
D. 14 cm, 18 cm

24. The cost of levelling a rectangular field at the rate of 85 paise per square metre is ₹ 624.75. Then the perimeter of the field if its sides are in the ratio of 5 : 3 is :

A. 35 m B. 21 m
C. 112 m D. 49 m

25. The diagonal of a rectangular field is 15 m and its area is 108 sq. m. What will be the total expenditure in fencing the field at the rate of ₹ 5 per metre?

A. ₹ 441 B. ₹ 420
C. ₹ 210 D. ₹ 120

26. The minute hand of a clock is 10 cm long. The area of the face of the clock described by the minute hand between 9 AM and 9.35 AM is :

A. 140 cm^2 B. 183.3 cm^2
C. 180 cm^2 D. 175.3 cm^2

27. The length of a rectangular plot is 60% more than its breadth. If the difference between the length and the breadth of that rectangle is 24 cm, what is the area of that rectangle?

A. 2400 sq. cm
B. 2480 sq. cm
C. 2560 sq. cm
D. Data inadequate

28. The area of a rectangle is 460 square metres. If the length is 15% more than the breadth, what is the breadth of the rectangular field?

A. 15 metres
B. 26 metres
C. 34.5 metres
D. None of these

29. The ratio between the length and the breadth of a rectangular field is 3 : 2. If only the length is increased by 5 metres, the new area of the field will be 2600 sq. metres. What is the breadth of the rectangular field?

A. 40 metres
B. 60 metres
C. 65 metres
D. Cannot be determined

30. If the length and breadth of a rectangular plot be increased by 50% and 20% respectively, then how many times will its area be increased?

A. $1\frac{1}{3}$ B. 2
C. $3\frac{2}{5}$ D. None of these

31. The length of a rectangle is decreased by r%, and the breadth is increased by $(r + 5)$%. Find r, if the area of the rectangle is unaltered.

A. 5 B. 8
C. 10 D. 20

32. The length and breadth of the floor of the room are 20 feet and 10 feet respectively. Square tiles of 2 feet length of different colours are to be laid on the floor. Black tiles are laid in the first row on all sides. If white tiles are laid in the one-third of the remaining and blue tiles in the rest, how many blue tiles will be there?

A. 16 B. 24
C. 32 D. 48

33. A park square in shape has a 3 metre wide road inside it running along its sides. The area occupied by the road is 1764 square metres. What is the perimeter along the outer edge of the road?

A. 576 metres
B. 600 metres
C. 640 metres
D. Data inadequate

34. What will be the length of the diagonal of that square plot whose area is equal to the area of a rectangular plot of length 45 metres and breadth 40 metres?

A. 42.5 metres
B. 60 metres
C. 75 metres
D. Data inadequate

35. The length of one pair of opposite sides of a square is increased by 5 cm on each side; the ratio of the length and the breadth of the newly formed rectangle becomes 3 : 2. What is the area of the original square?

A. 25 sq. cm B. 81 sq. cm
C. 100 sq. cm D. 225 sq. cm

36. What will be the ratio between the area of a rectangle and the area of a triangle with one of the sides of the rectangle as base and a vertex on the opposite side of the rectangle?
A. 1 : 2
B. 2 : 1
C. 3 : 1
D. None of these

37. A cow is tethered in the middle of a field with a 14 feet long rope. If the cow grazes 100 sq. ft. per day, then approximately what time will be taken by the cow to graze the whole field?
A. 2 days B. 6 days
C. 18 days D. 24 days

38. A circular ground whose diameter is 35 metres, has a 1.4 m broad garden around it. What is the area of the garden in square metres?
A. 160.16
B. 176.16
C. 196.16
D. None of these

39. The cost of the paint is ₹ 36.50 per kg. If 1 kg of paint covers 16 square feet, how much will it cost to paint outside of a cube having 8 feet each side?
A. ₹ 692 B. ₹ 768
C. ₹ 876 D. ₹ 972

40. The capacity of a cylindrical tank is 246.4 litres. If the height is 4 metres, what is the diameter of the base?
A. 1.4 m B. 2.8 m
C. 14 m D. 28 m

EXPLANATORY ANSWERS

1. D: ∵ Radius of the circle $= \frac{112}{4} = 28$ m

∴ Area of the circle $= \frac{22}{7} \times 28 \times 28 = 2464$ m^2.

2. A: Length of the rectangle $= \frac{112}{8} = 14$ cm.

∴ Perimeter of the rectangle = 2(14 + 8) = 44 cm.
∴ Circumference of the circle = 132 – 44 = 88 cm.

∴ $r = \frac{88 \times 7}{2 \times 22} = 14$ cm

∴ Area of the circle $= \frac{22}{7} \times 14 \times 14 = 616$ sq cm.

3. B: From question—

$\because$ Diameter of the circle = 28 cm.

$\Rightarrow$ Area of the circle = $\frac{22}{7}\times(14)^2$ = 616 cm^2

$\therefore$ Area of the rectangle = 1166 – 616 = 550 cm^2

$\Rightarrow$ Breadth of the rectangle = $\frac{550}{25}$ = 22 cm.

$\therefore$ Required sum = $2\times\frac{22}{7}\times(14)+2(25+22)$

= 88 + 94 = 182 cm.

4. A: Length of the floor = $\frac{212\times 32}{2\times(32+21)}$ = 64 ft.

and breadth the floor = $\frac{64\times 21}{32}$ = 42 ft.

$\therefore$ Area of the floor = 64 × 42 = 2688 sq. ft.

$\therefore$ Reqd. cost = ₹ 2688 × 2.5 = ₹ 6720.

5. A: Only statement A may be true or possibility.

6. A: Area of the circular field = 18634 m^2

$\therefore$ πr^2 = 18634

$\therefore$ $r^2 = 18634\times\frac{7}{22}$ = 5929

$\therefore$ r = 77 m

$\therefore$ Length of the fence = $2\times\frac{22}{7}\times 77$ = 484 m

$\therefore$ Total cost = 484 × 365 = ₹ 176660.

7. C: One side of the square = $\sqrt{196}$ = 14 cm

$\therefore$ Radius of the circle = 28 cm

$\therefore$Circumference of the circle = $2\times\frac{22}{7}\times 28 =$ 176 cm

$\therefore$Breadth of the rectangle = 176 cm

$\therefore$Length of the rectangle = $\frac{712}{2}-176 =$ 356 – 176 = 180 cm.

8. B: Let r be the radius of the circular plot then from problem,

$\because$ The circumference of the circular plot = 484 m

$$\Rightarrow \qquad 2\pi r = 484$$

$$r = 484 \times \frac{7}{22} \times \frac{1}{2} = 77 \text{ metres}$$

$\therefore$ Area of the circular plot $= \pi r^2 = \frac{22}{7} \times (77)^2 = 18634 \text{ m}^2$.

9. D.

10. A: Area of the whole paper ABCD = 22 × 14 = 308 cm^2

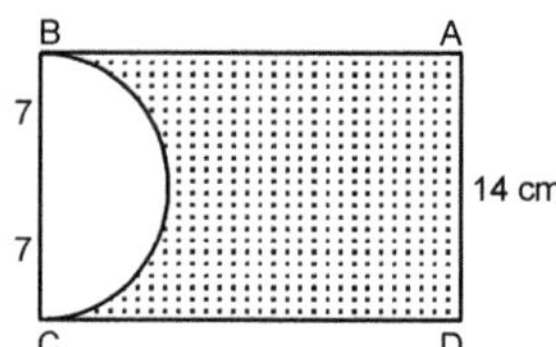

Radius of the semi-circle $= \frac{1}{2} \times 14 \text{ cm} = 7 \text{ cm}$

$\therefore$ Area of the semi-circle $= \frac{1}{2}\pi r^2 = \frac{1}{2} \times \frac{22}{7} \times 7 \times 7 = 77 \text{ cm}^2$

$\therefore$ Area of the remaining part of the paper

$$= 308 \text{ cm}^2 - 77 \text{ cm}^2 = 231 \text{ cm}^2.$$

11. B: Circumference of flower bed = 880 dm

$$\Rightarrow \qquad 2\pi r = 880 \text{ dm}$$

$$\Rightarrow \qquad r = \frac{880}{2\pi} \text{dm} = \frac{880 \times 7}{2 \times 22} = 140 \text{ dm}$$

Area of flower bed $= \pi r^2 = \frac{22}{7} \times (140)^2 \text{ dm}^2$

$\therefore$ Required number of plants

$$= \frac{\frac{22}{7} \times 140 \times 140}{35} \text{dm}^2$$

$$= \frac{22}{7} \times \frac{140 \times 140}{35} = 1760.$$

12. D.

13. A: Area of each quadrant = $\frac{\theta}{360} \times \pi r^2$

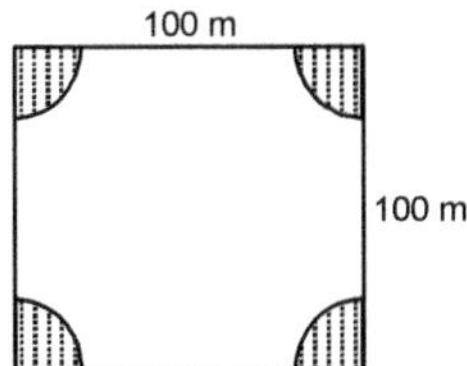

$$= \frac{90}{360} \times \frac{22}{7} \times 14 \times 14 \text{ m}^2 = 154 \text{ m}^2$$

$\therefore$ Area of 4 quadrants = 154 × 4 m^2 = 616 m^2

Area of park = $(100)^2$ = 10,000 m^2

Hence area of the remaining part of the park

$$= 10,000 - 616 = 9,384 \text{ m}^2.$$

14. D: Length of minute hand of clock = r = 14 cm

Central angle covered in 1 minute = $\frac{360}{60} = 6°$

$\therefore$ Area swept in one minute = Area of sector with central angle 6°

$$= \frac{\theta}{360} \times \pi r^2 = \frac{6}{360} \times \frac{22}{7} \times 14 \times 14$$

$$= \frac{154}{15} = 10.26 \text{ cm}^2.$$

15. C: Let R be the radius of outer circle and r the radius of inner circle.
Circumference of outer circle = 77 cm

$$\therefore 2\pi R = 77 \Rightarrow R = \frac{77}{2\pi} = \frac{77 \times 7}{2 \times 22} = \frac{49}{4} \text{ cm}$$

Circumference of inner circle = 55 cm

$$\therefore \quad 2\pi r = 55 \quad \Rightarrow r = \frac{55}{2\pi} = \frac{55 \times 7}{2 \times 22} = \frac{35}{4} \text{ cm}$$

$$\therefore \quad \text{Area of ring} = \pi(R^2 - r^2)$$

$$= \frac{22}{7} \times \left(\frac{49}{4} + \frac{35}{4}\right)\left(\frac{49}{4} - \frac{35}{4}\right) = 231 \text{ cm}^2$$

16. B: Volume of water that flows in one second

$= (18 \times 0.075 \times 0.045)\ m^3$

Volume of water that flows in 30 minutes

$= 18 \times 0.075 \times 0.045 \times 30 \times 60$

$= 109.35\ m^3$.

Area of the base of the reservoir $= 10.8 \times 3.75\ m^2$

$\therefore$ Height of water $= \dfrac{109.35}{10.8 \times 3.75} = 2.7$ metres.

17. D: Let r cm be the radius of the base and h cm be the height.

Then, $h = 18$ cm.

Now, circumference of the base = Length of the sheed

$\Rightarrow$ Circumference = 44 cm

$\Rightarrow \quad 2\pi r = 44$

$\Rightarrow \quad 2 \times \dfrac{22}{7} \times r = 44$

$\Rightarrow \quad r = 7$ cm

Volume of the cylinder= $\pi r^2 h\ cm^3$

$= \dfrac{22}{7} \times (7)^2 \times 18\ cm^3$

$= 2772\ cm^3$

18. B: Slant height, $l = \sqrt{r^2 + h^2}$

$= \sqrt{7^2 + 24^2} = 25$ metres

Area of curved surface of cone $= \pi rl$

$= \dfrac{22}{7} \times 7 \times 25 = 550\ m^2$

$\therefore$Area of the cloth required $= 550\ m^2$

$\therefore$ Length of the cloth $= \dfrac{550}{5} = 110$ metres.

19. A.

20. B.

21. C: Volume of the metallic rod $= 19 \times 4 \times 2 = 152$ cu.cm.

Volume of the cube $= 4^3 = 64$ cu. cm.

Total volume of both after melting them

$$= 152 + 64 = 216 \text{ cu.cm.}$$

$\therefore$ Volume of new cube = 216 cu. cm.

$\Rightarrow$ Side = 6 cm.

22. B.

23. C: Let S_1 and S_2 be the two squares. Let the side of the square S_1 be x cm. Then the side of the square $S_2 = (x + 4)$ cm.

$\therefore$ Area of square $S_1 = x^2$

and, Area of square $S_2 = (x + 4)^2$

$\therefore$ From question,

$\Rightarrow$ $x^2 + (x + 4)^2 = 400$

Solving the equation,

$\Rightarrow$ $x = -16$ and 12

But x cannot be negative

$\therefore$ Side of the square $S_1 = 12$ cm

$\therefore$ that of square $S_2 = x + 4 = 12 + 4 = 16$ cm.

24. C: Area of the field $= \left(\dfrac{\text{Total cost}}{\text{Rate/metre}^2}\right)$

$$= \frac{624.75}{0.85} = 735 \text{ sq. metres}$$

Let the length and breadth of the field be $5x$ and $3x$ metres respectively.

Then, its area $= 5x \times 3x = 15x^2$ sq. metres

$\therefore$ $15x^2 = 735$

$\Rightarrow$ $x^2 = \dfrac{735}{15} = 49$

$\Rightarrow$ $x = 7$

$\therefore$ Length $= 5x = 5 \times 7 = 35$ metres

and breadth $= 3x = 3 \times 7 = 21$ metres

$\therefore$ Perimeter $= 2\,(35 + 21) = 112$ metres.

25. C.

26. B: Angle described by minute hand in 60 minutes = 360°

Angle described by minute hand in 35 minutes $= \dfrac{360}{60} \times 35 = 210°$

$\therefore$ The required area swept by the minute hand = Area of sector $r = 10$ cm

and, $\theta = 210°$

$$= \frac{22}{7} \times 10 \times 10 \times \frac{210}{360}$$

$$= 183.3 \text{ cm}^2.$$

27. C: Let breadth = x cm. Then, length = $\left(\frac{160}{100}x\right)$ cm = $\frac{8}{5}x$ cm.

So, $\frac{8}{5}x - x = 24 \Rightarrow \frac{3}{5}x = 24$

$\Rightarrow \quad x = \left(\frac{24 \times 5}{3}\right) = 40.$

$\therefore$ Length = 64 cm, Breadth = 40 cm.

Area = (64×40) cm^2 = 2560 cm^2.

28. D: Let breadth = x metres. Then, length = $\left(\frac{115x}{100}\right)$ metres.

$\therefore \quad x \times \frac{115x}{100} = 460 \Rightarrow x^2 = \left(\frac{460 \times 100}{115}\right) = 400$

$\Rightarrow \quad x = 20.$

29. A: Let length = $(3x)$ metres and breadth = $(2x)$ metres.

Then, $(3x + 5) \times 2x = 2600$

$\Rightarrow \quad 6x^2 + 10x - 2600 = 0$

$\Rightarrow \quad 3x^2 + 5x - 1300 = 0$

$\Rightarrow \quad (3x + 65)(x - 20) = 0$

$\Rightarrow \quad x = 20.$

$\therefore \quad$ Breadth = $2x$ = 40 m.

30. D:

31. D: Let original length = x and original breadth = y.

Then, original area = xy.

$$\text{New area} = \left[\frac{(100 - r)}{100} \times x\right]\left[\frac{(105 + r)}{100} \times y\right]$$

$$= \left[\left(\frac{10500 - 5r - r^2}{10000}\right)xy\right]$$

$\therefore \left(\frac{10500 - 5r - r^2}{10000}\right)xy = xy \Rightarrow r^2 + 5r - 500 = 0$

$\Rightarrow (r + 25)(r - 20) = 0 \Rightarrow r = 20.$

32. A: Area left after laying black tiles = [(20 – 4) × (10 – 4) sq. ft = 96 sq. ft.

Area under white tiles = $\left(\frac{1}{3}\times 96\right)$ sq. ft = 32 sq. ft

Area under blue tiles = (96 – 32) sq. ft = 64 sq. ft

Number of blue tiles = $\frac{64}{(2\times 2)} = 16.$

33. B: Let the length of the outer edge be x metres. Then, length of the inner edge = $(x - 6)$ m.

$\therefore \quad x^2 - (x - 6)^2 = 1764$

$\Rightarrow \quad x^2 - (x^2 - 12x + 36) = 1764$

$\Rightarrow \quad 12x = 1800$

$\therefore \quad x = 150.$

$\therefore$ Required perimeter $= (4x)$ m = (4 × 150) m

= 600 m.

34. B: Area = (45 × 40) m^2 $\Rightarrow \frac{1}{2} \times (\text{diagonal})^2 = 1800$

$\Rightarrow$ diagonal = 60 m.

35. C: Let original length of each side = x cm.

Then, its area = (x^2) cm^2.

Length of rectangle formed = $(x + 5)$ cm and its breadth = x cm.

$\therefore \frac{x+5}{x} = \frac{3}{2} \Rightarrow 2x + 10 = 3x \Rightarrow x = 10.$

$\therefore$ Original length of each side = 10 cm and its area = 100 cm^2.

36. B: Area of rectangle = lb sq. units.

Area of the triangle = $\frac{1}{2}lb$ sq. units.

$\therefore$ Required ratio = $lb : \frac{1}{2}lb = 2 : 1.$

37. B: Area of the field grazed $= \left(\frac{22}{7} \times 14 \times 14\right)$ sq. ft

$= 616$ sq. ft.

Number of days taken to graze the field $= \frac{616}{100}$ days $= 6$ days (approx.).

38. D: Radius of the ground = 17.5 m.

Radius of inner circle = (17.5 – 1.4) m = 16.1 m.

Area of the garden $= \pi \times [(17.5)^2 - 16.1)^2]$ m^2

$= \left[\frac{22}{7} \times (17.5 + 16.1)(17.5 - 16.1)\right]$ m^2

$= \left(\frac{22}{7} \times 33.6 \times 1.4\right)$ m^2 = 147.84 m^2.

39. C: Surface area of the cube $= (6 \times 8^2)$ sq. ft = 384 sq. ft.

Quantity of paint required $= \left(\frac{384}{16}\right)$ kg = 24 kg.

∴ Cost of painting = ₹ (36.50 × 24) = ₹ 876.

40. D: Volume of the tank = 246.4 litres = 246400 cm^3.

Let the radius of the base be r cm. Then,

$\left(\frac{22}{7} \times r^2 \times 400\right) = 246400 \Rightarrow r^2 = \left(\frac{246400 \times 7}{22 \times 400}\right) = 196 \Rightarrow r = 14.$

∴ Diameter of the base = $2r$ = 28 cm.

15

ALGEBRAIC IDENTITIES

It is the branch of mathematics that uses letters and symbols to represent variable quantities and numbers, and to express generalizations about them.

SOME IMPORTANT FORMULAE

A. $a^2 - b^2 = (a + b)(a - b)$
B. $(a + b)^2 = a^2 + 2ab + b^2$
C. $(a - b)^2 = a^2 - 2ab + b^2$
D. $a^3 + b^3 = (a + b)(a^2 - ab + b^2)$
E. $a^3 + b^3 = (a + b)^3 - 3ab(a + b)$
F. $a^3 - b^3 = (a - b)(a^2 + ab + b^2)$
G. $a^3 - b^3 = (\mathrm{a} - \mathrm{b})^3 + 3ab(a - b)$
H. $(a + b)^2 = (a - b)^2 + 4ab$
I. $(a - b)^2 = (a + b)^2 - 4ab$
J. $a^3 + b^3 + c^3 - 3abc = (a + b + c)(a^2 + b^2 + c^2 - ab - bc - ca)$
K. If $a + b + c = 0$, then $a^3 + b^3 + c^3 = 3abc$

EXERCISE

1. If $x = 12$ and $y = 4$, the value of $(x+y)^{x/y}$ will be:

A. 4096 B. 3896
C. 4196 D. 5086

2. If $x = 9$, $y = \sqrt{17}$, then the value of $\left(x^2 - y^2\right)^{-1/2}$ will be:

A. 2^{-4} B. 2^2
C. 3^{-3} D. 2^{-3}

3. If $x + y = 2z$, then the value of $\left(\dfrac{x}{x-z} + \dfrac{z}{y-z}\right)$ will be:

A. 1 B. 4
C. 3/2 D. 2

4. If $x + y + z = 0$, then the value of $\dfrac{(x+y)(y+z)(z+x)}{xyz}$ will be:

A. –3 B. –2
C. 0 D. –1

5. If $x + \dfrac{1}{x} = 3$, the value of $x^4 + \dfrac{1}{x^4}$ will be:

A. 49 B. 47
C. 37 D. 42

6. If $x^2 + y^2 + z^2 = 115$ and $xy + yz + zx = 27$, then the value of $x + y + z$ will be:

A. ± 15 B. ± 13
C. ± 17 D. ± 19

7. If $x = 17$, $y = 15$ and $z = 13$, then the value of $x^2 + y^2 + z^2 - 2xy - 2xz - 2yz$ will be:

A. 111 B. 109
C. 121 D. 120

8. If $x + y = 1$, then the value of $x^3 + y^3 + 3xy$ will be:

A. 1 B. 4
C. 3 D. 7

9. What will be the value of $x^3 + y^3 + z^3 - 3xyz$ if $x + y + z = 16$ and $xy + yz + zx = 78$?

A. 352 B. 452
C. 342 D. 360

10. Which of the following is equivalent to $(x^4 + y^4)(x^2 + y^2)(x + y)(x - y)$?

A. $x^8 - y^8$
B. $x^{10} - y^{10}$
C. $x^6 - y^6$
D. $x^{12} - y^{12}$

11. If $x^2 = y + z$, $y^2 = z + x$ and $z^2 = x + y$, then the value of $\left(\frac{1}{x+1}+\frac{1}{y+1}+\frac{1}{z+1}\right)$ will be?

A. 4 B. 3
C. 1 D. 2

12. If $2x = a + 3$, then what will be the value of $8x^3 - 18ax$?

A. $a^3 + 27$ B. $a^3 - 27$
C. $a^3 + 25$ D. $a^3 - 36$

13. If $x + y = 8$ and $x - y = 2$, then the value of $x^2 + y^2$ will be:

A. 38 B. 40
C. 42 D. 34

14. If $a^2 + b^2 = 30$ and $a - b = 6$, then the value of ab will be:

A. –3 B. –5
C. 2 D. –6

15. If $a + b + c = 15$ and $a^2 + b^2 + c^2 = 77$, the what will be the value of $ab + bc + ca$?

A. 22 B. 74
C. 20 D. 18

EXPLANATORY ANSWERS

1. A: $(x+y)^{x/y} = (12+4)^{12/4} = (16)^3 = 4096.$ $[\because x = 12, y = 4]$

2. D: $(x^2 - y^2)^{-1/2} = (81-17)^{-1/2}$

$$= (64)^{-1/2} = \frac{1}{\sqrt{64}} = \frac{1}{8} = 2^{-3}.$$

3. A: $\because x + y = 2z \Rightarrow x - z = z - y = -(y - z)$

$$\therefore \frac{x}{x-z}+\frac{z}{y-z} = \frac{x}{-(y-z)}+\frac{z}{y-z} = \frac{z-x}{y-z} = 1. \quad [\because x - z = z - y]$$

4. D: $\because$ $x + y + z = 0 \Rightarrow x + y = -z$
$x + y + z = 0 \Rightarrow y + z = -x$
and $x + y + z = 0 \Rightarrow z + x = -y$

$$\therefore \quad \frac{(x+y)(y+z)(z+x)}{xyz} = \frac{-z.-x.-y}{xyz} = -1.$$

5. B:

6. B: $\because (x + y + z)^2 = x^2 + y^2 + z^2 + 2\,(xy + yz + zx)$

$\therefore (x + y + z)^2 = 115 + 2 \times 27$

$= 115 + 54 = 169$

$\therefore \ (x + y + z) = \sqrt{169} = \pm\, 13.$

7. C: The given expression is equivalent to $(x - y - z)^2$

$\therefore \quad (x - y - z)^2 = (17 - 15 - 13)^2$

$= (-11)^2 = 121.$

8. A: $\because \quad (x + y)^3 = x^3 + y^3 + 3xy\,(x + y)$

$\therefore \quad (1)^3 = x^3 + y^3 + 3xy \times 1$

$\therefore \quad 1 = x^3 + y^3 + 3xy.$

9. A: $\because (x + y + z) = 16 \Rightarrow (x + y + z)^2 = (16)^2$

$= x^2 + y^2 + z^2 + 2(xy + yz + zx) = 256$

$\therefore x^2 + y^2 + z^2 + 2{\times}78 = 256 \Rightarrow x^2 + y^2 + z^2$

$= 256 - 156 = 100$

$\therefore \ x^3 + y^3 + z^3 - 3xyz = (x + y + z)\,[(x^2 + y^2 + z^2) - (xy + yz + zx)]$

$= 16[100 - 78]$

$= 16 \times 22 = 352.$

10. A: $\because (x^4 + y^4)(x^2 + y^2)(x + y)(x - y)$

$= (x^4 + y^4)(x^2 + y^2)(x^2 - y^2)$

$= (x^4 + y^4)(x^4 - y^4)$

$= x^8 - y^8.$

11. C:

12. A: $\because \ 2x = a + 3$

$\Rightarrow \quad (2x)^3 = (a + 3)^3$

$\therefore \quad 8x^3 = a^3 + 27 + 3 \times a \times 3(a + 3)$

$= a^3 + 9a^2 + 27a + 27$

and $\quad 18ax = 9a \times 2x$

$= 9a \times (a + 3) = 9a^2 + 27a$

$\therefore \quad 8x^3 - 18ax = a^3 + 9a^2 + 27a + 27 - 9a^2 - 27a$

$= a^3 + 27.$

13. D: $\because \ x^2 + y^2 = \dfrac{(x+y)^2 + (x-y)^2}{2}$

$$= \frac{(8)^2 + (2)^2}{2} = \frac{64 + 4}{2} = \frac{68}{2} = 34.$$

14. A: $\because$ $(a - b)^2 = a^2 + b^2 - 2ab$

$\Rightarrow$ $$ab = \frac{a^2 + b^2 - (a-b)^2}{2}$$

$$= \frac{30 - (6)^2}{2}$$

$$= \frac{30 - 36}{2} = \frac{-6}{2} = -3.$$

15. B: $\because$ $(a + b + c)^2 = a^2 + b^2 + c^2 + 2(ab + bc + ca)$

$\therefore$ $$ab + bc + ca = \frac{(a+b+c)^2 - \left(a^2 + b^2 + c^2\right)}{2}$$

$$= \frac{(15)^2 - 77}{2} = \frac{225 - 77}{2}$$

$$= \frac{148}{2} = 74.$$

16

SURDS

Given a number, it is not always possible to find some whole number which when multiplied by itself will give the given number. In other words all given numbers are not perfect square numbers. For example, square root of 9, *i.e.*, $\sqrt{9}$ is 3, which is a whole number. But square root of 15, *i.e.*, $\sqrt{15}$ = 3.873, which is not a whole number.

Hence square roots of natural numbers which are not perfect squares are not rational numbers. These are irrational numbers and are called **Surds**. For example, $\sqrt{3}$, $\sqrt{7}$, $2+\sqrt{11}$, $4+\sqrt{13}$ ..... etc. are **Surds**.

Given below are a few formulas which are quite helpful in solving the problems related to surds:

1. $\sqrt{a} \times \sqrt{a} = a$

2. $\sqrt{a} \times \sqrt{b} = \sqrt{ab}$

3. $\left(\sqrt{a}+\sqrt{b}\right)^2 = a + b + \sqrt[2]{ab}$

4. $\left(\sqrt{a}-\sqrt{b}\right)^2 = a + b - \sqrt[2]{ab}$

5. $x\sqrt{a} + x\sqrt{b} = x\left(\sqrt{a}+\sqrt{b}\right)$

6. $\dfrac{1}{\sqrt{a}+\sqrt{b}} = \dfrac{1}{\sqrt{a}+\sqrt{b}} \times \dfrac{\sqrt{a}-\sqrt{b}}{\sqrt{a}-\sqrt{b}} = \dfrac{\sqrt{a}-\sqrt{b}}{a-b}$

7. $\dfrac{1}{\sqrt{a}-\sqrt{b}} = \dfrac{1}{\sqrt{a}-\sqrt{b}} \times \dfrac{\sqrt{a}+\sqrt{b}}{\sqrt{a}+\sqrt{b}} = \dfrac{\sqrt{a}+\sqrt{b}}{a-b}$

8. $a + \sqrt{b} = c + \sqrt{d} \Rightarrow a = c$ and $b = d$

9. $\sqrt{2}$ = 1.41421, $\sqrt{3}$ = 1.73205, $\sqrt{5}$ = 2.23607,

$\sqrt{6}$ = 2.4494

$\sqrt{7}$ = 2.64575, $\sqrt{8}$ = 2.82842, $\sqrt{10}$ = 3.16227,

$\sqrt{11}$ = 3.31662

EXERCISE

1. What will be the value of $\frac{1}{\sqrt{3}}$ upto 3 decimal places?

A. 0.577 B. 0.477
C. 0.673 D. 0.575

2. If $\sqrt{2} = 1.4122$, the value of $\frac{1}{2}\left(\frac{\sqrt{2}-1}{\sqrt{2}+1}\right)$ is:

A. .0768 B. .0658
C. .0858 D. .0458

3. If $\sqrt{1936} = 44$, the value of $\sqrt{19.36} + \sqrt{0.1936} + \sqrt{.001936}$ upto 3 decimal places will be:

A. 5.679 B. 4.884
C. 9.884 D. 6.778

4. Value of $\frac{\sqrt{2}-1}{\sqrt{2+1}}$ upto 3 decimal places will be:

A. 0.172 B. 0.158
C. 0.176 D. 0.188

5. $\sqrt[3]{8^4}$ is equivalent to:

A. 15 B. 9
C. 16 D. 25

6. If $\sqrt{6} = 2.45$, the value of $\sqrt{\frac{2}{3}} + 3\sqrt{3/2}$ will be equivalent to:

A. 3.942 B. 4.492
C. 4.942 D. 9.345

7. $\sqrt{72}$ is equivalent to:

A. $3\sqrt{5}$ B. $6\sqrt{2}$
C. $8\sqrt{2}$ D. $7\sqrt{3}$

8. What will be the value of $\left(\sqrt{80} + 3 \times \sqrt{245} - \sqrt{125}\right)$?

A. $18\sqrt{5}$ B. $20\sqrt{5}$
C. $22\sqrt{5}$ D. $28\sqrt{2}$

9. Value of $\left(\frac{\sqrt{5}+\sqrt{3}}{\sqrt{5}-\sqrt{3}}\right)$ will be equivalent to :

A. $4 + \sqrt{15}$ B. $3 - \sqrt{15}$
C. $2 + \sqrt{15}$ D. $4 - \sqrt{15}$

10. The expression $\left(\frac{\sqrt{7}+\sqrt{5}}{\sqrt{7}-\sqrt{5}}\right)$ is equivalent to:

A. $6 - \sqrt{35}$ B. $2 + \sqrt{35}$
C. $4 - \sqrt{35}$ D. $6 + \sqrt{35}$

EXPLANATORY ANSWERS

1. A: $\because \frac{1}{\sqrt{3}} = \frac{1}{\sqrt{3}} \times \frac{\sqrt{3}}{\sqrt{3}} = \frac{\sqrt{3}}{3} = \frac{1.732}{3} = 0.577$.

2. C: $\because \frac{1}{2}\left(\frac{\sqrt{2}-1}{\sqrt{2}+1}\right) = \frac{1}{2} \times \frac{\sqrt{2}-1}{\sqrt{2}+1} \times \frac{\sqrt{2}-1}{\sqrt{2}-1} = \frac{1}{2} \times \frac{\left(\sqrt{2}-1\right)^2}{\left(\sqrt{2}\right)^2 - 1^2}$

$$= \frac{1}{2} \times \frac{2+1-2\sqrt{2}}{2-1} = \frac{1}{2} \times \frac{3-2\sqrt{2}}{1} = \frac{1}{2} \times (3-2\times 1.4142)$$

$$= \frac{1}{2} \times 0.1716 = .0858$$

3. B: $\because \sqrt{1936} = 44 \Rightarrow \sqrt{19.36} = 4.4$

$\Rightarrow \sqrt{0.1936} = 0.44$

$\Rightarrow \sqrt{.001936} = .044$

$\therefore \sqrt{19.36} + \sqrt{0.1936} + \sqrt{.001936}$

$= 4.4 + 0.44 + .044 = 4.884.$

4. A: $\because \dfrac{\sqrt{2}-1}{\sqrt{2}+1} = \dfrac{\sqrt{2}-1}{\sqrt{2}+1} \times \dfrac{\sqrt{2}-1}{\sqrt{2}-1} = \dfrac{\left(\sqrt{2}-1\right)^2}{\left(\sqrt{2}\right)^2 - (1)^2} = \dfrac{2+1-2\sqrt{2}}{2-1}$

$$= \frac{3-2\sqrt{2}}{1} = 3 - 2 \times 1.414 = 0.172.$$

5. C: $\sqrt[3]{8^4} = (8)^{\frac{4}{3}} = \left(2^3\right)^{\frac{4}{3}} = 2^{3\times\frac{4}{3}} = 2^4 = 16\cdot$

6. B: $\because \sqrt{\dfrac{2}{3}} + 3\sqrt{\dfrac{3}{2}} = \dfrac{\sqrt{2}}{\sqrt{3}} \times \dfrac{\sqrt{3}}{\sqrt{3}} + 3 \times \dfrac{\sqrt{3}}{\sqrt{2}} \times \dfrac{\sqrt{2}}{\sqrt{2}}$

$$= \frac{\sqrt{6}}{3} + \frac{3\sqrt{6}}{2} = \sqrt{6}\left[\frac{1}{3} + \frac{3}{2}\right] = \sqrt{6} \times \frac{11}{6} = \frac{11}{6} \times 2.45 = 4.492\,.$$

7. B: $\because \sqrt{72} = \sqrt{6\times 6\times 2} = \sqrt{6^2 \times 2} = 6\sqrt{2}\,\cdot$

8. B: $\because \sqrt{80} + 3 \times \sqrt{245} - \sqrt{125}$

$= \sqrt{16\times 5} + 3\times\sqrt{49\times 5} - \sqrt{25\times 5}$

$= 4\sqrt{5} + 21\sqrt{5} - 5\sqrt{5} = 20\sqrt{5}\,.$

9. A: $\because \dfrac{\sqrt{5}+\sqrt{3}}{\sqrt{5}-\sqrt{3}} = \dfrac{\sqrt{5}+\sqrt{3}}{\sqrt{5}-\sqrt{3}} \times \dfrac{\sqrt{5}+\sqrt{3}}{\sqrt{5}+\sqrt{3}}$

$$= \frac{\left(\sqrt{5}+\sqrt{3}\right)^2}{\left(\sqrt{5}\right)^2 - \left(\sqrt{3}\right)^2} = \frac{5+3+2\sqrt{15}}{5-3}$$

$$= \frac{8+2\sqrt{15}}{2} = 4+\sqrt{15}$$

10. D: $\because \dfrac{\sqrt{7}+\sqrt{5}}{\sqrt{7}-\sqrt{5}} = \dfrac{\sqrt{7}+\sqrt{5}}{\sqrt{7}-\sqrt{5}} \times \dfrac{\sqrt{7}+\sqrt{5}}{\sqrt{7}+\sqrt{5}}$

$$= \frac{\left(\sqrt{7}+\sqrt{5}\right)^2}{\left(\sqrt{7}\right)^2 - \left(\sqrt{5}\right)^2}$$

$$= \frac{7+5+2\sqrt{35}}{7-5} = \frac{12+2\sqrt{35}}{2} = 6+\sqrt{35}.$$

17

TRIANGLES AND ITS VARIOUS KINDS

Properties of geometrical figures:

(*i*) **Equilateral triangle:** All sides are equal.

(*ii*) **Isosceles triangle:** Two sides are equal.

(*iii*) **Rhombus:** All sides are equal and no angle is a right angle, but diagonals are at right angles and unequal.

(*iv*) **Square:** All sides are equal and each angle is right angle. The diagonals are also equal.

(*v*) **Parallelogram:** Opposite sides are parallel and equal, diagonals bisect each other.

(*vi*) **Rectangle:** Opposite sides are equal and each angle is a right angle, diagonals are equal.

Co-ordinates of standard points:

(*i*) *Centroid of a triangle:*

The point is the intersection of the medians. This point divides each median in the ratio 2 : 1, its co-ordinates are

$$G_1\left(\frac{x_1+x_2+x_3}{3},\frac{y_1+y_2+y_3}{3}\right)$$

(*ii*) *Incentre of a triangle:*

This is the centre of the circle which touches the sides of a given triangle, it is the point of intersection of the internal bisectors of the angles of the triangle, its co-ordinates are given by the formula

$$I=(x,y) \text{ where } x=\frac{ax_1+bx_2+cx_3}{a+b+c}$$

$$y=\frac{ay_1+by_2+cy_3}{a+b+c}$$

where (a, b, c) are the lengths of the triangle

(*iii*) *Orthocentre of a triangle:*

The point H is the intersection of the altitudes.

(*iv*) The points O, G, H are collinear and G divides OH in the ratio 1 : 2.

EXERCISE

1. The points A (12, 8), B(–2, 6) and C (6, 0) are vertices of :

A. right angled triangle
B. isosceles triangle
C. equilateral triangle
D. None of these

2. The points (1, 1) (–1, –1) and $(-\sqrt{3}, \sqrt{3})$ are the angular points of a triangle, then the triangle is:

A. right angled
B. isosceles
C. equilateral
D. None of these

3. Two vertices of a triangle are the points (1, 4) and (7, 2). Its centroid is the point (5, 3), then the third vertex is :

A. (3, 7) B. (7, 3)
C. (1, 1) D. (0, 0)

4. Let the vertices of a triangle be (0, 0), (3, 0) and (0, 4), then its orthocentre is :

A. (0, 0)

B. $\left(1, \frac{4}{3}\right)$

C. $\left(\frac{3}{2}, 2\right)$

D. None of these

5. Distance of (2, 3) from origin is:

A. 2 B. 5
C. –1 D. $\sqrt{13}$

6. Find the values of y for which the distance between the points P(2, –3) and Q(10, y) is 10 units.

A. 8, 2 B. –9, 3
C. –9, 5 D. –8, 2

7. The centroid of the triangle whose vertices are A(4, –6), B(3, –2) and C(5, 2) is :

A. 3, 2 B. 4, 1
C. 4, –2 D. 4, 3

8. If (7, 3), (6, 1), (8, 2) and (P, 4) are the vertices of a parallelogram taken in order then the value of P is :

A. 4 B. 6
C. 7 D. 9

9. If the vertices of rhombus are (3, 0), (4, 5), (–1, 4) and (–2, –1) taken in order then area of rhombus is :

A. 20 square units
B. 24 square units
C. 22 square units
D. 26 square units

10. Find the value of P for which the points A(–1, 3), B(2, P) and C(5, –1) are collinear :

A. 3 B. 1
C. 2 D. 4

EXPLANATORY ANSWERS

1. A: $BC^2 + CA^2 = AB^2$.

2. C: $BC^2 = CA^2 = AB^2$.

3. B: $5 = \frac{\Sigma x}{3},\ 3 = \frac{\Sigma y}{3}$.

4. A: The two altitudes *i.e.*, x-axis and y-axis of ΔOAB meet at origin.

5. D: A(0, 0) ———— (2, 3)B

$AB = \sqrt{(2-0)^2 + (3-0)^2} = \sqrt{4+9} = \sqrt{13}$

6. B: $\because PQ = 10$

$\Rightarrow \sqrt{(10-2)^2 + (y+3)^2} = 10$

$\sqrt{64 + y^2 + 9 + 6y} = 10$

Squaring both sides,

$y^2 + 6y - 27 = 0$

$\Rightarrow y^2 + 9y - 3y - 27 = 0$

$\Rightarrow y(y + 9) - 3(y + 9) = 0$

$\Rightarrow (y + 9)(y - 3) = 0$

$\Rightarrow y = -9, y = 3$

$\therefore y = -9, 3$

7. C:

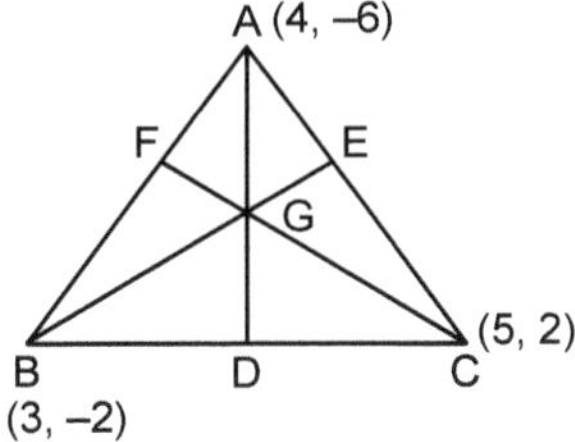

The centroid of the triangle G(x, y)

$= G\left(\frac{4+3+5}{3}, \frac{-6-2+2}{3}\right)$

$= G(4, -2)$

8. D: D(P, 4) C(8, 2)

A(7, 3) B(6, 1)

We know that the diagonals of a parallelogram bisect each other. Mid-point of AC and BD coincide.

Hence, $\left(\frac{7+8}{2}, \frac{3+2}{2}\right) = \left(\frac{6+P}{2}, \frac{1+4}{2}\right)$

$\Rightarrow \quad \left(\frac{6+P}{2}, \frac{5}{2}\right) = \left(\frac{15}{2}, \frac{5}{2}\right)$

Equating the *x*-co-ordinate, we get

$\frac{6+P}{2} = \frac{15}{2} \Rightarrow P = 9$

9. B: We know that area of rhombus

$= \frac{1}{2} \times AC \times BD = \frac{1}{2} \times \sqrt{(-1-3)^2 + (4-0)^2} \times \sqrt{(-2-4)^2 + (-1-5)^2}$

$= \frac{1}{2}\sqrt{32} \times \sqrt{72} = \frac{1}{2} \times 4\sqrt{2} \times 6\sqrt{2}$

$= \frac{1}{2} \times 48 = 24$ square units.

10. B: Points A, B, C are collinear

$\Rightarrow$ Area of $\Delta ABC = 0$

$\frac{1}{2}[-1\ (P + 1) + 2(-1 - 3) + 5(3 - P) = 0$

$\Rightarrow \frac{1}{2}[-6P + 6] = 0 \Rightarrow 3P = 3 \Rightarrow P = 1.$

18

SIMILARITY OF TRIANGLES

Two triangles are said to be similar, if

(*i*) their corresponding angles are equal and

(*ii*) their corresponding sides are in the same ratio (*i.e.* proportional).

Also, we know that :

(*i*) If corresponding angles of two triangles are equal, then they are known as equiangular triangles.

(*ii*) Two line segments are divided proportionally when the ratio of the lengths of the segments of one of them is equal to the ratio of the lengths of the segments of the other.

EXERCISE

1. Two similar triangles have
- A. equal sides
- B. equal areas
- C. equal angles
- D. None of these

2. Two congruent triangles have
- A. proportional sides
- B. equal sides
- C. equal corresponding sides
- D. equal corresponding angles

3. Which of the following is false for two congruent triangles
- A. Corresponding angles are equal.
- B. Two sides and included angles are equal.
- C. Corresponding sides are equal.
- D. Two angles and one side are equal.

4. If the sides of a triangle are 8 cm, 12 cm and 15 cm then the angle is
- A. Right angle
- B. Obtuse angle
- C. Acute angle
- D. None of these

5. If two triangles are on the same base and between the parallel lines then they will be
- A. equilaterals
- B. right angled
- C. equal in area
- D. congruent

6. If the three heights of a traingle are equal then it is
- A. right angled triangle
- B. obtuse angled triangle
- C. equilateral triangle
- D. None of these

7. If two corresponding sides and the angle between them of a traingle are equal to another triangle. Then the angles are :

A. congruent but not similar
B. similar but not congruent
C. neither congruent nor similar
D. congruent and similar.

8. Ratio of areas of two similar triangles is equal to :

A. ratio of squares of the corresponding altitudes
B. ratio of squares of corresponding medians.
C. Either (A) or (B)
D. (A) and (B) both

9. If the areas of two similar triangles are equal then the triangles :

A. are congruent
B. have equal length of corresponding sides
C. (A) and (B)
D. None of these

10. Two isosceles triangles have equal vertical angles and their areas are in the ratio of 9 : 25 then the ratio between their corresponding heights is :

A. 5 : 3 B. 25 : 9
C. 3 : 5 D. 16 : 9

EXPLANATORY ANSWERS

1. C: equal angles
2. C: equal corresponding sides
3. D: Two angles and one side are equal.
4. C: Acute angle
5. C: equal in area
6. C: equilateral triangle
7. C: neither congruent nor similar
8. D: (A) and (B) both
9. C. (A) and (B)
10. C: According to equestion

$$\angle A = \angle D \text{ and } \frac{\text{ar}(\Delta\, ABC)}{\text{ar}(\Delta\, DEF)} = \frac{9}{25}$$

Since, AB = AC (given) ....(*i*)

DE = DF (given) ....(*ii*)

Dividing (*i*) by (*ii*)

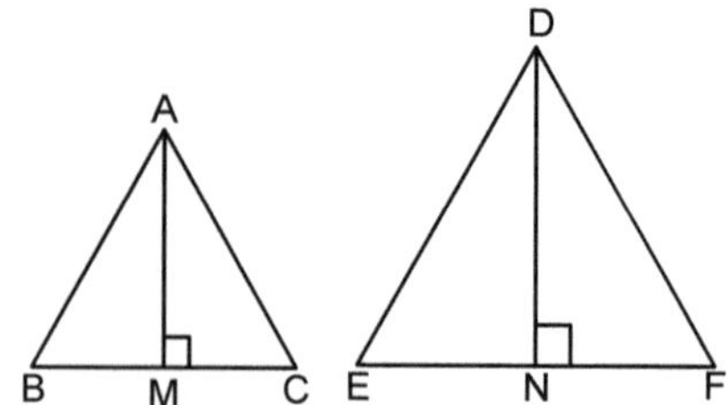

$$\frac{AB}{DE} = \frac{AC}{DF} \qquad ...(iii)$$

Hence, $\Delta ABC \sim \Delta DEF$ [By SAS criterion of similar Δs]

In ΔAMC and ΔDNF

$$\angle AMC = \angle DNF = 90°$$

$$\angle C = \angle F$$ (because $\Delta ABC \sim \Delta DEF$)

$\therefore$ $\angle AMC \sim DNF$ (By AA Criterion of similar Δs)

$$\therefore \quad \frac{AC}{DF} = \frac{AM}{DN}$$

and, $$\frac{ar\ (\Delta\ ABC)}{ar\ (DEF)} = \frac{AC^2}{DF^2} = \frac{AM^2}{DN^2}$$

$$\therefore \quad \frac{AM^2}{DN^2} = \frac{9}{25} \Rightarrow \frac{AM}{DN} = \frac{3}{5}$$

Hence required ratio = 3 : 5

19

CIRCLE AND TANGENTS

A circle is a set of those points in a plane that are at a given constant distance from a given fixed point in the plane. The fixed point is called the **centre of the circle** and the constant distance of every point on the circle from its centre of called the **radius of the circle**.

The fixed point O is called its centre and the constant distance r is called the radius.

Diameter is the longest chord of the circle.

Secant

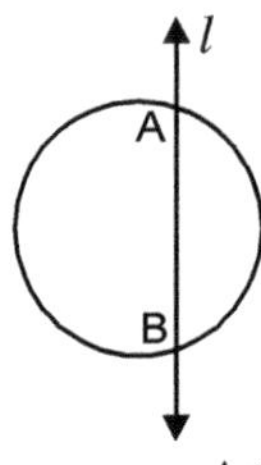

A line which interesects a circle in two distinct points is called a **secant** of the circle. In the fig. the line l intersects the circle in two distinct points A and B. The line l is a secant to the circle.

Tanget

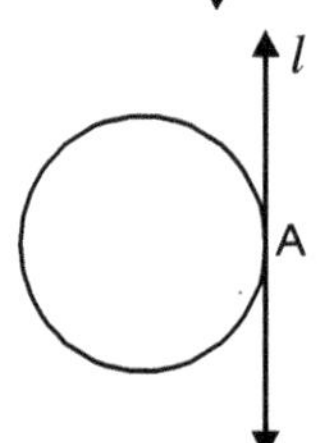

A tangent to a circle is a line that intersects the circle at exactly one point.

The point at which it meets the circle is called its point of contact and the line (tangent) is said to touch the circle at this point. In the figure, the line l meets the circle at only point A. Here A is the point of contact.

EXERCISE

1. PQ is a diameter and PQRS is a cyclic quadrilateral. If $\angle PSR = 150°$, then measure of $\angle RPQ$ is :

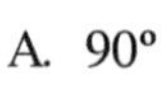

A. 90°

B. 60°

C. 30°

D. None of these

2. Determine the value of x in the figure given below.

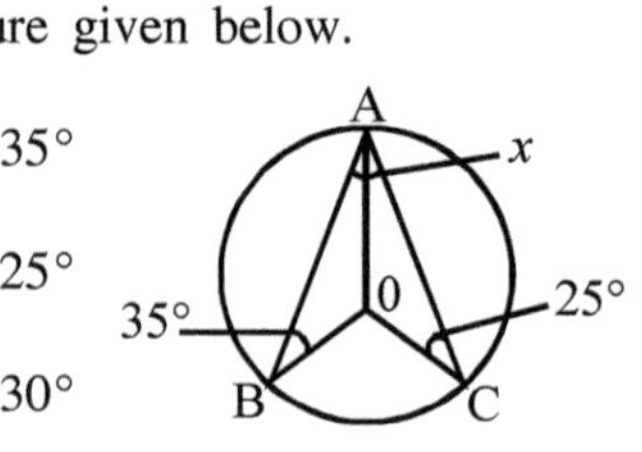

A. 35°

B. 25°

C. 30°

D. 60°

3. O is the centre of the circle. If $\angle OAB = 30°$ and $\angle OCB = 40°$, find $\angle AOC$.

A. 120°

B. 140°

C. 110°

D. 130°

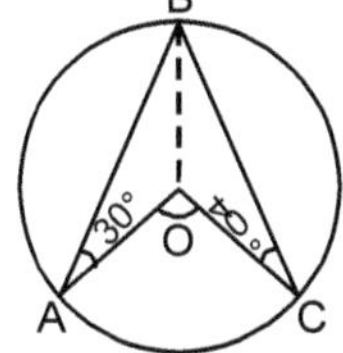

4. In fig. if $\angle ACB = 40°$, $\angle DPB = 120°$, then find y.

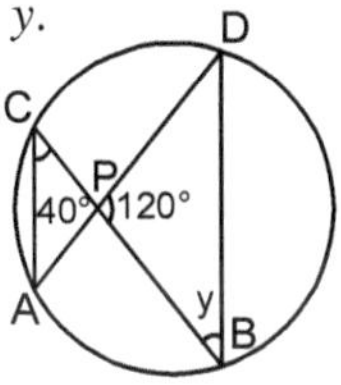

A. 10°

B. 20°

C. 15°

D. 25°

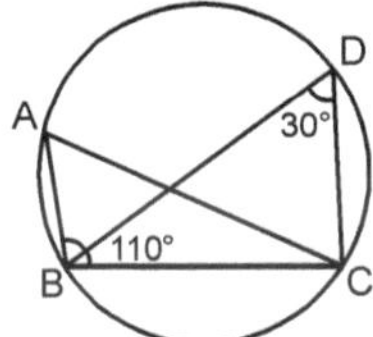

5. In the fig. if $\angle BDC = 30°$, $\angle CBA = 110°$, then find BCA.

A. 20°

B. 40°

C. 35°

D. 60°

6. From a point Q, the length of the tangent to a circle is 24 cm and the distance from the centre is 25 cm. The radius of the circle is

A. 7 cm B. 12 cm

C. 15 cm D. 24.5 cm

7. In the given figure, if TP and TQ are the two tangents to a circle with centre O and that $\angle POQ = 110°$, then $\angle PTQ$ is equal to

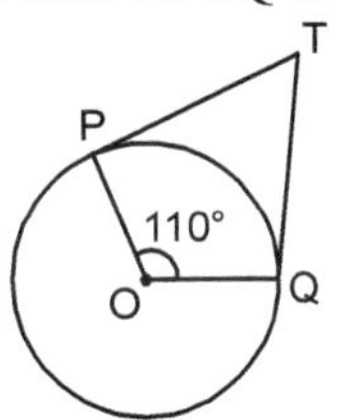

A. 60°

B. 70°

C. 80°

D. 90°

8. If tangents PA and PB from a point P to a circle with centre O are inclined to each other at angle of 80°, then $\angle POA$ is equal to

A. 50°

B. 60°

C. 70°

D. 80°

9. In Fig., a circle touches all the four sides of a quadrilateral ABCD whose sides AB = 6 cm, BC = 7 cm and CD = 4 cm. Find AD

A. 2 cm

B. 5 cm

C. 3 cm

D. 4 cm

10. If AB, AC, PQ are tangents in the figure and AB = 5 cm. The perimeter of ΔAPQ is

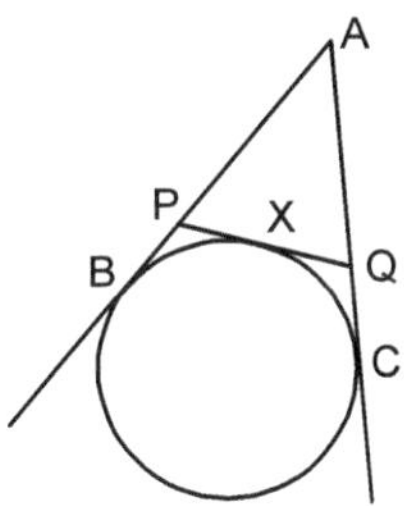

A. 8 cm

B. 6 cm

C. 10 cm

D. 5 cm

EXPLANATORY ANSWERS

1. B: $\angle PQR = 180° - 150° = 30°$

$\angle PRQ = 90°$ (Angle of a semicircle)

$\angle RPQ + 90° + 30° = 180°$

$\Rightarrow \angle RPQ = 60°$

2. D: $\angle OAB = \angle OBA \left(\because OA = OB\right)$

$\angle OAB = 35°$

Similarly, $\angle AOC = 25°$

$\therefore \quad \angle x = 35° + 25° = 60°$

3. B: O is the centre of the circle,

$\angle OAB = 30°$, $\angle OCB = 40°$. join OB

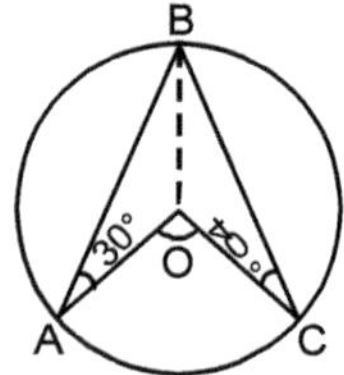

In ΔOAB,

$\therefore$ OA = OB (radii of the same circle)

$\therefore \angle OBA = \angle OAB = 30°$ ($\angle s$ opp. to equal sides of a Δ) ...(*i*)

Similarly, $\angle OBC = \angle OCB = 40°$ ...(*ii*)

Adding equations (*i*) and (*ii*), we get

$\angle OBA + \angle OBC = 30° + 40°$

$\Rightarrow \angle ABC = 70°$

$\because \widehat{AC}$ subtends $\angle AOC$ at the centre and

ΔABC at any point on the circumference

$\angle AOC = 2 \times \angle ABC$

$= 2 \times 70° = 140°$

4. B: $\angle D = \angle C$ [$\because \angle s$ in the same segment of a circle are equal]

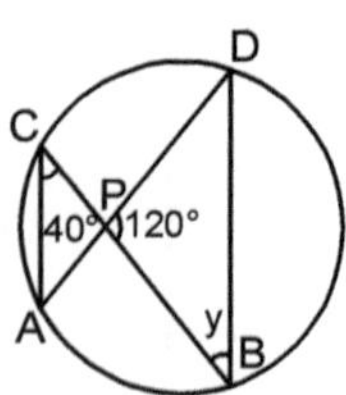

But $\angle C = 40°$ (Given)

$\therefore \angle C = 40°$

In Δ BPD, we have

$\angle BPD + \angle D + \angle B = 180°$ [$\because$ sum of three $\angle s$ of a $\Delta = 180°$]

$\Rightarrow 120° + 40° + y = 180°$

$\Rightarrow y = 180° - 160° = 20°$.

5. B: $\angle BAC = \angle BDC$ ($\angle$s in the same segment)

$= 30°$ (given)

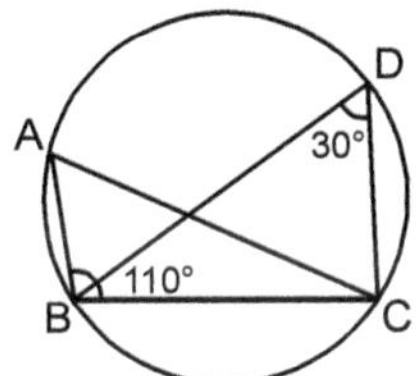

$\angle BAC + \angle CBA + \angle BCA = 180°$ ($\angle$s of ΔABC)

$\Rightarrow 30° + 110° + \angle BCA = 180°$

$\Rightarrow \angle BCA = 180° - 30° - 110° = 40°$

6. A: In rt. $\angle d$ ΔOTQ,

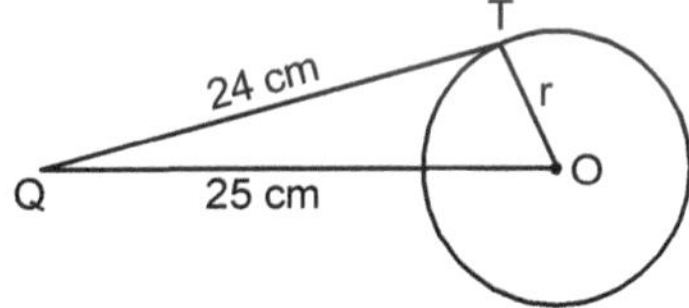

$$OT = \sqrt{OQ^2 - OT^2}$$

$$= \sqrt{25^2 - 24^2} = \sqrt{625 - 576}$$

$$= \sqrt{49} = 7 \text{ cm}.$$

7. B: Since $\angle POQ + \angle PTQ = 180°$ [$\because \angle OPT = 90°, \angle OQT = 90°$]

$\Rightarrow 110° + \angle PTQ = 180°$

$\Rightarrow \angle PTQ = 180° - 110° = 70°$.

8. A: Since $\angle APB = 80°$

$\angle AOB = 180° - 80° = 100°$

$\angle PAO = \angle PBO = 90°$

Since OP bisects $\angle AOB$

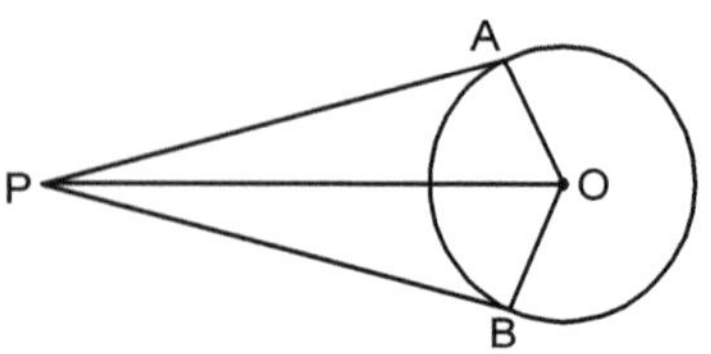

$$\angle AOP = \frac{1}{2}(100°) = 50°$$

i.e. $\angle POA = 50°$.

9. C: AD = AS + DS = AP + DR [∵ AS = AP and DS = DR]

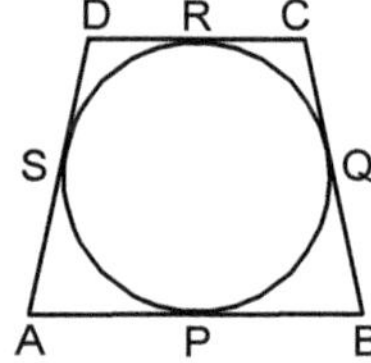

= (AB – BP) + (CD – RC)

= AB + CD – (BP + RC)

= AB + CD – (BQ + CQ) [∵ BP = BQ, RC = CQ]

= AB + CD – BC = 6 + 4 – 7 = 3 cm.

10. C: Since AB and AC are the tangents from the same point A

∴ AB = AC = 5 cm

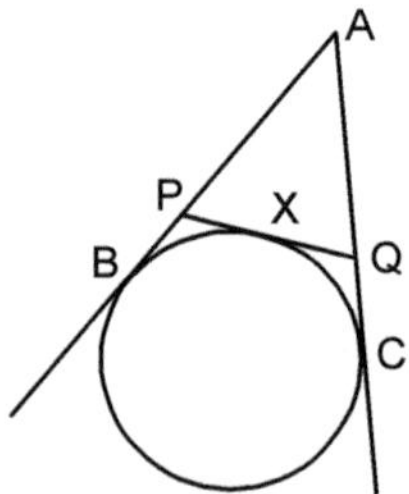

Similarly, BP = PX and XQ = QC

Perimeter of ΔAPQ = AP + AQ + PQ

= AP + AQ + (PX + XQ)

= (AP + PX) + (AQ + XQ)

= (AP + BP) + (AQ + QC)

= AB + AC = 5 + 5 = 10 cm.

20

TRIGONOMETRY

Trigonometric Ratios of Angles

There are six trigonometric ratios — sine, cosine, tangent, cotangent, secant and cosecant—upon which trigonometry is based.

ΔABC is a right- angled triangle in which $\angle$ACB = θ. The side AB is opposite to an angle θ and is called **opposide side**. BC is the **adjacent side** in relation to angle θ; AC is the **hypotenuse**.

The six trigonometric ratios of the acute angle θ are defined as follows :

$$\sin\theta = \frac{p}{h} = \frac{AB}{AC} \qquad \cos\theta = \frac{b}{h} = \frac{BC}{AC}$$

$$\tan\theta = \frac{p}{b} = \frac{AB}{BC} \qquad \cot\theta = \frac{b}{p} = \frac{BC}{AB}$$

$$\sec\theta = \frac{h}{b} = \frac{AC}{BC} \qquad \text{cosec}\theta = \frac{h}{p} = \frac{AC}{AB}$$

IMPORTANT FORMULAE

A. (*i*) $\tan\theta = \frac{\sin\theta}{\cos\theta} = \frac{1}{\cot\theta}$ (*ii*) $\cot\theta = \frac{\cos\theta}{\sin\theta} = \frac{1}{\tan\theta}$

(*iii*) $\sec\theta = \frac{1}{\cos\theta}$ (*iv*) $\text{cosec}\theta = \frac{1}{\sin\theta}$

B. (*v*) $\sin^2\theta + \cos^2\theta = 1$

$\sin^2\theta = 1 - \cos^2\theta \Rightarrow \sin\theta = \sqrt{1-\cos^2\theta}$

$\cos^2\theta = 1 - \sin^2\theta \Rightarrow \cos\theta = \sqrt{1-\sin^2\theta}$

(*vi*) $1 + \tan^2\theta = \sec^2\theta$

$\sec^2\theta - \tan^2\theta = 1$

$\sec^2\theta - 1 = \tan^2\theta$

(*vii*) $1 + \cot^2\theta = \text{cosec}^2\theta$

$\text{cosec}^2\theta - \cot^2\theta = 1$

$\text{cosec}^2\theta - 1 = \cot^2\theta$

C. (*viii*) $\sin(90 - \theta) = \cos\theta$

(*ix*) $\cos(90 - \theta) = \sin\theta$

(*x*) $\tan(90 - \theta) = \cot\theta$

(*xi*) $\cot(90 - \theta) = \tan\theta$

(*xii*) $\sec(90 - \theta) = \text{cosec}\theta$

(*xiii*) $\text{cosec}(90 - \theta) = \sec\theta$

D. (*i*) $\sin(A \pm B) = \sin A \times \cos B \pm \cos A \times \sin B$

(*ii*) $\cos(A \pm B) = \cos A \times \cos B \mp \sin A \times \sin B$

E. (*i*) $\sin 2\theta = 2\sin\theta \cdot \cos\theta$

(*ii*) $\cos 2\theta = \cos^2\theta - \sin^2\theta$

$= 1 - 2\sin^2\theta = 2\cos^2\theta - 1$

(*iii*) $\tan 2\theta = \dfrac{2\tan\theta}{1-\tan^2\theta}$

F. (*i*) $\sin 3\theta = 3\sin\theta - 4\sin^3\theta$

(*ii*) $\cos 3\theta = 4\cos^3\theta - 3\cos\theta$

T-Ratios of Standard Angles

θ	**0°**	**30°**	**45°**	**60°**	**90°**
sinθ	0	$\frac{1}{2}$	$\frac{1}{\sqrt{2}}$	$\frac{\sqrt{3}}{2}$	1
cosθ	1	$\frac{\sqrt{3}}{2}$	$\frac{1}{\sqrt{2}}$	$\frac{1}{2}$	0
tanθ	0	$\frac{1}{\sqrt{3}}$	1	$\sqrt{3}$	∞
cotθ	∞	$\sqrt{3}$	1	$\frac{1}{\sqrt{3}}$	0
secθ	1	$\frac{2}{\sqrt{3}}$	$\sqrt{2}$	2	∞
cosecθ	∞	2	$\sqrt{2}$	$\frac{2}{\sqrt{3}}$	1

HEIGHT AND DISTANCE

Our common use for trigonometry is to measure heights and distance that are either awkward or impossible to measure by ordinary means. One of the biggest triumphs of trigonometry is being able to find the size of an object or the distance to an object (such as the moon) without going to the object. In trigonometry, we develop methods for measuring sides and angles as well as for solving related applied problems. Because of the extensive use of these concepts, trigonometry is considered one of the most practical and relevant branches of mathematics.

The Angle of Elevation

If a person is looking up at an object, the acute angle measured from the horizontal to a line of sight observation of the object is called the angle of elevation.

In the given figure, α is the angle of elevation.

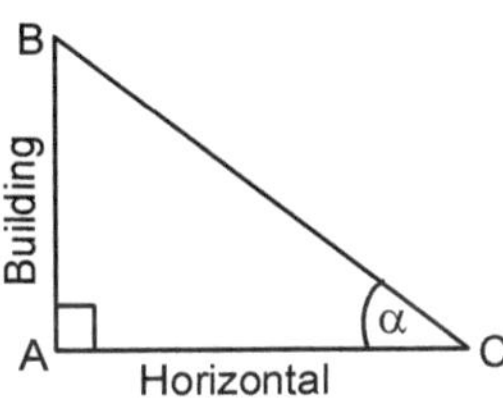

The Angle of Depression

The angle β for a point below a horizontal line is the angle formed by the horizontal line and the observer's line of sight through the point. In the following figure, β is the angle of depression.

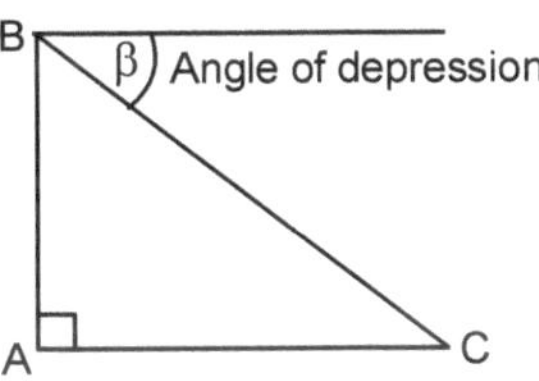

EXERCISE

1. If $2 \tan \theta = 1$, find the value of $\frac{3\cos\theta + 2\sin\theta}{2\cos\theta - \sin\theta}$

A. $\frac{8}{3}$ B. $\frac{5}{3}$

C. $\frac{2}{3}$ D. 2

2. $\cos^2 72° + \cos^2 18° = ?$

A. 0 B. 1

C. –1 D. 2

3. $3 \tan^2 30° + \sec^4 45° - \tan^2 60°$ is equal to :

A. 0 B. 1

C. 2 D. 3

4. The value of $\frac{\sin 10°}{\cos 80°}$ is :

A. 0 B. 1

C. 2 D. 3

5. If $\theta = 45$ then $\frac{2\tan\theta}{1+\tan^2\theta}$ is :

A. 1 B. 0

C. 2 D. 3

6. If $\theta = 30°$ then $\cos 2\theta$ is :

A. 0 B. 1

C. $\frac{1}{2}$ D. $\frac{\sqrt{3}}{2}$

7. What is the value of $\sin^2 35° + \sin^2 55°$?

A. 0 B. 1

C. $\frac{1}{2}$ D. 2

8. The value of tan 45° × cot 45° is :

A. 0 B. 1

C. 2 D. $\frac{1}{2}$

9. The value of sin(90° – θ) is :

A. cos θ B. sin θ

C. –cos θ D. None of these

10. What is the value of sin 30° × cosec 30°

A. 1 B. 0

C. $\frac{1}{2}$ D. 2

11. sin θ + cos θ = 1 where θ = ...

A. 30° B. 45°

C. 60° D. 90°

12. tan 45° × tan 82° is

A. 1 B. 0

C. 2 D. 3

13. The angle of elevation of the top of a tower from a point on the ground, which is 30 m away from the foot of the tower is 30°. The height of the tower is :

A. $8\sqrt{3}$ m B. $9\sqrt{3}$ m

C. $10\sqrt{3}$ m D. $12\sqrt{3}$ m

14. A kite is flying at a height of 60 m above the ground. The string attached to the kite is temporarily tied to a point on the ground. The inclination of the string with the ground is 60°. Find the length of the string, assuming that there is no slack in the string.

A. $40\sqrt{3}$ m B. $30\sqrt{3}$ m

C. $20\sqrt{3}$ m D. $10\sqrt{3}$ m

15. From a point on the ground, the angles of elevation of the bottom and top of a transmission tower fixed at the top of a 20 m high building are 45° and 60° respectively. The height of the tower is :

A. $25(\sqrt{3}-1)$ m

B. $20(\sqrt{3}-1)$ m

C. 20 m

D. 10 m

16. Two poles of equal heights are standing opposite to each other on either side of a road, which is 100 metres wide. From a point between them on the road, the angles of elevation of their tops are 30° and 60°. The height of each pole is

A. 44 m B. 43.25 m

C. 50 m D. 40.5 m

17. The angle of elevation of the top of a hill at the foot of a tower is 60° and the angle of elevation of top of the tower from the foot of the hill is 30°. If the tower is 50 m high, then the height of the hill is :

A. 148 m B. 150 m

C. 152 m D. 160 m

18. The angles of elevation of the top of a tower from two points a and b from the base and in the same straight line with it are complementary. The height of the tower is :

A. ab B. $\sqrt{ab}$

C. a^2b^2 D. None of these

19. The angles of elevation of the top of a tower from two points at the distances of 4 m and 9 m from the base of the tower and in the same straight line with it are complementary. The height of the tower is :

A. 8 m B. 5 m

C. 6 m D. 4 m

20. The value of $\frac{\tan 49°}{\cot 41°}$ is :

A. 1 B. 2

C. 0 D. 3

EXPLANATORY ANSWERS

1. A: $\frac{3\cos\theta + 2\sin\theta}{2\cos\theta - \sin\theta} = \frac{3\frac{\cos\theta}{\cos\theta} + 2\frac{\sin\theta}{\cos\theta}}{2\frac{\cos\theta}{\cos\theta} - \frac{\sin\theta}{\cos\theta}}$

[Dividing both the numerator and denominator by cos θ]

$= \frac{3 + 2\tan\theta}{2 - \tan\theta} = \frac{3 + 2 \times \frac{1}{2}}{2 - \frac{1}{2}}$ [Given 2 tan θ = 1 ∴ tan θ = $\frac{1}{2}$]

$= \frac{3+1}{3/2} = 4 \times \frac{2}{3} = 2\frac{2}{3}$.

2. B: $\cos^2 72° + \cos^2 18° = \cos^2 (90 - 18°) + \cos^2 18°$

$= \sin^2 18° + \cos^2 18° = 1$.

3. C: $3\left(\frac{1}{\sqrt{3}}\right)^2 + (\sqrt{2})^2 - (\sqrt{3})^2$

$= 3 \times \frac{1}{3} + 4 - 3 = 2$.

4. B: $\frac{\sin 10°}{\cos(90° - 10°)} = \frac{\sin 10°}{\sin 10°} = 1$.

5. A: $\frac{2\tan 45°}{1 + \tan^2 45°} = \frac{2 \times 1}{1+1} = \frac{2}{2} = 1$.

6. C: $\cos 2(30°) = \cos 60° = \frac{1}{2}$.

7. B: $\sin^2 35° + \sin^2(90° - 35°)$

$= \sin^2 35° + \cos^2 35° = 1.$ $[\because \sin^2\theta + \cos^2\theta = 1]$

8. B: $\tan 45° \times \cot 45° = 1 \times 1 = 1.$

9. A: $\sin (90° - \theta) = \cos \theta.$

10.A: $\sin 30° \times \text{cosec } 30° = \frac{1}{2} \times \frac{2}{1} = \frac{1}{1} = 1.$

11.D: Put $\theta = 90°$ then $\sin \theta + \cos \theta = \sin 90° + \cos 90° = 1 + 0 = 1.$

12.A: $\tan 45° \times \tan 8° \cdot \tan (90° - 8°)$

$= \tan 45° \times \tan 8° \times \cot 8° = 1 \times 1 = 1.$

13.C: Let AB be the tower. The angle of elevation of the top A of the tower from a point C on the ground which is 30 metres away from the foot of the tower is 30°.

$\therefore \quad \angle ACB = 30°$

and $\quad BC = 30$ m.

From right ΔABC, we have

$$\frac{AB}{BC} = \tan 30°$$

$$\Rightarrow \quad AB = BC \tan 30° = 30 \times \frac{1}{\sqrt{3}} = 10\sqrt{3} \text{ m.}$$

14.A: Let AB = height of kite = 60 m and the inclination of the string AC is 60°.

From right-angled ΔABC, we have

$$\frac{AC}{AB} = \text{cosec } 60°$$

$$\Rightarrow \quad \frac{AC}{60} = \frac{2}{\sqrt{3}} \Rightarrow AC = 60 \times \frac{2}{\sqrt{3}} = 40\sqrt{3} \text{ m.}$$

15.A: Let AB = 20 m be the building and AC be the transmission tower fixed at the top of building. From a point D on the ground, the angle of elevation of the bottom and top of transmission tower are 45° and 60°.

$\therefore \angle ADB = 45°$ and $\angle CDB = 60°$

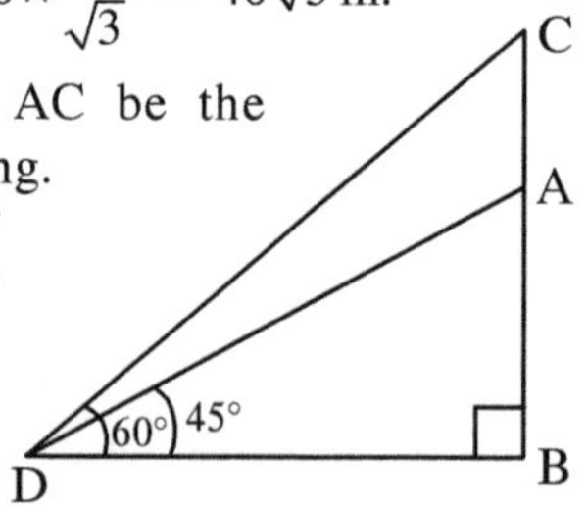

From right ΔABD, we have

$$\frac{AB}{BD} = \tan 45° = 1$$

$\therefore$ AB = BD

$\Rightarrow$ BD = 20 m [$\because$ AB = 20 m]

From right-angled ΔCBD, we have

$$\frac{BC}{BD} = \tan 60°$$

$\Rightarrow$ BC = BD tan 60°

$$= 20 \times \sqrt{3} = 20\sqrt{3}\,\text{m}$$

Now AC = BC – AB = $20\sqrt{3} - 20$

$$= 20(\sqrt{3} - 1)\,\text{m}.$$

Hence the height of the tower = $20(\sqrt{3} - 1)\,\text{m}$.

16.B: Let AB and CD be the two poles of equal height h metres standing on either side of the road AC = 100 metres.

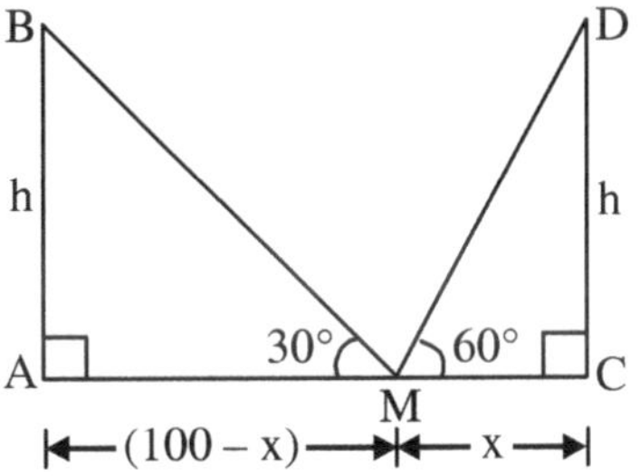

Let M be the point at which the poles AB, CD subtend angles of 30° and 60° respectively.

Let CM = x metres so that

AM = $(100 - x)$ metres

In right-angled ΔMCD, $\frac{h}{x} = \tan 60°$

$\Rightarrow$ $h = x\sqrt{3}$ ...(*i*)

In right-angled ΔMAB,

$$\frac{h}{100 - x} = \tan 30° \Rightarrow \frac{h}{100 - x} = \frac{1}{\sqrt{3}}$$

$\Rightarrow$ $h\sqrt{3} = 100 - x \Rightarrow (x\sqrt{3})\sqrt{3} = 100 - x$

$$3x = 100 - x$$

$$4x = 100;\ x = 100 \div 4 = 25 \text{ m}$$

$\therefore$ From (*i*), $h = x\sqrt{3} = 25 \times 1.73 = 43.25$ m

Hence, distance of point M from C = 25 m and distance of point from A = (100 – 25)m = 75 m. Height of each pole = 43.25 m.

17.B: Let AB be the hill and CD the tower.

$$\angle BDA = 60^\circ \text{ and } \angle DBC = 30^\circ$$

$$CD = 50 \text{ m.}$$

Let AB = h metres

In right-angled ΔADC,

$$\frac{CD}{BD} = \tan 30^\circ$$

$$\Rightarrow \qquad BD = \frac{CD}{\tan 30^\circ}$$

$$= CD \cot 30^\circ$$

$$\Rightarrow \qquad BD = 50\sqrt{3} \text{ metres}$$

Now in right-angled ΔABD, we have

$$\frac{AB}{BD} = \tan 60^\circ \Rightarrow AB = BD \tan 60^\circ$$

$$\Rightarrow AB = (50\sqrt{3})\sqrt{3} = 150 \text{ m.}$$

Hence, height of the hill is 150 m.

18.B: Let AB be the tower and C and D be the two points such that BD = a and BC = b.

If $\angle BDA = \theta$, then $\angle BCA = 90^\circ - \theta$

Now in right-angled ΔABD,

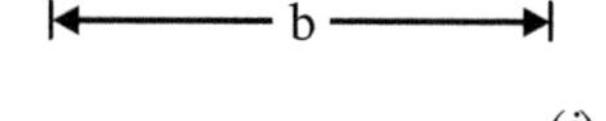

$$\frac{AB}{BD} = \tan\theta \Rightarrow \frac{h}{a} = \tan\theta$$

$$\therefore \qquad h = a \tan\theta \qquad \text{...}(i)$$

In right-angled ΔABC,

$$\frac{AB}{BC} = \tan(90^\circ - \theta) = \cot\theta$$

$$\Rightarrow \qquad \frac{h}{b} = \cot\theta \Rightarrow h = b \cot\theta \qquad \text{...}(ii)$$

multiplying (*i*) and (*ii*), we get

$$h^2 = ab \tan\theta \cot\theta = ab \tan\theta \times \frac{1}{\tan\theta} = ab.$$

$$\therefore \qquad h = \sqrt{ab}.$$

19.C: Let AB be the tower and C and D be the two points such that BD = 4 m and BC = 9 m.

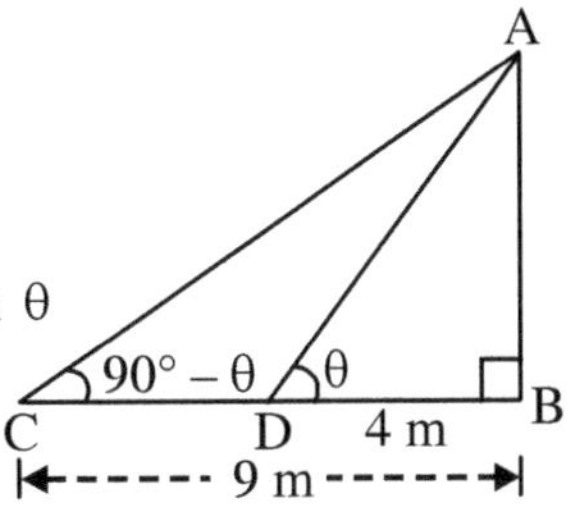

If ∠BDA = θ, then ∠BCA = 90° – θ

Now in right-angled ΔABD,

$$\frac{AB}{BD} = \tan\theta \Rightarrow \frac{h}{4} = \tan\theta$$

∴ $h = 4\tan\theta \quad ...(i)$

In right-angled ΔABC,

$$\frac{AB}{BC} = \tan(90° - \theta) = \cot\theta$$

$$\Rightarrow \quad \frac{h}{9} = \cot\theta \Rightarrow h = 9\cot\theta \quad ...(ii)$$

multiplying (*i*) and (*ii*), we get

$$h^2 = 36\tan\theta\cot\theta = 36\tan\theta \times \frac{1}{\tan\theta} = 36.$$

∴ $h = \pm\sqrt{36} = 6$ m.

20.A: $\dfrac{\tan 49°}{\cot 41°} = \dfrac{\tan(90° - 41°)}{\cot 41°} = \dfrac{\cot 41°}{\cot 41°} = 1$ $\quad [\because \tan(90° - \theta) = \cot\theta]$

21

DATA TABLES

TABLES

Tables are often used in reports, magazines and newspaper to present as set of numerical data. It is one of the easiest and most accurate ways of presenting data. One of the main purposes of tables is to make complicated information easier to understand. Hence, the advantage of presenting data in a table is that one can see the information at a glance. We present below an example of tabular presentation of annual expenditure of 5 families for last 5 years.

Annual Expenditure of 5 families (in ₹ Thousands)

Years → Families ↓	**2008**	**2009**	**2010**	**2011**	**2012**
A	35	50	55	60	70
B	40	60	65	75	80
C	45	50	70	80	95
D	30	40	45	50	75
E	50	55	60	70	90

Essentials of a Tables:

(*i*) **Title:** Heading of the table

(*ii*) **Stub:** The section of the table containing row headings in called Stub.

(*iii*) **Column Captions :** The heading of each column is designated as column caption.

(*iv*) **Body**

(*v*) **Footnotes**

(*vi*) **Source**

EXERCISE

Directions (Qs. 1 to 4) : *Study the table below to answer these questions.*

Rate of Interest, Dividend Payout Ratio and the Retained Earnings of Five Companies

Company	Interest (₹ 000)	Rate of Interest (%)	Dividend Payout Ratio (%)	Retained Earnings (₹ lakh)
A	234	18	22.50	155
B	576	24	19.60	402
C	129.6	16	8.75	365
D	144	9	32.50	270
E	180	15	28.00	216

Profit earned is either paid out as dividend or ploughed back in business as retained earnings. Interest is paid on borrowings.

1. What is the sum of profits made by Companies A & B?
A. ₹ 700 lakh B. ₹ 500 lakh
C. ₹ 600 lakh D. None of these

2. What is the sum of the borrowings of all five companies?
A. ₹ 14.6 crore
B. ₹ 146 lakh
C. ₹ 14.6 lakh
D. None of these

3. By how much do the borrowings of Company B exceed that of Company A?
A. ₹ 1,000,000
B. ₹ 1,210,000
C. ₹ 1,320,000
D. ₹ 1,100,000

4. By how much does the dividend paid by Company D exceed the dividend paid by Company B?
A. ₹ 320 lakh
B. ₹ 23 lakh
C. ₹ 32 lakh
D. ₹ 230 lakh

Directions (Qs. 5 to 9) : *Study the following table to answer these questions.*

Average Hourly Wage (in ₹) by Age Group

Years	18 – 20 years		21 – 23 years	
	Male	Female	Male	Female
2007	15.1	15.1	29.7	25.1
2008	12.4	13.4	21.0	19.1
2009	10.0	13.8	14.7	16.9
2010	11.0	13.4	18.0	20.5
2011	21.2	16.3	29.1	32.7
2012	15.0	21.0	32.1	33.9

5. In 2011, for the 21-23 years age group, the wages for the females was approximately what per cent of that of the males?
A. 220 B. 30
C. 85 D. 110

6. What was the difference between the average wages of males and of females for the 21 – 23 years age group?
A. 0.80 B. 0.60
C. 0.40 D. 0.20

7. In how many years was the wage for the females higher than that of males in both the age groups?
A. Three B. Four
C. Two D. One

8. In the age group of 18–20 years, in which year was the wage-disparity maximum?
A. 2010 B. 2011
C. 2009 D. 2012

9. In the age group of 21–23 years, in which year was the wage-disparity minimum?
A. 2008 B. 2012
C. 2009 D. 2007

Directions (Qs. 10 to 15) : *Answer these questions on the basis of the data given in the following table indicating the trend in sales of four companies. The amounts given are in lakhs of rupees :*

Year	Name of the Company			
	Dowby	Alpha	Baron	Celia
2004	12.00	2.00	18.50	12.00
2005	10.00	5.00	15.00	16.00
2006	18.00	7.50	16.50	15.00
2007	20.00	11.50	14.50	36.00
2008	25.00	15.00	50.00	48.00

10. Which company has shown consistently an increasing sales average?
A. Alpha B. Baron
C. Celia D. Dowby

11. The cumulative sales of all the companies put together in 2005 was how much of the sales of 2008?
A. $\frac{3}{7}$ B. $\frac{2}{5}$
C. $\frac{1}{4}$ D. $\frac{1}{3}$

12. What was the average sales of Baron over the 5 years?
A. 22.90 B. 21.90
C. 23.90 D. 20.90

13. Which company faced a decline in sales in 2007 over its previous year?
A. Alpha B. Baron
C. Celia D. Dowby

14. The ratio of the highest turnover of any company in any year to the lowest turnover of any company in any year is
A. 25 B. 15
C. 2.5 D. 0.25

15. How many companies had the same turnover in the same year?
A. 1 B. 2
C. 3 D. 4

EXPLANATORY ANSWERS

1. A:

2. D:

3. D: Required difference = 2400000 – 1300000 (From solutions of 179)
= ₹ 1100000

4. C: Dividend paid by company B = $\frac{402}{80.4} \times 19.6$ = ₹ 98 lakh

Dividend paid by company D = $\frac{270}{67.5} \times 32.5$ = ₹ 130 lakh

Their difference = 130 – 98 = ₹ 32 lakh.

5. D: Required percentage = $\frac{32.7}{29.1} \times 100 = 112.37 \approx 110\%$.

6. B:

7. A:

Year	Wage for male 18-20 years + 21-23 years	Wage for female 18-20 years + 21 – 23 years
2007	₹ 44.8	₹ 40.2
2008	₹ 33.4	₹ 32.5
2009	₹ 24.7	₹ 30.7
2010	₹ 29.0	₹ 33.9
2011	₹ 50.3	₹ 49.0
2012	₹ 47.1	₹ 54.9

Hence, in three years the wage of females was higher than that of male.

8. D: In 2012 wage for male (18-20 years) was ₹ 15.0 white wage for female was ₹ 21.0. Obviously it is maximum wage disparity.

9. B: In 2012 wage for male (21-23 years) was ₹ 32.1 white wage for female was ₹ 33.9. Obviously it is minimum wage-disparity.

10. A: Of course, Alpha has shown consistently increasing sales average.

11. C:

Year	Total Sales of all the Companies	Cumulative Sales
2004	44.50	44.50
2005	46.00	90.50
2006	57.00	147.50
2007	82.00	229.00
2008	138.00	367.50

Let, $90.50 = K \times 367.50$

$\Rightarrow \quad K = \frac{90.50}{367.50} = \frac{181}{735} \approx \frac{1}{4}$.

12. A: $\frac{18.50 + 15.00 + 16.50 + 14.50 + 50.00}{5} = \frac{114.50}{5} = 22.90$.

13. B: Obviously, Baron faced a decline in sales.

14. A: $\frac{50}{2} = 25$

15. B: In 2004, Celia and Dowby.

22

BAR GRAPHS

BAR GRAPHS

Given quantity of a bar graph can be compared by the height or length. A bar graph can have either vertical or horizontal bars. You can compare different quantities or the same quantity at the different times. The bars may be placed adjacent to each other or may be separated from each other by spaces depending upon the problem.

For Illustration:

Registration of New Vehicles in Delhi (in thousands)

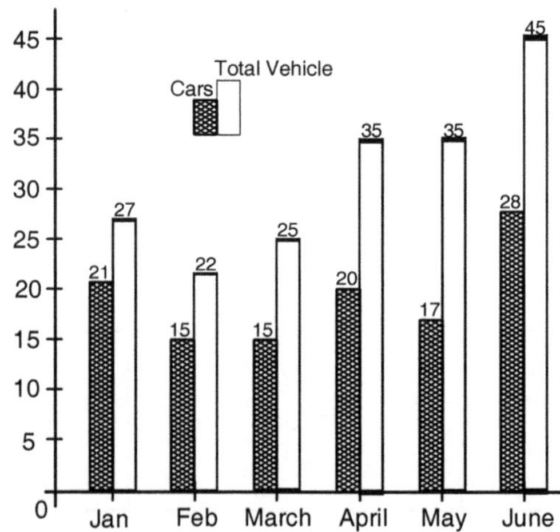

CUMULATIVE GRAPH

These are usually bar or line graphs where the height of the bar or line is divided up proportionally among various quantities presented in the graph. The representation of quantities may be done in terms of either percentage of the total or in absolute figures. These are also called sub-divided graphs. Thus, cumulative graph may be conveniently used for making comparisons.

For Illustration:

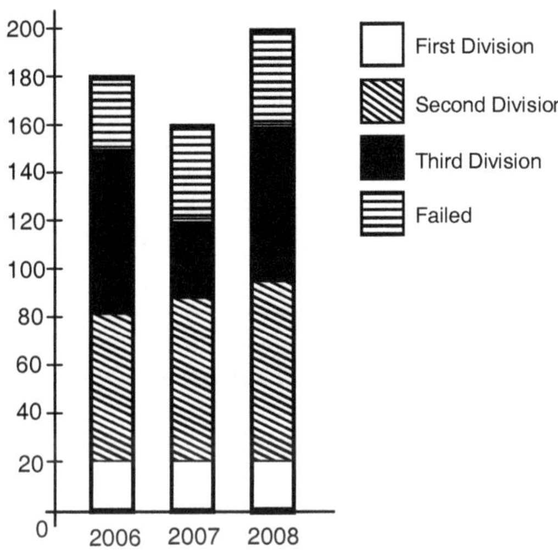

EXERCISE

Directions (Qs. 1 to 4) : *Study the following bar graph giving Economic Indices for the period 1961-62 to 2001-02 to answer these questions.*

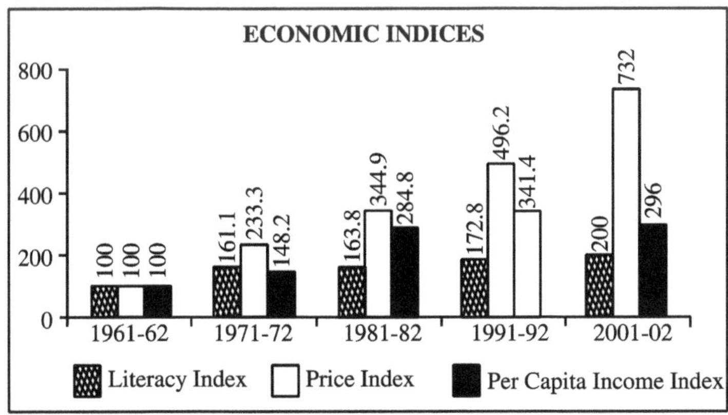

1. What is the average annual percentage increase in literacy index from 1961-62 to 2001-02?

A. 25% B. 15.8%
C. 18.3% D. 4.9%

2. Of the three economic indices which index for which period shows the maximum percentage increase as compared to the previous period?

A. Literacy, 1971-72
B. Price, 2001-02
C. Per capita income, 1981-82
D. Price, 1971-72

3. In which period the per capita income index increases at a faster rate than the price index as compared to the preceding period?
A. 1971-72 B. 2001-02
C. 1981-82 D. 1991-92

4. What are the respective indices of literacy, price and per capita income for 2001-02 taking 1971-72 as the base period?
A. 124.1, 313.8, 200
B. 313.8, 124, 201
C. 313.8, 124.1, 190
D. 124.1, 313.8, 194

Directions (Qs. 5 to 9) : *The following bar graph indicates the production of sugar (in lakh tonnes) by three different sugar companies P, Q and R over the years 2003 to 2007.*

Production of Sugar by Companies P, Q and R during 2003–2007.

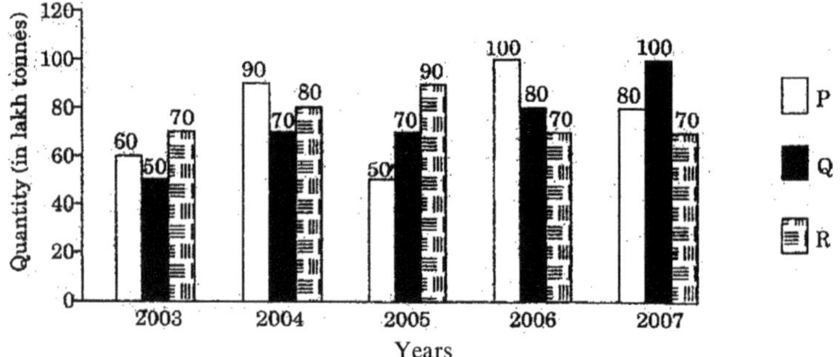

5. The percentage of production of Company R to production of Company Q is the maximum in the year
A. 2005 B. 2004
C. 2003 D. 2006

6. The ratio of the average production of Company P during the years 2005 to 2007 to the average production of Company Q for the same period is
A. 15 : 17 B. 23 : 25
C. 27 : 29 D. 9 : 11

7. The percentage increase in production of Company Q from the year 2003 to the year 2007 is
A. 60% B. 80%
C. 90% D. 100%

8. The average production over the years 2003–2007 was maximum for the Company(ies)
A. R B. Q
C. P D. None of these

9. The percentage rise or fall in production of Company Q as compared to the previous year is the maximum in the year
A. 2006 B. 2005
C. 2004 D. 2007

Directions (Qs. 10 to 13) : *Study the following graph to answer these questions.*

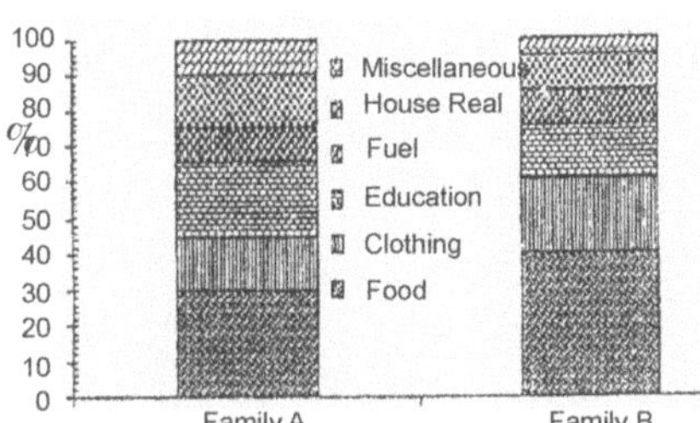

10. What fraction of the total expenditure is spent on education in family A?

A. 9/13

B. 2/3

C. 13/21

D. 1/5

11. If the total expenditure of family B is ₹ 10,000, then money spent on clothes by this family during the years is

A. ₹ 2,000 B. ₹ 600

C. ₹ 200 D. ₹ 6,000

12. If the total annual expenditure of family A is ₹ 30,000, the money spent on food, clothes and house rent is

A. ₹ 21,000 B. ₹ 18,000

C. ₹ 18,500 D. ₹ 15,000

13. What percentage is B's expenditure on food over A's expenditure on food, taking equal total expenditure?

A. 133.33% B. 70%

C. 10% D. 75%

EXPLANATORY ANSWERS

1. A: Average percentage increase $= \dfrac{200 - 100}{4} = 25\%$.

2. D: Price index of 1971-72 shows 133.3% increase which is maximum.

3. C:

Years	Per Capita Income Index	Price Index
71-72	48.20%	133.30%
81-82	67.88%	47.83%
91-92	19.87%	43.87%
01-02	Negative	47.52%

According to above table in 81-82. The Per capita income index increases at faster rate than the price index.

4. A:

5. C: In 2003, required percentage $= \dfrac{70}{50} \times 100 = 140\%$

In 2004, required percentage $= \dfrac{80}{70} \times 100 = 114.2\%$

In 2005, required percentage = $\frac{90}{70} \times 100 = 128.57\%$

Thus, in 2003 required percentage was maximum.

6. B: Required ratio = (50 + 100 + 80) : (70 + 80 + 100)
= 230 : 250 = 23 : 25

7. D: Required increase percentage

$$= \frac{100-50}{50} \times 100 = 100\%$$

8. A: Obviously that is R.

9. D: Obviously that year is 2007.

10. D: Required ratio = $\frac{20}{100} = \frac{1}{5}$.

11. A: Money spend on clothes by family B = $1000 \times \frac{20}{100}$ = ₹ 2000.

12. B: Required expenditure = $30000 \times \frac{(30+15+15)}{100}$ = ₹ 18000.

13. A: Required percentage = $\frac{40}{30} \times 100$ = 133.33%.

23

FREQUENCY POLYGON

FREQUENCY POLYGON

Frequency Polygon are used to show how a quantity changes continuously. If the line goes up, the quantity is increasing; if the line goes down, the quantity is decreasing; if the line is horizontal, the quantity is not changing.

For Illustration:

Demand and Production of rubber (in thousand tons) in various years

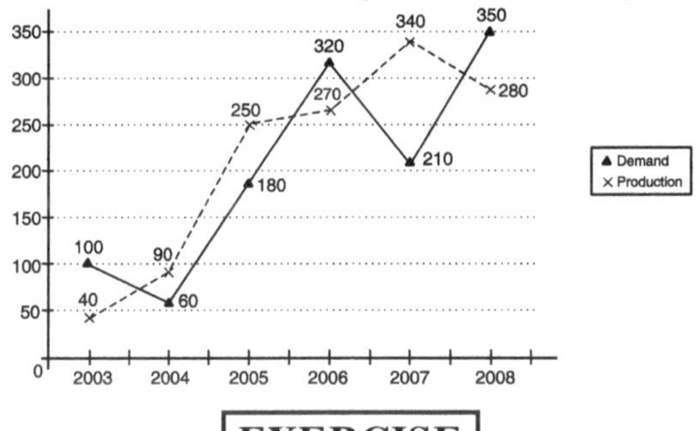

EXERCISE

Directions (Qs. 1 to 4) : *Study the given graph carefully to answer these questions.*

The following graph shows the ratio of imports to exports by two companies A and B over the years.

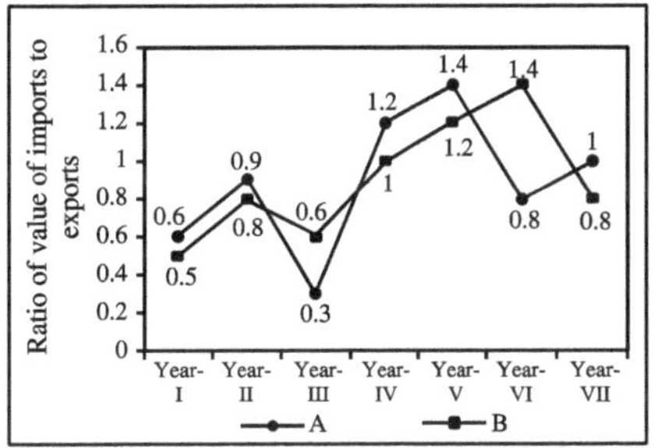

1. If the imports of company A in Year – VI were ₹ 10.40 crore, what were the exports of company A in the same year?

A. 13 crore B. 12.75 crore

C. 12.50 crore D. 13.75 crore

2. It is supposed that Imports – Exports = 'x' for company A in Year-I and the imports of company A in Year-I were ₹ 3.6 crore, and it is also supposed that Imports – Exports = 'a' for company B in Year-V and the exports of company B in Year-V were ₹ 5 crore. What is the relationship between 'a' and 'x'?

A. $x > a$ B. $x = a$
C. $a > x$ D. $x \neq a$

3. If the exports of company B in Year-III were ₹ 2.19 crore, what were the imports of company B in the same year?

A. 3.65 crore
B. 1.314 crore
C. 1.214 crore
D. 1.414 crore

4. If the imports of company A in Year-V were ₹ 8.40 crore, what were the exports of company B in Year-VII?

A. 6 crore
B. 7.40 crore
C. 7.20 crore
D. Data inadequate

Directions (Qs. 5 to 8) : *The following graph shows the number of successful candidates from different schools (A to F) in different disciplines. Study the graph carefully to answer these questions.*

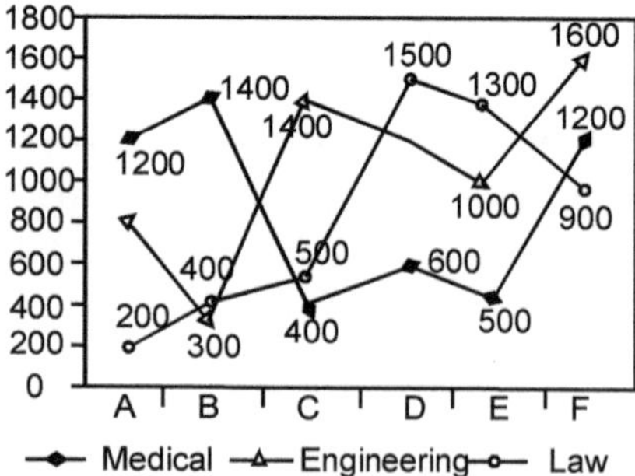

5. In which of the following institutes is the difference between the number of successful candidates in Engineering and that in Medical discipline the maximum?

A. F B. C
C. B D. D

6. The total number of successful candidates from Medical discipline is approximately what per cent more than that from Law?

A. 8% B. 15%
C. 12% D. 10%

7. The number of successful candidates from F in Engineering discipline is what per cent more than the number of successful candidates from A in Medical discipline?

A. 30% B. 25%
C. $33\frac{1}{3}\%$ D. 20%

8. In which of the following institutes is the sum of the number of successful candidates in Engineering and Law disciplines 50% of the number of Medical students of the same institute?

A. C B. E
C. D D. B

Directions (Qs. 9 to 12) : Consider the following graph where the prices of timber are given for the period 1997-2003. The prices for plywood and sawn timber are given in ₹/m^3 while the price of logs is given in ₹/tonne. Assume 1 ton is equal to 1,000 kg and one cu.m of log weigh 800 kg.

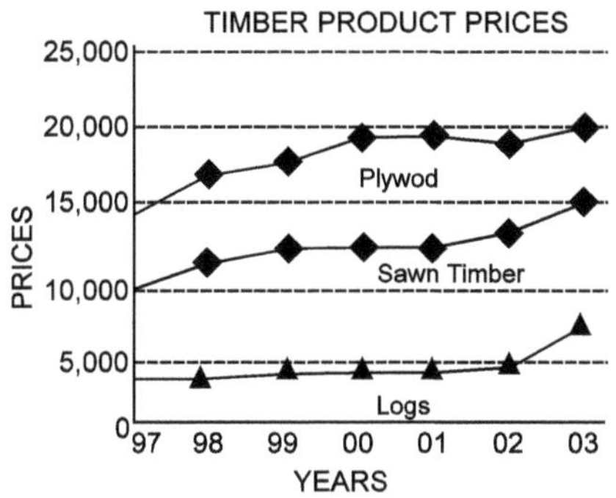

9. Which product had the largest percentage increase in price per cubic meter over the 7-year period ?

A. Sawn timber

B. Logs

C. Plywood

D. None of these

10. The maximum increase in price per cubic metre for any product over any two successive years was :

A. ₹ 2,500 B. ₹ 3,125

C. ₹ 2,000 D. ₹ 4,125

11. In 2003, the total sales of the company measured in cubic metres was made up of 40% plywood, 30% sawn timber and 30% logs. The average realisation per cubic metre in 2003 was closest to :

A. ₹ 16,500 B. ₹ 13,500

C. ₹ 15,000 D. ₹ 18,000

12. In 2004, the prices of plywood, sawn timber and logs went up by 5%, 1% and 10%, respectively, and the total sales were made up of 40% plywood, 30% sawn timber and 30% logs. The average realisation per cubic metre in 2004 was closest to :

A. ₹ 15,500 B. ₹ 16,500

C. ₹ 14,500 D. ₹ 18,500

EXPLANATORY ANSWERS

1. A:

2. C: x = ₹ 3.6 crore – ₹ $\frac{3.6}{0.6}$ crore = – ₹ 2.4 crore

a = ₹ 5 crore × 1.2 – ₹ 5 crore = ₹ 1 crore

Thus, $a > x$.

3. B: Required exports = ₹ 2.19 crore × 0.6 = ₹ 1.314 crore.

4. D: There is no relation between imports of company A in year-V and exports of company B in year-VIII and the given data is not sufficient to answer the question.

5. B:

Institute	Required difference
A	1200 – 800 = 400
B	1400 – 300 = 1100
C	1400 – 400 = 1000
D	1200 – 600 = 600
E	1000 – 500 = 500
F	1600 – 1200 = 400.

6. D: Total number of successful candidates in Medical = 5300, Law = 4800

Required percentage = $\frac{5300 \times 4800}{4800} \times 100$ = 10.4% = 10%.

7. C: Successful candidates from F in Engineering = 1600
Successful candidates from A in Medical = 1200

Required percentage = $\frac{1600 - 1200}{1200} \times 100$

$= \frac{100}{3} = 33\frac{1}{3}\%$.

8. D:

	A	B	C	D	E	F
Medical	1200	1400	400	600	500	1200
Engineering	800	300	1400	1200	1000	1600
Law	200	400	500	1500	1300	900

Hence, in B the total number of successful candidates of Engineering and Law is 50% of the number of candidates of Medical.

9. B: Increase in plywood = $\frac{(20{,}000 - 14000)}{14000} \times 100 = 42.86\%$

Increase in Sawn Timber = $\frac{15000 - 10000}{10000} \times 100 = 50\%$

Increase in Logs = $\frac{\frac{7500}{1.25} - \frac{4000}{1.25}}{\frac{4000}{1.25}} \times 100$ = 87.5%

Hence, Logs had the largest increase in prices.

10. A: In plywood during 97 to 98 the price rise is about ₹ 2500 and it is maximum.

11. C: 40% of ₹ 20000 = $20000 \times \frac{40}{100}$ = ₹ 8000

30% of ₹ 15000 = $15000 \times \frac{30}{100}$ = ₹ 4500

30% of ₹ 7500 = $7500 \times \frac{30}{100}$ = ₹ 2250

Total = ₹ 8000 + ₹ 4500 + ₹ 2250 = ₹ 14750 ≈ ₹ 15000.
Hence, correct answer in C

12. A:

24

PIE CHARTS

PIE CHARTS

These are used to show the share of various sectors in the total. They usually show the percentage share of each sector in the whole (taken as 100%). In such representation the total quantity in question is distributed over a total angle of 360°. The area of each sector is proportional to the relative frequency of the class represented by the sector.

$$\text{Sector angle} = \frac{\text{Class frequency}}{\text{Total frequency}} \times 360°$$

For Illustration:

Distribution of Expenditure of a family

EXERCISE

Directions (Qs. 1 to 4) : *Study the pie-chart carefully to answer the questions that follow:*

Percentage-wise Break up of Students in terms of Specialization in MBA

TOTAL NUMBER OF STUDENTS = 8000

1. What is the total number of students having specialization in IR, Marketing and IT?
A. 4640 B. 4080
C. 4260 D. 4400

2. Students having IB as specialization forms **approximately** what per cent of students having Marketing as specialization?
A. 116 B. 86
C. 124 D. 74

3. What is the total number of students having IB as specilization?
A. 1520 B. 1280
C. 1360 D. 1120

4. What is the respective ratio of the students having Finance as specialization to that of students having HR as specialization?
A. 11 : 19 B. 18 : 13
C. 6 : 7 D. 12 : 21

Directions (Qs. 5 to 8) : *Study the graph below to answer these questions.*

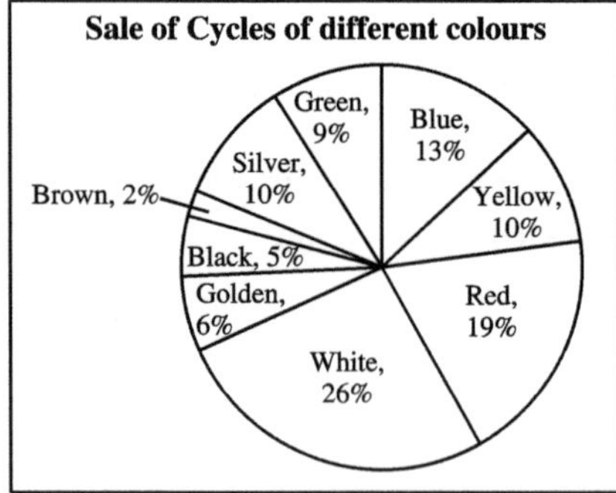

5. 50% of all the cycles consisted of which colours?
A. Black, Golden, Blue, Red
B. Blue, Black, Red, Silver
C. White, Golden, Blue, Black
D. Golden, Green, Black, White

6. Cycles of which colour when increased by two per cent and then combined with that of red cycles will make 30 per cent of the total?
A. Golden
B. Blue
C. Black
D. None of these

7. If in certain period the total production of all cycles was 95400 then how many more blue cycles were sold than green?
A. 2580 B. 3618
C. 2850 D. 3816

8. Cycles of which colour are 20% less popular than white coloured cycles?
A. Black
B. Golden
C. Blue
D. None of these

Directions (Qs. 9 to 12) : *Study the pir-chart below to answer these questions. The chart gives the composition of solar radiation.*

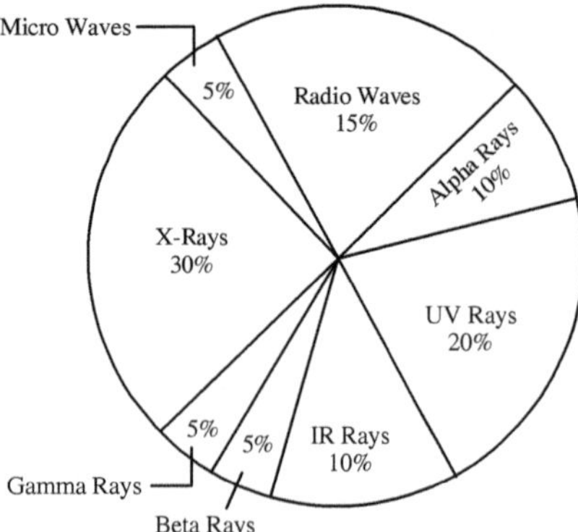

Total sun rays received in one minute = 3600 units

9. If the human body can withstand a maximum of 9720 units of IR rays when exposed to the sun continuously, then what is the maximum time in minutes that any person could stand in the sun without crossing the threshold limit of IR rays?

A. 23 B. 19
C. 27 D. 29

10. The amount of Beta rays in 10 minutes of the sun rays is how many times the amount of IR rays in 3 minutes of the sun rays?

A. 1.44 B. 1.33
C. 1.66 D. None of these

11. How many minutes of exposure to the sun in a day would be enough to ensure that the body receives enough amount of Vitamin D, given that the body requires 40 units of Vitamin D every day and that 30 units of Beta rays generate one unit of Vitamin D?

A. $5\frac{1}{3}$ B. $5\frac{2}{3}$
C. $6\frac{1}{3}$ D. $6\frac{2}{3}$

12. The amount of Alpha rays received in two minutes is how much more/ less than the amount of Radio waves received in 4 minutes?

A. 1320 units more
B. 1200 units less
C. 1440 units less
D. 1600 units more

EXPLANATORY ANSWERS

1. D:

2. B: Required percentage = $\frac{19}{22} \times 100 = 86.36\% \approx 86\%$

3. A: Required number of Students = $\frac{19}{100} \times 8000 = 1520$

4. C: Required ratio = 12 : 14 = 6 : 7

5. C: Obviously, White, Golden, Blue and Black colours consists 50% of cycles.

6. D: Clearly, there is no such colours.

7. D: Required difference = $95400 \times \frac{(13-9)}{100} = 954 \times 4 = 3816.$

8. D: There is no such coloured cycle which is exactly 20% less popular than White coloured cycles.

9. C: The maximum time = $\frac{9720}{\frac{3600 \times 10}{100}} = 27.$

10. D:

11. D: 40 units of vitamin D generate from

$$= 40 \times 30 = 1200 \text{ units of } \beta\text{-rays}$$

The amount of β-rays received in 1 min.

$$= \frac{5}{100} \times 3600 = 180 \text{ units}$$

Hence, required time $= \frac{1200}{180} = 6\frac{2}{3}$ min.

12. C: The amount of a-rays received in 2 min.

$$= \frac{10}{100} \times 3600 \times 2 = 720 \text{ units}$$

The amount of radio waves received in 4 min.

$$= \frac{15}{100} \times 3600 \times 4 = 2160 \text{ units}$$

Required difference = 2160 – 720 = 1440 units less.

25

MISCELLANEOUS QUESTIONS

1. When three right hand side digits of a number are 1,000 the number is divisible by:
   A. 4
   B. 5
   C. 9
   D. All the above

2. When the two right hand side digits of a number are 100, the number is divisible by:
   A. 2
   B. 4
   C. 5
   D. All the above

3. When the last digit of a number is 5, the number is divisible by:
   A. 3
   B. 5
   C. 25
   D. All the above

4. The H.C.F. of the product of first six odd numbers and the product of first six even numbers is:
   A. 45 B. 40
   C. 34 D. 30

5. $1\frac{1}{2}+\frac{1}{7}\times 10\frac{1}{2}-2\frac{1}{3}\div 1\frac{3}{4}$ of $1\frac{1}{3}$ is equal to:
   A. 1 B. 2
   C. 3 D. 4

6. $6\frac{1}{2}-\left[5\frac{1}{2}-\left\{4\frac{1}{2}-\left(3\frac{1}{2}-2\overline{\frac{1}{2}-\frac{1}{2}}\right)\right\}\right]$ is equal to:
   A. 4 B. 3
   C. 2 D. 1

7. $\frac{1}{2}+\frac{2}{3}/\frac{3}{7}-\frac{1}{6}$ is equal to:
   A. $5\frac{4}{11}$ B. $3\frac{5}{11}$
   C. $4\frac{5}{11}$ D. $7\frac{6}{21}$

8. The sum of $\frac{1}{2}, \frac{1}{4}, \frac{1}{8}$ of a number is 28. The number is:
   A. 24 B. 28
   C. 32 D. 36

9. If 20 men can finish a piece of work in 10 days, how many persons can finish the same job in 4 days?
   A. 20 B. 30
   C. 40 D. 50

10. If 15 men can finish a job in 20 days, 25 men will finish the same job in:
    A. 8 days B. 12 days
    C. 16 days D. 12 days

EXPLANATORY ANSWERS

1. D: For example, consider the number 1000. The multiples of 1000 are 125 and 8, while the multiples of 125 and 8 are 5 and 4. Hence, the number is divisible by 4, 5 as well as 8.

2. D.

3. B.

4. A: First six odd numbers are 1, 3, 5, 7, 9, 11

Product of first six odd numbers $= 1 \times 3 \times 5 \times 7 \times 9 \times 11$

$= 1 \times 3 \times 5 \times 7 \times 3 \times 3 \times 11$

First six even numbers are 2, 4, 6, 8, 10, 12

Product of first six even numbers $= 2 \times 4 \times 6 \times 8 \times 10 \times 12$

$= 2 \times 2 \times 2 \times 2 \times 3 \times 2 \times 2 \times 2 \times 2 \times 5 \times 2 \times 2 \times 3$

The common factors are 3, 3, 5.

$\therefore$ H.C.F. $= 3 \times 3 \times 5 = 45$.

5. B: $1\frac{1}{2}+\frac{1}{7}\times 10\frac{1}{2}-2\frac{1}{3}\div 1\frac{3}{4}$ of $1\frac{1}{3} = \frac{3}{2}+\frac{1}{7}\times\frac{21}{2}-\frac{7}{3}\div\frac{7}{4}$ of $\frac{4}{3}$

$$=\frac{3}{2}+\frac{3}{2}-\frac{7}{3}\div\frac{7}{3}=\frac{3}{2}+\frac{3}{2}-\frac{7}{3}\times\frac{3}{7}=\frac{3}{2}+\frac{3}{2}-1=\frac{3}{2}+\frac{1}{2}=2.$$

6. A: $$6\frac{1}{2}-\left[5\frac{1}{2}-\left\{4\frac{1}{2}-\left(3\frac{1}{2}-2\overline{\frac{1}{2}-\frac{1}{2}}\right)\right\}\right]$$

$$=\frac{13}{2}-\left[\frac{11}{2}-\left\{\frac{9}{2}-\left(\frac{7}{2}-2\right)\right\}\right]=\frac{13}{2}-\left[\frac{11}{2}-\left\{\frac{9}{2}-\frac{3}{2}\right\}\right]$$

$$=\frac{13}{2}-\left[\frac{11}{2}-3\right]=\frac{13}{2}-\frac{5}{2}=4.$$

7. C: $\frac{1}{2}+\frac{2}{3}/\frac{3}{7}-\frac{1}{6}=\frac{7}{6}/\frac{11}{42}=\frac{7}{6}\times\frac{42}{11}=\frac{49}{11}=4\frac{5}{11}$.

8. C: Let the number be x.

$\therefore \frac{x}{2}+\frac{x}{4}+\frac{x}{8}=28$, or $\frac{7}{x}=28$ $\quad\therefore x=\frac{28\times 8}{7}=32$.

9. D: Work can be finished in 10 days by 20 men

Work can be finished in 1 day by 20×10 men

Work can be finished in 4 days by $\frac{20\times 10}{4}=50$ men.

10. B: 15 men can finish the job in 20 days

25 men can finish the job in $\frac{20\times 15}{25}=12$ days.

1310

GENERAL ENGLISH

Error Detection

Directions : *In the following questions indicate which portion of the sentence marked A, B, C or D contains an error. If there is no error, mark E (Ignore punctuation errors, if any).*

1. They went (A)/to college (B)/ after the rain (C)/stopped (D)/No error (E).
2. She had met (A)/me twice (B)/a week during (C)/the summer holidays (D)/No error (E).
3. Why does he (A)/not attend (B)/ with what (C)/I am saying? (D)/ No error (E).
4. We must (A)/not deviate (B)/of the (C)/right path (D) /No error (E).
5. The temperature (A)/has been (B)/upon (C)/the average recently (D)/No error (E).
6. They have (A)/enjoyed to talk (B)/to her about (C)/old times (D)/No error (E).
7. She made me (A)/to admire her (B)/to admire her for her beauty (C)/and intelligence (D)/ No error (E).
8. She asked her son (A)/if he was (B)/going to (C)/college today (D)/No error (E).
9. The doctor said to (A)/the patient (B)/not to eat (C)/fried things (D)/ No error (E).
10. He is one of (A)/those boys (B)/ who is (C)/physically strong (D)/ No error (E).
11. Those who is (A)/punctual in attendence (B)/will be (C)/well rewarded (D)/No error (E).
12. If your mother (A)/will come again (B)/I shall report (C)/ against you (D)/No error (E).
13. He is very poor (A)/to buy clothes/(B)/for his children (C)/ and wife (D)/No error (E).
14. He is one of (A)/my those friends (B)/ who have achieved (C)/ tremendous success in life (D)/ No error (E).
15. Mumps are (A)/a disease (B)/ with painful swelling (C)/in the neck (D)/No error (E).
16. No sooner (A)/I reached (B)/the station, (C)/than the train started (D)/No error (E).
17. Though he worked (A)/hard, still he (B)/could not pass (C)/the examination (D)/No error (E).
18. She is (A)/too happy (B)/to see you (C)/after so many days (D)/ No error (E).
19. My friend has (A)/been living in London (B)/with her parents (C)/ for the past three years (D)/No error (E).

20. He sat (A)/in the cafe (B)/when I met him (C)/the other day (D)/ No error (E).

21. All human beings (A)/have their roles (B)/to play in (C)/the theatre of this world (D)/No error (E).

22. Though lot of (A)/work has been done (B)/in the country, (C)/it is not enough (D)/No error (E).

23. Education can play (A)/an important role (B)/in creating (C)/communal harmony (D)/No error (E).

24. He felt that (A)/it was no longer necessary (B)/for him to hunt (C)/ down a job (D)/No error (E).

25. I know many men (A)/who had marked (B)/physical courage, but (C)/lacked moral courage (D)/No error (E).

26. Life is dear (A)/to a mute creature (B)/as it is (C)/to a man (D)/No error (E).

27. He walked up (A)/the end of (B)/ the road but (C)/found no flourist (D)/No error (E).

28. He has been (A)/appointed as (B)/President of (C)/the ruling party (D)/No error (E).

29. Fashion is very (A)/fickle, and keeping up (B)/with trends can (C)/be trying and expensive proposition (D)/No error (E).

30. The doctors told the family (A)/ that if the patient (B)/could survive for 24 hours (C)/he will have a chance (D)/No error (E).

31. They took (A)/more time (B)/for reaching there (C)/than we (D)/ No error (E).

32. Neither I nor (A)/she am to (B)/ apply for (C)/this teaching post (D)/No error (E).

33. Ten rupees are (A)/surely not a (B)/big sum to (C)/reckon with (D)/No error (E).

34. The speed of (A)/the sports car (B)/ is greater than the (C)/ other one (D)/ No error (E).

35. This dictionary is (A)/as good if (B)/not better than (C)/the other one (D)/No error (E).

36. None but (A)/those having (B)/ three years' experience (C)/need apply (D)/No error (E).

37. My father got (A)/angry before (B)/I said (C)/a word (D)/No error (E).

38. Tapan is the most (A)/irresponsible person (B)/and does not (C)/care for his belongings (D)/No error (E).

39. In spite of Jaya's (A)/faults my mother (B)/can not help (C)/but like her (D)/No error (E).

40. If she would have (A)/worked hard/(B)/she would have (C)/ passed the examination (D)/No error (E).

41. As the child is not (A)/feeling well, so he (B)/will not be able (C)/to attend the school (D)/No error (E).

42. After he returns (A)/from his official tour (B)/I will go and (C)/see him (D)/No error (E).

43. The maximum (A)/number of persons (B)/a boat (C)/is ten (D)/ No error (E).

44. If the day (A)/after tomorrow (B)/ is Friday, what day (C)/was yesterday (D)/No error (E).

45. Only well read person (A)/can make (B)/proper use (C)/of the English language (D)/No error (E).

46. She is one of (A)/the fashion designers (B)/which have (C)/ become famous (D)/No error (E).

47. Not only Harish (A)/but also Nikhil (B)/is involved in (C)/the social service programme (D)/No error (E).

48. Neither he (A)/or I have (B)/been called (C)/for the interview (D)/ No error (E).

49. We all know (A)/that he is (B)/ wiser (C)/than hardworking (D)/ No error (E).

50. I wish (A)/I was (B)/the Prime Minister (C)/of the country (D)/ No error (E).

51. Too calmly (A)/the hunter took (B)/careful aim (C)/and fired the bullets (D)/No error (E).

52. The court presented (A)/rigorous imprisonment to (B)/all the seven accused (C)/in the bank robbery case (D)/No error (E).

53. Amar was conscious to (A)/all that was (B)/going on (C)/around his place (D)/No error (E).

54. Hurry up (A)/if not (B)/you miss the bus (C)/to school! (D)/No error (E).

55. Till it stops raining (A)/I can not (B)/go to the (C)/market for shopping (D)/No error (E).

56. Only if (A)/I were rich (B)/ enough to buy I can (C)/buy my favourite car (D)/No error (E).

57. The thief mother (A)/pleaded (B)/for her (C)/son's innocence (D)/No error (E).

58. They plan their products (A)/and strategies little by little (B)/rather than (C)/take a long leap (D)/No error (E).

59. The last decade (A)/had witnessed a shift (B)/in business strategies (C)/all about the world (D)/No error (E).

60. Experience, good (A)/analytical skills (B)/and flair for innovation (C)/are called (D)/No error (E).

61. The Worker Union (A)/has given (B)/a written complaint (C)/to the Chairman (D)/No error (E).

62. Five armed miscreants (A)/broke through the house (B)/and decamped with (C)/jewellery and cash (D)/No error (E).

63. He is (A)/not scholar, (B)/he is (C)/an engineer (D)/No error (E).

64. On every (A)/Saturday night (B)/ we go (C)/to cinema (D)/No error (E).

65. I shall (A)/go to the library (B)/ to return books (C)/before the due date (D)/No error (E).

66. Her mother (A)/is an interior designer (B)/and earns thousands of rupees (C)/a month (D)/No error (E).

67. The leaf (A)/is always (B)/the green (C)/in colour (D)/No error (E).

68. The lion (A)/saw his (B)/shade in (C)/the water (D)/No error (E).

69. The child (A)/was walking (B)/ in the (C)/centre of the road (D)/ No error (E).

70. The fire (A)/that broke out (B)/ last night (C)/caused many damage (D)/No error (E).

71 Many people (A)/lost their life (B)/in the train accident (C)/last year (D)/No error (E).

72. The number of (A)/members of the club (B)/are increasing (C)/ day-by-day (D)/No error (E).

73. The colour (A)/of her hairs (B)/ is as black (C)/as coal (D)/No error (E).

74. The news (A)/of her recovery (B)/ from coma (C)/are unbelievable (D)/No error (E).

75. Very little (A)/people attended (B)/the function (C)/yesterday night (D)/No error (E).

76. Our long trip (A)/by train (B)/ was not (C)/at all comfortable (D)/No error (E).

77. All his savings (A)/are kept (B)/ in the locker (C)/of a nearby bank (D)/No error (E).

78. Jaya and me (A)/would rather (B)/ go to (C)/the library (D)/No error (E).

79. Just between (A)/you and I, (B)/ I do not want (C)/to meet him (D)/No error (E).

80. One should be (A)/aware of (B)/ his responsibility (C)/towards elders (D)/No error (E).

81. Divya is (A)/more beautiful (B)/ than (C)/her (D)/No error (E).

82. Rinku (A)/is intelligent (B)/than (C)/I (D)/No error (E).

83. Neither of (A)/the participants (B)/managed to score (C)/the qualifying points (D)/No error (E).

84. Any of (A)/these two dresses (B)/ has been tailored (C)/by the Choicest Tailors (D)/No error (E).

85. Mary has grown (A)/into (B)/a (C)/handsome woman (D)/No error (E).

86. Pinki is (A)/four years (B)/smaller (C)/than Asha (D)/No error (E).

87. The building (A)/on the next block (B)/is several metres (C)/ tall (D)/No error (E).

88. Children must (A)/keep (B)/their teeth (C)/clear (D)/No error (E).

89. All the students (A)/passed the examination (B)/accept the one (C)/who cheated (D)/No error (E).

90. Farther information (A)/on the matter (B)/is eagerly awaited (C)/ by all (D)/No error (E).

91. Mayank has been (A)/sick for (B)/ over (C)/two months (D)/No error (E).

92. He is (A)/my elder brother (B)/ and the man with him (C)/is his best friend (D)/No error (E).

93. Lie this (A)/book on (B)/the shelf (C)/over there (D)/No error (E).

94. He told (A)/me he (B)/would come back (C)/to Delhi (D)/No error (E).

95. This bank (A)/was stolen (B)/last night (C)/by some men (D)/ No error (E).

96. He wanted (A)/to lend a book (B)/from my (C)/best friend (D)/ No error (E).

97. He learnt (A)/me how (B)/to drive (C)/a car (D)/No error (E).

98. Can I (A)/be of (B)/some help (C)/to you? (D)/No error (E).

99. None fortunately (A)/saw us (B)/ there at (C)/the club (D)/No error (E).

100. Unless you (A)/do not (B)/leave early (C)/you can't catch the train (D)/ No error (E).

101. The teacher (A)/came always (B)/ late to (C)/our class (D)/No error (E).

102. Many remote areas (A)/are (B)/ rarely (C)/populated (D)/No error (E).

103. He is living (A)/in Patna (B)/ before he moved (C)/to Delhi (D)/No error (E).

104. I am sorry (A)/for not able to (B)/come to (C)/your Birthday Party (D)/No error (E).

105. Alas! (A)/the train (B)/stops (C)/ suddenly (D)/No error (E).

106. She is (A)/went to (B)/meet her (C)/parents after a long time (D)/ No error (E).

107. The child (A)/picked (B)/the ball (C)/from the ground (D)/No error (E).

108. God helps (A)/them (B)/who help (C)/themselves (D)/ No error (E).

109. Once on a time (A)/there lived (B)/a very wise (C)/and handsome king (D)/No error (E).

110. He thought (A)/that he could (B)/ win the first prize (C)/in the painting competition (D)/No error (E).

111. I refrained (A)/myself (B)/from expressing (C)/my views (D)/No error (E).

112. The official excuse (A)/was that (B)/the fourth general election (C)/was only 4 months aloof (D)/ No error (E).

113. Seven years (A)/was long (B)/a time (C)/to wait (D)/No error (E).

114. There are three major factors (A)/ which a recruiter (B)/must look for (C)/in a candidate (D)/No error (E).

115. Her mother had died (A)/when she was (B)/not yet (C)/two year old (D)/No error (E).

116. The sole objective (A)/of the trust (B)/is the warfare (C)/of mentally retarded children (D)/ No error (E).

117. All you have (A)/been hoping for (B)/will finally (C)/get accomplished (D)/No error (E).

118. Students are (A)/warned to (B)/ pay attention to (C)/their studies (D)/No error (E).

119. I have seen (A)/a beautiful (B)/ girl walking (C)/down the stairs yesterday (D)/No error (E).

120. Once he decided to (A)/build the temple (B)/the search for (C)/a suitable site started (D)/No error (E).

121. The robber was (A)/in poor shape (B)/but his spirit (C)/were not broken (D)/No error (E).

122. Inside a week (A)/I was asked (B)/to report to the Headquarters (C)/on deputation (D)/No error (E).

123. There is (A)/a clear division (B)/of opinion (C)/amidst the political parties (D)/No error (E).

124. The fighting (A)/broke out (B)/ later (C)/a dispute (D)/No error (E).

125. His lawyers (A)/have forbade (B)/ him to say (C)/anything (D)/No error (E).

EXPLANATORY ANSWERS

1. D : It should be 'had stopped'.

2. A : It should be 'she met'.

3. C : It should be 'to what'.

4. C : It should be 'from the'.

5. C : It should be 'above'.

6. B : It should be 'enjoyed talking'.

7. B : It should be 'admire her'.

8. D : It should be 'college that day'.

9. A : It should be 'The doctor advised'.

10. A : It should be 'who are'.

11. A : It should be 'Those who are'.

12. B : It should be 'comes again'.

13. A : It should be 'He is too poor'.

14. E :

15. A : It should be 'Mumps is'.

16. B : It should be 'did I reach'.

17. B : It should be 'hard, he'.

18. B : It should be 'very happy'.

19. D : It should be 'for the last three years'.

20. A : It should be 'He was sitting'.

21. C : It should be 'to play on'.

22. A : It should be 'Though a lot of'.

23. E :

24. D : It should be 'for a job'.

25. A : It should be 'I have known many men'.

26. A : It should be 'Life is as dear'.

27. B : It should be 'to the end of'.

28. B : It should be 'appointed'.

29. D : It should be 'be a trying and expensive proposition'.

30. D : It should be 'he would have a chance'.

31. C : It should be 'to reach there'.

32. B : It should be 'she is to'.

33. A : It should be 'Ten rupees is'.

34. C : It should be 'is greater than that of the'.

35. B : It should be 'as good as if'.

36. E :

37. C : It should be 'I had said'.

38. D : It should be 'take care of his belongings'.

39. D : It should be 'liking her'.

40. A : It should be 'If she had'.

41. B : It should be 'feeling well he'.

42. C : It should be 'I will go to'.

43. C : It should be 'on each boat'.

44. D : It should be 'was it yesterday'.

45. A : It should be 'only a well read person' OR 'only well read persons'.

46. C : It should be 'who have'.

47. E :

48. B : It should be 'nor I have'.

49. C : It should be 'more wise'.

50. B : It should be 'I were'.

51. A : It should be 'very calmly'.

52. A : It should be 'the court awarded'.

53. A : It should be 'Amar was conscious of'.

54. B : It should be 'lest'.

55. A : It should be 'Unless the rain stops'.

56. C : It should be 'I could'.

57. A : It should be 'The thief's mother'.

58. D : It should be 'taking a long leap'.

59. D : It should be 'all over the world'.

60. D : It should be 'are called for'.

61. A : It should be 'The Workers' Union'.

62. B : It should be 'broke into the house'.

63. B : It should be 'not a scholar'.

64. D : It should be 'to the cinema'.

65. C : It should be 'to return the books'.

66. E :

67. C : It should be 'green'.

68. C : It should be 'image in'

69. D : It should be 'middle of the road'.

70. D : It should be 'caused much damage'.

71. B : It should be 'lost their lives'.

72. C : It should be 'is increasing'.

73. B : It should be 'of her hair'.

74. D : It should be 'is unbeliev-able'.

75. A : It should be ' very few'.

76. A : It should be 'Our long journey'.

77. E :

78. A : It should be 'Jaya and I'.

79. B : It should be 'you and me'.

80. C : It should be 'one's responsi-bility'.

81. D : It should be 'she'.

82. B : It should be 'is more intelligent'.

83. A : It should be 'None of'.

84. A : It should be 'Either of'.

85. D : It should be 'beaufiful woman'.

86. C : It should be 'younger'.

87. D : It should be 'high'.

88. D : It should be 'clean'.

89. C : It should be 'except the one'.

90. A : It should be 'Further information'.

91. B : It should be 'ill for'.

92. E :

93. A : It should be 'Lay this'.

94. B : It should be 'me that he'.

95. B : It should be 'was robbed'.

96. B : It should be 'to borrow a book'.

97. A : It should be 'He taught'.

98. E :

99. A : It should be 'Fortunately no one'.

100. B : 'do not' is not needed in the sentence.

101. C : It should be 'always came'.

102. C : It should be 'scarcely'.

103. A : It should be 'He had been living'.

104. B : It should be 'for not being able to'.

105. C : It should be 'had stopped'.

106. B : It should be 'going to'.

107. B : It should be 'picked up'.

108. B : It should be 'those'.

109. A : It should be 'Once upon a time'.

110. E :

111. B : 'myself' is not needed in the sentence.

112. D : It should be 'was only four months away'.

113. B : It should be 'was too long'.

114. B : It should be 'that a recruiter'.

115. A : It should be 'Her mother died'.

116. C : It should be 'is the welfare'.

117. A : It should be 'All that you have'.

118. B : It should be 'advised to'.

119. B : It should be 'I saw'.

120. E :

121. D : It should be 'was not broken'.

122. A : It should be 'Within a week'.

123. D : It should be 'among the political parties'.

124. C : It should be 'after'.

125. B : It should be 'have forbidden'.

Synonyms

Directions : *In each questions below, out of the four alternatives, choose the one which best expresses the meaning of the given word.*

1. Odious
A. unpleasant B. dirty
C. silly D. constant

2. Hybrid
A. clean B. cross
C. superb D. serious

3. Detract
A. to redo B. delete
C. diminish D. change

4. Connoisseur
A. trustworthy B. expert
C. cheat D. corrupt

5. Luminous
A. quiet B. unbound
C. pressed D. glowing

6. Fractious
A. irritable B. shattered
C. partitioned D. unfair

7. Wanton
A. strict B. desired
C. playful D. unwanted

8. Spurious
A. genuine
B. false
C. readily available
D. outstanding

9. Verity
A. truth B. change
C. wholesome D. differ

10. Spendthrift
A. emptied B. consumer
C. worried D. wasteful

11. Vestibule
A. directed
B. investment
C. lobby
D. idling

12. Gullible
A. hungry B. foolish
C. insane D. cheeky

13. Bedeck
A. get off B. worker
C. decorate D. transfer

14. Infringe
A. filter B. disobey
C. boundary D. shrink

15. Adjourn
A. delay B. trip
C. bind D. court

16. Wobble
A. elastic B. heated
C. tremble D. jumpy

17. Drudgery
A. magic B. treatment
C. doubtful D. labour

18. Fugitive
A. crucial B. stormy
C. unstable D. mature

19. Profane
A. impure B. proud
C. survey D. certified

20. Niche
A. cost B. place
C. mark D. grip

21. Quirk
A. easy B. fancy
C. dumb D. recall

22. Mandatory
A. human B. heroic
C. required D. polite

23. Foster
A. cultivate B. dedicate
C. train D. achieve

24. Antiquity
A. age B. old
C. ancient D. thought

25. Complacent
A. confused B. unseen
C. thick D. pleased

26. Erudite
A. harsh B. strain
C. quick D. learned

27. Zenith
A. modest B. height
C. tussle D. shameful

28. Grimy
A. unclean B. shiny
C. greased D. slippery

29. Kindle
A. soft B. pity
C. fire D. make

30. Tedious
A. lively B. minute
C. tiring D. single

31. Yoke
A. embryo B. shout
C. desire D. bond

32. Jocular
A. faulty B. funny
C. idiotic D. uneven

33. Nefarious
A. evil B. friendly
C. ignorant D. many

34. Incur
A. gain B. arrive
C. speak D. force

35. Resolve
A. cancel B. total
C. decide D. balance

36. Overcast
A. announce B. project
C. dull D. carry

37. Vouch
A. rest B. certify
C. cheque D. purse

38. Supple
A. dark B. silly
C. agree D. elastic

39. Jeopardy
A. fun B. action
C. merry D. danger

40. Fidelity
A. manner B. faith
C. story D. charge

41. Zone
A. point B. issue
C. belt D. object

42. Decoy
A. spy B. ruin
C. trap D. fact

43. Amplify
A. boost B. remove
C. test D. value

44. Random
A. casual B. will
C. order D. limit

45. Extol
A. ending B. widen
C. force D. celebrate

46. Thorny
A. sharp
B. frightening
C. thorough
D. disable

47. Rugged
A. matted B. rough
C. strong D. grand

48. Forage
A. aged B. scare
C. food D. weak

49. Hoodwink
A. cheat B. viewer
C. honest D. decent

50. Smother
A. plain B. envelop
C. giggle D. hurry

Directions : *In the questions that follow, a set of three words is given with different meanings of a certain word. Choose that word from the options given after each set.*

51. Absurd, Droll, Comic
A. dainty B. insane
C. jocular D. stormy

52. Gracious, Daring, Manful
A. clanger B. gallivant
C. gallant D. wager

53. Lovable, Enchanting, Cuddly
A. beloved B. amiable
C. sonorous D. forage

54. Overwhelm, Crush, Destroy
A. overdue B. oppress
C. downfall D. engulf

55. Decode, Simplify, Interpret
A. observe
B. calculate
C. erase
D. translate

56. Mark, Note, Sign
A. symptom B. issue
C. letter D. order

57. Relish, Smack, Swallow
A. hurt B. praise
C. taste D. scold

58. Dreadful, Hellish, Titanic
A. uneven
B. monstrous
C. difficult
D. hated

59. Reduce, Cheaper, Exhaust
A. finish B. burn
C. wipe D. depress

60. Fancy, Request, Desire
A. covet B. worry
C. haste D. caution

61. Rough, Crude, Sharp
A. edged B. harsh
C. uneven D. witty

62. Devalue, Corrupt, Weaken
A. unwell B. alter
C. adulterate D. praise

63. Fence, Defend, Protect
A. barricade B. curtail
C. storm D. reserve

64. Graceful, Tender, Refined
A. pure B. lively
C. elegant D. legal

65. Lodge, Abide, Dwell
A. rule B. reside
C. dominate D. complain

66. Credit, Dignity, Glory
A. crown B. decent
C. mannerly D. honour

67. System, Method, Fashion
A. technique B. famous
C. unitary D. ability

68. Titan, Huge, Jumbo
A. time B. ample
C. fast D. gaint

69. Absurd, Amazing, Wonderful
A. silly
B. handsome
C. incredible
D. praise

70. Distant, Aloof, Careless
A. lazy
B. indifferent
C. away
D. secondary

71. Die, Expire, Vanish
A. perish B. last
C. want D. due

72. Thoughtful, Grave, Serious
A. ideal B. sacred
C. angry D. pensive

73. Sum, Number, Amount
A. whole B. count
C. quantity D. finance

74. Legal, Official, Lawful
A. court B. justice
C. valid D. rule

75. Insane, Dumb, Crazy
A. bright B. idiotic
C. clown D. wise

76. Reign, Empire, Kingdom
A. sovereignty
B. command
C. destruction
D. union

77. Nurse, Feed, Attend
A. nourish B. consume
C. present D. protect

78. Daily, Register, Gazette
A. journal
B. regular
C. attendance
D. always

79. Friendly, Warm, Cheerful
A. manly B. tepid
C. excited D. cordial

80. Cry, Moan, Sigh
A. wail B. groan
C. lease D. clamp

81. Imitate, Phoney, Counterfeit
A. mimic B. double
C. constitute D. forge

82. Creation, Inception, Source
A. genesis B. beget
C. sculpture D. trace

83. Protege, Aspirant, Entrant
A. nominee B. scholar
C. orator D. disposed

84. Force, Compel, Bind
A. solder B. unite
C. oblige D. activate

85. Derision, Contempt, Despite
A. ladle B. deface
C. berate D. scorn

86. Unfruitful, Barren, Unproductive
A. wasted B. marooned
C. pilfered D. sterile

87. Vanity, Arrogance, Pride
A. maturity B. exclusive
C. conceit D. terse

88. Douse, Satiate, Cool
A. freeze B. simplify
C. quench D. relax

89. Candid, Artless, Ingenuous
A. drab B. naive
C. fadded D. cheap

90. Guide, Symptom, Clue
A. measure B. index
C. effect D. aide

91. Baron, Mogul, Magnate
A. lure B. princely
C. tycoon D. genre

92. Mesmerize, Spellbind, Fascinate
A. hypnotize B. scrape
C. remember D. attract

93. Custom, Style, Trend
A. vogue B. tradition
C. lively D. fancy

94. Juvenile, Callow, Unfledged
A. shrewd
B. inexperienced
C. young
D. cunning

95. Struggle, Tussle, Scuffle
A. toil B. wrestle
C. debate D. error

96. Spiritual, Heavenly, Divine
A. learned
B. celestial
C. mythological
D. scholistic

97. Provide, Bestow, Reveal
A. convey B. engage
C. clear D. furnish

98. Husky, Gruff, Croaky
A. revile B. tactless
C. hoarse D. evident

99. Expression, Remark, Locution
A. distinct B. speech
C. phrase D. appeal

100. Contract, Guarantee, Pledge
A. undertake
B. soothe
C. offer
D. appropriate

101. Gauze, Swathe, Plaster
A. passage B. clean
C. fortify D. bandage

102. Opulence, Treasure, Prosperity
A. attainment
B. saving
C. fortune
D. support

103. Panic, Startle, Unnerve
A. dread B. release
C. corner D. alarm

104. Remove, Abstract, Recall
A. erase
B. unbound
C. remember
D. withdraw

105. Free, Frank, Direct
A. available
B. outspoken
C. orderly
D. approachable

106. Evildoer, Wrongdoer, Transgressor
A. corrupt B. killer
C. malefactor D. slave

107. Cripple, Hack, Disfigure
A. mutilate B. exercise
C. decrease D. beat

108. Baffle, Confuse, Bewilder
A. blend B. surprise
C. puzzle D. madden

109. Delight, Pleasure, Comfort
A. please B. luxury
C. happiness D. deceit

110. Slit, Gash, Notch
A. untie B. separate
C. stimulate D. incision

111. Core, Grain, Marrow
A. centre B. reality
C. kernel D. solid

112. Bolt, Lock, Hasp
A. rough B. latch
C. bound D. close

113. Notification, Statement, Account
A. presentation B. reminder
C. bulletin D. logic

114. Scrutinize, Investigate, Analyse
A. violate B. promote
C. explore D. exhibit

115. Precise, Methodical, Efficient
A. perfect B. calculated
C. systematic D. accurate

116. Sunny, Joyful, Debonair
A. Showy B. rampart
C. brisk D. buoyant

117. Academic, Speculative, Theoretical
A. hypothetical
B. educative
C. overwrought
D. unanimous

118. Confound, Dishevel, Tangle
A. jumble B. exchange
C. disobey D. affix

119. Paroxysm, Spasm, Outbreak
A. agony B. outburst
C. outset D. entry

120. Murmur, Breathe, Rustle
A. disturb B. whisper
C. inhale D. noise

ANSWERS

1	**2**	**3**	**4**	**5**	**6**	**7**	**8**	**9**	**10**
A	B	C	B	D	A	C	B	A	D
11	**12**	**13**	**14**	**15**	**16**	**17**	**18**	**19**	**20**
C	B	C	B	A	C	D	C	A	B
21	**22**	**23**	**24**	**25**	**26**	**27**	**28**	**29**	**30**
B	C	A	A	D	D	B	A	C	C
31	**32**	**33**	**34**	**35**	**36**	**37**	**38**	**39**	**40**
D	B	A	A	C	C	B	D	D	B
41	**42**	**43**	**44**	**45**	**46**	**47**	**48**	**49**	**50**
C	C	A	A	D	A	B	C	A	B
51	**52**	**53**	**54**	**55**	**56**	**57**	**58**	**59**	**60**
C	C	B	D	D	A	C	B	D	A

61	**62**	**63**	**64**	**65**	**66**	**67**	**68**	**69**	**70**
B	C	A	C	B	D	A	D	C	B
71	**72**	**73**	**74**	**75**	**76**	**77**	**78**	**79**	**80**
A	D	C	C	C	A	A	A	D	B
81	**82**	**83**	**84**	**85**	**86**	**87**	**88**	**89**	**90**
D	A	A	C	D	D	C	C	B	B
91	**92**	**93**	**94**	**95**	**96**	**97**	**98**	**99**	**100**
C	A	A	C	B	B	D	C	C	A
101	**102**	**103**	**104**	**105**	**106**	**107**	**108**	**109**	**110**
D	C	D	D	B	C	A	C	B	D
111	**112**	**113**	**114**	**115**	**116**	**117**	**118**	**119**	**120**
C	B	C	C	C	D	A	A	B	B

Antonyms

Directions : *In each questions below, out of the four alternatives, choose the word that is most nearly the opposite in meaning to the given word.*

1. Transient
A. passing B. brief
C. lucid D. eternal

2. Effective
A. potent B. able
C. futile D. sharp

3. Oust
A. spoil B. renew
C. induct D. outdo

4. Sustain
A. rule B. uphold
C. impose D. resist

5. Lofty
A. sublime B. flat
C. shrill D. terse

6. Venerable
A. similar B. young
C. accurate D. wise

7. Anticipation
A. surprise B. foresee
C. revival D. assurance

8. Embellish
A. obscure B. enrich
C. deface D. lavish

9. Deter
A. circulate B. induce
C. hamper D. encourage

10. Luscious
A. shining B. tasty
C. eerie D. sour

11. Revenue
A. income B. outlay
C. construct D. repeal

12. Tangible
A. independent B. unreal
C. material D. salient

13. Fiendish
A. corrupt B. angelic
C. valuable D. reverent

14. Headstrong
A. complaisant
B. mastermind
C. unorthodox
D. ponderous

15. Nebulous
A. clear B. confused
C. careful D. central

16. Questionable
A. subjective B. disputed
C. certain D. deductive

17. Slender
A. silky B. grim
C. stout D. coarse

18. Upright
A. inferior B. crooked
C. wrong D. engage

19. Tyrant
A. quiet B. accord
C. kind D. unjust

20. Sporadic
A. genuine B. blithe
C. peculiar D. frequent

21. Blemish
A. acclaim B. spotless
C. advance D. retard

22. Extravagant
A. frank B. credible
C. partial D. stingy

23. Stretch
A. prevail B. fondle
C. object D. curtail

24. Persecute
A. sanction B. patronize
C. authorise D. transact

25. Eternal
A. finite B. mystic
C. perpetual D. disjunct

26. Deviate
A. obscure B. magnify
C. persist D. restore

27. Vicious
A. moral B. chaste
C. faulty D. peevish

28. Subtle
A. artful B. coarse
C. delicate D. fragile

29. Ferocious
A. prolific B. strong
C. modest D. wild

30. Pertinent
A. relevant B. graphic
C. unfit D. prompt

31. Mighty
A. frail B. godly
C. potent D. uneasy

32. Onerous
A. exacting B. crushing
C. facile D. arduous

33. Transact
A. afflict B. loiter
C. waver D. persist

34. Mourn
A. maim B. deplore
C. revel D. truncate

35. Claim
A. quote B. waive
C. lively D. bright

36. Solemn
A. sedate B. cordial
C. artless D. vulgar

37. Zealot
A. devoted B. fickle
C. fanatic D. highest

38. Bewilder
A. astonish B. damage
C. enlighten D. distrust

39. Contempt
A. grace B. scorn
C. share D. accord

40. Hypocrisy
A. flattery B. charm
C. deceit D. honesty

41. Protract
A. refute B. clarify
C. curtail D. conceal

42. Uncouth
A. clownish B. attractive
C. unbiased D. reliable

43. Scarcity
A. pleasure B. galore
C. retrieval D. amass

44. Rejoice
A. neglect B. drain
C. obtuse D. lament

45. Partake
A. whole B. allot
C. divide D. sever

46. Just
A. unlawful B. partial
C. discreet D. fraction

47. Myth
A. legend B. story
C. fable D. fact

48. Unanimity
A. unity B. agreement
C. discord D. deception

49. Ghastly
A. inconstant B. spectral
C. gratified D. corporeal

50. Loathe
A. undress B. prefer
C. compromise D. dominate

ANSWERS

1	**2**	**3**	**4**	**5**	**6**	**7**	**8**	**9**	**10**
D	C	C	C	B	B	C	C	D	D
11	**12**	**13**	**14**	**15**	**16**	**17**	**18**	**19**	**20**
B	B	B	A	A	C	C	B	C	D
21	**22**	**23**	**24**	**25**	**26**	**27**	**28**	**29**	**30**
B	D	D	B	A	C	A	B	C	C
31	**32**	**33**	**34**	**35**	**36**	**37**	**38**	**39**	**40**
A	C	B	C	B	D	B	C	A	D
41	**42**	**43**	**44**	**45**	**46**	**47**	**48**	**49**	**50**
C	B	B	D	B	A	D	C	D	B

One Word Substitution

Directions : *Choose the most suitable 'one word' for each of the following expressions given below.*

1. The belief that good must prevail over evil in the end
A. Optimism
B. Sophtism
C. Truism
D. Radicalism

2. Hater of women
A. Misochist
B. Misogamist
C. Misogynist
D. Misanthropist

3. That cannot be seen through
A. Transparent
B. Translucent
C. Evanscent
D. Opaque

4. One who will never cease to exist
A. Immoral
B. Impassable
C. Immortal
D. Impassive

5. Custom or condition of marriage to more than one person at a time
A. Bigamy
B. Polygamy
C. Monogamy
D. Matriomony

6. Habit of walking in sleep
A. Sophtism
B. Somnambulism
C. Scepticism
D. Somniloquism

7. Person who talks too much or too often only about himself
A. Optimist
B. Critic
C. Egoist
D. Stoic

8. A summary or outline of a book
A. Precis
B. manuscript
C. Preface
D. Synopsis

9. Neat and smart in dress and appearance
A. Shabby B. Spruce
C. Rustic D. Sophist

10. Arrangement of events according to dates or times of occurrence
A. Chronology
B. Catalogue
C. Chronicle
D. Choreography

11. A person who has no means of livelihood
A. Beggar B. Refugee
C. Convict D. Pauper

12. A post supporting the handrail of a staircase
A. Banister B. Barrage
C. Barrister D. Barouche

13. A person who firmly believes that all the events are decided by fate

A. Forte B. Florist

C. Fugitive D. Fatalist

14. Easily cheated or duped

A. Naive B. Deceived

C. Gullible D. Forged

15. Things that can be easily set on fire

A. Inflammable B. Sparkler

C. Fiery D. Rabid

16. Instrument for testing the quality of milk

A. Altimeter

B. Lactometer

C. Barometer

D. Chronometer

17. A person who believes in the existence of God

A. Atheist B. Baptist

C. Theist D. Cynicist

18. Of, or like a cat

A. Furry B. Agile

C. Feline D. Canine

19. Extermination of a race or community by mass murder

A. Arson B. Coup

C. Pilferage D. Genocide

20. Given, done or obtained without payment

A. Award

B. Endowment

C. Gratuity

D. Grant

21. A cardboard box for holding goods

A. Carton B. Trunk

C. Chest D. Package

22. Person relying on experience and observation

A. Examiner

B. Eccentric

C. Empiric

D. Executioner

23. Group of lions

A. Shoal B. Pride

C. Flock D. Pack

24. An exceptionally brilliant or successful young person

A. Genius B. Maestro

C. Intellect D. Whiz-kid

25. Ruler who has absolute authority to run the government

A. Monarch

B. Dictator

C. Bureaucrat

D. Theocrat

26. Agreement during a war or battle to stop fighting for a time

A. Alliance

B. Treaty

C. Armistice

D. Concordant

27. A person who eats human flesh

A. Cannibal B. Obese

C. Dossier D. Laggard

28. An illusion or hope that cannot be realized

A. Mirage

B. Fantasy

C. Misconception

D. Perception

29. Something outdated or no longer in use or fashion

A. Absolute B. Obsolete

C. Retarded D. Regale

30. Complete failure to reach an agreement to settle a quarrel or grievance
A. Mishap B. Wreck
C. Omission D. Deadlock

31. Person who eats too much
A. Famished B. Glutton
C. Hungry D. Starved

32. Contrary to law
A. Inimical B. Adverse
C. Illegal D. Precept

33. A criminal who has often been in prison
A. Jailbird B. Jailor
C. Prisoner D. Jockey

34. Person using more words than needed
A. Gullible B. Talkative
C. Verbose D. Extrovert

35. Building where grain is stored
A. Stockyard B. Modicum
C. Iota D. Granary

36. A woman head of a family or tribe
A. Matriarch B. Patriarch
C. Frateral D. Ladybird

37. Crime of killing a small babe
A. Insensate
B. Infanticide
C. Innuendo
D. Infidel

38. Person of good appearance and manners
A. Debonair B. Adonis
C. Courteous D. Social

39. A change which is proposed or made to a rule, regulation etc.
A. Enhancement
B. Reform
C. Clarification
D. Amendment

40. A dull, slow or mindless person
A. Insane B. Zombie
C. Deranged D. Lunatic

41. A place where people often meet
A. Rendezvous
B. Club
C. Joint
D. Association

42. Reaching a conclusion from two statements
A. Reasoning
B. Comparison
C. Syllogism
D. Deduction

43. Being the only one of its sort
A. Specimen
B. Sample
C. Unique
D. Outstanding

44. Exposed to being attacked or harmed
A. Volatile
B. Vulnerable
C. Versatile
D. Voluptuary

45. Egg laying animals that creep or crawl
A. Reptiles B. Creepers
C. Primers D. Insects

46. A person who is free from national prejudices and feels at home in any country of the world
A. Orthodox
B. Conservative
C. Crusader
D. Cosmopolitan

47. Speech delivered without previous thought or preparation
A. Oration B. Jargon
C. Extempore D. Harangue

48. Irrelevant talk about God and sacred things
A. Sacrilege
B. Blasphemy
C. Profanity
D. Oblation

49. Company of persons making a journey together for safety
A. Travellers
B. Tourists
C. Campaign
D. Caravan

50. Animals feeding on flesh or other animal matter
A. Carnivore B. Omnivore
C. Barbarian D. Cannibal

ANSWERS

1	**2**	**3**	**4**	**5**	**6**	**7**	**8**	**9**	**10**
A	C	D	C	B	B	C	D	B	A
11	**12**	**13**	**14**	**15**	**16**	**17**	**18**	**19**	**20**
D	A	D	C	A	B	C	C	D	C
21	**22**	**23**	**24**	**25**	**26**	**27**	**28**	**29**	**30**
A	C	B	D	B	C	A	A	B	D
31	**32**	**33**	**34**	**35**	**36**	**37**	**38**	**39**	**40**
B	C	A	C	D	A	B	A	D	B
41	**42**	**43**	**44**	**45**	**46**	**47**	**48**	**49**	**50**
A	C	C	B	A	D	C	B	D	A

Idioms and Phrases

Directions : *From the alternatives given below each idiom/phrase select the one that best brings out the meaning of the idiom/phrase.*

1. By leaps and bounds
A. majority B. rapidly
C. easily D. fairly

2. In a daze
A. in bright light
B. ill and bedridden
C. facing a problem
D. confused and shocked

3. A broken reed
A. a broken affair
B. an unreliable person
C. discord
D. an easy task

4. Round the corner
A. curved
B. drift
C. easily available
D. not far off

5. A black sheep
A. a person of bad reputation
B. a breed of sheep
C. a dark room
D. unpleasant feeling

6. To cross one's mind
A. to get confused
B. to occur
C. to create tension
D. to tell a lie

7. Yeoman's service
A. render help
B. poor service
C. slavery
D. late delivery of goods

8. To lead a dog's life
A. to live in a small house
B. to behave inhumanly
C. to be loyal to others
D. to live in misery

9. An early bird
A. one who catches worms
B. a cock or hen
C. a lucky person
D. an early riser

10. A fool's errand
A. to work very slowly
B. to waste time
C. a useless task
D. a silly mistake

11. Fair and square
A. give reason
B. honest
C. smart person
D. a white cube

12. A feather in one's cap
A. a hole in the cap
B. an achievement
C. a light object
D. a dirty cap

13. A queer fish
A. a strange person

B. a dead fish
C. a secret plan
D. biased person

14. Flying colours
A. victory
B. modern art
C. rainbow
D. good news

15. Gift of the gab
A. well learned
B. an unexpected visitor
C. fluency in speech
D. a costly gift

16. Game for anything
A. prefer playing games to studies
B. full of life
C. easily impressed
D. a good player

17. To give a slip
A. to fall
B. to go unnoticed
C. to bunk the class
D. to escape

18. A white collar worker
A. a person doing a labourer's work
B. a person doing an officer's job
C. a person in white uniform
D. a foreign dignatory

19. By and large
A. expanded
B. without any trouble
C. an easy situation
D. in general

20. Dress someone up
A. get ready for a party
B. prepare to do something
C. disguise
D. plan

21. Let someone down
A. disappoint
B. push away
C. humiliate
D. say goodbye

22. To take after
A. to chase
B. to resemble
C. to follow
D. to walk behind

23. Fret and fume
A. shout loudly
B. burn a large fire
C. start a fight
D. show angry impatience

24. Practise what you preach
A. become a teacher
B. do what is right
C. do what one advises others to do
D. follow the leader

25. The top brass
A. a rich dealer of brass product
B. high ranking military officer
C. good trumpet player
D. of great value or importance

26. The ins and outs
A. entry and exit gates
B. secret information
C. the good and the bad
D. the full details

27. Hit the jackpot
A. have a great success
B. slap a foolish person
C. win in a gamble
D. hit the target

28. A casanova
A. to have fun
B. a sincere wish
C. an unfaithful lover
D. an unexpected good news

29. Straight from the horse's mouth
A. very outspoken
B. most powerful
C. heart warming speech
D. first hand news

30. To set forth
A. to impress
B. to express
C. to follow
D. to clear all doubts

31. Lay off
A. dismiss temporarily
B. to fall asleep
C. feel tired
D. postpone

32. To fall in with
A. form a group
B. work together
C. to decline
D. to agree to

33. Bring round
A. persuade
B. encircle
C. trap
D. draw a circle

34. Yawning gap
A. parted lips
B. a wide gap
C. on the other side
D. more than needed

35. A word of honour
A. an award
B. a sincere promise
C. a high military rank
D. an effort to win

36. Even walls have ears
A. holes in walls
B. very poor condition
C. there are spies around
D. face trouble

37. A stepping stone
A. a rung of ladder
B. to finish a given task
C. source of success
D. an opportunity

38. To smell a rat
A. to have a suspicion
B. foul smell
C. to be scared of
D. to sense trouble

39. Turning point
A. a busy crossroad
B. a point of change for the better
C. an important factor
D. a kind of bend

40. One of these days
A. recently B. recent past
C. finally D. shortly

41. To see eye to eye with
A. to cause a fight
B. to reason out
C. to get friendly with
D. to agree

42. Red tape
A. power
B. official delay
C. danger sign
D. unlucky person

43. To be in a saddle
A. to be in control

B. to ride a horse
C. to be in trouble
D. to be very excited

44. Under the table
A. unknown
B. secretly
C. well hidden
D. not in view

45. A rainy day
A. a time of trouble
B. the day of the onset of monsoon
C. a day when it rained continuously
D. the time to have fun

46. To put on
A. to mimic
B. to stay on
C. to offer for sale
D. to wear

47. To hold on
A. catch on to something
B. to save
C. to let someone wait
D. to continue

48. To read between the lines
A. to correct the errors
B. to see the hidden meaning
C. to study hard
D. to discover something new

49. Look after
A. to overlook
B. to ignore
C. to attend to
D. to take charge

50. Tom, Dick and Harry
A. three musketeers
B. many sided
C. ordinary person
D. three different pairs

ANSWERS

1	**2**	**3**	**4**	**5**	**6**	**7**	**8**	**9**	**10**
B	D	B	D	A	B	A	D	D	C
11	**12**	**13**	**14**	**15**	**16**	**17**	**18**	**19**	**20**
B	B	A	A	C	B	D	B	D	C
21	**22**	**23**	**24**	**25**	**26**	**27**	**28**	**29**	**30**
A	B	D	C	B	D	A	C	D	B
31	**32**	**33**	**34**	**35**	**36**	**37**	**38**	**39**	**40**
A	D	A	B	B	C	C	A	B	D
41	**42**	**43**	**44**	**45**	**46**	**47**	**48**	**49**	**50**
D	B	A	B	A	D	D	B	C	C

Mis-Spelt Words

Directions : *In each question below, groups of four words are given. In each group, one word is not spelt correctly. Find this mis-spelt word.*

1. A. bouquet B. eternal
C. criple D. blurred

2. A. lodge B. rigime
C. inhabit D. conduit

3. A. hostile B. entrence
C. fervent D. typically

4. A. terminator B. border
C. censer D. juicer

5. A. ruffian B. distortion
C. brighten D. comedean

6. A. conterary B. persuade
C. nostalgia D. proficient

7. A. spectators B. condemn
C. priority D. analisis

8. A. percolate
B. delimma
C. fierce
D. overwhelm

9. A. fabricate B. ethical
C. optimist D. armistise

10. A. absente B. genuine
C. heartily D. agitated

11. A. allot B. occurance
C. faithful D. nativity

12. A. contradict B. realistick
C. abstract D. brutal

13. A. profitable B. construct
C. salwage D. authentic

14. A. engredients B. personal
C. ruthless D. discrete

15. A. temprate B. virtuous
C. fanfare D. smoulder

16. A. idling B. consumer
C. protrution D. oblique

17. A. illegal B. condensed
C. culpable D. boundry

18. A. prespire B. dribble
C. acutely D. wither

19. A. stagnant B. profession
C. quater D. inverted

20. A. ettiquete B. intrinsic
C. probable D. crusading

21. A. reciprocate
B. dehidration
C. tournament
D. circumvent

22. A. evacuate B. converge
C. dissembark D. elegance

23. A. exemplary
B. submerging
C. cooperative
D. managable

24. A. inundate B. smoulder
C. stimulus D. generosity

25. A. dexterous B. kernel
C. pagentry D. novice

26. A. wrestler B. numeros C. festivity D. baptism

27. A. remorseful B. journalism C. gurilla D. youngster

28. A. filanthropy B. ravenous C. detergent D. unforeseen

29. A. inoccupied B. ensure C. anatomy D. unwary

30. A. luminous B. abhorrent C. vibrasion D. wretched

ANSWERS (WITH CORRECT SPELLING)

1. C : cripple
2. B : regime
3. B : entrance
4. C : censor
5. D : comedian
6. A : contrary
7. D : analysis
8. B : dilemma
9. D : armistice
10. A : absentee
11. B : occurrence
12. B : realistic
13. C : salvage
14. A : ingredients
15. A : temperate
16. C : protrusion
17. D : boundary
18. A : perspire
19. C : quarter
20. A : etiquette
21. B : dehydration
22. C : disembark
23. D : manageable
24. D : generosity
25. C : pageantry
26. B : numerous
27. C : guerilla
28. A : philanthropy
29. A : unoccupied
30. C : vibration

Word Usage

Directions : *In each question below, sentences are given with blanks to be filled in with appropriate words. From the given four alternatives, choose the correct word which meaningfully completes the given sentence.*

1. The suspect was too ..... to admit that he had committed the crime.
   A. nervous B. clever
   C. shy D. obstinate
2. The patient's condition would become ..... if timely medication is not given.
   A. pathetic B. deadly
   C. serious D. grave
3. He was ..... of his valuables.
   A. cheated B. snatched
   C. looted D. deprived
4. The child picked up the toy which ..... on the ground.
   A. laid B. lay
   C. lying D. was lie
5. I ..... a certain grace about the way she carried herself.
   A. marked B. found
   C. noticed D. assumed
6. The fact is that men in uniform make a ..... audience.
   A. distinguished
   B. cheerful
   C. encouraging
   D. experimental
7. Try to be ..... about your objectives.
   A. clear B. confused
   C. worried D. ignorant
8. One evening, all the children in the family ..... to go to a picnic.
   A. fought B. panicked
   C. decided D. needed
9. High pitched noises ..... the reader's mind.
   A. crackled B. disturbed
   C. dampened D. crossed
10. After the control, the ..... winner celebrated by partying with her friends.
    A. eager B. solitary
    C. expected D. radiant
11. Medication will also be ..... at the time of examination.
    A. advised
    B. made available
    C. prescribed
    D. distributed
12. Too much work will ..... your energy.
    A. drain B. boost
    C. enhance D. filter
13. The water ..... in a silver stream down on mountain slope.
    A. seeped B. rushed
    C. flowed D. drained
14. The film was ..... the 'Best Film' for its magnificent portrayal of the complex and moving emotions.
    A. described B. directed
    C. adjudged D. projected

15. He will not study ..... he is compelled to do so.
A. unless B. till
C. since D. until

16. Women have ..... strongly in our freedom movements during the Civil Disobedience Movement in 1930.
A. focussed
B. participated
C. protested
D. improved

17. The ..... he eats, the fatter he becomes.
A. less B. most
C. more D. lots

18. I felicitated him on his grand ..... at the Defence Service Examination.
A. party
B. success
C. authority
D. appointment

19. He ..... your helping him to do the sums.
A. criticises
B. praises
C. accomplishes
D. appreciates

20. The word 'caste' is ..... from the Portuguese word 'casta' signifying breed, race or kind.
A. extracted B. imposed
C. derived D. taken

21. She walked past us with her ..... in the air.
A. chin B. attention
C. nose D. hands

22. He ..... his back on his friends when he became a celebrity.
A. forced B. showed
C. detained D. turned

23. That multinational firm seeks to ..... engineers from all walks of disciplines to its various departments.
A. offer B. recruit
C. lay off D. impress

24. We all believe that change is the ..... of nature.
A. law B. force
C. habit D. part

25. Only ..... will you find a girl that combines both looks and is good at other things.
A. rarely B. often
C. naturally D. in films

26. There are a few parents, who can ..... to send their children to boarding schools.
A. reason out B. admit
C. afford D. try

27. His achievements in the field of social welfare are .....
A. creditable
B. exceptional
C. underestimated
D. manifold

28. The palatial building was ..... for the wedding occassion.
A. ignited
B. enlightened
C. lighted
D. illuminated

29. This is the ..... of the two questions.
A. hardest
B. unexpected
C. complex
D. easier

30. The court has ..... the final judgement.
A. decided B. awaited
C. examined D. passed

31. Nearly fifty countries are expected to ..... in the trade fair this year.
A. collaborate B. participate
C. franchise D. unite

32. The actor's fine performance undoubtedly deserved a great ..... from the audience.
A. applause B. criticism
C. proposal D. reward

33. The army offers exciting career ..... for the adventurous young people.
A. promotions B. perks
C. providents D. prospects

34. The model's face was ..... with heavy make-up.
A. coated B. painted
C. glued D. shaded

35. India is the largest ..... of films in the world.
A. producer B. maker
C. inventor D. creator

36. The naughty child was ..... by his mother.
A. loved B. defended
C. rebuked D. threatened

37. Even after hours of discussion the Board failed to reach a ..... decision.
A. biased
B. unanimous
C. unique
D. perplexed

38. He refused to sell that dress unless the price offered was .....
A. right B. true
C. correct D. realistic

39. Women in rural areas are capable of progressive thinking and have the ..... for viable social participation.
A. potential B. heart
C. knowledge D. courage

40. The unemployment rate in the country is ..... and ample measures should be taken to solve the problem.
A. stagnant
B. controversial
C. alarming
D. distinct

ANSWERS

1	2	3	4	5	6	7	8	9	10
D	C	D	B	C	A	A	C	B	D
11	**12**	**13**	**14**	**15**	**16**	**17**	**18**	**19**	**20**
C	A	B	C	A	B	C	B	D	C
21	**22**	**23**	**24**	**25**	**26**	**27**	**28**	**29**	**30**
C	D	B	A	A	C	A	C	D	D
31	**32**	**33**	**34**	**35**	**36**	**37**	**38**	**39**	**40**
B	A	D	A	A	C	B	A	A	C

Sentence Completion

Directions : *Following exercise is meant to test your ability to choose the right words to fill in the gaps of sentences. Read the sentence carefully and choose suitable preposition for the purpose.*

1. She is proud ..... her beauty.
A. at B. on
C. of D. about

2. Mohan belongs ..... the upper strata of the society.
A. from B. for
C. to D. of

3. They have invited us ..... attend the function.
A. for B. to
C. upto D. at

4. We offer heartiest congratulation ..... your success.
A. at B. on
C. upon D. for

5. M/s Ram Avtar & Sons are the famous dealers ..... sugar and wheat.
A. of B. in
C. at D. for

6. He showed much affection ..... me when I met him recently.
A. for B. to
C. with D. towards

7. He entered ..... the gate without any dificulty.
A. by B. from
C. in D. into

8. He aimed ..... the target and fired.
A. to B. at
C. on D. up

9. The trend ..... price rise is unfortunate.
A. in B. of
C. for D. with

10. Adulteration ..... food stuff is going unchecked.
A. with B. of
C. in D. into

11. So far that case is concerned, I have not dealt ..... it.
A. no preposition is required
B. in
C. into
D. with

12. The man killed ..... road accident was a stranger.
A. of B. by
C. in D. on

13. He did not go ..... the right direction.
A. to B. by
C. into D. in

14. The train reached ..... the station right time.
A. to
B. by
C. on
D. no preposition is required

15. Punjab Mail arrived ..... New Delhi Railway Station three hours late.
A. no preposition is required
B. on
C. at
D. to

16. He slipped away ..... the crowd to avoid arrest.
A. of B. from
C. by D. with

17. The man died ..... heart attack without receiving any treatment.
A. of B. with
C. in D. by

18. He called ..... me late at night to communicate the message.
A. upon B. on
C. to D. up

19. The accused ran away ..... the police custoday.
A. from B. off
C. by D. off

20. My friend called ..... me to offer congratulations on my success.
A. to B. upon
C. on D. off

21. This remark is not ..... your favour.
A. to B. for
C. in D. of

22. He acted well ..... accordance with law.
A. with B. by
C. in D. to

23. There is a provision ..... law to bail out the accused.
A. by B. of
C. with D. in

24. Parole can be granted ..... any convict under the provisions of law.
A. for B. to
C. into D. upon

25. The appeal has been moved ..... High Court by the party.
A. in B. to
C. for D. with

26. He filed an appeal ..... the higher court.
A. with B. to
C. in D. for

27. An appeal has been admitted ..... the Supreme Court.
A. by B. into
C. with D. in

28. The absentee was reported to be ..... bed since last three days.
A. at B. in
C. on D. into

29. When I entered the room he was lying ..... bed.
A. over B. at
C. on D. in

30. Please accompany me ..... my room to collect the material.
A. for B. to
C. upto D. into

31. He met me ..... the way near the park after a long time.
A. in B. by
C. on D. into

32. This item has been included ..... the agenda of the meeting.
A. into B. in
C. on D. with

33. He has made good progress ..... English now.

A. with B. in
C. into D. of

34. The colour of your coat is matching ..... that of the pant.

A. with
B. by
C. to
D. no preposition is required

35. Our team played a match ..... the Young Men's.

A. by B. with
C. to D. against

36. Will you go ..... the market just now?

A. in B. to
C. for D. into

37. Indian team had played ..... the M.C.C. last year.

A. with B. upon
C. against D. off

38. I am not going to contest Lok Sabha seat ...... Raebareli.

A. off B. from
C. by D. at

39. The substract can also be injected ..... human body.

A. with B. upon
C. into D. in

40. You must be very careful ..... reading the question paper.

A. for B. in
C. with D. against

41. The fare to Mumbai has been increased ..... sixty rupees from here recently.

A. to B. by
C. with D. upto

42. Fare to Chennai has now increased ..... eighty rupees from here instead of seventy-three.

A. by B. to
C. for D. upto

43. He is going to Kolkata ..... Punjab Mail.

A. by B. with
C. in D. through

44. Diwali is a festival ..... light.

A. of B. for
C. with D. by

45. I am not responsible ..... your personal safety.

A. of B. for
C. with D. about

46. He was run over ..... a speedy train.

A. of B. off
C. by D. under

47. The train reached the station ..... right time.

A. by
B. at
C. on
D. no preposition is required

48. He is good ..... chess.

A. for B. at
C. on D. with

49. Payments were made ..... cash at the Head Office.

A. in
B. by
C. through
D. no preposition is required

50. He called ..... John in the street and insulted him.

A. up B. at
C. down D. away

51. Preface ..... this book is very impressive.
A. for B. of
C. to D. on

52. Headlines of a newspapers are helpful ..... understanding the intro and follow-up of the news.
A. in B. for
C. about D. with

53. Title cover counts much ..... sale of any book.
A. in B. for
C. to D. on

54. He sent ..... his resignation last night.
A. for B. up
C. in D. to

55. He gave a ring ..... me yesterday.
A. for B. to
C. about D. by

56. He wants to appear ..... the university examination.
A. at B. in
C. for D. to

57. Respondent had appeared ..... the tribunal.
A. in B. at
C. before D. to

58. Witness was produced ..... the court today by the police.
A. to B. before
C. in D. at

59. The films produced ..... India lack of technical accomplishment.
A. by B. in
C. at D. from

60. In respect of films, India is ..... the largest producer of the world.
A. no preposition is required
B. from
C. among
D. into

61. Syce let ..... the horse from the carriage.
A. off B. away
C. up D. out

62. The cup was broken ..... pieces.
A. to B. into
C. with D. by

63. They are not ..... friendly terms now.
A. on B. with
C. in D. at

64. He was wearing a cap ..... his head.
A. over B. upon
C. on D. at

65. He had wrapped a handkerchief ..... his head.
A. over B. upon
C. around D. on

66. Who knocked at the door ..... this hour of night?
A. by B. in
C. at D. on

67. Alas! his ailing friend passed ..... last night.
A. off B. away
C. on D. out

68. Do not put ..... this urgent work on tomorrow.
A. away B. out
C. off D. down

69. An extra bogie was attached ..... Punjab Mail to accommodate the marriage party.

A. with B. to
C. by D. into

70. He pulled ..... the chain to stop the train.
A. up B. down
C. away D. off

71. They put ..... the cigarette before entering into the shrine.
A. down B. off
C. out D. away

72. There is a danger of epidemic break ..... in the flooded area.
A. out B. up
C. away D. off

73. There is an apprehension ..... breach of peace in the town.
A. for B. of
C. with D. into

74. The train was packed ..... capacity.
A. beyond B. upto
C. over D. to

75. The accused were awarded death penalty ..... the triple murder case.
A. for B. in
C. into D. against

76. He was listening ..... my advice attentively.
A. to B. for
C. by D. at

77. Servant put ..... the lights and went to sleep.
A. off B. out
C. away D. in

78. Due to on-rush ..... the traffic streets are jammed.
A. off B. of
C. with D. by

79. Survival of civil polity without fair administration justice cannot be imagined .....
A. at
B. by
C. no preposition is required
D. of

80. Aspirations ..... the people have remained unfulfilled in spite of much progress through planning.
A. by B. of
C. in D. for

81. We have entered ..... partnership of a reputable firm.
A. into B. in
C. for D. to

82. ..... the influence of wine, the man quarrelled with the conductor.
A. in B. by
C. under D. for

83. Our train will pass ..... that station during late hours of night.
A. through B. by
C. from D. with

84. Industrial production ..... the country has fallen due to labour trouble and power crisis.
A. in B. of
C. into D. within

85. Unemployment in the country is ..... the pitch of it.
A. on B. at
C. to D. in

86. Superfast trains are useful ..... long journey.
A. to B. for
C. in D. into

87. Don't take ill ..... it! my friend.
A. for B. of
C. on D. upon

88. Newspapers are an effective medium ..... public opinion in a democratic country.
A. for B. of
C. to D. into

89. All democratic governments show great respect ..... public opinion.
A. in B. for
C. to D. on

90. An independent judiciary is a must ..... social justice.
A. for B. to
C. unto D. upon

91. The facts as stated above are true ..... the best of my knowledge and belief.
A. in B. by
C. to D. from

92. He does not think ..... his future at all.
A. for B. on
C. upon D. of

93. Mohan is actively thinking ..... his future course of action.
A. of B. for
C. about D. upon

94. Wine is injurious ..... health.
A. for B. to
C. upon D. about

95. She alighted ..... the bus at Connaught Place.
A. off B. from
C. with D. by

96. He went abroad ..... the morning flight.
A. by B. from
C. with D. off

97. Orders have been issued to inquire ..... the matter.
A. about B. into
C. of D. off

98. One of your friends met me last night and inquired ..... your health.
A. into B. for
C. about D. of

99. Government has setup a court ..... inquiry to ascertain the facts.
A. for B. of
C. about D. on

100. He is a candidate ..... B.A. examination.
A. to B. for
C. in D. at

ANSWERS

1	2	3	4	5	6	7	8	9	10
C	C	B	B	B	B	D	B	B	C
11	**12**	**13**	**14**	**15**	**16**	**17**	**18**	**19**	**20**
D	C	D	D	C	B	A	D	A	C
21	**22**	**23**	**24**	**25**	**26**	**27**	**28**	**29**	**30**
C	C	B	B	A	C	A	C	D	B

31	**32**	**33**	**34**	**35**	**36**	**37**	**38**	**39**	**40**
B	A	B	D	D	B	C	B	C	B
41	**42**	**43**	**44**	**45**	**46**	**47**	**48**	**49**	**50**
B	B	A	A	B	C	D	B	A	C
51	**52**	**53**	**54**	**55**	**56**	**57**	**58**	**59**	**60**
B	A	B	C	B	B	C	C	B	A
61	**62**	**63**	**64**	**65**	**66**	**67**	**68**	**69**	**70**
A	B	A	C	C	C	B	C	B	B
71	**72**	**73**	**74**	**75**	**76**	**77**	**78**	**79**	**80**
C	A	B	D	B	A	B	B	D	B
81	**82**	**83**	**84**	**85**	**86**	**87**	**88**	**89**	**90**
A	C	B	B	B	B	B	B	B	A
91	**92**	**93**	**94**	**95**	**96**	**97**	**98**	**99**	**100**
C	D	C	B	B	A	B	C	B	B

Ordering of Sentences

Directions : *In the questions given below, the first and the last part of the sentences are numbered 1 and 6. The rest of the sentence is split into four parts P, Q, R and S which are not given in their proper order. From the given options after each questions, find out which of the four combinations is correct.*

1. 1. Looking at the history
P. can help us remember
Q. and perhaps encourage us
R. of everyday life
S. that every day is history
6. to live a little more intensely.
A. SQPR B. PQSR
C. QRPS D. RPSQ

2. 1. There are seven precautions.
P. of being a lightning casualty
Q. that can minimise your chances
R. if you cannot seek shelter
S. in a substantial building
6. or a hard-topped vehicle
A. SQRP B. SQPR
C. QSPR D. QPRS

3. 1. A large man
P. stood stiffly in the back
Q. to meet the wildly
R. of the vehicle
S. wearing a battered grey hat
6. cheering thousands
A. SPRQ B. SQPR
C. SQRP D. QSPR

4. 1. When it was learnt
P. the world price,
Q. that the cost of production
R. was more than three times
S. the government offered
6. lavish subsidies to farmers.
A. QRPS B. PQRS
C. PRQS D. QSRP

5. 1. Someone who has
P. sports or physical activity
Q. may not be
R. excelled only in studies
S. but has completely ignored
6. a good team player
A. PRQS B. SQRP
C. RSPQ D. QRPS

6. 1. Many top management executives
P. and therefore the pre-interview stage
Q. have realised the inadequacies
R. of the interview process
S. has become an important process

6. in weeding out the weaker candidates.

A. RPQS B. PRSQ
C. QSPR D. QRPS

7. 1. A large number

P. of party leaders feel

Q. only the judiciary

R. that it is

S. which can finally pave the way

6. for his selection as party chief.

A. SPQR B. PRQS
C. SQRP D. RQPS

8. 1. Fed up with

P. the villagers took turns staying awake

Q. in their neighbourhood,

R. the spate of robberies

S. to collar the uninvited visitor

6. on his next attempt to rob.

A. SPQR B. QSPR
C. RQPS D. PRSQ

9. 1. Law and order

P. who eliminate government officials

Q. terrorists and militants

R. are virtually at ransom

S. in the hands of

6. and panic crowds.

A. PRSQ B. RSQP
C. SQPR D. PSRQ

10. 1. It is not

P. but whether we can

Q. a question of whether

R. we can afford

S. to make nuclear weapons

6. afford not to

A. PQSR B. SRQP
C. QRSP D. RSPQ

11. 1. The most interesting feature

P. of the emancipation of women

Q. is that the woman's claim

R. accepted without any

S. to equality has been

6. demur or challenge.

A. PRQS B. SRQP
C. PQSR D. RQPS

12. 1. Hindi has

P. modern language and

Q. medium of instruction in

R. it is doing better as

S. rapidly developed as

6. schools and colleges.

A. SPRQ B. SRQP
C. PQRS D. PRSQ

13. 1. Cinema as a

P. used to educate childern

Q. as well as illiterates

R. can very effectively be

S. medium of instruction

6. under adult education scheme.

A. QRPS B. SQRP
C. PSQR D. SRPQ

14. 1. Most people with a layman's

P. do not go to a witchdoctor for one.

Q. is created by books and media

R. an awarness of which

S. knowledge of science,

6. but have recourse to medicine.

A. QSRP B. RQPS
C. SRQP D. PSQR

15. 1. The theories of Charles Darwin that

P. man was a special creation

Q. man was descended from the ape

R. of God and Adam and Eve

S. shook the religious belief that

6. were the first humans

A. RQPS B. QSPR
C. PSQR D. QRPS

16. 1. It is hard

P. responsibility for doing

Q. to work, to accept

R. often unpleasant

S. to teach youngsters

6. but necessary chores

A. SQPR B. RSPQ
C. PSRQ D. SRPQ

17. 1. Action speaks louder

P. provide the first

Q. parents need to be

R. conscious that they

S. than words and

6. role models for their children

A. PQSR B. SRQP
C. SQRP D. QRPS

18. 1. As a teenager

P. her singing talents

Q. under the watchful eye

R. Whitney Houston cultivated

S. of her mother, Cissy

6. founder of the 1960s group The Sweet Inspiration.

A. QPRS B. SQRP
C. PRSQ D. RPQS

19. 1. If however,

P. travel in winter, and

Q. do not mind

R. the cold and the snow,

S. you plan to

6. how about Europe?

A. PRSQ B. SPQR
C. RQSP D. RPSQ

20. 1. Talking excitedly,

P. the two walked on,

Q. eventually meeting

R. to be the father

S. a man who seemed

6. of one of them

A. SPRQ B. RQPS
C. PQSR D. QSPR

21. 1. Essentially, a mutual fund is

P. provided by

Q. a collective pool

R. purchased from money

S. of assets

6. a large number of investors.

A. QRPS B. QSRP
C. QPRS D. QSPR

22. 1. Renowned carnatic vocalist, T.R. Balamani,

P. teaching music for

Q. who has been

R. says that group lessons

S. the last 27 years,

6. have a certain advantage over private lessons.
A. QPSR B. SQRP
C. PQSR D. SRPQ

23. 1. A lot of friends
P. of their lives
Q. have made a shambles
R. I grew up with
S. and have got
6. into drugs and violent crime
A. RQPS B. QRSP
C. SQPR D. PSRQ

24. 1. Far more attention is
P. planning of kitchens today
Q. due to
R. than ever before,
S. being given to the
6. space constraints and modern appliances.
A. QRPS B. SPRQ
C. RSPQ D. PSQR

25. 1. A happy family is
P. the lessons of giving
Q. and sharing
R. the members learn
S. one in which
6. each other joys and sorrows.
A. QRSP B. SRQP
C. SRPQ D. RSQP

26. 1. It is important to keep
P. to maintain
Q. the various components
R. of nature in full harmony
S. a balance
6. in the environment
A. QRPS B. PSRQ
C. SQPR D. RQSP

27. 1. Not only
P. better than cats,
Q. the one better
R. are dogs
S. but in many ways
6. than humans
A. PSQR B. QSPR
C. RPSQ D. PQRS

28. 1. The mechanic was very busy
P. when I took my car
Q. in the waiting room
R. I settled down
S. for repairs, so
6. with a book I'd brought along.
A. PQRS B. RSQP
C. PSRQ D. RPQS

29. 1. Dressing up can be
P. an easy task of
Q. an honest manner
R. you can look at your figure
S. as its faults in
6. and then go about choosing something that's just right for you.
A. PQSR B. SPQR
C. QRPS D. PRSQ

30. 1. Some people
P. certainly they enjoy
Q. unhappy today but
R. may be
S. far greater comforts
6. than their forefathers ever did.
A. RQPS B. PSQR
C. SPRQ D. QSRP

ANSWERS

1	2	3	4	5	6	7	8	9	10
D	D	A	A	C	D	B	C	B	C
11	**12**	**13**	**14**	**15**	**16**	**17**	**18**	**19**	**20**
C	A	D	C	B	A	C	D	B	C
21	**22**	**23**	**24**	**25**	**26**	**27**	**28**	**29**	**30**
B	A	A	B	C	A	C	C	D	A

Comprehension

Directions : *Read the following passage carefully and choose the best answer to each of the questions out of the four alternatives given.*

PASSAGE-I

We talk about two people fighting like wild cats, but this is nothing compared to angry mongooses fighting. They grip each other with their mouths and front paws and they roll over and over, all the time screaming at each other. They seem to be tearing each other to pieces. Yet, when they finally part, neither of them shows even a scratch.

Mongooses can move as quickly as lightning. That is why they can kill snakes without hurting themselves. They sink their needle-sharp teeth into the back of the neck of a poisonous snake. Apart from its speed, its tail helps the mongoose when it fights with snakes. When the mongoose is angry the hairs on its tail stand out so that it looks like a brush. When it attacks it keeps wiping this brush across the face of its enemy.

Although, they kill snakes, the usual food of mongooses is rats, mice, lizards, insects and other small animals. They are also very fond of eggs. If it is caught when it is young, the mongoose can become very tame and it is a delightful pet. In India, many people keep mongooses in their homes as protection against snakes.

QUESTIONS

1. When two mongooses fight
   A. they kill each other
   B. they keep screaming
   C. they tear each other to pieces
   D. they scratch each other

2. A mongoose moves
   A. only when asked to do so
   B. very fast
   C. all the time
   D. round and round

3. When it fights a snake the mongoose uses
   A. some needles
   B. its nose
   C. its sharp teeth
   D. its ears

4. 'Apart from' (in paragraph 2), means
   A. different from
   B. away from
   C. in addition to
   D. far from

5. The mongoose uses its tail
   A. to clean itself
   B. to clean the face of the snake
   C. instead of a brush
   D. as a weapon

6. The ..... food of a mongoose is rats and mice
   A. special B. ordinary
   C. only D. raw

7. The mongoose likes to ..... eggs.
   A. lay B. bury
   C. hide D. eat

8. People, in India, keep mongooses at home
   A. to guard the home
   B. to catch mice
   C. to protect themselves from snakes
   D. to fight other mongooses

PASSAGE-II

The mosquito is a nuisance. It annoys people when they are sleeping and it is also dreaded as a carrier of malaria. For many years, all kinds of methods have been used to get rid of mosquitoes. In some parts of the world, people rub themselves with an oil that will keep mosquitoes away. The health authorities spend a lot of money spraying stagnant ponds and other places where mosquitoes breed, with a powerful fluid that kills all the harmful insects, including mosquitoes. In many tropical countries, people sleep under mosquito nets. If they sleep out in the open, they make sure that there is a fire to keep away mosquitoes.

The latest device for mosquito eradication is a machine called the 'Zapper' which is produced and sold by an American company. It kills mosquitoes and other small insects. A coloured light inside the machine attracts the mosquitoes. When they enter the Zapper a powerful ray kills the insects at once.

The machine which must be made to stand on the floor is four feet high and weighs thirty pounds. The Zapper does not cause any harm to human beings. The inventor of Zapper thinks that his machine is the best way to get rid of mosquitoes as well as other insects that bite human beings. Of course, insects such as flies and moths will also be killed if they enter the Zapper. The Zapper now works only on electricity. It is likely that in a few years somebody will invent a similar machine operated on battery.

QUESTIONS

1. Zapper is the ..... of a new machine.
   A. inventor B. title
   C. name D. colour

2. The Zapper is used for
   A. catching mosquitoes
   B. trapping flies
   C. burning insects
   D. killing mosquitoes

3. The mosquitoes are attracted by the ..... in the machine.
   A. colours B. noise
   C. beauty D. light

4. The Zapper should be
   A. nailed to the wall
   B. hung from the ceiling
   C. placed on the ground
   D. buried in the ground

5. Flies will be killed if they ..... the Zapper.
   A. fly near

B. see
C. touch
D. come into

6. The Zapper can only be used in homes which have
A. electricity B. batteries
C. insects D. lights

7. The Zapper is a safe invention because it
A. is only four feet high
B. does not harm people
C. does not make noise
D. works on electricity

PASSAGE-III

Just as some men like to play football or cricket, so some men like to climb mountains. This is often very difficult to do, for mountains are not just big hills. Paths are usually very steep. Some mountain sides are straight up and down, so that it may take many hours to climb as little as one hundred feet. There is always the danger than you may fall off and be killed or injured. Men talk about conquering a mountain. It is a wonderful feeling to reach the top of a mountain after climbing for hours and may be, even for days. You look down and see the whole country below you. You feel god-like. Two Italian prisoners of war escaped from a prison camp in Kenya during the war. They did not try to get back to their own country, for they knew that was impossible. Instead, they climbed to the top of Mount Kenya, and then they came down again and gave themselves up. They had wanted to get that feeling of freedom that one has, after climbing a difficult mountain.

QUESTIONS

1. Some men like to climb a mountain because
A. they do not like to play football or cricket
B. they know the trick of climbing
C. they want to have a wonderful feeling
D. they like to face danger

2. To climb mountains is often difficult because
A. mountains are big hills
B. it consumes more time
C. prisoners often escape from camps and settle there
D. paths are steep and uneven

3. 'It is a wonderful feeling .....' 'It' refers to
A. the steep path
B. the prisoner
C. the mountain
D. mountaineering

4. Two Italian prisoners escaped from the camp and climbed to the top of Mount Kenya
A. to escape to Italy
B. to come down and give up
C. to get the feeling of freedom
D. to gain fame as mountaineers

5. Mountaineering is not a very popular sport like football or cricket because
A. there are no spectators in this sport
B. it may take many hours or even days

C. not many people are prepared to risk their lives
D. people do not want to enjoy a god-like feeling

PASSAGE-IV

Once, an ant who had come to drink at a stream fell into the water and was carried away by the swift current. He was in great danger of drowning. A dove, perched on a nearby tree, saw the ant's danger and dropped a leaf into the water. The ant climbed on to this, and was carried to safety.

Sometimes after this, a hunter, creeping through the bushes, saw the dove asleep, and took careful aim with his gun. He was about to fire when the ant, who was nearby, crawled forward and bit him sharply in the ankle. The hunter missed his aim, and the loud noise of gun awakened the dove from her sleep. She saw her danger and flew swiftly away to safety. Thus, the ant repaid the dove for having saved his life in the foaming current of the stream.

QUESTIONS

1. The ant came to stream to
A. fall into it
B. look at the swift current
C. to carry back some water
D. drink at it

2. The dove dropped a leaf into the water to
A. save the ant
B. drown the ant
C. help itself
D. perch on it

3. The dove was in danger because
A. a hunter wanted to care for it
B. there was a bush nearby
C. a hunter was about to shoot it
D. it had fell off the branch

4. The word 'aim' in this passage means
A. to point a gun at something or someone
B. to have an ambition
C. to try to reach somewhere
D. to look at something

5. The ant repaid the dove by
A. biting the hunter
B. warning the dove
C. crawling near the hunter
D. biting the dove

PASSAGE-V

Throughout in recorded history, India was celebrated for her fine textiles, her muslins and brocades of silver and gold. As a matter of fact, there is evidence that her textile industry goes back at least five thousand years, for Indian muslins were found urapped around mummies in Egyptian pyramids dating back to 3000 BC. The ancient Indian iron and steel industry was equally famous. The well-known Damascus steel for swords and armour used in the Crusades came from India. Thus, in countless industries and crafts, the Indian craftsman, worker, builder and artist created and prospered, and their products found favour both at home and abroad. And then, political disintegration and foreign conquest closed the long golden chapter of India's advancement and creative achievement.

QUESTIONS

1. India had a flourishing textile industry in the past, is proved by the fact, that
   A. India produced muslins and brocades of silver and gold
   B. the country was already famous for its fine textiles
   C. the industry claims to be five thousand year old
   D. Indian muslins were used for covering Egyptian mummies in 3000 BC.

2. According to the writer, the ancient Indian iron and steel industry was famous, because
   A. India supplied swords and armour to Damascus
   B. India provided steel with which swords and armour were made for the Crusaders
   C. Indian steel was famous among those fighting the Crusades
   D. Products of iron and steel were shipped to Damascus from India

3. Which one of the following statements is not true?
   A. There is a long history of excellence that the Indian craftsmen had achieved in various crafts
   B. Creations of Indian craftsmen brought to them prosperity
   C. Even after foreign conquest these crafts ensured India's industrial progress
   D. Indian crafts died out due to political division of the country

4. Which of the following is opposite in meaning to the word 'advancement' occurring in the passage?
   A. deterioration
   B. backwardness
   C. poverty
   D. failure

5. Which one of the following would be the most suitable title for the passage?
   A. The rise and fall of Indian crafts
   B. Ancient India's textile industry
   C. Indian iron and steel industry in the past
   D. Indian exports in the ancient times

PASSAGE-VI

A man may usually be known by the books he reads, as well as by the company he keeps; for there is a companionship of books as well as of men; and one should always live in the best compamy, whether it be of books or of men. A good book may be among the best of friends. It is the same today that it always was and it will never change. It is the most patient and cheerful of companions. It does not turn its back upon us in times of adversity or distress. It always receives us with the same kindness; amusing and interesting us in youth, comforting and consoling us in age.

QUESTIONS

1. According to the writer, 'a man may usually be known by the books he reads', because
   A. his reading habit shows that he is a scholar
   B. the books he reads affect his thinking and character
   C. books provide him a lot of knowledge
   D. his selection of books generally reveals his temperament and character
2. Which one of the following statements is not true?
   A. Good books as well as good men always provide the finest company
   B. A good book never betrays us
   C. We have sometimes to be patient with a book as it may bore us
   D. A good book serves as a permanent friend
3. The statement 'A good book may be among the best of friends', in the middle of the passage means that
   A. there cannot be a better friend than a good book
   B. books may be good friends, but not better than good men
   C. a good book can be included amongst the best friends of mankind
   D. our best friends read the same good books
4. Which of the following is opposite in meaning to the word 'adversity' occurring in the passage?
   A. happiness
   B. prosperity
   C. progress
   D. misfortune
5. Which one of the following would be the most suitable title for the passage?
   A. Books show the reader's character
   B. Books as man's abiding friends
   C. Books are useful in our youth
   D. The importance of books in old age

PASSAGE-VII

Honey bees make their own hives in hollow trees, or they use the hives that men make for them.

In each hive, there are worker bees who make the honey-comb out of wax and others who guard the beehive and collect food. There is a queen who lays an eggs in each cell of the honey-comb.

The young bees are fed on nectar and pollen. Honey is made in the bodies of the worker bees from the nectar and pollen of flowers.

Every year the old queen leaves the hive and she is followed by a 'Swarm' of bees.

QUESTIONS

1. Honey bees normally live
   A. on trees
   B. in houses
   C. in hives
   D. on roofs
2. The queen bee
   A. rules the other bees
   B. feeds on the other bees
   C. trains the worker bees
   D. lays the eggs
3. The honey-comb is made out of
   A. nectar
   B. flowers
   C. wax
   D. sugar
4. Honey is made by
   A. working men
   B. worker bees
   C. men in hives
   D. queens
5. Which of the following titles would be most suitable for the passage?
   A. The Queen
   B. Honey Bees
   C. Insects
   D. Worker Bees

PASSAGE-VIII

Birds are alike in many ways. Because they all have backbones. They are all vertebrates. They all have two legs and two wings. they all have lungs and are warm blooded. This means that their bodies are warm even when the weather is cold. All birds have feathers.

There are many different kinds of birds. Some, like the ostrich, are taller and heavier than a man. Some are very small, like the humming-bird. Many birds can fly very well. Swallows and ducks are excellent flyers. Some birds cannot fly at all. The pengum's wings cannot lift him off the ground.

QUESTIONS

1. According to the passage, all birds are vertebrates because they have
   A. feathers
   B. two legs and two wings
   C. backbones
   D. warm blood
2. When a bird is alive and well, its body is
   A. cold B. warm
   C. light D. heavy
3. One very large bird mentioned in the passage is the
   A. penguin
   B. humming-bird
   C. swallow
   D. ostrich
4. According to the passage, the humming-bird
   A. sings beautifully
   B. can fly very high
   C. is very small
   D. can fly very well
5. A penguin cannot
   A. fly in cold water
   B. stay on the ground
   C. fly very well
   D. fly at all

PASSAGE-IX

In order to measure distances, the surveyor lays out a series of straight lines which he calls survey lines. To do this, he uses his chain and ranging rods. The rods are not unlike broomsticks only longer, and they are usually coloured black and white or red and white so that they can be easily seen. Assuming that the surveyor wished to measure the distance between X and Y, he would place a rod at X while his assistant would walk towards Y. The surveyor would stand two or three yards behind X. Keeping X and Y in line; his assistant would then place one or more rods at intervals and in the same line, the surveyor guiding him as to whether or not all rods were in line.

QUESTIONS

1. Survey lines help a surveyor to
   A. make straight lines
   B. see easily and clearly
   C. range some rods
   D. measure distances
2. Two different things used by the surveyor to lay out his survey lines are
   A. a chain and some rods
   B. broomsticks and rods
   C. a tape and a chain
   D. a chain and broomsticks
3. Because they have to be easily seen, ranging rods are
   A. striaght
   B. carefully measured
   C. guided
   D. brightly coloured
4. When measuring the distance from X to Y, the surveyor stands
   A. in front of X
   B. behind X
   C. on a line between X and Y
   D. two or three yards behind Y
5. The surveyor has to guide his assistant to
   A. stand behind Y
   B. walk towards X
   C. find the rods
   D. keep the rods in a straight line

PASSAGE-X

Any person who wishes to be a candidate for election to the National Assembly must prepare four copies of the nomination paper in the prescribed form (Form E). He must also make a declaration in the prescribed form (Form F) stating that he is qualified to be a member of the Assembly. A day is specified in the election notice for the receipt of nominations. The nomination papers and the declaration must be delivered to the Returning Officer between 9 AM and 12 mid-day on that day. Delivery may be made by the candidate himself, or by the person who proposed or the person who seconded him.

QUESTIONS

1. The prospective candidate for elections has to
   A. make sure that he will win
   B. fill in a nomination paper

C. be a member of the Assembly
D. have a duplicate machine

2. How many different forms must be completed by the candidate?
A. Three
B. One
C. Two
D. Four

3. A candidate completes Form F to declare that he:
A. wants to vote
B. has paid the required deposit
C. is qualified to be a candidate
D. cannot vote

4. Nominations must be handed in
A. in nine o'clock on the day stated
B. at 12 mid-day on the day stated
C. during the afternoon of the day stated
D. during first half of the day stated

5. The completed forms can be delivered to the Returning Officer by
A. one of three people
B. any member of the candidate's family
C. the person who came second in the election
D. no-one but the candidate

PASSAGE-XI

Electricity is very useful as long as we do not get in its way. But it can make trouble for us if we do. Luckily, we have a way of avoiding this. We can wrap electric wires in coats of rubber or plastic. These coats are called insulation. Electricity cannot travel through a coat of insulation, and so it runs along safely inside the wire.

If a current of electricity runs through you, it gives you a shock and strong shocks are dangerous. They can kill you. So it is safest not to meddle with electric wires or machines. An electrician knows how to work with electricity, and he does not get hurt. Usually, he turns a switch so that no current at all comes into the wire on which he is working.

QUESTIONS

1. According to the passage, electricity becomes dangerous when
A. it is too hot
B. it is interfered with
C. the power fails
D. it cannot travel

2. Electric wires covered with rubber or plastic are
A. dangerous
B. insulated
C. live
D. troublesome

3. If a current of electricity runs through a person's body
A. it always kills him
B. he does not get hurt
C. it lights him up
D. he gets a shock

4. The advice given in the passage about electric wires and machines is

A. to cover them with rubber or plastic
B. to turn them off
C. to make them safe to meddle with
D. not to interfere with them

5. Electricians avoid getting shocks from electric wires by
A. switching off the current
B. not touching wires
C. going against the current
D. wearing insulated coats

PASSAGE-XII

Glaciers are formed by the continuous collection of snow on high peaks. The weight of additional snow compresses the earlier falls into ice which is slowly forced down into valleys.

Continental glaciers, or ice-sheets covering whole continents, are now found only in Greenland and the Polar regions. However, at one time similar ice-sheets covered most of Northern Europe, Canada and Northern USA. In the Southern Hemisphere, because of the smaller land surfaces, the effect of the ice-sheets was limited.

Much study has been devoted recently to the glaciers on Mt. Kenya. Here there are ten glaciers which appear to be slowly shrinking in size and five others have disappeared altogether. It is thought that the climate in this part of Africa may be getting progressively warmer, the giant groundsel plants on the slopes of Mt. Kenya were at one time known to grow much lower down but are now isolated plants near the peak.

QUESTIONS

1. According to the passage, glaciers are first formed
A. high up on mountains
B. in valleys
C. on ice
D. in ice-sheets

2. According to the passage, continental glaciers can now be fournd
A. on the continent
B. in northern Europe
C. in Greenland and at the Poles
D. on ice-sheets

3. The effect of te ice-sheets was limited in the Southern Hemisphere because
A. it is warmer than the Northern Hemisphere
B. it is smaller than the Northern Hemisphere
C. there is less land than in the Northern Hemisphere
D. there is more land than in the Northern Hemisphere

4. According to the passage, how many glaciers were there on Mt. Kenya at one time?
A. Ten B. Fifteen
C. Five D. None

5. What, according to the author, may be the cause of the disappearance of some of the glaciers on Mt. Kenya?
A. The climate is becoming colder
B. There is too much rain
C. Not enough snow is falling
D. The climate is becoming warmer

ANSWERS

Passage-I

1	2	3	4	5
B	B	C	C	D
6	**7**	**8**		
B	D	C		

Passage-II

1	2	3	4	5
C	D	D	C	D
6	**7**			
A	B			

Passage-III

1	2	3	4	5
C	D	D	C	A

Passage-IV

1	2	3	4	5
D	A	C	A	A

Passage-V

1	2	3	4	5
C	B	C	B	A

Passage-VI

1	2	3	4	5
B	C	C	B	B

Passage-VII

1	2	3	4	5
C	D	C	B	B

Passage-VIII

1	2	3	4	5
C	B	D	C	D

Passage-IX

1	2	3	4	5
D	A	D	B	D

Passage-X

1	2	3	4	5
B	C	C	D	A

Passage-XI

1	2	3	4	5
B	B	D	D	A

Passage-XII

1	2	3	4	5
A	C	C	B	D

Closet Test

Directions : *In the following passages, some of the words have been left out. First, read each passage over and try to understand what it is about, then fill in the blanks with the help of alternatives given.*

PASSAGE-I

He mentioned two factors being responsible ... (1) ... this telecom revolution. One is the ... (2) ... technological change, beginning ... (3) ... microelectronics ... (4) ..., the budget problems of most industrial countries ... (5) ... with free trade agreements ... (6) ... resulted in major liberalisation moves. Their aim ... (7) ... to increase the world economy through a ... (8) ... market at lower prices. In the process, most countries were, and still are, ... (9) ... to privatise part of their national telecom operator companies ... (10) ... order to survive.

1. A. to B. with C. from D. for

2. A. easy B. rapid C. real D. fast

3. A. with B. at C. by D. along

4. A. firstly B. truly C. rarely D. secondly

5. A. combination B. combined C. combine D. confusion

6. A. was B. will be C. had D. have been

7. A. are B. is C. was D. will be

8. A. many B. bigger C. busy D. largest

9. A. forcible B. pushed C. to go D. being forced

10. A. in B. at C. by D. with

PASSAGE-II

A long line of women were waiting ... (1) ... a shop. A man approached and immediately pushed ... (2) ... the front of the line. Angry shouts sent ... (3) ... retreating to the back. He tried again, ... (4) ... once more the women jostled and ... (5) ... him back again. Finally, giving ... (6) ..., he ... (7) ... his tie, ... (8) his ruffled hair and, with dignity, ... (9) ... , "Very well, ladies, ... (10) ... that's what you want, I won't open the shop."

1. A. beside B. outside C. against D. before

2. A. at B. forward
C. to D. behind

3. A. her B. his
C. she D. him

4. A. and B. also
C. because D. but

5. A. pushed B. broke
C. shook D. threw

6. A. in B. up
C. into D. on

7. A. straightened
B. messed
C. pressed
D. crushed

8. A. soothed
B. organised
C. smoothed
D. closed

9. A. told B. cried
C. said D. said that

10. A. all B. then
C. for D. if

PASSAGE-III

The skin is the body's ... (1) ... organ. With the exception of the palms and soles, the skin is ... (2) ... with hair follicles. The skin's ... (3) ... is to protect the body ... (4) ... regulating its temperature. The skin ... (5) ... of three layers. For a lovely skin one should ... (6) ... caring for it. Refresh the skin with a face mask from ... (7) ... . To prevent skin from losing vital oils use a moisturiser ... (8) ... cleansing. Moisturising prevents ... (9) ... loss of water from the skin ... (10) ... protecting and nourishing it.

1. A. longest B. larger
C. largest D. longer

2. A. scratched
B. covered
C. toned
D. dabbed

3. A. function B. reason
C. habit D. ability

4. A. by B. with
C. for D. unless

5. A. kinds B. parts are
C. is found D. consists

6. A. start B. detest
C. allow D. hate

7. A. morning till night
B. days
C. time to time
D. yesteryears

8. A. later B. beyond
C. ahead of D. after

9. A. undue B. wanted
C. little D. rare

10. A. hereby B. thereby
C. therefore D. hence

PASSAGE-IV

Many accidents take place at home, ... (1) ... it is up to the parents to take ... (2) ... . Open windows ... (3) ... dangerous ... (4) ... them with bars or grills. Also use child-proof electric circuits ... (5) ... the wall to ... (6) ... inquisitive little hands ... (7) ... getting shocks. Better ... (8) ... ensure ... (9) ... your home ... (10) ... earth-leak circuit breakers installed.

1. A. so B. also
C. for D. as

2. A. care
B. precaution
C. advise
D. help

3. A. are B. can be
C. prove D. appear

4. A. break B. seal
C. cover D. fill

5. A. inside B. over
C. on D. in

6. A. prevent B. let
C. allow D. encourage

7. A. against B. for
C. from D. behind

8. A. still B. thus
C. not D. quickly

9. A. regarding B. than
C. about D. that

10. A. had B. has
C. have D. may have

PASSAGE-V

He had lived nearly his ... (1) ... life not ... (2) ... from the house in ... (3) .. he was born and raised, and from the ... (4) ... of his brothers and sisters. That working class neighbourhood ... (5) ... big and rich ... (6) ... for him. Our family eventually joined him ... (7) ..., and on trips ... (8) ... the neighbourhood, he proudly ... (9) ... me ... (10) ... friends.

1. A. total B. complete
C. entire D. maximum

2. A. afar B. away
C. far off D. far

3. A. where B. what
C. why D. which

4. A. houses B. homes
C. dwelling D. inhabitat

5. A. was B. were
C. is D. are

6. A. only B. supply
C. enough D. amount

7. A. over B. together
C. there D. with

8. A. inside B. near
C. into D. through

9. A. threw
B. introduced
C. handed
D. presented

10. A. for B. to
C. like D. as

PASSAGE-VI

The boy was hurt ... (1) ... confused. What ... (2) ... seemed so beautiful now looked ... (3) ... the plastic, cheap thing ... (4) .... it was. He ... (5) ... outside to the back porch and ... (6) ... to cry ... (7) ... his mother appeared and ... (8) gently what was wrong. He explained ... (9) ... best he could. She listened, and then they ... (10) ... inside.

1. A. too B. and
C. so D. also

2. A. have B. has
C. has been D. had

3. A. alike B. like
C. same as D. as

4. A. that B. what
C. which D. who

5. A. brushed B. scurried
C. walked D. narrated

6. A. start B. acted
C. began D. got

7. A. early B. quick
C. fast D. soon

8. A. told B. cried
C. said D. asked

9. A. as B. it
C. on D. so

10. A. went B. go
C. will go D. were going

PASSAGE-VII

His appetite ... (1) ... research continued to set him apart from other investors. He ... (2) ... the heavy business manuals ... (3) ... the zest of a small boy reading comics. Line ... (4) ... line, he soaked up financial pages. His friends cheerfully accepted that he knew ... (5) ... about stocks than ... (6) ... . Nobody was going to tell you ... (7) ... stocks were a bargain; you had to ... (8) ... there on your own. And, so he ... (9) ... his homework. His independence of mind and ability to focus on his work ... (10) ... served him well.

1. A. for B. of
C. above D. with

2. A. weighed B. read
C. collected D. bought

3. A. around B. under
C. with D. like

4. A. from B. by
C. inside D. between

5. A. most B. more
C. all D. much

6. A. somebody
B. nobody
C. everybody
D. anybody

7. A. what B. that
C. which D. when

8. A. go B. come
C. arrive D. get

9. A. did B. do
C. made D. does

10. A. too B. also
C. together D. both

ANSWERS

Passage-I

1	2	3	4	5	6	7	8	9	10
D	B	A	D	B	C	C	B	D	A

Passage-II

1	2	3	4	5	6	7	8	9	10
B	C	D	D	A	B	A	C	C	D

Passage-III

1	2	3	4	5	6	7	8	9	10
C	B	A	A	D	A	C	D	A	B

Passage-IV

1	2	3	4	5	6	7	8	9	10
A	B	B	C	D	A	C	A	D	B

Passage-V

1	2	3	4	5	6	7	8	9	10
C	D	D	A	A	C	C	D	B	B

Passage-VI

1	2	3	4	5	6	7	8	9	10
B	D	B	A	C	C	D	D	A	A

Passage-VII

1	2	3	4	5	6	7	8	9	10
A	B	C	B	B	D	C	D	A	B

Miscellaneous Questions

Directions : *Choose the right question-word with which a question can be framed in respect to each of the following sentences. The italicised part of each sentence could be the answer to such a question.*

1. *Two clerks* had failed to report for duty.
A. Who B. What
C. Whom D. How

2. She is leaving the country *tomorrow.*
A. Why B. Where
C. When D. What

3. *Mr. Shah* is the Chairman of the newly-found committee.
A. Who B. What
C. How D. Why

4. The function was held *at the club.*
A. Whose B. Where
C. Whom D. Why

5. He scolded *the servant* for breaking the glass.
A. Who B. Whom
C. Whose D. What

6. This is *her* book.
A. Who B. Can
C. How D. Whose

7. The Dentist *told her to open the mouth.*
A. What B. Whom
C. Where D. Why

8. *This Grammar Book* is the better of the two books.
A. How B. Who
C. Which D. What

9. He went to the village *to visit his grand parents.*
A. Why B. Where
C. How D. What

10. *Yes,* I like it.
A. Will B. Do
C. Can D. have

Directions : *Choose the most appropriate meaning of each of the sentences given below.*

11. He secured 89% marks.
A. He stood first in class
B. He had faired well in his exams
C. He has done better than his friends
D. He will get the scholarship

12. The child is now cured.
A. The doctor is checking the child's pulse
B. The child is running around with joy
C. The child is eating chocolates
D. The child had been ill

13. Minni cannot sit on this chair.
A. There is dirt on the chair
B. Minni does not like the colour of the chairs

C. The chair is too small for Minni to sit on
D. Minni is sitting on the sofa

14. He only plays cricket.
A. He plays cricket and nothing else
B. He and nobody else plays cricket
C. He cannot play any other game
D. He plays cricket and nothing else worth-mentioning

15. Our guest came early.
A. Our guest came before the scheduled time
B. Our guest came earliest
C. Our guest came already
D. Our guest came too soon

16. She is Rhea's mother.
A. Rhea is her daughter
B. Only Rhea and nobody else is her daughter
C. She is not only Rhea's mother but also Ritu's mother
D. She is proud of her daughter

17. We missed the train.
A. The train had left the platform at 9.30 pm
B. The train had left right on time
C. We were late in reaching the station
D. The train did not wait for us

18. He is the richest man in the town.
A. A few men in the town are richer than him
B. No other man in the town is as rich as him
C. The town is full of rich men
D. He has recently purchased acres of land in this town

19. I want this book.
A. This book is very much in demand
B. This book is written by my favourite author
C. I want to present this book to my best friend
D. This book contains information useful for my research

20. She is drinking lemonade.
A. She is thirsty
B. She only drinks lemonade
C. She does not like any other drink
D. Only lemonade is served in the restaurant where she is sitting

Directions : *In the following questions, there are some bold words or phrase which have been given with four options. If another word or better expression is required for the bold part choose it from the group. If no change is required, choose 'D' as the answer.*

21. He **had left** for Kolkata tomorrow.
A. will go
B. is leaving
C. left already
D. no change is required

22. He is such **a clown man** that he can make anybody laugh.
A. clownish
B. a funny clown man
C. a serious joker
D. no change is required

23. **Many less** people attended the function.
A. very few
B. lesser
C. the least
D. no change is required

24. She is seventeen **ages** old.
A. age
B. year
C. years
D. no change is required

25. He is **a well student** and is admired by all
A. an expert student
B. a healthy student
C. a good student
D. no change is required

26. I **knocked at** the door before opening it.
A. banged
B. shouted at
C. kicked hard
D. no change required

27. **A much** pollution is caused by smoke from factories.
A. much
B. more
C. most
D. no change is required

28. You **are viewing at** the most beautiful girl.
A. are seeing at
B. are looking at
C. are viewing over
D. no change is required

29. Do not go near the fire, your clothes **may get burning.**
A. may get fired
B. may get burns
C. may catch fire
D. no change is required

30. The star **is burning** in the sky.
A. shines
B. is shone
C. was twinkling
D. no change is required

ANSWERS (WITH EXPLANATION)

1. D : How many clerks failed to report for duty?

2. C : When is she leaving the country?

3. A : Who is the Chairman of the newly found committee?

4. B : Where was the function held?

5. B : Whom did he scold for breaking the glass?

6. D : Whose book is this?

7. A : What did the Dentist tell her?

8. C : Which is the better of the two books?

9. A : Why did he go to the village?

10. B : Do you like it?

11	12	13	14	15	16	17	18	19	20
B	D	C	D	A	A	C	B	D	A
21	**22**	**23**	**24**	**25**	**26**	**27**	**28**	**29**	**30**
B	B	A	C	C	D	A	B	C	A

ESSAY WRITING

IMPORTANT TIPS

An essay is a written composition containing an expression of one's personal opinions or ideas on a subject. A good essay must hold its readers' attention from the beginning to the end. For this, it must possess certain qualities, which make a piece of writing readable and enjoyable.

Every essay depends on two things: (*a*) its subject matter, and (*b*) its language.

To write an essay you require 'material'—clear ideas based on experience, reading and observation. These ideas have to be put into words and these words must convey what you wish to say. For this you should know the right words and the most appropriate way to put them together.

An essay is generally divided into three parts:

1. The Introduction. **2.** The Body. **3.** The Conclusion. And each of these requires careful attention.

(*i*) **The Introduction Paragraph:** It is the first paragraph of your essay. It introduces the main idea of your essay. A good opening paragraph captures the interest of your reader and tells why your topic is important. The introduction should be designed to attract the reader's attention and give the reader an idea of the essay's focus. Begin with an attention grabber.

(*ii*) **The Body or Supporting Paragraphs:** Supporting paragraphs make up the main body of your essay. They develop the main idea of your essay.

To form a perfect body of your essay, you should:

1. List the points that develop the main idea of your essay. 2. Place each supporting point in its own paragraph. 3. Develop each supporting point with facts, details and examples. To connect your supporting paragraphs, you should use special transition words. Transition words link your paragraphs together and make your essay easier to read. Use them at the beginning and at the end of your paragraphs.

(*iii*) **The Conclusion or Summary Paragraph:** It comes at the end of your essay after you have finished developing your ideas. It summarises or restates the main idea of the essay. You want to leave the reader with a sense that your essay is complete. Restate the strongest points of your essay that support your main idea. Conclude your essay by restating the main idea in different words. Give your personal opinion or suggest a plan for action. Use a summary statement rather than phrases like the following: "In summary...," "To conclude...," "To summarise...," or "In closing....". These are too obvious and vague to be effective. Use a transitional phrase, which summarises a point in your essay instead.

In a short essay, you can deal with a very few points only. It is of no use to write down a lot of things that have nothing to do with the subject. Write down facts that will help you in your essay. Write down your own ideas. Find the main idea of your essay. Choose the most important point you are going to present. Organise your facts and ideas in a way that develops your main idea. Once you have chosen the most important point of your essay, you must find the best way to tell your reader about it. Develop each supporting paragraph and make sure to follow the correct paragraph format. Write simple sentences to express your meaning. Use simple words; be clear as well as brief. Focus on the main idea of your essay. Check your essay for mistakes and correct them. Make sure that your handwriting is clear and legible. The examiner may not have enough time to take pains to try and read illegible words carefully. An illegible handwriting might only put off his interest in reading your essay even though it might be good. An essay can be written just about anything, even a poem. Hence, it will be difficult to predict which essay you may be asked to write about in your exam. Here are a few selected essays for your study.

PRICE RISE

India is a land of problems. One of the most serious problems is the problem of price rise. Whenever we go to market, we often find that the prices of all the essential articles have risen. Now, the situation has become more serious because of unprecedented rise in the prices of food items.

It is very difficult for a common man to make both ends meet. The income of the common people does not rise so much as the prices of goods. The salaried people and those who live on pensions are hit the most as they have only a fixed income. The condition of those who live on interest income is even worse as the interests have so many times been decreased during the last few years.

One great reason for the rise in prices is the rapid increase in population. Another reason is that most of the people are trying to raise their standards of living. Now people are giving more attention to food, clothing, health, housing, entertainment, education of children, etc. Many people have ACs, cars, desert coolers, geysers, mixers, refrigerators, television sets, telephones, etc. in their homes which previously they did not have. All this increases their expenditure and prices of goods.

Goods are not produced at the same rate as the population and demand rise. Many people waste money on luxuries and functions and marriages. The government does not care to control its expenditure. Taxation system is also defective in our country. Then, there are so many ministers and legislators and government employees who have to be paid from treasury. Not much money is left with the government for development purposes.

India has to import a lot of petroleum products and gas to meet her energy requirements. There is much wastage of petrol on running luxury cars. Black money and corruption also lead to price rise. Some traders hoard essential items and raise prices to earn more profits. Famines, floods and strikes also cause price rise.

To check prices, population should be controlled. Strikes should be avoided. Taxation system should be overhauled. Wastage should be avoided. Black money and corruption should be dealt with strictly. Unnecessary imports should be avoided, particularly the imports of luxury items. More attention should be given to exports. Production should be increased. More attention should be given to energy resources.

Much expenditure has to be done on defence. This cannot be helped. However, it should be avoided wherever the security of the country is not compromised. Good relations with neighbouring countries should be established to minimise expenditure on wars and encounters.

With the coming of the VAT system of taxation, people hoped that the prices of goods would by and large go down to a considerable extent. But this has not happened. Let the government and people cooperate with each other to solve all problems, including the problem of price rise.

CORRUPTION

Corruption is one of the burning topics of today. It is also one of the most serious problems of society these days.

Corruption is there in all the government departments. It is there from the lowest to the highest level. If you want to get any work done in any department, you have to grease the palms of many officials there. The peons, the clerks and the officers, all are corrupt. It has, however, to be admitted that some exceptions are also there. Those who do not take bribes can be counted on fingers.

Corruption is there in many countries. But it is not so common in developed countries. India is one of the most corrupt countries in the world. In this respect, her place is with Pakistan, Bangladesh, Nigeria, etc. The European countries are the least corrupt in the world.

In India, it is said, nobody can get a government job without paying bribe. This became clear when the biggest recruitment scam was unearthed a few years ago in Punjab. Only the UPSC and the like may be an exception. As far as the state public service commissions are concerned, nothing can be said with certainty unless their working is thoroughly scrutinised by some investigative agency.

India has become a land of scams. During the last few decades, we have seen a number of scams unearthed. Some of them are 2G Spectrum scam, Coalgate, Railways scam, Securities scam, Hawala scam, Fodder scam, Bofors scam, Housing scam, Sugar scam, Wheat scam, Urea scam, Recruitment scam, Petrol pump scam, Coffingate, etc. Indeed, the list is endless. So many frauds are committed in banks. The money meant for the pension to the aged, widows, orphans and the handicapped is swindled. Unfortunately, this virus of corruption has spread even in the judiciary, at least at the lower level. It is heartening to note that the Supreme Court and the High Court are trying to root it out from judiciary. Let us hope for the best.

The biggest den of corruption is the political field. There is criminalisation of politics at the highest level. A fairly large number of our central and state legislators have a criminal background. The cases of corruption against many of them are going on in courts. The courts and the Election Commission are doing their best to end this criminalisation of politics.

We have the CBI, the central and state vigilance commissions and other investigative agencies. The Lok Pal, the Consumer Courts and other Courts and Tribunals are there to end corruption and injustice. But the corrupt people are very cunning. They can easily find loopholes in laws. They have the money and muscle power. They can get the laws twisted to their advantage.

Besides the loopholes in laws, the most serious thing is that the punishments are not harsh. Even when a person is convicted, he either goes scot free or gets very little punishment. The people are losing faith in the investigative agencies and even in the judiciary. It is common knowledge that only those who commit petty thefts and frauds, are punished. Those who indulge in most serious scams or crimes, hardly ever get any punishment. It is because they can engage famous, crafty lawyers who can prolong the case till it loses its teeth.

Laws are made and passed by the legislators. In many of them they themselves are criminals, how can we hope that they will make and pass good laws? They will always pass laws which are in their own favour and which can save them if they are caught.

If the democratic process has to be continued in the country and if the people are to be saved from losing all faith in the government, investigative agencies and the judiciary, something serious will have to be done. Otherwise, this country will go to the dogs, sooner or later.

DRUG-ADDICTION

When the Hippies came to India, they brought not only strange dresses but also drugs. It is common knowledge that the young people are greatly influenced by anything strange and new.

At present, our country is under the grip of drug-addiction. Most of the drug-addicts live in cities. They include both boys and girls. University, college and school hostels are particularly full of drug-addicts.

Drug-addiction is, however, not restricted to urban areas only. Even in the rural areas there are so many drug-addicts. There are not only men but also women in large numbers who take drugs. This vice has invaded all sections of society. Many rickshaw-pullers, factory workers, government employees and even businessmen can be seen who are given to the habit of drug-taking.

Most often it so happens that a person takes a drug just for the thrill of it. Then he takes it the second or third time to repeat the experience. When he takes it a number of times, he forms the habit. Then a time comes when he wants to get rid of it. But he cannot do so because he feels restlessness if he does not take the drug.

Most of the young people start this habit in the company of their friends in hostels. One reason for this wide-spread practice is that drugs are easily available everywhere. There are so many peddlers who sell drugs. Drugs are of many kinds such as heroin, smack, LSD, opium, ganja, charas, etc. All drugs are habit-forming.

A drug-addict gets his health spoiled. He also wastes his precious money on drugs. Some of these drugs such as heroin are very costly. But those who are addicted to drugs cannot get rid of them easily. If they do not have money to purchase a drug, they steal money from home or from wherever they can. They can even commit some more serious crime to get money for drugs.

Drug-taking makes a person lazy. It can cause even death. Young people should be taught in schools and colleges to avoid this bad habit. If a youth falls a prey to this habit, he should be taken to the drug-deaddiction centre as early as possible. Strict action should be taken against drug-peddlers, chemists, and others who sell drugs.

One reason for this menace is that the young people feel frustrated. They find the education system worthless. They do not get proper love from parents. They are unemployed and have no hope of getting a job. The parents, teachers, NGO's, social workers, government agencies and media should join hands to save the youth of our country from this menace.

DOWRY SYSTEM

Dowry system is a curse. It degrades women. Women have to suffer due to many wrong or evil social practices. Dowry system is one of such practices.

Dowry system is present in the entire Hindu society. The rich and the poor, all have to give dowry on the marriage of their daughters. Those who do not practise this system on the marriage of their son or daughter can be counted on the fingers of the hand. Sometimes, people of other communities also follow this system, but the practice is not common among them.

On the marriage of the boy and the girl, the couple has to start a new home. For this, the main responsibility is that of the boy's parents. But there is nothing wrong in it if the girl's parents also give some gifts. Indeed the giving of small gifts by relatives and friends on a marriage is common all over the world. It is even allowed by the law. But there is no compulsion in such a case.

At present, the situation in India is very alarming. On the marriage of a daughter the parents have to give a rich dowry. For this, they sometimes have to borrow money at a high rate of interest. Sometimes, they even have to mortgage or sell their property.

The serious thing is that the boy and his parents cannot be satisfied in any way. Even if they are given a rich dowry, they demand still more. They demand a car, a refrigerator, a colour TV, a microwave oven, a mixer, an AC set, luxurious furniture and so many other household and luxury items besides a hefty amount in the form of cash and jewellery. Then, they go on demanding one thing after the other all their life. All the parents cannot afford to do this, even if they love their daughters more than their hearts and may be ready to make any sacrifice for them.

The girls who do not bring rich dowry are tortured all their life. Some of them are burnt alive. Others commit suicide as they do not want to be a burden to their parents.

This demand for dowry is not limited to a particular section. Even the highly educated people are under its grip. Even if a girl is highly educated and has many skills and virtues and is very beautiful, rich dowry must be given.

Surprisingly, the more the qualifications and earning capacity of a boy, the more is the demand for dowry. It is still more surprising that even when a girl is employed and is earning or has the capacity to earn according to her qualifications and skills, dowry has to be given.

There are a number of anti-dowry acts passed by the union and state legislatures. But they are not implemented strictly. Even if this is done, dowry system does not seem to get eliminated. It is because the people in general are not prepared to do so. The rich people give rich dowry on the marriage of their daughters to make it a social show. The poor and middle-class people have to follow suit for the sake of custom and tradition. Sometimes, the people, the elderly people in particular, say that if they do not give or accept dowry, they will lose their respect in society.

How can we get rid of this evil? The only answer is that a general opinion against this evil should be framed in society. The conscience of the people should be aroused. The anti-dowry acts should be strictly implemented. The media should play its role positively and sincerely. Students in schools and colleges should be made to vow against this evil which is a blot on society. Dowry-seekers should be boycotted by all.

CLEAN INDIA DRIVE

Prime Minister Narendra Modi launched the Swachch Bharat sanitation programme on October 2, 2014. It was a befitting tribute to the Father of the Nation who was concerned about sanitation issues. The proposed sanitation programme will reframe the social and economic face of India and prove to be a great game changer. Sanitation has a direct link with the spread of communicable diseases which are prevalent in India. The basic cause of frequent epidemics in India is insanitation. The country can attain Health for All by October 2, 2019, if the programme is implemented in totality.

Living in an insanitary environment, like poverty, degrades the quality of human life and it is a curse and a social stigma as well. Therefore, the accomplishment of the total Sanitation Programme (TSP) will improve the living standard of the poorest of the poor on the one hand and improve the Human Development Index (HDI) of India on the other. Presently, India is positioned 134 in the UN's HDI. Poverty is less painful if one gets a chance to live in a sanitary environment. In fact, a sanitary environment is the basic necessity of human life like air, water and food for its aesthetic and psychological development. That is why we say, "Cleanliness is next to godliness". If India ensures total sanitation by 2019, our stock will rise in the comity of nations.

Up to the 1960s, carrying human excreta as head load was the worst social stigma. Now open defecation has taken its place. Women go for nature's call at night in the open and they are frequently molested and even raped. The coverage for use of in-house sanitary latrines varies from state to state, depending upon the percentage of BPL families.

According to the proposed Swachh Bharat scheme, the government will build individual toilets in 1.04 crore households and 5 lakh community/public toilets in urban areas. Around 8.8 crore toilets will be built in rural areas and a majority of these are to be provided in individual households. The total sanitation programme includes programmes that are to be executed under the umbrella programme.

Provision of 100 per cent sewerage and a drainage system in all urban towns together with innocuous disposal or recycling of the finally treated effluent for irrigation with a total ban on discharge into the drains or rivers. An effective sewerage and drainage system forms the backbone of urban sanitation.

There is need for 100 per cent solid waste management, both in urban and rural areas and recycling of the final waste product. Around 100 per cent coverage of rural households and slum areas with sanitary latrines. All the open areas in urban and rural communities will be either paved or grassed. All the streets to be paved with concrete blocks or paver blocks. There should be zero tolerance to dumping or littering of solid waste matter (mostly paper and plastic matter) in open spaces, both in urban and rural areas. It should be the same for stagnation of sullage or any other waste water in urban or rural areas. There should be daily sweeping of streets, roads or public places both in rural and urban areas. The vacant plots should be provided with boundary walls and kept neat, clean and green.

Pursuit of Swachh Bharat also requires strengthening public health services. Services such as good drainage systems, absence of swamps and ponds that are home to stagnant water, and the supply of safe drinking water—all of which reduce exposure to and spread of diseases—are classic examples of public goods and require effective government intervention. Swachh Bharat would do well to encourage each state to restart a separate public health department, accountable for the delivery of public health services.

MAKE IN INDIA CAMPAIGN

Prime Minister Narendra Modi launched the 'Make in India' campaign at a high-profile event on September 25, 2014. Unveiling the campaign PM Modi said FDI should be understood as 'First Develop India' along with 'Foreign Direct Investment' while encouraging investors not to just look at India as merely a market but also as an opportunity. The Prime Minister pointed out that it was crucial to increase the purchasing power of the common man to boost demand and thus spur development. Key thrust of the programme would be on cutting down in delays in manufacturing projects clearance, develop adequate infrastructure and make it easier for companies to do business in India.

The national programme aims at time-bound project clearances through a single online portal which will be further supported by the eight-member team dedicated to answering investor queries within 48 hours and addressing key issues including labour laws, skill development and infrastructure.

The objective of the mega programme is to ensure that manufacturing sector which contributes around 15% of the country's Gross Domestic Products is increased to 25% in next few years.

Notwithstanding the challenges faced in making India a manufacturing hub, the country is poised to reap rich dividend for being one of the youngest nations in the world. According to reports by 2020, India is set to become the world's youngest country with 64% of its population in the working age group. Although a sound beginning has been made for the Make in India campaign, now the ball is in the government's court to ensure its success.

The major objective behind the initiative is to focus on 25 sectors of the economy for job creation and skill enhancement. Some of these sectors are: automobiles, chemicals, IT, pharmaceuticals, textiles, ports, aviation, leather, tourism and hospitality, wellness, railways, auto components, design manufacturing, renewable energy, mining, biotechnology, and electronics. The initiative hopes to increase GDP growth and tax revenue. The initiative also aims at high quality standards and minimising the impact on the environment. The initiative hopes to attract capital and technological investment in India.

Under the initiative, brochures on the 25 sectors and a web portal were released. Before the initiative was launched, foreign equity caps in various sectors had been relaxed or removed. The application for licences was made available online. The validity of licenses was increased to 3 years. Various other norms and procedures were also relaxed.

DIWALI

A festival plays a great role as it brings new joy and hope to the people. Of all the festivals I like Diwali. Diwali or Deepawali which means rows of lights is an important festival not only of Hindus but of almost all the communities living in India. It is celebrated with great enthusiasm all over the country.

This festive day falls on the Amavasya of the month of Kartik every year exactly twenty days after Dussehra by the Hindu Calendar. This festival of lights, sweets and crackers is celebrated with fun and frolic by all. In this day, the return of Lord Rama to Ayodhya after gaining victory over Ravana is memorable. To welcome him back and to express their joy, the people of Ayodhya lighted rows of earthen lamps. Some others believe that Goddess Lakshmi of wealth and prosperity visits every house on this night. To welcome her the lights are lit throughout the night. Jains believe that in the early morning of this day Lord Mahavir attained 'Moksha or Salvation.'

The preparations start with cleaning their houses and shops. This is the best time for the manufacturers and sellers of sweets, toys and idols of gods and goddesses, crackers, candles etc. As people are eager to purchase new clothes, utensils, greeting cards and other things, there is great hustle-bustle in every market. These market areas are decorated and they undoubtedly draw a lot of crowd.

On the day of Diwali, everyone is happy and mirthful. Clad in new clothes they visit their friends and relatives. Sweets and greetings are exchanged.

At night people worship Lord Ganesh and Goddess Lakshmi with great devotion. People decorate their houses with illuminating lamps, candles and electric bulbs. The sight of these glittering lights is very enchanting as the night appears to be under the spell of a full moon. Children let off fireworks. All the variety of crackers like anars, rockets, lighting pencils, etc. is seen.

Fireworks must be under the supervision of elders as any folly can lead to injuries, burns and fire hazards. Many fire tenders are placed at different areas for ready help in case of need. All people, young and old, who take part in the happy occasion must be careful so that accidents of such harm do not occur.

Some people wrongly believe that they should gamble on the day of Diwali. Gambling is a social evil and people must keep away from this practice.

Diwali is the festival of wealth, prosperity and happiness. It is the festival celebrated by the majority of Indians in every nook and corner of the country. As such, it has become a symbol of unity in diversity.

UNEMPLOYMENT

At present, our Employment Exchanges have registers containing long lists of unemployed youth. There are skilled, unskilled and educated youth who are unemployed. As per Employment Exchanges, there are more than four crore people unemployed and many more underemployed in India at present.

The educated ones run after white collared jobs which are hard to seek because of fewer jobs, reservations, glut of the qualified people, corruption, nepotism, favouritism and so many other factors. Our universities are turning out graduates like nuts and bolts in factories.

There is a glut of not only arts graduates, but also commerce, engineering, medical and other graduates in several technical, technological and managerial fields and disciplines.

However, there are emerging on the horizon, thanks to globalisation and Information Technology revolution, several new diplomas and courses which can help the young people to become proficient in them and get alternative jobs. But all the people cannot avail themselves of this opportunity. It is because they lack awareness, will, means, resources, guidance, etc.

The problem of unemployment can be solved only if our government and the society are both seriously interested in doing so. The upper class, to which the bureaucrats, politicians and industrialists of our country belong, is getting a whopping chunk of the exchequer in the form of pay, profits and other facilities. The bureaucrats' pay scales may be cut down and with the amount saved the unemployed can feed their families.

At present, whereas unemployment in general is a serious problem, higher posts are manned by either rich and powerful families, or person from reserved categories. Those who are economically weaker and do not fit in any reserved category have been left high and dry.

The problem of unemployment can be solved by bringing about a comprehensive planning system for many years may be, two decades or so, keeping in view the likely rise in population and expected changes in the social set-up and scientific and other spheres.

The best way is to start new courses which are relevant to the times. New development schemes both in urban and rural areas should be started. The youth should be employed there.

Some self-financing schemes should also be started. The youths should be given liberal loans on easy terms to start their own enterprises on small-scale. Such youths should be provided free training and guidance and supervision in starting and running their plants at suitable places.

It is in the fitness of things that the government have already started some useful Rozgar Yojna. But in India there is still much scope for development. In rural areas in certain states, conditions are pretty bad. In slum areas almost everywhere, they are far from satisfactory.

Young people should be sent to work in slum areas, health resorts, rural development works, illiteracy, poverty, disease eradication programmes. For this, they must be paid adequately. Some means should be adopted for their absorption or rehabilitation in one or the other field, as the case may be, keeping in view their qualifications, experience, aptitude, family circumstances, etc.

EDUCATION FOR ALL

Education is a tool that can play a vital role in improving the socio-economic condition of the nation. It empowers citizens with analytical abilities, leads to better confidence levels and fortifies one with will power and goal setting competencies.

Education involves not only textbook learning but also a growth of values, skills and capacities. This helps individuals to plan for their career as well as play a useful part in building a new society with progressive values. Hence, education results in changing both individual lives as well as that of the entire community for the better. The education sector has been of vital importance to the Indian Government which has been regularly formulating provisions and schemes for promoting elementary education.

The Right to Education has also been enshrined as a Fundamental Right by the Constitution of India. It states that "The State shall provide free and compulsory education to all children of the age of six to fourteen years in such a manner as the State may, by law, determine."

To promote literacy among its citizens, the Government of India has launched several schemes such as the Kasturba Gandhi Balika Vidyalaya Scheme, Mid-day Meal Scheme and the National Program for Education of Girls at Elementary Level (NPEGEL). One of the most fundamental and promising of these schemes is the Sarva Shiksha Abhiyan. The Sarva Shiksha Abhiyaan is also known as the Education for All movement or 'Each One Teach One'. It was introduced in 2000-2001 as the flagship programme run by the Government of India. This scheme is framed to provide useful and relevant elementary education for all children in the age group of six to fourteen. The Sarva Shiksha Abhiyan aims to bridge social, regional and gender gaps, with the active participation of the community in the management of schools.

NATIONAL INTEGRATION

India is a sovereign democratic secular State. Here, all the people have equal rights and duties without discrimination on the basis of religion, caste, colour, creed, region, language, etc.

India is a multi-racial and multi religious country. It is a pluralist State. It is a secular country where the people of all religions worship, without any let or hindrance, according to their religious practices, though subject to law and order.

Geographically and linguistically, India has a vast variety. It is a unity in diversity. The Indian people in different States and regions eat different kinds of food. They wear different clothes. They speak different languages. They have different castes and they observe different religious practices. Still, they are all Indians.

It is a pity that communal riots take place in different parts of our country off and on. Mostly, the innocent, gullible people are incited by political leaders and religious bigots to indulge in acts of violence and resort to arson, murder, loot, mayhem, etc.

The result is untold loss to life and property, mostly of innocent people. Such people should be dealt with sternly.

An awakening and love for the country should be brought about among the common people. These are the innocent illiterate people who are most gullible and most likely to be led astray. Therefore, the literacy campaign should be intensified.

Intercaste and inter-religious marriages should be less encouraged. People should be encouraged to celebrate together festivals sacred to all religions. Ancient monuments whether temples or mosques should be considered national monuments.

Students should be given patriotic lectures in colleges and the school and college curricula should include lives of great national leaders. Practice of pilgrimages, fairs, etc. where members of all communities participate should be encouraged.

ADULTERATION

Adulteration is one of the trickiest problems we are facing today. It is because the adulterators are too cunning people to be caught easily. Moreover, they seem to be hand and glove with the police and health authorities that be.

It is most unfortunate that today we can hardly get anything in pure form. Milk which is a kind of nectar from God and is meant most for children, expectant mothers, invalids and old people is one of the most adulterated things. What we get is not pure milk of the cow or the buffalo but the chemical milk prepared by mixing several obnoxious things such as caustic soda, fertilizers, detergent powders, shampoo, etc. with refined oil.

The seeds of papaya are mixed in black pepper. There is corn flour or maida or wheat flour mixed in besan. We find the horse dung in tea leaves. There is sand in sugar. There are toxic insecticides in spices. The vegetables are washed in dangerous colouring chemicals and so on.

In fact, we can't get any eatable in pure form. Then there are medicines which instead of curing a disease can deteriorate it. The fake toilet soap we get in the market can cause rashes on skin and perhaps even cancer. Similarly, we find several carcinogenic ingredients mixed in eatables. Sweets are coloured with most harmful colours. Surprisingly, toxic elements have been found even in items of well-established renowned multinational companies manufacturing cold drinks, chocolates, etc.

Clearly, if urgent, drastic steps against the adulterators are not taken, the health of the whole nation may be in danger. These adulterators should be given severe punishments, including capital punishment.

POVERTY

Poverty is one of the toughest problems that India is facing today. Quite oddly, in spite of all the progress that India has made during the years, the monster of poverty has not been eliminated. A great segment of our society is still living below the poverty line.

The most distressing feature of our social system is that we have at present all the more glaring contrasts and disparities in incomes and life styles. Whereas on the one hand we have millionaires and even billionaires, on the other hand, we have teeming millions who cannot make both ends meet. And then with the rise in prices of essential commodities, their real incomes are further shrinking.

Nothing is without cause. Similarly, there are definite causes for this stark poverty. Illiteracy is one of such causes. The world has moved fast during the last some years. But the illiterate or semi-literate people are unable to keep pace with the world. Hence, they cannot find a job. Even if they are able to find one, it is not lucrative enough to enable them to earn enough for themselves and for their family. Hence, they have to lead a marginal life.

Many parents, particularly in rural areas and those belonging to lower strata of life are superstitious. They do not allow their children to learn new arts and services. They consider some arts such as singing, dancing, painting, etc. to be immoral even if their child has a strong aptitude for it.

Many people are lethargic and they do not want to do anything. Then there is so much corruption at all levels that they dare not take a risk in investing in any venture. Also cut-throat competition in every field discourages new entrants.

The remedy lies in a house to house survey. Seats in services should be reserved for economically weaker persons. Those who want to set up a small scale industry or start a business should be given liberal loans at low interests. Really indigent and helpless persons, particularly the senior citizens, the disabled and the widows should be given pensions and grants and subsidies.

AIDS

AIDS is a deadly disease for which so far no foolproof treatment has been discovered. Of course, great research is going on in this field. It is said that a vaccine has now been discovered but how far it is successful, is still doubtful. But its efficacy in saving the new born babies is said to have been proved to an acceptable measure.

The best safeguard against this devastating disease is the precautions that we should take and bear in mind. The first reason how a man gets AIDS is through infected blood transfused into his body. So, if we need transfusion of blood for any reason, we should make sure that it is AIDS free and has conclusively been tested as such.

In is quite understandable that we should use only disposable syringes if we want to have an injection. A non-disposable syringe might have got infected.

Another reason for the spread of AIDS is unprotected sex. We must take care that we are never to indulge in unprotected sex. The best thing is that we should never have extra-marital relations.

A baby may be infected with AIDS if any of the parents has got the infection or is HIV positive. It should be confirmed from specialists if the new vaccine developed for the protection of babies against AIDS is effective. If found so, it should be administered to the baby under the guidance and supervision of the specialist concerned.

If a person has at all developed AIDS, we should not discard him like a hot potato. He should be shown due regard and affection and we should take measures that we can for his comfort and recovery, if possible. We should remember that certain acts such as shaking hands, kissing, using same towels, etc. does not spread AIDS.

We should not fight shy of getting our blood tested for HIV. It is done at nominal rates and even free at certain places. In case of HIV positive, we should take the counsel, help and guidance of experts in the matter.

A RAILWAY JOURNEY

Children generally love to go out. As such, they are very fond of making journeys frequently. They love all kinds of journeys. I have frequently travelled by bus with my parents to different places. However, last Sunday I had a memorable journey by rail.

We reached the station at about 10.00 a.m. The train was to start at 10.15 a.m. My father bought tickets for mother and me as also for himself.

Immediately, we moved to platform No. 1 where the train was to arrive shortly. We had not been there on the platform for more than a minute or two when the train arrived. We at once boarded it. We had first class tickets with us. So, we found no difficulty in boarding the train.

I got a seat near the window. Soon, the train started. I felt thrilled. I saw the platform moving backwards. At first the train was slow but soon it gathered speed. Within a few minutes, it gained the speed of the wind.

All the houses, poles, fields and trees seemed to be running backwards. I saw farmers working in the fields. Animals were also grazing there. Some women were picking up weeds from the fields.

It was an express train. So, it did not halt at small stations. Even at big stations and junctions, it halted only for a few minutes. As the train halted some people bought eatables and drinks from the vendors at the platforms. Some vendors also came within the compartments. A travelling ticket Examiner came and checked our tickets.

It was late in the afternoon that the train reached Kolkata. We alighted from it and through the exit gate came out. Again our tickets were checked, now at the gate. We left for our uncle's house where we had to go.

A VISIT TO THE TAJ

The Taj Mahal is a world famous mausoleum. It is situated on the bank of the river Yamuna near Agra. It was built by the Mughal Emperor Shah Jahan in the middle of the seventeenth century.

Shah Jahan built this monument in memory of his beloved wife, Mumtaz Mahal. It is said that more than twenty thousand masons and workers took more than twenty years in building this monument.

The Taj is made of pure white marble. It is one of the wonders of the world. Tagore called it "a tear frozen on the face of eternity."

Even after about four centuries when it was built, it has not lost its beauty. When the Mathura Oil Refinery was set up, there was a wide-spread fear about the safety of the glory of the Taj. However, at the instance of the Supreme Court, timely remedial measures were taken.

Before we reach the main building of the Taj, we walk on a path which has tall attractive cypress trees on either side. Behind the cypress trees there are vast luxurious grassy lawns.

There is a large central dome over the main building, having four spiralling minarets on each of the four sides of the building. The graves of Shah Jahan and Mumtaz Mahal lie in a dark chamber beneath the central dome.

Thousands of visitors and tourists visit the Taj annually. It is a sight to see in the moonlight, especially on the full moon night.

I visited the Taj last Monday and I would like to visit it more than once again.

A ROAD ACCIDENT

Road accidents are very common these day. Some people drive vehicles very rashly. Others drive them in a drunken state and cannot easily control them.

Yesterday, I was going along the GT Road on a bicycle. As the traffic was very fast, I decided to avoid the macadamized road. So, I went on the kutcha path along the road.

Suddenly, a truck came at full speed. A bus was coming from the opposite direction. The truck was not following the rules of the road. It simply rammed into the bus.

The driver of the bus was killed on the spot. A large number of passengers were seriously injured. Half of the bus was smashed. The same was the condition of the truck. The luggage which the truck was carrying, spread on the road.

It was later learnt that the truck driver was dead drunk. He was also seriously injured. He was taken to the local civil hospital by the police not only for treatment but also for alcohol test.

It was later learnt that the truck driver who had tried to run away, was fined heavily by the court. The injured passengers and the bus passengers who had died in the accident, had to be paid adequate compensation. However, no amount of compensation can ever bring back a life which is lost. The best remedy is to avoid accidents altogether. It is rightly said safety saves. All the necessary steps should be taken to check the alarming rise in the number of road accidents.

SCIENCE AND HUMAN HAPPINESS

Modern age is the age of science. Wherever we go, we find articles based on some or the other scientific formulas. For instance, many of the students and office-goers get awakened with the help of an alarm clock. The factory goers learn about the factory time through the buzzing of a hooter.

People generally go to places of work by using one or the other vehicle. The food they eat is prepared on the stove or gas oven. The clothes they wear are prepared in big factories and mills.

Science has enabled the modern man to fly in air like birds and swim in the sea like fishes. Even more than that he can even travel in space which the birds can't do. All the modern means of travel and other devices are the inventions of science.

Some of important devices and inventions and discoveries used by the common man are electric bulb, fluorescent tube, mixer, juicer, oven, grinder, refrigerator, TV, cinema, paper, printing press, bus, car, ship, tractor, aeroplane, microscope, telescope, X-Ray, A.C, railway train computer, telephone, telegraph system, etc.

One important discovery of science is electricity which has made the working of so many factories and mills possible.

Inventions and discoveries in agriculture and irrigation methods have enabled food for the teeming millions on earth. Means of travel and communication have become faster and cheaper. Inventions in medical science have led to longevity and reduction in the ratio of child mortality. Life has become comfortable for the common man.

RENEWABLE ENERGY

Ex-Prime Minister Atal Bihari Vajpayee said in an address to people through leading newspapers on December 25, 2003. "Just as the last two centuries were driven by coal and oil, it is my belief that the next century will belong to renewables."

He also said, "Our expanding economy, and the strong growth expected in the next few decades, will require substantial addition to our energy generating capacity."

We can, indeed, come over energy crisis that we have been facing for quite long by reducing dependence on fossil fuels and focussing our attention on renewable energy sources. This we can do by expanding and diversifying our energy supply mix.

This shift towards renewable energy can provide a greater of national energy security and offer greater opportunity for sustainability as well as environmental and social responsibility.

Some of the important renewable energy sources can be listed in two main categories. The first system which may be called 'Grid Connected System' may involve wind power, small hydro power, Biomass/cogeneration power, urban and industrial waste power and solar photovoltaic power.

The second category system which may be captioned 'Decentralized System', may involve systems which come in closer touch of the common man such as biogas plants, nightsoil based biogas plants (Which may be community or institution-based) improved chulhas, solar home lighting, solar street lighting, solar lanterns, SPV pumps, solar water heating, etc.

The use of renewable energy has been started in various forms at several places (number of which may expand in the near future) such as Sunderbans, Ladakh, Bastar, North East, Bangalore, Tirupati, Tirumale Devasthanam, etc.

ULTRAVIOLET (UV) RADIATION

The sun spreads its rays of light in the form of electromagnetic radiation. These have different names and forms such as ultraviolet rays, gamma rays, infrared rays, radiowaves, microwaves, visible rays, etc.

The most dangerous among all the rays mentioned above are the ultraviolet (UV) rays. These rays are invisible except that when they fall on certain kinds of material they can make them emit visible light by emitting electromagnetic radiation of lower energy.

The earth has a high intensity oxygenated zone layer as its cover which absorbs most of the ultraviolet rays. But if the ozone layer becomes thin as, indeed, it has, some of the UV rays reach the earth and may be a hazard to human life and health.

UV rays can cause sunburn, alteration of connective tissue of dermis, tanning of skin and even skin cancer and other diseases.

Ordinarily, we can get only limited protection against UV rays even by sitting in shade as under a tree.

Curiously, however, the UV rays cannot penetrate glass. Thus we can protect our eyes against UV rays by wearing sun-glass of various kinds. If eyes are not protected against UV rays, we can contract even cataract. If we consult a doctor or a scientific expert, he may tell us about several hazards which may be caused by UV radiations.

We can take certain steps to protect ourselves against the fury of UV radiations, such as keeping infants in shade, limiting midday sun, wearing hat, sunglasses, protective clothing, applying sunscreen, etc.

It is rightly said that we should not look at the sun at the time of solar eclipse as that way, we can get our eyes harmed by the UV rays emitted by the sun.

HORRORS OF WAR

It is admitted on all hands that war is a terrible thing. In olden times, wars were fought with bows and arrows and clubs and spears. Then wars were not so dangerous.

Then came guns, cannon, rifles, pistols and small bombs. Then wars became more horrible. With the manufacturing of warplanes, warships, gunboats, torpedoes and missiles wars became even more destructive. There was more loss of life and property in the first and second world wars than perhaps in all human history taken together prior to that.

With the making of the atom bomb and the hydrogen bomb and innumerable other destructive explosive things including nuclear, bacteriological and chemical weapons and other weapons of mass destruction (WMD), the destructive power of the war machinery has assumed unimaginable proportions.

Now a number of countries like the USA, the UK, France Russia, China, India, Pakistan, etc. have nuclear weapons and missiles of various categories on which nuclear warheads can be mounted.

The destruction which modern wars cause is immense. Crops are destroyed. Cities are levelled. Even educational institutions and hospitals are not spared. Thousands of women become widows. Millions of children become orphans.

May God forbid, if nuclear war takes place, the whole of mankind may be wiped off the face of the earth. So, effective steps must be taken to banish war altogether.

ELECTRICITY

Electricity is one of the most important discoveries of science in the modern age. Electricity is there in the charged clouds and that is why they thunder so loudly. Probably, man took an idea from the clouds and this helped him in discovering electricity.

Electricity is a blind energy and is thus ruthless in its power, working and effect. Man has, however, found out the means to harness it with the help of insulators which he has discovered through experiments for the purpose.

Today, electricity is produced in several ways, that is, through hydraulic means, through wind power, through the use of coal, through nuclear power and so on. Now, even house waste is being used to generate electricity and energy. Solar energy is a common word these days. Energy comes to us mostly in the form of electricity, though some other shapes and forms may also be there.

In the modern age, we cannot think of life without electricity. Day in and day out, we are always surrounded by objects and machines which work with electricity. Some of these common household objects and devices are the electric bulb, the fluorescent tube, the electric fan, the desert cooler, the air conditioner, the room heater, the electric microwave oven, the mixer, the juicer, the toaster, the refrigerator, the geyser, etc.

Almost all the factories run with electricity. Computer which has changed the face of life on earth is also run with electricity. Even objects such as the mobile phone, etc. which work with the help of satellite use computer for certain purposes such as recording, bill charging, etc.

Thus, it is basically electricity which has revolutionized life on earth and other revolutionary things get sustenance from electricity.

AN EARTHQUAKE

So far, no foolproof method has been devised to predict an approaching earthquake. Some people, especially in China, believe that just before an earthquake occurs, birds and animals start behaving in strange manner.

Scientist have created artificial earthquakes in the laboratories to apprise the people of their various aspects. But, it is not essential that the earthquakes should always occur in the same manner. Some earthquakes are said to start from 30 to 100 kilometres below the surface of the earth and others from 100 to 650 kilometres below it. The earthquake that started, as recorded in history, at the deepest level under the earth so far, occurred in Bolivia in 1994.

A violent earthquake shook the city of Bam, 1285 km southeast of Teheran in Iran at 5.28 a.m. (07.28 IST) on 26 December 2003. The earthquake was of the magnitude of 6.3 on the Richter scale. Its epicenter was outside Bam, about 1000 km southeast of Tehran. The quake hit the city when most of the people were in bed.

The city had a population of 80,000 and death toll was high. It was estimated that more than 40,000 people had died. The citadel of Bam was destroyed. The oldest part of the fortress dates to about 2000 years ago, but most of it was built in the 15th to 18th centuries and attracted thousands of tourists every year.

Telephone links with Bam were severed and the authorities were in contact with the city area through radio and satellite phone links. More than 90 percent buildings in the city were demolished. Thousands of people were injured. Power and water supplies were also snapped. This hampered relief efforts.

The international community came to the rescue of the Iranian people and tents, blankets, canned food, bread, clothing and medicines were donated liberally by some countries and sent to affected area.

Another quake rock South Asia. Jammu & Kashmir and Pakistan are badly hit by the killer quake raising the death toll to 80000 in Pakistan and more than 1500 in Batalik village of Jammu & Kashmir. India extended her hands for help of earthquake victims in Pakistan also.

HEALTH IS WEALTH

There is a well-known saying : If wealth is lost, nothing is lost. If health is lost, something is lost. If character is lost, everything is lost.

It can be reasonably believed that no person in a sound mind would like to lose something even.

A healthy man can work hard and earn wealth, whereas an unhealthy man can't do this. Moreover, it is said and that rightly so, that a sound mind lives only in a sound body. In the modern world brain is everything to get all that man desires, but health is a prerequisite for having a good brain.

A student who works hard throughout the year has to bring out his knowledge on the paper on the day of examination. But if he does not enjoy good health, he may fall ill on the day of examination and thus all the labour done by him the whole year may just go down the drain.

In normal cause, even to pursue one's studies in a sustained manner may not be possible for one who doesn't enjoy good health.

It is for this reason that it is said that students and all young people should take part in sports and games and have regular walks and exercise on daily basis.

Those people who run after money excessively and lose their health, are no gainers in any way. A man having a lot of money, may not even be able to enjoy the fruits of his labour because death and disease can overpower him any time. So, the first and foremost thing for us is to take care of our health. Wealth-earning and other motives must take only a secondary place in our scheme of things.

THE VALUE OF TREES / FORESTS

It is rightly said that for the earth to be a healthy place, at least one third of the whole land area should be covered with forests. Trees absorb carbon from the air in the sunlight and turn it into food for themselves. In return, they release oxygen in the air which is so essential for human and animal world. The existence of men, animals and even the plants is impossible without a fair amount of oxygen in the air. If the trees are cut down ruthlessly, the balance of oxygen in the atmosphere is disturbed and it has serious repercussions.

Trees check floods and soil erosion. In forests the dense undergrowth ensures preservation of water which gets released slowly into plains, valleys and living habitations.

A large number of wild animals also live in forests. Birds build their nests in trees. If there are no trees, the life of these birds and animals will be endangered.

Trees provide us so many things such as shade, fuel, timber for houses, wood for furniture, gum, fodder for animals, medicines etc. So many industries are based on the trees. Among them we have paper industry, match-making industry, making of wooden and cardboard boxes for packing purposes, etc.

Recently, there has started the cultivation of a plant known as "diesel plant", the oil of the seeds of which gives fuel like diesel. It is being grown in Maharashtra and Punjab.

So, trees are so essential for us. They should not be cut, but more and more trees should be grown instead.

THE VALUE OF BOOKS

Books are a store-house of knowledge. All that men have observed, learnt and experienced over the centuries has been enshrined in books. In other words, it is in books that the great minds of the past ages are kept safe for generations to come.

Books are our best friends. Even our closest friends and nearest relatives may part company with us in time of adversity, but books always stand by us. They stand by us through thick and thin. They never betray us.

When the dark clouds of misery engulf us from all sides and we feel helpless, books come to our rescue. We read them, consult them and regain hope and confidence which no living human being could impart.

In earliest times, man was uncivilized and barbarian. Someone thought of writing and when he joined the written pages to form a unit, the first book took its birth.

Previously, books were handwritten and were sometimes lost. As the printing press came, books began to be printed in thousands such that if one book or some books were lost there were almost always a few more left to keep the author's ideas alive.

Now, we have books of all kinds on all branches of life. We have books on literature, philosophy, sports, history, astronomy, astrology, physiology, hygiene, geography, poetry, cookery, doll-making, soap making, mathematics, fiction, science, technology, painting, photography, drama, indeed, on any and every conceivable subject. Much depends on our own aptitude and necessity which type of books we want to read.

In the modern computer age, some people fear that the device like the internet may spell the end of books. But, as we have seen, it is a fallacy as books have their own place in our life. They are indeed, indispensable and that is an indisputable fact.

LIFE IN A BIG CITY

Life in a big city is often said to be very tiring. It is because distances are long and those who have to go some other place for the purpose of purchases, seeing some relative or friend or work, have to remain on the road for a long time, sometimes, for hours together.

There is too much traffic on the roads in a big city. There is always the possibility of an accident if we loosen the grip over our vehicle even for a moment.

Then there is so much pollution in a big city. So many vehicles which run on petrol or diesel pollute the atmosphere. There is also so much noise on the roads and in markets. There is also an acute housing problem in a big city. Many people have to live in slums, huts, shanties, and small houses.

There are often so many places worthseeing in a big city. One does not generally get bored. There are also great employment avenues in a big city for all kinds of people educated, skilled, semi-skilled and even unskilled.

In a big city, there are so many schools, colleges, universities and institutions of all kinds where one can get good education according to one's taste and aptitude. Then there are so many libraries where one can gain more and more knowledge.

There are so many hospitals and dispensaries in a big city where one can get quick medical aid of all kinds. Then there are also so many nursing homes run by specialists of various diseases.

There are so many museums, exhibitions and magic and other shows where one can get recreation as well as an opportunity to enhance one's knowledge.

So, a big city has some merits as well as demerits. It depends upon our own attitude how we look at a big city.

DELHI

Delhi is one of the four biggest cities of India. The other three such cities are Mumbai, Kolkata and Chennai. In one respect at least, Delhi tops all the other three cities. It is in the matter of the number of auto- vehicles. The number of vehicles that ply on the roads of Delhi is more than their number in the other three big cities all put together.

Delhi is the Capital of India It has for centuries been the Capital of India except for certain brief breaks here and there. It was because before partition, it lay almost in the heart of the country. Its importance, however, has not diminished after Independence.

Delhi is sometimes called the city of kings. Having been the Capital of various dynasties in the past, it has several monuments and places worth-seeing. Some of such famous places are the Red Fort, the Jama Masjid, the Birla Mandir, the India Gate, the Qutub Minar, the Connaught Place, Gurdwara Bangla Saheb, the Gurdwara Sis Ganj, Gurdwara Rakab Ganj, Jantar Mantar, etc.

Some of the famous universities in Delhi are – Delhi University, Jawaharlal Nehru University, Jamia Millia Islamia, Guru Gobind Singh University, Indira Gandhi National Open University, etc.

There are also a large number of libraries, museums and art galleries in Delhi. Some of the famous hospitals of Delhi are All India Institute of Medical Sciences, Ram Manohar Lohia Hospital, Mool Chand Hospital, Sir Ganga Ram Hospital, Safdarjang Hospital, Kalawati Hospital, Sucheta Kripalani Hospitial, Loknayak Jayaprakash Hospital, etc.

Life in Delhi is very tiring. It has a population of over 16 million. The seat of legislature, the Parliament, is situated in Delhi. Rastrapati Bhawan, the President's residence is also located in Delhi. It is the Secretariat – the North Block and the South Block – where the policies of the government are formulated. Various government departments have their headquarters in Delhi. Delhi is a great centre of trade. Nobody can feel bored there. One should have money enough to entertain oneself, besides finding the employment and hobby of his taste there.

COMMUNAL HARMONY

Communal harmony is of utmost importance to our country for peace and progress.

Before independence, the Indian people by and large lived in peace. There were hardly any fanatics to arouse the religious feelings of people then. There existed composite cultures in several then Indian cities such as Lahore, Karachi, Amritsar, Delhi, Ahmedabad, Hyderabad, Kanpur, etc. There were hardly any communal riots then. Unfortunately, Muslim Leage's two nation theory divided the innocent Indian masses into two broad camps of Hindus and Muslims and thus started the diabolical communal riots which led to the disturbance of communal peace on a large scale and finally to division of the country.

After Independence, Indian people largely lived in communal harmony except rarely when some people were incited in the name of religion by the malicious Pakistani agents.

This communal harmony took an ugly turn in terrorist movement in Punjab which was largely engineered by the ISI of Pakistan.

There have grown up some staunch hawks in all religious organisations now and one concrete surfacing of this attitude has been witnessed in demolition of the Babri structure and burning of Rambhaktas in a train and its aftermath in Gujarat.

We should remember that our great religious preachers and scriptures have always stood for oneness of mankind and we should adhere to this doctrine. Moreover, national progress which is essential for all, is possible only if we maintain communal harmony.

LEISURE

Human body is a machine. Like any other machine, it requires rest after working for some time. W.H. Davies has expressed his views about the modern life which is full of stress and strain in the following words:

"What is this life if full of care?
We have no time to stand and stare."

Excessive worry about time is the bane of modern man. The doctrine that not a minute should be wasted is fraught with danger. It simply exhorts continuous work day and night and negates the idea of leisure.

Leisure is essential for our physical and mental health. A person who has done strenuous physical work for a few hours, needs rest after that. Similar is the case with one who has engaged himself in some mental work or intellectual activity for some time. This is the reason in all schools, colleges and other institutions, in offices and factories there is recess or lunch period. Even shops in posh markets close for an hour or so for lunch which also includes period for recess and refreshment.

One who has done hard physical work for some time, may study some interesting story book or have a look at the pages of an illustrated magazine during the leisure time. He may watch T.V if he doesn't have a book or is not inclined to read.

A person who has done some hard mental or intellectual work for sometime, may indulge in some physical activity such as a game of badminton, gardening, etc. for the purpose of replenishing the mental stamina.

The period of leisure should not be considered waste of time, even if one just spends this time in gossiping instead of indulging in any useful physical or mental activity. It should be regarded as worthwhile. However, the leisure time should be limited and should not be prolonged inordinately so as to encroach upon the working hours.

THE POSTMAN

The postman is a very useful member of society. He brings us dak from our friends and relatives who live at long distances from us. He brings us messages of joy and sorrow. He does his duty in sun and shower.

The postman is perhaps at the lowest level in the posts and telegraphs set up. He is the least literate and accordingly gets the lowest pay per month. He is only a step higher than sweepers and khalasis.

A postman is not a totally illiterate person. Otherwise, he would not be able to read even the address on letters. He is perhaps at least a matriculate. If a postman is hardworking and continues his studies during his spare time and passes graduation, he can rise at least to the post of a clerk in a post office.

The postman has to do his duty whether he is appointed in an urban or a rural area. His duty starts in the morning and ends late in the afternoon or in the evening.

The postman often goes to far off places on his bicycle. He should be provided at least less with a moped. He gets a uniform annually, but his pay is very low whereas his duty is hard and strenuous.

In rural areas, the postman has sometimes to read letters to illiterate recipients. Rarely, he may even have to write a letter for them.

He brings letters, inland letters, postcards, money orders, parcels and telegrams. People wait for him eagerly. Though he is fobidden to accept any gift from anybody, some people force him to accept a gift on certain occasions such as Diwali, New Year's Day or some marriage or birth in the family.

In any case, he is a lovable person who deserves better treatment from the authorities in the matter of pay-fixation, allowances, etc.

AN IDEAL CITIZEN

We are all the citizens of India. We are the children of Mother India. We hence have equal rights and duties. In spite of this, it is not certain that all of us are ideal citizens. We should all try to become ideal citizens of India. That is the best thing for us as well as our country.

Mr. Prem Kumar is an ideal citizen. He is every inch a patriot. He is ready to die for the country. He pays all his taxes regularly. He is very honest in his dealings. He works sincerely. He never wastes his own or others' time.

Mr. Kumar has a great civic sense. He never wastes water, electricity, petrol or gas. He does not try to spread pollution. He uses only lead free petrol in his scooter.

He does not adopt corrupt and underhand methods to become rich overnight. He works hard to achieve success.

He believes in spreading education, literacy and healthcare, cleanliness, and population-control awareness. He participates in all national and social activities and schemes and campaigns such as pulse polio, adult education, poverty removal, etc.

He goes to slum areas during his free time to teach the slum - dwellers the importance of literacy, small family, cleanliness etc.

In time of national and natural calamities such as earthquakes, floods, famines, fires, war, etc. he donates whatever he can to the National Relief Fund.

He is a highly educated man and strains every nerve to uphold the values of human rights, social equality, non-violence, universal brotherhood, national integration, democracy, transparency in public affairs, a non-polluted globe, etc. by raising his voice through the mass media.

SUBHASH CHANDRA BOSE

Subhash Chandra Bose was one of the greatest freedom fighters of India. He was born on January 23,1897 at Cuttack in Odisha. His father, Jankinath Bose was a renowned lawyer of the area. His mother, Prabhavati, was a highly learned religiously-minded lady.

Subhash Chandra imbibed many of his religious views from her. Some other persons who influenced him greatly were his teacher Beni Prasad Madho, C.R. Das and Swami Vivekananda.

He was a very intelligent, precocious, patriotic child with revolutionary ideas in his mind from the very beginning. He did his graduation from the Presidency College in 1919. Later, he appeared and passed the ICS examination only to please his father. But actually his heart was framed for serving his motherland and getting it liberated from the foreign rule.

In politics, his real mentors were Lokmanya Tilak and Sri Aurobindo Ghose more than Gandhi. Hence he was not much attracted towards the Non-Cooperation Movement which was started by Gandhiji in the 1920's.

In Bengal, the National Movement was being spearheaded by C.R. Das and Subhash Chandra was especially attracted towards him. The young Subhash arranged demonstration in Calcutta and was put behind the bars. Later, he had to be released. He was appointed the Chief Executive Officer of the Calcutta Corporation. Earlier in 1924, he had been arrested under the special ordinance and sent to Mandalay.

He was elected President of The Congress at the 1938 Haripur Session. Thereafter, he formed the Forward Bloc. Actually, he was in favour of fixing a deadline for freedom and giving an ultimatum to the British government to leave India. He led the Indian National Army. On July 2, 1943, he gave the famous slogan "Delhi Chalo". His words, "Give me your blood and I will give you freedom" can never be forgotten by his Countrymen.

He went in disguise as a Pathan first to Germany and then managed to reach Japan. The radio Tokyo declared that Netaji (by which name he is commonly known to his countrymen) died in an air crash in 1945. His death is still a matter of controversy for some people. They think he's still alive and is living in disguise as a priest somewhere.

MAN AND MACHINE

Man is a machine no doubt. He is a marvellous piece of work. The only difference is that man has got life and consciousness which machines don't have. Except for this difference, now we have robots which are machines but look like men and can do a lot of chores which seem difficult to men.

Thus, machines are time-saving devices. They increase man's life and, if properly used, they add comfort to man's life. Such are innumerable electrical and electronic devices.

However, when we use machines as labour-saving devices, we are also prone to cause unemployment on a large-scale. When one machine is used to do the jobs of a number of people, naturally, many hands will become surplus.

So, this is the tendency of throwing the workers on the roads for which Gandhiji criticized machines, otherwise he was not opposed to them. Let us have a look at his own words.

"I am not fighting machinery as such but the madness of thinking that machinery saves labour. Men save labour until thousands of them are without work and die of hunger on the streets. I want to secure employment and livelihood not only to part of a few at the expense of the money. At present the machine is helping a small minority to live on the exploitation of the masses. The motive force of his minority is not humanity and love of their kind, but greed and avarice. This state of things I am attacking with all my might." Gandhiji said. He also said, "I must refuse to insult the naked by giving them clothes they do not need instead of giving them the work they sorely need. The ill-clad or the naked millions of India need no charity, but work."

SMS GREETINGS

The system of sending greetings to friends and relatives on various occasions such as festivals, birthdays, marriage anniversaries, new year, etc. is quite old now.

In present times, this sending of cards costs a lot. The greeting card is quite a costly item and, besides, the postal charges are heavy. A person who has to send so many messages has to spend a lot of money.

It was perhaps for the first time that the computer-savvy Generation-X took to SMS in a big way by sending over One Crore SMS greetings on the occasion of New Year 2006.

There was an unprecedent rush of SMS messages on the occasion and One crore messages were delivered on or before the New Year Day while thousands more were delivered within the next few days.

This sudden popularity of the SMS greetings emerged from the fact that such greetings cost only 60 paise to Re 1 per SMS.

As reported, apart from young customers and IT guys, even the public relations companies, corporate sector, armymen and millions of cellular users all over the country used their handsets to convey their best wishes and greetings to their relatives, friends and clients.

A PICNIC

Picnicking is a very good source of recreation as well as instruction. I try my best to have at least one picnic party in a month. Last Sunday I alongwith a number of my friends, went out for a picnic. I had persuaded them two days earlier and all the neccessary arrangements had been made a day earlier.

On the fixed day, two of my friends, Sushil and Anil left very early in the morning for the canal. They took with them a number of mats, a stove, a kerosene can, some wheat flour, a pastry board, a pastry roller, a big can of purified water and a number of necessary articles which had been jointly listed by all the friends. They left for the venue on a tempo. The renowned cook, Mr. Devi Dayal, who had been engaged by us also reached the place at the time he was asked to do. He had already cut up the vegetables and prepared the fire before we reached there.

There were a dozen friends in all. We, the remaining friends reached the place on our bikes.

On reaching the lake, we decided to boat for a while. We had already engaged a boatsman and his boat. We had a very hilarious time. Then we decided to sing and dance on the mats to the tune of deck which Anil and Sushil had taken with them.

Meanwhile, Devi Dayal, had prepared hot puris with a fresh mixed vegetable dish. Thereafter we took sweet pudding.

Then we had a session of titbits and quizzes and other cultural items. We enjoyed ourselves a lot for a few hours and then returned home. We were full of enthusiasm, joy and happiness that the moments of interaction and cooperative spirit had lent us.

NUCLEAR WAR

Only a mad man will think of nuclear war. But the bitter truth is that there can, indeed, be some mad men who wield power in the world. Thus, we had Hitler.

It cannot be denied that if Hitler had atom bombs, he would have destroyed the whole world and "shut the doors on mankind" as he and his aides used to assert during the Second World War.

The diabological episode of 9/11 did take place and if the concerned terrorists had an atom bomb, they would have used it. So, the most dangerous thing is that the nuclear weapons can one day fall in the hands of terrorists.

At present, it is estimated and that perhaps correctly, that the most dangerous flashpoint in the world for the start of the nuclear war is the Indian subcontinent where India and Pakistan, both nuclear powers, are at loggerheads with each other.

God forbid, if the nuclear war takes place in any part of the world, the whole world will automatically be engulfed in it because of the oneness of the atmosphere and the rotation of the earth.

Such a war would cause untold destruction and misery. The buildings and crops would be engulfed in flames of fire. The human, animal and plant life will be destroyed on a large scale. Mankind may even get annihilated.

After the war there would be eternal winter. Those who survive would die of cold, starvation and radiation. If still some people survive, they would have to face a miserable fate. They would get incurable diseases such as cancer because of radiation and thus they would die by inches facing a situation of life-in-death.

A NATIONAL INTEGRATION CAMP

A National Integration camp was organised by the Ministry of Youths Affairs and Sports in our school campus during the last winter vacation. About two hundred students from different schools and colleges of the area attended the camp. It was a one week camp which started on December 22 and ended on December 28.

The volunteers remained busy in different activities. They served the locality with projects like cleaning dharamashalas, cremation ground, stadium, panchayat homes as well as planting saplings in the locality.

As it was a national-level camp, volunteers from other States had also come to participate in the camp. There were lectures by specialists in various fields on health awareness, national integration, communal harmony, environmental science and awareness.

Some lecturers also highlighted various problems being faced by our country such as terrorism, unemployment, poverty, AIDS, cancer, TB, Polio, etc. Volunteer also collected ₹ 20,000 from the adjoining villages to help the poor.

The grand finale of the camp was a trip to the Golden Temple, Jallianwala Bagh and Wagah border.

POWER OF THE PRESS

If one thing of which even the crookedest politicians and bureaucrats may be afraid is the press. It is rightly called the fourth estate. In any government, especially that having a democrative set-up, the three important organs are the legislature, the judiciary and the executive. The press may be regarded as the fourth organ.

The press brings to surface all the machinations of the clever politicians through simple informative statements and comments. The word Newspapers is almost synonymous with the word press. These newspapers are widely read even by the commonest people. Thus, if a politician falls in the eyes of the newspapers, he also loses favour with the common people whom he has to go for votes sooner or later.

The newspapers carry news, advertisements, readers' views, editorials, book reviews, cartoons, pictures, quizzes, etc. The word news is sometimes written in capital letters NEWS to convey the sense of North, East, West and South respectively which implies that they bring news from all directions or from all over the world. But we know that the newspapers carry information even from the skies. For instance, they tell us when an eclipse is to take place, when a storm is likely to approach a particular sea-coast, when the sun is going to flare up, when a comet will touch the atmosphere of the earth, etc. They also tell us about the weather.

In the newspapers we read editorials which carry comments on different policies of the government and other matters. Sometimes, these editorials are biased in favour of or against a particular political party or other organisation. So, we must read them most objectively. If we want to express our views, we can write a simple letter to the editor. Thus, newspapers are something useful, unavoidable and even indispensable in the modern age.

COMPREHENSION PASSAGE

(1)

India has signed the International Treaty on Plant Genetic Resources for Food and Agriculture.

The treaty will facilitate conservation and sustainable use of plant genetic resources of food and agriculture and fair and equitable sharing of the benefits arising out of their use for sustainable development of agriculture and food security.

"Access to plant genetic resources for creating new plant varieties is to be ensured all over the world through this treaty. Developing nations which are gene rich but economically poor will get adequate compensation through fair and equitable share of benefits arising out of the use of plant genetic resources which have been conserved by the farmers over centuries. The "Farmers' Right" concept will help in global recognition of the important role played by farmers in crop improvement activities."

QUESTIONS

1. What is the name of the treaty which India has signed?
2. What will the treaty facilitate?
3. What kind of sharing will it ensure?
4. Over what part of the world will it have its effect?
5. How will the developing nations be benefited by it?
6. In what context are the "Farmers' Rights" mentioned in the passage?

ANSWERS

1. The name of the treaty which India has signed is "International Treaty on Plant Genetic Resources for Food and Agriculture."
2. The treaty will facilitate conservation and sustainable use of plant genetic resources of food and agriculture.
3. It will ensure the fair and equitable sharing of the benefits derived from the use of plant genetic resources.

4. It will have its effect all over the world.
5. The developing nations will be greatly benefitted by it. Many of these nations are rich in genetic resources though they are economically poor. They will be greatly benefited by getting adequate compensation.
6. "Farmers' Rights" are mentioned in the passage in connection with the important role played by them in crop improvement activities.

(2)

In a significant judgement, the Punjab and Haryana High Court ruled on 29 May 2002.

"A hire purchase agreement may in substance be a loan transaction and the label of such an agreement is not conclusive. It is open to the court to determine whether a particular agreement is loan transaction or a hire-purchase agreement. In a loan agreement for financing goods on hypothecated basis, the creditor cannot forcibly repossess the hypothecated item, though he can enforce the security through the court."

The judge delivering the verdict further held: "If a specific clause is inserted in an agreement authorising the repossession of a vehicle or any other goods by the hypothecatee, such a clause may be unconscionable, unless otherwise shown by the hypothecatee".

QUESTIONS

1. What ruling did the court give regarding a loan transaction?
2. Who is to determine a transaction?
3. What can a creditor do and what can't he do in a loan agreement for financing goods on hypothecated basis?
4. About what clause did the court say that it may be "unconscionable"?
5. Which court gave the said judgement and when?

ANSWERS

1. The court ruled that the hire purchase agreement may in substance be a loan transaction and the value of such a transaction is not conclusive.
2. It is the court who is to determine such a transaction.
3. When there is a loan agreement for financing goods on hypothecated basis, the creditor cannot forcibly repossess the item that is hypothecated, but he can enforce the security through the court.

4. If in the agreement a specific clause is inserted which authorises the repossession of the hypothecated item by the hypothecatee, such a clause may be unconscionable except when it is shown otherwise by the hypothecatee.
5. The said judgement was given by the Punjab and Haryana High Court on 29 May 2002.

(3)

They had not been long together before. Darcy told her that Bingley was also coming to wait on her; and she had barely time to express her satisfaction and prepare for such a visitor, when Bingley's quick step was heard on the stairs, and in a moment he entered the room. All Elizabeth's anger against him had been long done away; but had she still felt any, it could hardly have stood its ground against the unaffected cordiality with which he expressed himself. On seeing her again, he inquired in a friendly, though general way, after her family, and looked and spoke with the same good-humoured ease that he had ever done.

QUESTIONS

1. For whom do you think has the word 'they' been used in the first line of the given passage?
2. For whom do you think has the word 'her' been used in the same line?
3. Why had the lady mentioned in the passage barely time to express her satisfaction?
4. In what tone did the gentleman talk to the lady?
5. What was the effect of this talk on the lady?

ANSWERS

1. The word "They" has been used in the first line of the passage for Darcy and Elizabeth.
2. The word "her" has been used in the same line for Elizabeth.
3. She had barely time to express her satisfaction because Bingley's step was suddenly heard on the stairs.
4. The gentleman talked to the lady in a genuinely cordial tone.
5. The effect of this talk was positive in the sense that the lady's anger, if any, was over.

(4)

In this way Indian mythology and old tradition crept into my mind and got mixed up with all manner of other creatures of the imagination. I do not think I ever attached very much importance to these stories as factually true, and I even criticized the magical and supernatural element in them. But they were just as imaginatively true for me as were the stories from the Arabian Nights or the Panchatantra, that storehouse of animal tales from which Western Asia and Europe have drawn so much. As I grew up other pictures crowded into my mind: fairy stories, both Indian and European, tales from Greek mythology, the story of Joan of Arc, Alice in Wonderland, and many stories of Akbar and Birbal, Sherlock Holmes, King Arthur and his Knights, the Rani of Jhansi-the young heroine of the Indian Mutiny-and tales of Rajput chivalry and heroism. These and many others filled my mind in strange confusion, but always there was the background of Indian mythology which I had imbibed in my earliest years.

—J. L. Nehru

QUESTIONS

1. What crept into author's mind during the earliest years of his life?
2. Did he ever consider these things to be factually true?
3. What did he criticize?
4. What crowded into his mind as he grew up?
5. In what context does the author mention the Arabian Nights and the Panchtantra?
6. What was always there as background in the author's mind?

ANSWERS

1. Indian mythology and old tradition crept into author's mind during the earliest years of his life.
2. Perhaps he never considered these things to be factually true.
3. He criticized the magical and supernatural element in the old Indian mythology and tradition.
4. As he grew up, several other pictures crowded into his mind, much as Indian as well as Greek fairy tales, tales from Greek mythology, the story of Joan of Arc, Alice in Wonderland, stories of Akbar and Birbal, Sherlock Holmes, King Arthur and his knights, the Rani of Jhansi, Rajput chivalry and heroism, etc.

5. The author makes a mention of the Arabian Nights and the Pachtantra to inform the readers that he considered the Indian mythology and tradition in the same view.
6. It was the Indian mythology which was always there as the background in the author's mind.

(5)

The new food policy, to be announced shortly, will provide special incentives for edible oil producers, especially rice bran oil producers in the country. Since the country is importing more than 40 lakh tonnes of edible oil annually the government plans to encourage farmers to plant cash crops on a large scale especially oilseeds instead of following the traditional wheat-paddy rotation.

This was stated today by Union Minister for Consumer Affairs, Food and Public Distribution Supply on June 30, 2002.

Responding to the demand to cut down duties on edible oils, he said: "The Centre is aware of the fact that high level of state and central duties is affecting the interests of producers, traders and consumers. That is one of the reasons the Central government in the last budget had tried to rectify the import duty structure. It has given positive results."

QUESTIONS

1. When will the new food policy be announced?
2. What will it provide?
3. What does the government plan to encourage and why?
4. What is the designation of the governmental authority mentioned in the passage?
5. Whose interests are mentioned in the passage and what is affecting them?
6. What had the central government tried in the last budget and what has been the effect?

ANSWERS

1. The new food policy will be announced shortly.
2. It will provide special incentives for edible oil producers, especially rice bran producers in the country.
3. The government plans to encourage the planting of cash crops on a large scale, especially oil seeds.

4. The designation of the governmental authority mentioned in the passage is the Union Minister for Consumer Affairs, Food and Public Distribution Supply.
5. The interests of producers, traders and consumers are mentioned in the passage. The high level of state and central duties is affecting them.
6. The government had tried to rectify the import duty structure in the last budget. It has given positive results.

(6)

A Particular Woman

Has she come a full circle from her "liberated spirit" day? It would seem so. Once making strident call for freedom for women, she predicts today that there will be no great change in women's status in the next century. "They have to work out problems with men not without them," she says. "My good times today are eating and shopping to get rid of negative thoughts. But I want a marriage to go home to. I need a good man to take care of me. I need a solid base to my life. Work is one side of life. Emotional security is the other and both are necessary for every woman!"

QUESTIONS

1. From where has "A Particular Woman" come a full circle?
2. What was once her call?
3. What is her present prediction?
4. How does she think about men?
5. What does she think to be her good times at present?
6. Why does she want to marry?
7. What two things does she consider important for every woman?

ANSWERS

1. "A Particular Woman" has come a full circle from her "liberated spirit" day.
2. Once her call was for freedom for women.
3. Her present prediction is that there will be "no great change" in women's status in the next century.
4. She thinks that women need men to take care of them. She believes that women can't get emotional security without men.

5. She thinks eating and shopping to get rid of negative thoughts are her good times at present.
6. She wants to marry to go home to and to get emotional security.
7. She thinks that work and emotional security are the two things which are important for every woman.

(7)

As the unbelievable news regarding Hansie Cronje's involvement in "match-fixing" spread, the most affected were those nearest to him.

"A lot of us were shocked. It is a blow for us and we just have to refocus. I am going to go out there and try and do the best job I can," Pollock told Reuters at the ground.

"He [Cronje] is an integral part of the team and an always-reliable all-rounder. He is a top-class player and he is going to be a hard person to replace".

"There won't be a shortage of motivation when you play against Australia. We will be missing Hansie but I'm sure the guys will be able to motivate themselves," he said.

Australia's team manager Steve Bernard told AAP news agency in Durban that the match-fixing scandal had reduced the three-match series to a sideshow.

"People aren't talking about the cricket. They are talking about this controversy. It is a shadow over the series. This takes some glass away" Bernard said.

QUESTIONS

1. What unbelievable news is mentioned in the passage?
2. Briefly describe Pollock's reaction to the news.
3. Who was Steve Bernard?
4. What were his views in this connection.
5. Assign a suitable heading to the passage.

ANSWERS

1. The unbelievable news mentioned in the passage is Hansie Cronje's involvement in "match-fixing."
2. Pollock got shocked on hearing the news. He had a high opinion of Cronje as being a good player who was an all-rounder. During the ensuing match with Australia, although Cronje's absence will be greatly felt by the South African team, Pollock thinks that the guys will come over it through self-motivation.

3. Steve Bernard was Australia's team manager.
4. According to him the match-fixing scandal has reduced the three match series to a sideshow.
5. Hansie Cronje and Match-fixing.

(8)

And rising as she thus spoke, she would have quitted the room, had not Mr. Collins thus addressed her:

"When I do myself the honour of speaking to you next on the subject. I shall hope to receive a more favourable answer than you have now given me; though I am far from accusing you of cruelty at present, because I know it to be the established custom of your sex to reject a man on the first application, and perhaps you have even now said as much to encourage my suit as would be consistent with the true delicacy of the female character."

"Really, Mr. Collins," cried Elizabeth with some warmth, "you puzzle me exceedingly. If what I have hitherto said, can appear to you in the form of encouragement, I know not how to express my refusal in such a way as may convince you of its being one."

"You must give me leave to flatter myself, my dear cousin, that your refusal of my addresses is merely words of course. My reasons for believing it are briefly these: It does not appear to me that my hand is unworthy of your acceptance, or that the establishment I can offer would be any other than highly desirable. My situation in life, my connections with the family of de Bourgh, and my relationship to your own, are circumstances highly in my favour; and you should take it into further consideration, that in spite of your manifold attractions, it is by no means certain that another offer of marriage may ever be made to you. Your portion is unhappily so small that it will in all likelihood undo the effects of your loveliness and amiable qualifications. As I must therefore conclude that you are not serious in your rejection of me, I shall choose to attribute it to your wish of increasing my love by suspense, according to the usual practice of elegant females."

"I do assure you, sir, that I have no pretensions whatever to that kind of elegance which consists in tormenting a respectable man. I would rather be paid the compliment of being believed sincerely. I thank you again and again for the honour you have done me in your proposals, but to accept them is absolutely impossible. My feelings in every respect forbid it. Can I speak plainer? Do not consider me now as an elegant female, intending to plague you, but as a rational creature, speaking the truth from her heart."

QUESTIONS

1. Between which two characters does the dialogue as given in the passage take place?
2. Why did the lady not quit the room?
3. How does the man mentioned in the passage take the rejection?
4. Mention briefly his reasons for delivering that his suit had not actually been rejected by the lady.
5. Explain briefly how the lady tried to convince the man that her rejection of him was genuine and not fake or pretended.

ANSWERS

1. The dialogue as given in the passage takes place between Mr. Collins and Elizabeth.
2. The lady did not quit the room as Mr. Collins started addressing her in the manner as given in the passage.
3. The man mentioned in the passage took the rejection as a positive sign of the lady's finally accepting him after the first reaction was over.
4. He believed that his rejection of him by Elizabeth was only a manifestation of the true delicacy of the female character. He believed that there were sever factors encouraging his belief as such, such as his situation in life, his connections with the family of de Bourgh, his relationship to Elizabeth's family, etc.
5. The lady tried to convince Mr. Collins that her rejection of him was real and not feigned. She thanked him repeatedly for his proposal, but she told him that she was a rational creature and was not interested in torment him by making a pretended rejection of him. So, she should be taken seriously.

(9)

All the heat or uproar generated by the entry of global insurance players into the Indian market seems to be fizzling out in at least one important sector-health insurance. The insurance players are wary of going full steam into the sector citing "moral hazards" as one of the primary reasons, the other being unattractive terms set by the Insurance Regulatory Development Authority.

Interestingly, most of the nursing homes in India are not registered, thus forcing the insurance giants to set up a parallel infrastructure of their own nursing homes and hire medical professionals, leading to an escalation in costs for entering the health arena.

Despite life expectancy in the country being still lower than the global average and immense growth potential in the health sector, many global giants have not accepted the bait owing to the earlier mentioned reasons, thus defeating the social objectives behind the privatisation of insurance.

QUESTIONS

1. What was all the heat or uproar mentioned in the passage?
2. What two reasons are mentioned in the first paragraph for the global insurance companies being wary of going full steam into the sector?
3. What impact on the insurance giants has been mentioned in the passage for most of the nursing homes in India?
4. What factors could attract the global insurance players the Indian market?
5. How have social objectives behind the privatisation of insurance been defeated in India?

ANSWERS

1. All the heat or uproar mentioned in the passage was about the entry of global insurance players into the Indian market.
2. The two reasons in this context are "moral hazards" and unattractive terms set by the Insurance Regulatory Development Authority.
3. Most of the nursing homes in India not being registered has prompted the insurance giants to set up a parallel infrastructure of their own nursing homes and hire medical professionals. This has led to an increase in costs for entering the health sector.
4. The factors which could attract the global insurance giants were life expeditionary in India being still lower than the global average and the scope for immense growth in the health sector.
5. The social objectives behind the privatisation of insurance have been defeated in India because of the reasons mentioned in the first paragraph of the passage.

(10)

It is often said that we should give particular attention to what we eat. Even if we do so, we have the tendency to eat excessively on certain occasions. Among such occasions, we have marriages, birthday parties, feasts at hotels and so on. These excesses often lead to indigestion and several related problems. In such emergencies, some people take recourse to fasting. That is not bad in itself. But, they should take care that they do not fast for too long a period. One thing which can help them a lot is the taking of abundance of water. Water can clean the body system as nothing else can.

QUESTIONS

1. What is often said?
2. What tendency do we have to do on certain occasions?
3. Name a few such occasions.
4. How can water be helpful when one is fasting?

ANSWERS

1. The thing which is often said is that we should give particular attention to what we eat.
2. We have the tendency to overeat on certain occasions.
3. Some of such occasions are marriages, birthday parties, feasts at hotels and so on.
4. When one is fasting water can be helpful in the sense that it cleanses the body system.

(11)

The growth of the private training sector in India has been closely intertwined with that of our IT industry. In the early nineties, there was a lot of interest among students to pursue a career in information technology. This was the period when large IT training and educational organisation were instituted and started. They offered long-duration career-oriented courses that became popular with undergraduates. Many students even pursued these IT courses in tandem with their regular graduate degrees. It was because they believed that this dual certification would give them a better choice of securing employment in IT sector.

QUESTIONS

1. What has been the relationship between the growth of the private training sector in India and that of our IT industry?
2. What kind of interest among the students in early nineties does the writer mention here?
3. What became popular with undergraduates?
4. Why did many students pursue IT courses in tandem with their regular graduate degrees?

ANSWERS

1. Their growth has been intertwined.
2. The writer mentions here the interest among the students to pursue a career in information technology.
3. The long-duration career-oriented courses offered by IT training and educational organisation became popular with undergraduates.
4. They did so with the belief that thus they would get a better chance of securing employment in IT sector.

(12)

Cockroaches have not changed much since they appeared more than 30 crore years ago in the warm forests of the distant past. They are armed with a tough, shiny shell and mouth parts well adapted for chewing. They can run at the speed of 3 km per hour. They can smell food with their long, pointed antennae and eat almost anything that could be eaten. Their flattened body is very helpful for crawling under floorboards or between narrow cracks and crevices. They often live in the company of human beings where they get plenty of food items. However, they can survive in tropical rain forests and desert conditions alike.

QUESTIONS

1. When and where did the cockroaches first appear?
2. What are their eating habits?
3. Where and how do they crawl?
4. Where and why do they often live?

ANSWERS

1. The cockroaches first appeared in the warm forests of the distant past.
2. Their mouth parts are well adapted for chewing. They can smell food with their long pointed antennae and eat almost anything eatable.
3. They crawl under floorboards or between narrow cracks and crevices. Their flattened body is very helpful to them for crawling.
4. They often live in the company of human beings. It is because in their company they can get plenty of food items.

(13)

Autumn is the season of the year when the dampness of the monsoon air is over and the nights are fragrance-laden. Spring unleashes a riot of colour, the most prominent being gold and yellow, but autumn is richly textured in subdued shades. During this season blooms soothe rather than excite. They create a sense of well-being and heady intoxication. In the dry summer season, the rivers are dry or they contain very little water. In the rainy season, many of them overflow their banks. But in the autumn season, rivers contain water only to a reasonable degree.

QUESTIONS

1. What is the difference between colour scheme of nature in spring and that in autumn?
2. What role is played by the blooms in spring and autumn?
3. What is the condition of rivers in summer and rainy seasons?
4. What is their condition in the autumn season?

ANSWERS

1. In spring, a riot of colour, prominently gold and yellow is unleashed. In autumn, we have richly subdued shades.
2. In spring the blooms excite but in autumn they soothe.
3. In summer the rivers are dry or have very little water in them. In the rainy season, many of them overflow their banks.
4. In autumn, rivers contain only a reasonable amount of water.

(14)

Le Corbusier was a profound and original thinker. When he said that a house was "a machine for living", he meant that when one designs a house, one must think of it, first and foremost, as an object that can effectively mediate between human beings and the environment that they live in.

Although French by citizenship and residence, Le Corbusier was born and brought up in Switzerland. He is the man who planned and designed Chandigarh, but today his relevance lies less in his specific architectural and urban designs than it does in some of his principles, and more so, in his example as an independent thinker of modernity.

QUESTIONS

1. Who was Le Corbusier and what kind of man was he?
2. What was his definition of a house?
3. What did he mean by this definition?
4. Wherein lies his real relevance today?

ANSWERS

1. Le Corbusier was the man who planned and designed Chandigarh. He was born and brought up in Switzerland but by citizenship and residence, he was a French. Above all, he was a profound and original thinker.
2. He defined a house "a machine for living".
3. By this definition, he meant that a house was an object that can effectively mediate between human beings and the environment they live in.
4. His real relevance today lies in his being an independent thinker of modernity.

(15)

Special effects are used to create photographic actions that simulate real or imaginary events that are otherwise dangerous, expensive or rather impossible to perform. There is a great demand these days for the people who can create or are concerned with the skill of special effects.

In the application of this technique, a supervisor controls movement of cameras, film, models and painting, with precision, in order to create film effects.

Today, science graduates, electrical engineers, computer programmers and hardware experts, all are involved in this trade.

QUESTIONS

1. For what purpose are special effects used?
2. Demand for what kind of personnel does the writer refer to here?
3. What is the role of a supervisor in the application of this technique?
4. Who are involved in this trade now-a-days?

ANSWERS

1. The purpose of special effects is to create photographic actions that simulate real or imaginary events which may be otherwise risky, expensive or impossible to perform.

2. The writer refers here to the great demand these days for that kind of personnel who can create or are concerned with the skill of special effects.
3. In the application of the technique of special effects, it is the duty of the supervisor to control movement of cameras, films, models and paintings with precision.
4. Now-a-days, all such personnel as science graduates, electrical engineers, computer programmers and hardware experts are involved in this trade.

(16)

Democracy has struck deep roots in the Indian soil. The credit should go to the Indian people who have steadfastly upheld the democratic spirit. No doubt, there are certain negative factors which can derail the democratic process. Among such factors we have communalism, casteism, nepotism, illiteracy, slowness of the judicial process, corruption, haughtiness of the politicians and bureaucrats and the like. Sometimes, we see that the votes are actually bought or even snatched by the bullies. Money and muscular power play a powerful role during the election times. But, fortunately for the Indian people, judiciary, election commission, vigilance departments and some other powerful institutions are there to check all such malpractices. But the real credit should go to the brave Indian people for showing so much patience and faith in the democratic institutions for over half a century.

QUESTIONS

1. What do you think about the success or otherwise of democracy in India?
2. Mention some of the negative factors which can derail the democratic process.
3. Point out a few powerful institutions which are there to check all such malpractices.
4. To whom should the real credit go and why?

ANSWERS

1. Democracy is a grand success in India. Indeed, it has struck deep roots in the Indian soil.
2. Some of the negative factors which can derail the democratic process in India are communalism, casteism, nepotism, illiteracy, slowness of the judicial process, corruption, haughtiness of the politicians and the bureaucrats, etc.

3. Some of the powerful institutions which are there to check all such malpractices are judiciary, election commission, vigilance departments, etc.
4. The real credit for the success of democracy in India should go to the Indian people. It is because they have shown much patience and faith in the democratic institutions for over half a century.

(17)

The modern man is surrounded by scientific discoveries and inventions wherever he goes. The men who are traditionally minded still swear to show abhorrence to the very word 'science'. They do not care to know that they themselves are overwhelmed by science everywhere and even in their daily routine. The men of all faiths and creeds now live in houses in which they make use of all kinds of scientific gadgets such as the refrigerator, the TV set, the room-heater, the A.C., the desert cooler, the juicer, the electric bulb, the telephone, the computer, etc. Above all, if we want to know who is the greatest scientist in the universe we will be surprised to know that it is God Himself, since the whole of this universe is based on nothing but sound scientific principles.

QUESTIONS

1. What is the modern man surrounded by?
2. What is wrong with the traditionally minded men?
3. In what kind of houses do men of all faiths and creeds live?
4. Who is the greatest scientist in the universe and how do we know it?

ANSWERS

1. The modern man is surrounded everywhere by scientific discoveries and inventions.
2. The traditionally minded men still hate the very word 'science'. They do not try to understand that they themselves are making use of scientific devices and gadgets in their daily routine.
3. The men of all faiths and creeds live in houses where scientific devices and gadgets are used. Some of them are the refrigerator, the TV., the computer, the telephone, the A.C., the desert cooler, the room-heater, the juicer, the electric bulb, etc.
4. God is the greatest scientist in the universe. It is because the whole of this universe is based on sound scientific principles.

❑ ❑ ❑

www.ingramcontent.com/pod-product-compliance
Ingram Content Group UK Ltd.
Pitfield, Milton Keynes, MK11 3LW, UK
UKHW021708190726
13853UKWH00001B/468

9 789350 122778